ADOLESCENCE AND PUBERTY

THE KINSEY INSTITUTE SERIES

June Machover Reinisch, General Editor

Volume I
MASCULINITY/FEMININITY: *Basic Perspectives*
Edited by
June Machover Reinisch, Leonard A. Rosenblum,
and Stephanie A. Sanders

Volume II
HOMOSEXUALITY/HETEROSEXUALITY:
Concepts of Sexual Orientation
Edited by
David P. McWhirter, Stephanie A. Sanders, and
June Machover Reinisch

Volume III
ADOLESCENCE AND PUBERTY
Edited by
John Bancroft and June Machover Reinisch

ADOLESCENCE
AND PUBERTY

Edited by

John Bancroft, M.D.
June Machover Reinisch, Ph.D.

New York   Oxford
OXFORD UNIVERSITY PRESS
1990

Oxford University Press

Oxford   New York   Toronto
Delhi   Bombay   Calcutta   Madras   Karachi
Petaling Jaya   Singapore   Hong Kong   Tokyo
Nairobi   Dar es Salaam   Cape Town
Melbourne   Auckland

and associated companies in
Berlin   Ibadan

Published by Oxford University Press, Inc.,
200 Madison Avenue, New York, New York 10016

Oxford is a registered trademark of Oxford University Press

Library of Congress Cataloging-in-Publication Data
Adolescence and puberty /
edited by John Bancroft, June Machover Reinisch.
p. cm.—(Kinsey Institute series ; v. 3)
Based on a symposium held Nov. 20–23, 1986 at the Kinsey Institute,
Indiana University, Bloomington, Ind.
Includes bibliographical references. ISBN 0-19-505336-2
1. Teenagers—Sexual behavior—Congresses.
2. Puberty—Congresses.
I. Bancroft, John. II. Reinisch, June Machover.
III. Series.
[DNLM: 1. Adolescent Psychology—congresses.
2. Puberty—congresses.
3. Sex Behavior—in adolescence—congresses.
WS 462 A23235   1986]
HQ27.A235 1990 612.6'61—dc20
DNLM/DLC for Library of Congress
89-23160

2 4 6 8 9 7 5 3 1

Printed in the United States of America
on acid-free paper

To Professor Igor Kon, Institute of Ethnography, USSR Academy of Sciences, Moscow, for his seminal and courageous scholarly and scientific work on Soviet youth and sexology.

Preface

Adolescence and Puberty is the third volume in the Kinsey Institute Series. In each volume, researchers from a wide range of academic disciplines draw on their own data and on the viewpoints of their own area of expertise to address the central issues in a specific arena of discourse. The chapters for each volume were written after the contributors participated in a Kinsey Symposium on the topic. As a result, they reflect the diverse perspectives that emerge during sustained discussions among colleagues from many different fields. The editors of each volume provided an introduction based on the full range of discussions at the Symposium and the contents of the final contributions. This overview highlights the central themes and research findings of the volume as well as major issues for future consideration.

We would like to acknowledge the support of Indiana University. Special thanks go to Stephanie Sanders, Mary Ziemba-Davis, Kathryn Fisher, Sandra Ham, Elizabeth Roberge, Janet Rowland, Terry Sare, J. Susan Straub, and the other members of The Kinsey Institute staff for their assistance in planning and conducting the Third Kinsey Symposium and for helping to prepare this book. We also thank Joan Bossert and Louise Chang at Oxford University Press.

Bloomington, Ind.   J.B.
May 1990   J.M.R.

Contents

II Social and Cultural Aspects of Adolescent Sexuality

Contributors

John Bancroft, M.D.
Clinical Consultant
Reproductive Biology Unit
MRC Centre for Reproductive
  Biology
Edinburgh, Scotland

Inese Z. Beitins, M.D.
Division of Pediatric
  Endocrinology
University of Michigan Medical
  Center
Ann Arbor, Michigan

Judy L. Cameron, Ph.D.
University of Pittsburgh
Western Psychiatric Institute and
  Clinic
Pittsburgh, Pennsylvania

George P. Chrousos, M.D.
Developmental Endocrinology
  Branch
National Institute for Child
  Health and Human Services
Bethesda, Maryland

Jacqueline Darroch Forrest, Ph.D.
Director of Research
The Alan Guttmacher Institute
New York, New York

Carol M. Foster, M.D.
Division of Pediatric
  Endocrinology
University of Michigan Medical
  Center
Ann Arbor, Michigan

Paula M. Hale, M.D.
Division of Pediatric
  Endocrinology
University of Michigan Medical
  Center
Ann Arbor, Michigan

Sandra L. Hofferth, Ph.D.
Senior Research Associate
The Urban Institute
Washington, D.C.

Nancy J. Hopwood, M.D.
Professor of Pediatrics
University of Michigan Medical
  School
Ann Arbor, Michigan

Mary E. Hotvedt, Ph.D.
Counseling, Research &
  Consultation Associate
Department of Family and
  Community Medicine
University of Arizona Health
  Science Center
El Dorado Psychological
  Associates
Tucson, Arizona

Gale Inoff-Germain
Laboratory of Developmental
  Psychology
National Institutes of Mental
  Health
Bethesda, Maryland

Robert P. Kelch, M.D.
Division of Pediatric
  Endocrinology
University of Michigan Medical
  Center
Ann Arbor, Michigan

Tarina M. Mendes, M.D.
Division of Pediatric
  Endocrinology
University of Michigan Medical
  Center
Ann Arbor, Michigan

Editha D. Nottelmann, Ph.D.
Laboratory of Developmental
  Psychology
National Institutes of Mental
  Health
Bethesda, Maryland

Harriet F. Pilpel, P.C.
Legal Counsel
Weil, Gotshal & Manges
New York, New York

D. Malcolm Potts, Ph.D.
President
Family Health International
Research Triangle Park, North
  Carolina

June M. Reinisch, Ph.D.
Director and Professor
The Kinsey Institute for Research
  in Sex, Gender, and
  Reproduction
Indiana University
Bloomington, Indiana

Hyman Rodman, Ph.D.
Director, Family Research Center
University of North Carolina at
  Greensboro
Greensboro, North Carolina

Leonard A. Rosenblum, Ph.D.
Professor, Department of
  Psychiatry
State University of New York
Health Sciences Center at
  Brooklyn
Brooklyn, New York

Robert T. Rubin, M.D., Ph.D.
Professor of Psychiatry
Division of Biological Psychiatry
Department of Psychiatry
Harbor U.C.L.A. Medical Center
Torrance, California

Michael Rutter, C.B.E., M.D.
Professor of Child Psychiatry
Institute of Psychiatry
London, England

Stephanie A. Sanders, Ph.D.
Assistant Director
The Kinsey Institute for Research
  in Sex, Gender, and
  Reproduction
Indiana University
Bloomington, Indiana

Elizabeth J. Susman, Ph.D., RN
The Penn State University
State College, Pennsylvania

Jan E. Trost, Ph.D.
Professor
Department of Sociology
Uppsala University
Uppsala, Sweden

J. Richard Udry, Ph.D.
Director
Carolina Population Center
University of North Carolina
Chapel Hill, North Carolina

Gail Elizabeth Wyatt, Ph.D.
Associate Professor
Neuropsychiatric Institute
University of California at Los
    Angeles
Los Angeles, California

ADOLESCENCE AND PUBERTY

Introduction

John Bancroft

The purpose of The Kinsey Institute Series is to examine issues relating to sex, gender, and reproduction that require an interdisciplinary approach. Adolescence is a prime example of such an issue. It is the stage of development at which the individual is capable of reproduction, reorganizes and reasserts gender, and displays the early unfolding of the sexual adult—a time of complex and often obscure interaction between biological and sociopsychological influences.

The Symposium on Adolescence and Puberty was the third in the series and took place November 20–23, 1986, at The Kinsey Institute, Indiana University, Bloomington. There were nineteen scientists representing ten different disciplines. The program allowed considerable time for discussion, which has been taken into account by the authors in preparing their final manuscripts.

Inevitably, we have sampled only a few of the key issues of adolescence, but they do provide a broad scope. The chapters can be categorized under the following headings:

1. Factors influencing the onset of puberty
2. The interactive effect of hormonal and social influences on the emergence of adolescent sexuality
3. Emotional changes associated with adolescence
4. Patterns of adolescent sexual behavior in cross-cultural perspective
5. Legal aspects of the adolescent role

I will give a few brief comments about each of the contributions to help the reader form an overview of the volume.

The control of the onset of puberty still remains a mystery. While neuroendocrine mechanisms are obviously involved, we are aware of the extent to which social, psychological, and nutritional factors can impinge on the process. In a clear introduction to this field, Judy Cameron reviews the relevant evidence from primates. She convinces us that, although the final pathway depends on an increase in pulsatile gonadotropin-releasing hormone, the precise mechanisms bringing that about, whether involving stimulation or reduced inhibition of release, and under what influences, still remain uncertain. Nancy Hopwood complements this picture with a rich source of human clinical evidence, which leads us to broadly similar conclusions. In discussing these two chapters, Stephanie Sanders and June Reinisch introduce another important dimension to the picture—the longer term developmental perspective, which starts with early sexual differentiation in the brain and the influence this has on the subsequent onset of puberty. They also discuss the role of signals such as pheromones, which in lower mammals have important functions in regulating ovarian cyclicity and probably the onset of puberty itself. These three chapters provide an excellent up-to-date review of this field.

Leonard Rosenblum has provided us with a useful summary of some of the evidence of interactions between hormonal and nonhormonal mechanisms in primate adolescent development. A particularly striking example is the effect of adding adult males and females to a mixed-sex group of young squirrel monkeys—a dramatic alteration of the peer group sexual interaction. This chapter is a salutary reminder that, even when there is clear evidence of hormonal control of sexual behavior, the expression of that behavior can still be radically affected by environmental and social factors.

It is therefore particularly interesting to read Rosenblum's contribution in conjunction with that of Richard Udry. Udry and his colleagues have completed a remarkable study of boys and girls around the age of puberty in which the sexual behavior and peer group relationships were assessed by questionnaire, together with hormonal parameters in a subgroup of their subjects. Such research is very difficult to carry out, and the results are striking. The best predictor of sexuality in the study for boys in early adolescent was the level of circulating free testosterone. This appeared to be a direct effect of rising androgen levels on behavior rather than an indirect effect via physical maturation. The picture in the girls studied was somewhat different. Whereas there was some association between androgen levels and sexual interest, their likelihood of engaging in sexual intercourse appeared to be much more influenced by the types of friends they had than by their hormone levels. These findings, which are sufficiently important to deserve replication, provide us with clear evidence that social learning has a greater influence on the sexual development of girls than it does on that of boys. Such a sex difference could go quite a long way in explaining the extraordinary discrepancy in the evidence of hormone–sexual behavior relationships between men and women. For men the evidence is consistent, indicating that androgens are necessary for normal sexual desire. For women the evidence is inconsistent and often contradictory (Bancroft, 1989).

The stereotype of the adolescent includes emotional perturbation, and certainly a proportion of adolescents have an emotionally uncomfortable time before settling into adulthood. What are the relative contributions of biological and social learning factors in accounting for this aspect of development? Editha Nottelmann and George Chrousos with their colleagues report an ambitious study that explores this question. They have started to look at the relationship between hormonal changes preceding puberty and the common behavioral disturbances at that stage of development. As explorers venturing into unchartered waters, they have taken on a difficult task and, not surprisingly, their results are difficult to interpret in several respects. Robert Rubin considers in his discussion some of the methodological issues at stake. Even if this NIMH-based study raises as many questions as it answers, however, it still represents an important first step in a difficult field of research. Subsequent studies should profit considerably from their efforts.

Another aspect of the emotional upheaval of adolescence is the changing pattern of psychiatric illness in that age group—for example, an increase in the incidence of depression and a change in the sex ratio of depressive illness. Michael Rutter, with his exceptional grasp of the field, has carefully weighed the various factors that have to be taken into account and provides us with an authoritative review of the literature.

The sexual behavior of adolescents is considered from various viewpoints. Mary Hotvedt uses anthropological evidence from preindustrial societies to convince us how important it is to examine our own social structure during adolescence with a cross-cultural perspective. The time allowed for the adolescent transitional phase clearly varies considerably across cultures, as do various rituals and procedures that societies use to denote and institutionalize this crucial process of entry into the adult world. I have looked at some of the implications for our own society in my chapter.

Another type of cross-cultural perspective is provided by Jacqueline Forrest and her colleagues from the Alan Guttmacher Institute. Their comparison of the statistics of adolescent reproductive behavior across modern societies has been illuminating, especially the in-depth study of the United States, Canada, England and Wales, France, Sweden, and the Netherlands. This evidence points forcefully to the conclusion that adolescents in the United States have special problems with regard to sexuality, and Forrest marshals the reasons why this might be so—with particular emphasis on the mixed and confusing messages about sexual morality to which the U.S. teenager is so often exposed. Sandra Hofferth complements this report with a more detailed analysis of trends of sexual behavior and pregnancy among U.S. teenagers. Jan Trost examines some of the social mechanisms that might account for these contrasts between modern societies.

Gail Wyatt uses yet another approach to look at teenage sexuality in the United States. In her carefully sampled survey of Californian women, she encourages them to reflect back on their own adolescent sexuality. In doing so, she examines another cultural question that is of particular relevance in the United States—the black/white comparison—and points out the methodological shortcomings of many previous ethnic comparisons of that type. She also confronts us with the disturbing extent of sexual abuse during childhood and adolescence, a previously underestimated influence in adolescent sexual development.

Hyman Rodman, a family lawyer, looks at the legal status of the adolescent in American society. His comments are especially interesting to compare with the cross-cultural analysis of Hotvedt. Rodman dwells on a central dilemma of American parenthood: when and to what extent to give teenagers responsibility for their own lives. Moreover, he raises the possibility that American (and probably many European) societies err in being overcautious. The problems of teenage behavior in the United States certainly need to be looked at in that light.

Finally, Malcolm Potts concludes the book with a characteristically provocative piece in which he explores several of the themes that have emerged in the chapters.

Reference

Bancroft, J. (1989). *Human sexuality and its problems* (2nd ed.). Edinburgh: Churchill-Livingston.

I

INTERACTION OF BIOLOGICAL AND ENVIRONMENTAL FACTORS IN PUBERTY AND ADOLESCENCE

1

Factors Controlling the Onset of Puberty in Primates

Judy L. Cameron

There has been considerable debate over the years regarding how to define puberty, in that it is a stage of development that spans an extended period of time (in humans and higher primates a period of years) and encompasses a large variety of morphological, physiological, and behavioral changes. However, this chapter will specifically focus on the maturational changes in the reproductive system that occur during puberty. In this context, puberty can be defined as the period of transition from a state of reproductive immaturity to a state of full reproductive competence.

Much of what is known about the physiology of puberty in humans has been derived from studies utilizing nonhuman primate species. The anatomical and the physiological organization of the reproductive system are quite similar in humans and higher primates, both prior to puberty and in adulthood. Moreover, our limited understanding of the initiating and modulating influences in the pubertal process suggests that the mechanisms controlling the onset of puberty are similar in humans and certain nonhuman primate species. Much of the work discussed in this chapter has utilized two species of Old World monkeys, *Macaca mulatta* (rhesus monkeys) and *Macaca fascicularis* (cynomolgus monkeys). In both these species, the initial phases of puberty occur between 2 and 3 years of age and adulthood is attained by approximately 4 years of age.

This chapter discusses the mechanisms involved in reproductive maturation at puberty in primate species. It is intended to provide an overview of the subject for behaviorists, psychologists, and epidemiologists interested in studying the relationships between the physiological changes at puberty and the behavioral, psychological, and psychosocial changes that occur during pubertal maturation.

Intrinsic Control of Reproductive Function in Adulthood

In mature adult humans and nonhuman primates the activity of the gonads (the ovaries in the female and the testes in the male) are under the control of two hormones produced by the anterior pituitary (see Fig. 1-1). These hormones—follicle-stimulating hormone (FSH) and luteinizing hormone (LH)—are also commonly referred to as gonadotropins (for review, see Steiner & Cameron, 1989).

In the adult female, ovarian activity is cyclic in nature with ovulation occurring approximately once a month. FSH acts within the ovaries primarily to stimulate growth of ovarian follicles (the ovarian structures that contain the female germ cells, the ova). By a week into each cycle, a single follicle has usually been selected and begins growing rapidly, secreting copious amounts of the steroid hormone estrogen. Around the end of the second week in each cycle, the rising level of estrogen acts at the pituitary to cause release of a surge of LH and FSH. The gonadotropin surge, in turn, triggers the ovulatory process in which the mature follicle ruptures and releases its ovum into the nearby fallopian tube. Under LH stimulation, the ruptured follicle undergoes biochemical and structural reorganization to become a corpus luteum. Cells of the corpus luteum secrete estrogen and progesterone, hormones that act on the endometrial lining of the uterus to ready it for implantation of a fertilized ovum. If fertilization does not occur, the corpus luteum regresses after approximately 2 weeks. Withdrawal of hormonal support to the endometrium at the end of each nonpregnant cycle leads to sloughing of the endometrial tissue (i.e., menstruation).

Testicular function in the adult is also stimulated by LH and FSH. LH acts at the Leydig cells of the testes to stimulate testosterone production. Testosterone, in turn, acts within the seminiferous tubules, in conjunction with FSH, to stimulate spermatogenesis. Testosterone also plays an important trophic role in stimulating the accessory ducts and glands of the male reproductive tract, the secretory products of which are critical for maintaining the functional integrity of sperm.

LH and FSH production and release are controlled by a small peptide hormone, gonadotropin-releasing hormone (GnRH). GnRH is produced by neurons in the hypothalamus (the brain region located directly above the pituitary), the axons of which terminate in the capillary bed of the median eminence. GnRH released from the axon terminals is transported to the anterior pituitary by veins of the hypothalamo-

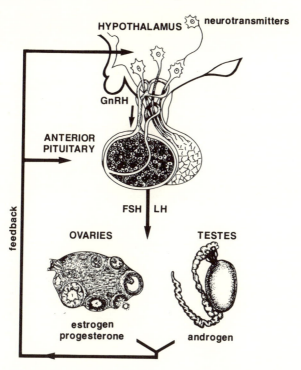

Figure 1–1. Schematic representation of the interactions between the hormones of the hypothalamic-pituitary-gonadal axis in adult primates (left side, female; right side, male). (Adapted from figure from E.S.E. Hafez, *Human Reproductive Physiology*, Ann Arbor Publishers, 1988.)

hypophyseal portal system. GnRH neurons sending axons to the median eminence appear to fire in a coordinated fashion, sending pulses of GnRH to the anterior pituitary, and resulting in pulsatile release of the pituitary gonadotropins. The mechanism(s) by which GnRH neurons are stimulated to fire in a coordinated pulsatile manner remains unknown at this time. The frequency and amplitude of pulsatile gonadotropin release varies depending on the physiological state, presumably resulting from changes in the frequency of GnRH release. For example, in the midfollicular phase of the menstrual cycle low-amplitude LH pulses occur approximately once every 90 minutes, whereas during the midluteal phase LH is released in large-amplitude pulses at a slow frequency of about once every 8 hours.

We have only a limited understanding of the mechanism(s) of GnRH production and release. It is known that a number of neuronal systems within the central nervous system can modulate the activity of GnRH neurons, including neuronal systems that release such neurotransmitters as norepinephrine, serotonin, and endogenous opiate peptides. Hormones produced by the gonads (i.e., estrogen and progesterone in females and testosterone in males) have an inhibitory influence on GnRH neuronal activity. Gonadal steroids also exert a negative-feedback effect directly at the level of the anterior pituitary to suppress activity of the cells that secrete LH and FSH. Females have an additional positive-feedback system by which very high levels of estrogen produced by a mature ovarian follicle act at the pituitary to stimulate the release of a surge of LH and FSH.

Changes in Gonadal Function at Puberty

The changes in the reproductive system that most obviously characterize puberty involve the maturation of the gonads and the ensuing development of secondary sexual characteristics, resulting from increased production of the gonadal steroid hormones. Female pubertal maturation involves amplification of the processes of ovarian follicular growth and steroidogenesis, which occur to a limited extent prior to puberty (Van Wagenen & Simpson, 1973). The increased production of steroid hormones by the ovaries stimulates proliferation of the uterine lining, and withdrawal of steroid support at the end of each cycle leads to menstruation. The first menstruation is referred to as menarche and is commonly used as a marker of puberty, although it is a relatively late event in the cascade of events that lead to pubertal maturation of the reproductive system. Increased ovarian steroid production also stimulates breast enlargement, pubic hair growth, and deposition of body fat in a characteristic female pattern. Ultimately, pubertal maturation of the ovaries leads to establishment of cyclic ovarian function, with regular ovulations. Generally the first ovulatory cycle occurs some months after menarche, and establishment of successive ovulatory cycles does not occur for months to years after menarche (Rowell, 1977; Apter, Viinikka, & Vihko, 1978).

In the male, pubertal development of the testes entails stimulation of Leydig cells to produce increasing quantities of testosterone, testicular growth resulting from proliferation of tubules and cellular elements involved in sperm production, and ultimately the production of mature sperm (Van Wagenen & Simpson, 1954; August, Grumbach, & Kaplan, 1972; Dang & Meussy-Dessolle, 1984). In addition to playing an important role in testicular maturation and sperm production, increased production of testicular hormones stimulates growth of the male external genitalia, causes development of masculine hair patterns (including beard growth and baldness), and leads to an increase in muscle mass.

Changes in Gonadotropin Secretion at Puberty

Gonadal maturation in both males and females results from increased secretion of the anterior pituitary gonadotropins, LH and FSH (Styne & Grumbach, 1978; Steiner & Bremner, 1981; Plant, 1983). Not only do the mean circulating levels of LH and FSH increase, but the amplitude of individual LH pulses also increases (Boyar et al., 1974a; Steiner & Bremner, 1981). However, studies in humans suggest that LH pulse frequency is similar in prepubertal children and adults (Penny, Olambiwonnu, & Frasier, 1977; Jakacki et al., 1982). Pubertal maturation of pulsatile gonadotropin secretion is distinguished by a very distinct pattern of LH release, with a nocturnal elevation of pulse amplitude (Boyar et al., 1974a; Beck & Wuttke, 1980; Steiner & Bremner, 1981). In humans, this nocturnal amplification of LH secretion is unique to puberty and is not observed during childhood or in the mature adult (Boyar et al., 1972). In rhesus and cynomolgus monkeys, nocturnal amplification of LH secretion continues throughout adulthood (Steiner et al., 1980; Plant & Zorub, 1982). In humans, the nighttime increase in LH secretion has been shown to be associated with sleep (Kapen et al., 1974), and presumably reflects a sleep-associated increase in GnRH secretion. Interestingly, a similar pattern of elevated nighttime LH secretion is seen in adults recovering from anorexia nervosa, a psychiatric disorder in which the activity of the reproductive system regresses to a prepubertal state during periods of self-inflicted starvation (Boyar et al., 1974a; Pirke et al., 1979). Despite the striking nature of this developmental pattern of LH secretion, it does not appear to be essential for gonadal maturation (Wildt, Marshall, & Knobil, 1980), and we still do not understand the correlation, if any, between the developmental pattern of LH secretion and the triggers for the pubertal increase in gonadotropin secretion (Figs. 1-2 and 1-3).

Studies in castrate monkeys (Plant, 1985) and humans with gonadal dysgenesis (Conte, Grumbach, & Kaplan, 1975; Levine, Loriaux, & Cutler, 1983) have shown that the pubertal increase in gonadotropin secretion occurs with or without the gonads at essentially the same time. These findings suggest that the timing of puberty onset is not dependent on gonadal activities.

The pubertal increase in gonadotropin secretion appears to be driven by an increase in GnRH secretion. Excellent support for this concept came from studies showing that administration of exogenous GnRH (in hourly pulses) to prepubertal female rhesus monkeys stimulated adult-like menstrual cycles (Wildt et al., 1980). These findings and similar studies in prepubertal male macaques, showing that exogenous GnRH can initiate premature testosterone secretion and spermatogenesis (Marshall, Wickings, & Nieschlag, 1985), clearly indicate that reproduc-

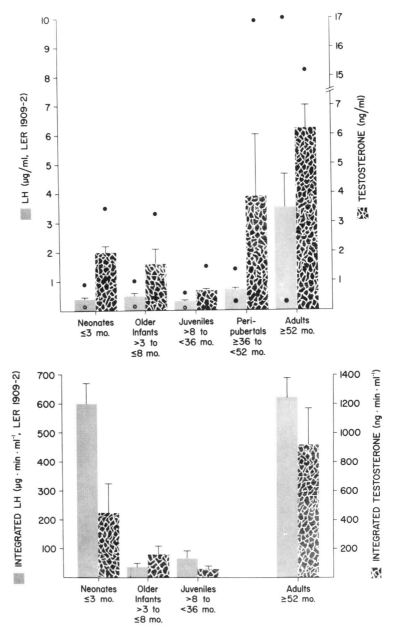

Figure 1–2. Mean (± SEM) serum LH and testosterone levels (top panel) measured in morning blood samples in groups of neonates, older infants, juveniles, peripubertals, and adult cynomolgus monkeys (●, range of values observed). (Bottom panel) Integrated (0–90 minutes) LH and testosterone responses to luteinizing hormone-releasing hormone (LHRH) (5 μg/kg, IV dose). (Taken from Steiner & Bremner, 1981.)

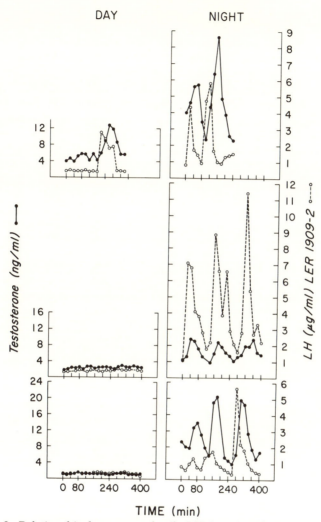

Figure 1–3. Relationship between pulsatile LH (○---○) and testosterone secretion (●——●) in the adult male macaque during selected segments of the morning and evening sampling intervals in three different monkeys. (Taken from Steiner et al., 1980.)

tive quiescence prior to puberty is not due to limitations in the functional capacity of the pituitary or the gonads, but rather appears to result from insufficient GnRH secretion. It is thus clear that the central issue in understanding the physiological control of the pubertal process is identification of the mechanism by which activity of the hypothalamic GnRH neurons increases at the time of puberty.

Factors Controlling the Pubertal Increase in GnRH Secretion

As indicated in Figure 1-4, the brains of prepubertal monkeys and humans contain GnRH neurons that are similar in number, morphology, and distribution to those in the adult brain (Barry, 1977; Goldsmith, Lamberts, & Brezina, 1983; Cameron et al., 1985a). However, studies in cynomolgus monkeys suggest that the amount of GnRH-containing cytoplasm, as measured by immunocytochemical techniques, is slightly less in neurons of prepubertal animals than in adult GnRH neurons (Cameron et al., 1985a). Nevertheless, it does not appear that low GnRH secretion prior to puberty is due to inadequate supply of GnRH in neurons of the prepubertal hypothalamus. This notion is supported by observations that the hypothalamic content of biologically active GnRH in castrate rhesus monkeys is not lower prior to puberty than in adulthood (Fraser, Pohl, & Plant, 1986).

Not only are GnRH neurons present in the hypothalamus prior to puberty, but they also appear to be responsible for driving the limited prepubertal gonadotropin secretion. This has been demonstrated by studies showing that the administration of a GnRH antiserum to prepubertal cynomolgus monkeys suppresses the scarcely detectable levels of circulating LH (Fig. 1-5); Cameron et al., 1985a). Further evidence that GnRH neurons are capable of driving LH and FSH secretion prior to puberty comes from studies showing that administration of an excitatory neurotransmitter, N-methyl-D,L-aspartic acid (NMA), releases adultlike pulses of LH in prepubertal rhesus monkeys (Gay & Plant, 1987). NMA appears to be acting to release LH via stimulation of GnRH neurons, in that prior treatment of the monkeys with a GnRH antagonist blocks the LH-releasing action of NMA (Gay & Plant, 1987).

Additional support for the concept that GnRH neurons of the hypo-

Figure 1–4. Mean cross-sectional areas of LHRH-containing cytoplasm in hypothalamic cells of three adult and three prepubertal macaques, *Macaca fascicularis*. (Taken from Cameron et al., 1985b.)

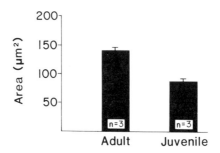

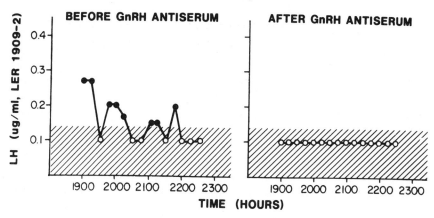

Figure 1–5. Plasma LH concentrations in blood samples collected from one juvenile monkey the night before (15 samples at 15-minute intervals) and the night after GnRH antiserum (Fraser #94, 2 mg/kg at 5 a.m.) administration. Open circles and hatched zone represent LH values below the level of detectability of the LH assay (0.15 μg/ml). (Taken from Cameron et al., 1985a.)

thalamus have the capability of producing and secreting adequate amounts of GnRH to drive adultlike gonadotropin secretion prior to puberty has been provided by studies examining gonadotropin secretion in neonatal humans and monkeys. For a short period of time after birth (6–8 months in humans and 2–3 months in rhesus monkeys), the hypothalamic-pituitary-gonadal axis operates at a level of heightened activity that is similar to the level of activity seen in adulthood (Winter et al., 1975; Frawley & Neill, 1979; Plant, 1980; Steiner & Bremner, 1981). This heightened activity is associated with circulating concentrations of LH and FSH that are much higher than those measured during later childhood and with levels of gonadal steroids that can be as high as those measured in adults (Fig. 1-2). The activity of the reproductive axis during the neonatal period appears to be driven by GnRH, in that treatment of neonatal monkeys with a regimen of continuous GnRH agonist-administration, which is believed to result in down-regulation of GnRH receptors, completely suppresses the activity of the reproductive axis (Mann et al., 1984). Likewise, the decrease in activity of the reproductive axis at the end of the neonatal period appears to result from decreased GnRH secretion. Taken together, the studies just discussed clearly indicate that GnRH neurons are capable of stimulating activity of the reproductive axis long before puberty. One must conclude, therefore, that the quiescence of the reproductive axis during childhood is due to either the presence of an inhibitory signal impinging on GnRH neurons or the lack of a stimulatory signal to these neurons.

It has frequently been suggested that a heightened sensitivity to the negative feedback of steroid hormones may be the mechanism by which GnRH neuronal activity is inhibited during the prepubertal period of reproductive quiescence. This hypothesis (commonly referred to as the "gonadostat hypothesis") further predicts that the stimulus for puberty onset is a decrease in sensitivity to steroid hormone negative feedback (Dohrn & Hohlweg, 1931). Indeed, experiments with ovariectomized female rhesus monkeys have shown that increasingly larger amounts of estradiol are necessary to suppress gonadotropin secretion as puberty draws near (Rapisarda et al., 1983). However, the fact that increasing amounts of steroid hormone are required to suppress gonadotropin secretion during pubertal development may reflect a change in sensitivity of the GnRH neuronal system to steroid hormone negative feedback, or may simply result from a requirement of more steroid hormone to suppress an increased amount of GnRH secretion. In fact, results from other studies strongly suggest that even if a reduction in sensitivity to steroid hormone negative feedback occurs at puberty, it is probably not the primary stimulus responsible for puberty onset. In particular, studies examining the patterns of gonadotropin secretion in neonatally castrated monkeys and humans with gonadal dysgenesis (Plant, 1980; Plant & Zorub, 1982; Conte et al., 1975; Levine et al., 1983) have shown that there is a suppression of gonadotropin secretion during childhood even in the absence of gonadal steroids. Furthermore, the possibility that the negative-feedback signal is supplied by steroid hormones produced by the adrenal glands is contradicted by studies showing that neonatal rhesus monkeys that have been both gonadectomized and adrenalectomized do not exhibit premature onset of puberty (Plant, 1988).

Numerous efforts have been made to identify neuronal systems that may inhibit GnRH secretion during the childhood period of reproductive quiescence. In particular, interest has focused on the hypothesis that a decrease in secretion of opioid peptides may play a role in triggering puberty onset, in that opioid peptides have strong inhibitory influences on gonadotropin secretion in adults. However, studies showing that administration of opioid antagonists to prepubertal children do not trigger puberty onset, provide evidence against this hypothesis (Fraioli et al., 1984; Sauder et al., 1984; Mauras, Veldhuis, & Rogol, 1986). Likewise, there is no good evidence that changes in activity of noradrenergic, dopaminergic, or serotonergic neurotransmitter systems play a role in triggering puberty onset. Interestingly, there are reports that pathological or experimentally placed lesions of the posterior hypothalamus in humans (Barnes, Cloutier, & Hayles, 1972) and monkeys (Terasawa et al., 1984) can advance the age of menarche and first ovulation. These findings suggest that a neuronal system in the posterior hypothalamus may play a role in suppressing GnRH neuronal activity during the period between infancy and puberty. However, the nature of such a neuronal system remains to be elucidated.

Studies suggesting that puberty onset is triggered by some aspect of the processes involved in physical growth and maturation lend support to the hypothesis that reproductive quiescence in the juvenile results from the absence of a stimulatory signal to the GnRH neurons. Observations by Frisch and Revelle (1970), noting a close correlation between the attainment of a particular body weight (i.e., 47 kg) and menarche in normal healthy American girls, stimulated increased interest in this hypothesis during the past two decades. These investigators proposed that attainment of a "critical body weight" triggered puberty onset. Subsequently, their theory was refined to postulate that a minimum percentage of body fat is the critical factor signaling the initiation of puberty (Frisch & McArthur, 1974). Other investigators have suggested that a change in basal metabolic rate, rather than a change in body weight or body composition per se, may provide a signal that triggers puberty onset in young women (Crawford & Osler, 1975). Although there is now a substantial body of data suggesting a link between these proposed "critical factors" and puberty onset, only a few investigators have performed experiments testing the existence of this "growth–metabolism link" for puberty onset.

In addressing this issue, Steiner, Cameron, and colleagues (Steiner et al., 1983; Cameron et al., 1985b) suggested that because of their higher metabolic rates (Kleiber, 1947; Bier et al., 1977) and lower metabolic reserves (Chaussain et al., 1977; Haymond et al., 1982; Cameron, Koerker, & Steiner, 1985c), children and prepubertal monkeys are subjected to a decreased availability of certain metabolic hormones or substrates that are critical for adultlike activity of GnRH neurons. To test this hypothesis, a sustained intravenous infusion of a "mixed meal" of glucose and amino acids was administered to castrate juvenile monkeys (*M. fascicularis*) to provide a continuous supply of metabolic substrates and provoke a continuous release of hormones that play roles in metabolizing nutrients (Steiner et al., 1983; Cameron et al., 1985b). In the initial study, three of six juvenile monkeys responded to the glucose–amino acid infusion with increased gonadotropin secretion (Figure 1-6). One of the three responders was subsequently given a 3-week infusion of saline, during which time circulating gonadotropin levels decreased, followed by a second period of glucose–amino acid infusion, which was again accompanied by increased gonadotropin secretion (Fig. 1-7). Although it appears from this that circulating metabolic factors may be able to modulate GnRH neuronal activity at pu-

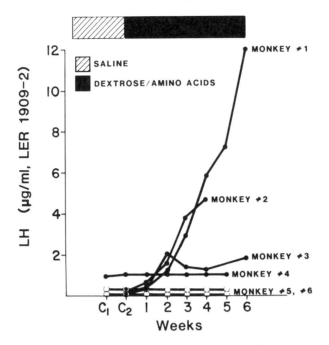

Figure 1–6. Plasma LH concentrations in samples collected weekly from six prepubertal macaques receiving IV infusions of saline (C_1, C_2: two control weeks, hatched bar), followed by chronic IV infusions of dextrose and amino acids (4–6 weeks; solid bar). Plasma LH increased significantly ($p < .05$) in monkeys 1, 2, and 3 during dextrose–amino acid infusion. Open circles represent values below the limit of assay detectability. (Taken from Cameron et al., 1985b.)

berty, several serious reservations remain in interpreting the significance of these results. First, although there was a rise in gonadotropin levels in castrate juvenile monkeys receiving the glucose–amino acid infusion into the range of intact adult monkeys, levels were about an order of magnitude lower than those of castrate adult monkeys. Second, in subsequent studies very few juvenile monkeys have responded to glucose–amino acid infusion with elevated gonadotropin secretion (J. L. Cameron and R. A. Steiner, unpublished observations). These latter points suggest that metabolic signals may provide only one of several signals that are necessary for the pubertal increase in GnRH neuronal activity, or that the metabolic signal provided by the glucose–amino acid infusion was not optimal for stimulation of GnRH neurons.

Further support for the concept that circulating metabolic signals may play a role in gating activity of GnRH neurons comes from studies on the effects of food restriction in adult monkeys. Monkeys placed on a

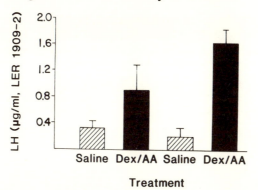

Figure 1–7. Mean plasma LH concentrations in samples collected from monkey 2 during alternating infusions of saline (2 weeks), dextrose–amino acids (6 weeks), saline (3 weeks), and dextrose–amino acids (6 weeks). Plasma LH concentrations during both periods of dextrose–amino acid infusion were significantly ($p < .05$) greater than during periods of saline infusion. (Taken from Cameron et al., 1985b.)

restricted diet for several weeks (Dubey et al., 1986; Cameron, 1987), like patients with anorexia nervosa (Boyar et al., 1974b; Warren & Vande Wiele, 1973), have marked decrease in circulating levels of gonadotropins. Gonadotropin secretion can generally be normalized by increased food intake (Warren et al., 1975; Morimoto et al., 1980). Studies showing that GnRH replacement can restore gonadotropin secretion in undernourished monkeys (Dubey et al., 1986) and anorexic patients (Nillius, Fries, & Wide, 1975; Zgliczynski et al., 1984) suggest that decreased gonadotropin secretion results from decreased activity of GnRH neurons. Undernutrition is, of course, accompanied by weight loss and changes in body composition, as well as by changes in availability of circulating metabolic substrates and hormones (Brasel, 1980). Recovery from undernutrition usually involves a gradual increase in calorie consumption and results in weight gain, changes in body composition, and changes in circulating levels of metabolic hormones and substrates. Thus, it has generally not been possible to dissociate the effects of these various factors on the activity of GnRH neurons. However, in a study examining whether dietary protein was necessary for the increase in GnRH neuronal activity seen with refeeding, monkeys on a reduced food intake regimen were abruptly refed with a diet lacking protein but isocaloric with their normal food intake (Fig. 1-8; Cameron, 1987). Gonadotropin secretion rose significantly in these monkeys within 24 hours, prior to any detectable change in body weight. Not only does this result indicate that dietary protein is not necessary for the restoration of GnRH neuronal activity, but it also provides strong

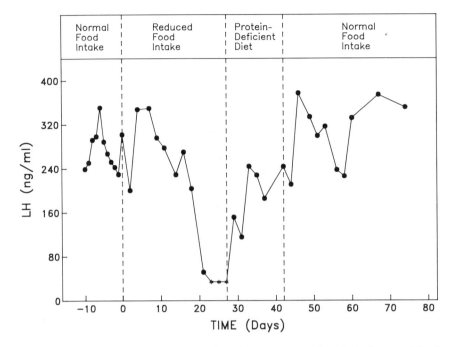

Figure 1–8. Circulating LH in a monkey during a control period of normal food intake, a 3- to 4-week period of reduced food intake, a 1- to 2-week period of a protein-deficient diet, and a 4-week recovery period of normal food intake. Plasma LH concentrations declined significantly ($p < .01$) at the end of the reduced food intake period. Consumption of protein-deficient diet caused a rise in plasma LH levels within 24 hours. Plasma LH concentrations continued to rise up to normal castrate levels during the 1- to 2-week period of protein-deficient diet consumption. Asterisks represent LH levels below assay detectability.

support for the concept that circulating "metabolic factors," rather than changes in body weight or body composition, provide a signal that links GnRH neuronal activity to the metabolic status of the body. The nature of these "metabolic factors," however, remains unknown at this time.

Environmental Influences on Puberty Onset

Many primates, including rhesus monkeys, exhibit a seasonal pattern of reproductive activity in adulthood (Walker, Wilson, & Gordon, 1984). Studies in the rhesus monkey by Wickings and co-workers (1981), showing that exogenous GnRH can stimulate the quiescent reproductive axis during the nonbreeding season, indicate that seasonal influences affect the reproductive system by modulating GnRH neuronal activity. In rhesus monkeys, the timing of puberty onset can also be influenced by seasonal factors (Wilson et al., 1984). However, regardless of seasonal influences, puberty does not occur before 18 months of age in the species (Wilson et al., 1984). Thus, although seasonal factors can modulate the timing of puberty, other factors appear to be responsible for holding the reproductive axis in a prepubertal state from 6 months to 18 months of age. In humans, there is no readily apparent seasonal influence on reproductive function.

Undernutrition has been reported to retard sexual development and delay attainment of adult reproductive capacity in many species (Cameron et al., 1985b). Protein–calorie malnutrition can markedly delay puberty onset in children (Dreizen, Spirakis, & Stone, 1967). Nutritionally delayed puberty is associated with low circulating levels of LH and FSH (Chakravarty et al., 1982) and is believed to result from a decrease in GnRH secretion similar to that which occurs in malnourished adults (as discussed in the previous section).

Strenuous physical training in adolescent girls is also associated with a high incidence of delayed puberty onset (Malina et al., 1978; Warren, 1980; Frisch et al., 1981). Warren (1980) has reported low and low-normal serum LH, FSH, and estrogen concentrations in highly trained ballet dancers with delayed puberty onset. Athletes with delayed puberty onset have reportedly lower weights than athletes in whom puberty occurs within the normal age range. However, a report that menarche occurs, without any change in body weight or composition, in dancers whose exercise regimen is sharply decreased (Warren, 1980) suggests that factors such as stress and altered metabolism may play a role in exercise-induced puberty delay.

Summary

Reproductive maturation in primates appears to result from increased activity of hypothalamic neurons that secrete GnRH. Neurons present in the hypothalamus prior to puberty contain biologically active GnRH; they have functional connections with the anterior pituitary gland and can be stimulated to produce and secrete GnRH. It is therefore likely that the quiescence of GnRH neurons prior to puberty results from the presence of an inhibitory signal impinging upon the GnRH neurons or the lack of a stimulatory drive to these neurons. Inhibitory signals such as gonadal or adrenal steroids and opioid peptides do not appear to be responsible for inhibiting puberty onset. There is some evidence for a neuronal system in the posterior hypothalamus that holds GnRH neuronal activity in check, but the nature of this system has not been characterized. Signals that may provide a stimulatory cue for puberty onset include attainment of a critical body weight, body composition, basal metabolic rate, or stimulatory metabolic milieu. Although there are ample clinical data showing correlations between these factors and puberty onset, few experiments addressing whether such factors actually play a causal role in the pubertal increase in GnRH secretion have been performed. The timing of puberty onset can also be influenced by various environmental factors including season (in monkeys but apparently not humans), nutrient intake, and physical activity.

Acknowledgments

Work performed in the author's laboratory was supported by U.S. Public Health Service grants Nos. R23 HD20887 and RO1 HD20789; work performed in Robert Steiner's laboratory was supported by U.S. Public Health Service grants Nos. RO1 HD 12625, P50 HD 12629, and RR00166. The author is grateful for the excellent technical assistance provided by Connie Nosbisch in studies performed in both Robert Steiner's and the author's laboratories.

References

Apter, D., Viinikka, L., & Vihko, R. (1978). Hormonal pattern of adolescent menstrual cycles. *Journal of Clinical Endocrinology and Metabolism, 47,* 944–954.

August, G. P., Grumbach, M. M., & Kaplan, S. L. (1972). Hormonal changes in puberty. III. Correlation of plasma testosterone, LH, FSH, testicular size, and bone age with male pubertal development. *Journal of Clinical Endocrinology and Metabolism, 34,* 319–326.

Barnes, N. D., Cloutier, M. D., & Hayles, A. B. (1972). The central nervous system and precocious puberty. In M. M. Grumbach, G. D. Grave, and F. E. Mayer (Eds.), *Control of the onset of puberty* (pp. 213–228). New York: Wiley.

Barry, J. (1977). Immunofluorescence study of LRF neurons in man. *Cell Tissue Research, 181,* 1–14.

Beck, W., & Wuttke, W. (1980). Diurnal variations of plasma luteinizing hormone, follicle-stimulating hormone, and prolactin in boys and girls from birth to puberty. *Journal of Clinical Endocrinology and Metabolism, 50,* 635–639.

Bier, D. M., Leake, R. D., Haynond, M. W., Arnold, K. J., Gruenke, L. D., Sperling, M. A., & Kipnis, D. M. (1977). Measurement of "true" glucose production rates in infancy and childhood with 6,6-dideuteroglucose. *Diabetes, 26,* 1016–1023.

Boyar, R. M., Katz, J., Finkelstein, J. W., Kapen, S., Weiner, H., Weitzman, E. D., & Hellman, L. (1974b). Anorexia nervosa: Immaturity of the 24-hour luteinizing hormone secretory pattern. *New England Journal of Medicine, 291,* 861–865.

Boyar, R., Perlow, M., Hellman, L., Kapen, S., & Weitzman, E. (1972). Twenty-four hour pattern of luteinizing hormone secretion in normal men with sleep stage recording. *Journal of Clinical Endocrinology and Metabolism, 35,* 73–81.

Boyar, R. M., Rosenfeld, R. S., Kapen, S., Finkelstein, J. W., Roffwarg, H. P., Weitzman, E. D., & Hellman, L. (1974a). Human puberty. Simultaneous augmented secretion of luteinizing hormone and testosterone during sleep. *Journal of Clinical Investigation, 54,* 609–618.

Brasel, J. A. (1980). Endocrine adaptation to malnutrition. *Pediatric Research, 14,* 1299–1303.

Cameron, J. L. (1987). Effects of dietary protein deficiency on the function of the hypothalamic GnRH pulse generator in castrated male rhesus monkeys. *Endocrine Society Abstract, 908.*

Cameron, J. L., Hansen, P. P., McNeill, T. H., Koerker, D. J., Clifton, D. K., Rogers, K. V., Bremner, W. J., & Steiner, R. A. (1985b). Metabolic cues for the onset of puberty. In C. Flagmini, S. Venturoli, and J. R. Givens (Eds.), *Adolescence in females* (pp. 59–78). Chicago: Yearbook Medical Publishers.

Cameron, J. L., Koerker, D. J., & Steiner, R. A. (1985c). Metabolic changes during maturation of male monkeys *(Macaca fascicularis)* and their possible implications for signaling puberty onset. *American Journal of Physiology, 12,* E385–E391.

Cameron, J. L., McNeill, T. H., Fraser, H. M., Bremner, W. J., Clifton, D. K., & Steiner, R. A. (1985a). The role of endogenous gonadotropin-releasing hormone in the control of luteinizing hormone and testosterone secretion in the juvenile male monkey, *Macaca fascicularis. Biology of Reproduction, 33,* 147–156.

Chakravarty, I., Sreedhar, R., Ghosh, K. K., & Bulusu, S. (1982). Circulating gonadotropin profile in severe cases of protein calorie malnutrition. *Fertility and Sterility, 37,* 650–654.

Chaussain, J. -L., George, P., Calzada, L., & Job, J. C. (1977). Glycemic response to 24-hour fast in normal children. III. Influence of age. *Journal of Pediatrics, 91,* 711–714.

Conte, F. A., Grumbach, M. M., & Kaplan, S. L. (1975). A diphasic pattern of gonadotropin secretion in patients with the syndrome of gonadal dysgenesis. *Journal of Clinical Endocrinology and Metabolism, 40,* 670–674.

Crawford, J. D., & Osler, D. C. (1975). Body composition at menarche: The Frisch–Revelle hypothesis revisited. *Pediatrics, 56,* 449–458.

Dang, D. C., & Meusy-Dessolle, N. (1984). Quantitative study of testis histology and plasma androgens at onset of spermatogenesis in the prepubertal laboratory-born macaque *(Macaca fascicularis). Archives of Andrology, 12(Suppl.),* 43–51.

Dohrn, M., & Hohlweg, W. (1931). Hormonale Beziehungen zwischen Hypophysenvorderlappen und Keimdrüsen. *Proceedings of the Second International Congress on Sex Research,* 436–442.

Dreizen, S., Spirakis, C. N., & Stone, R. E. (1967). A comparison of skeletal growth and maturation in undernourished girls before and after menarche. *Journal of Pediatrics, 70,* 256–263.

Dubey, A. K., Cameron, J. L., Steiner, R. A., & Plant, T. M. (1986). Inhibition of gonadotropin secretion in castrated male rhesus monkeys *(Macaca mulatta)* induced by dietary restriction: Analogy with the prepubertal hiatus of gonadotropin release. *Endocrinology, 118,* 518–525.

Fraioli, F., Cappa, M., Fabbri, A., Gnessi, L., Moretti, C., Bonelli, P., & Isidori, A. (1984). Lack of endogenous opioid inhibitory tone on LH secretion in early puberty. *Clinical Endocrinology, 20,* 299–305.

Fraser, M. O., Pohl, C. R., & Plant, T. M. (1989). The hypogonadotropic state of the prepubertal male rhesus monkey *(Macaca mulatta)* is not associated with a decrease in hypothalamic gonadotropin-releasing hormone content. *Biology of Reproduction 40,* 972–980.

Frawley, L. S., & Neill, J. D. (1979). Age-related changes in serum levels of gonadotropins and testosterone in infantile male rhesus monkeys. *Biology of Reproduction, 20,* 1147–1151.

Frisch, R. E., Gotz-Welbergen, A. V., McArthur, J. W., Albright, T., Witschi, J., Bullen, B., Birnholz, J., Reed, R. B., & Herman, H. (1981). Delayed menarche and amenorrhea of college athletes in relation to age of onset of training.

Frisch, R. E., & McArthur, J. W. (1974). Menstrual cycles: Fatness as a determinant of minimum weight for height necessary for their maintenance or onset. *Science, 185,* 949–951.

Frisch, R. E., & Revelle, R. (1970). Height and weight at menarche and a hypothesis of critical body weights and adolescent events. *Science, 169,* 397–399.

Gay, V. L, & Plant, T. M. (1987). N-methyl-D,L-aspartate elicits hypothalamic gonadotropin-releasing hormone release in prepubertal male rhesus monkeys *(Macaca mulatta). Endocrinology, 120,* 2289–2296.

Goldsmith, P. C., Lamberts, R., & Brezina, L. R. (1983). Gonadotropin-releasing hormone neurons and pathways in the primate hypothalamus and forebrain. In R. L. Norman (Ed.), *Neuroendocrine aspects of reproduction* (pp. 7–45). New York: Academic Press.

Haymond, M. W., Karl, I. E., Clarke, W. L., Pagliara, A. S., & Santiago, J. C. (1982). Differences in circulating gluconeogenic substrates during short-term fasting in men, women, and children. *Metabolism, 31,* 33–42.

Jakacki, R. I., Kelch, R. P., Sauder, S. E., Lloyd, J. S., Hopwood, N. J., & Marshall, J. C. (1982). Pulsatile secretion of luteinizing hormone in children. *Journal of Clinical Endocrinology and Metabolism, 55,* 453–458.

Kapen, S., Boyar, R. M., Finkelstein, J. W., Hellman, L., & Weitzman, E. D. (1974). Effect of sleep–wake cycle reversal on luteinizing hormone secretory pattern in puberty. *Journal of Clinical Endocrinology and Metabolism, 39,* 293–299.

Kleiber, M. (1947). Body size and metabolic rate. *Physiological Reviews, 27,* 511–541.

Levine, R. J., Loriaux, D. L., & Cutler, Jr., G. B. (1983). Developmental changes in neuroendocrine regulation of gonadotropin secretion in gonadal dysgenesis. *Journal of Clinical Endocrinology and Metabolism, 57,* 288–293.

Malina, R. M., Spirduso, W. W., Tate, C., & Baylor, A. M. (1978). Age at menarche and selected menstrual characteristics in athletes at different competitive levels and in different sports. *Medicine and Science in Sports, 10,* 218.

Mann, D. R., Davis-DaSilva, M., Wallen, K., Coan, P., Evans, D. E., & Collins, D. C. (1984). Blockade of neonatal activation of the pituitary-testicular axis with continuous administration of a gonadotropin-releasing hormone agonist in male rhesus monkeys. *Journal of Clinical Endocrinology and Metabolism, 59,* 207–211.

Marshall, G. R., Wickings, E. J., & Nieschlag, E. (1985). Pulsatile GnRH administration in immature male monkeys. *Acta Endocrinologica, 108 (Suppl. 267),* 179.

Mauras, N., Veldhuis, J. D., & Rogol, A. D. (1986). Role of endogenous opiates in pubertal maturation: Opposing actions of naltrexone in prepubertal and late pubertal boys. *Journal of Clinical Endocrinology and Metabolism, 62,* 1256–1263.

Morimoto, Y., Oishi, T., Hanasaki, N., Miyatake, A., Sato, B., Noma, K., Kato, H., Yano, S., & Yamamura, Y. (1980). Interrelations among amenorrhea, serum gonadotropins and body weight in anorexia nervosa. *Endocrinologica Japonica, 27*, 191–200.

Nillius, S. J., Fries, H., & Wide, L. (1975). Successful induction of follicular maturation and ovulation by prolonged treatment with LH-releasing hormone in women with anorexia nervosa. *American Journal of Obstetrics and Gynecology, 122*, 921–928.

Penny, R., Olambiwonnu, N. O., & Frasier, S. D. (1977). Episodic fluctuations of serum gonadotropins in pre- and postpubertal girls and boys. *Journal of Clinical Endocrinology and Metabolism, 45*, 307–311.

Pirke, K. M., Fichter, M. M., Lund, R., & Doerr, P. (1979). Twenty-four hour sleep–wake pattern of plasma LH in patients with anorexia nervosa. *Acta Endocrinologica, 92*, 193–204.

Plant, T. M. (1980). The effects of neonatal orchidectomy on the developmental pattern of gonadotropin secretion in the male rhesus monkey *(Macaca mulatta)*. *Endocrinology, 106*, 1451–1454.

Plant, T. M. (1983). Ontogeny of gonadotropin secretion in the rhesus macaque *(Macaca mulatta)*. In R. L. Norman (Ed.), *Neuroendocrine aspects of reproduction* (pp. 133–147). New York: Academic Press.

Plant, T. M. (1985). A study of the role of the postnatal testes in determining the ontogeny of gonadotropin secretion in the male rhesus monkey *(Macaca mulatta)*. *Endocrinology, 116*, 1341–1350.

Plant, T. M. (1988). Puberty in primates. In E. Knobil and J. D. Neill (Eds.), *The physiology of reproduction* (chap. 41, pp. 1763–1788). New York: Raven.

Plant, T. M., & Zorub, D. S. (1982). The role of nongonadal restraint of gonadotropin secretion in the delay of the onset of puberty in the rhesus monkey *(Macaca mulatta)*. *Journal of Animal Science, 55 (Suppl. 2)*, 43–55.

Rapisarda, J. J., Bergman, K. S., Steiner, R. A., & Foster, D. L. (1983). Response to estradiol inhibition of tonic luteinizing hormone secretion decreases during the final stage of puberty in the rhesus monkey. *Endocrinology, 112*, 1172–1179.

Rowell, T. E. (1977). Variation in age at puberty in monkeys. *Folia Primatologia, 27*, 284–290.

Sauder, S. E., Case, G. D., Hopwood, N. J., Kelch, R. P., & Marshall, J. C. (1984). The effects of opiate antagonism on gonadotropin secretion in children and in women with hypothalamic amenorrhea. *Pediatric Research, 18*, 322–328.

Steiner, R. A., & Bremner, W. J. (1981). Endocrine correlates of sexual development in the male monkey, *Macaca fascicularis*. *Endocrinology, 109*, 914–918.

Steiner, R. A., & Cameron, J. L. (1989). Endocrine control of reproduction. In B. Hille, A. Fuchs, R. Steiner, & A. Scher (Eds.), *Textbook of physiology* (pp 1289–1342). Philadelphia: Saunders.

Steiner, R. A., Cameron, J. L., McNeill, T. H., Clifton, D. K., & Bremner, W. J. (1983). Metabolic signals for the onset of puberty. In R. L. Norman (Ed.), *Neuroendocrine aspects of reproduction* (pp. 183–337). New York: Academic Press.

Steiner, R. A., Peterson, A. P., Yu, J. Y. L., Conner, H., Gilbert, M., ter-Penning, B., & Bremner, W. J. (1980). Ultradian luteinizing hormone and testosterone rhythms in the adult male monkey, *Macaca fascicularis*. *Endocrinology, 107*, 1489–1493.

Styne, D. M., & Grumbach, M. M. (1978). Puberty in the male and female: Its physiology and disorders. In S. S. C. Yen & R. B. Jaffe (Eds.), *Reproduc-

tive endocrinology, physiology, pathophysiology and clinical management (pp. 189–235). Philadelphia: Saunders.

Terasawa, E., Noonan, J. J., Nass, T. E., & Loose, M. D. (1984). Posterior hypothalamic lesions advance the onset of puberty in the female rhesus monkey. *Endocrinology, 115,* 2241–2250.

Van Wagenen, G., & Simpson, M. E. (1954). Testicular development in the rhesus monkey. *Anatomical Records, 118,* 231–251.

Van Wagenen, G., & Simpson, M. E. (1973). *Postnatal development of the ovary in Homo sapiens and Macaca mulatta.* New Haven, CT: Yale University Press.

Walker, M. L., Wilson, M. E., & Gordon, T. P. (1984). Endocrine control of the seasonal occurrence of ovulation in rhesus monkeys housed outdoors. *Endocrinology, 114,* 1074–1081.

Warren, M. P. (1980). The effects of exercise on pubertal progression and reproductive function in girls. *Journal of Clinical Endocrinology and Metabolism, 51,* 1150–1157.

Warren, M. P., Jewelewicz, R., Dryenfurth, I., Ans, R., Khalaf, S., & Vande Wiele, R. L. (1975). The significance of weight loss in the evaluation of pituitary response to LH-RH in women with secondary amenorrhea. *Journal of Clinical Endocrinology and Metabolism, 40,* 601–611.

Warren, M. P., & Vande Wiele, R. L. (1973). Clinical and metabolic features of anorexia nervosa. *American Journal of Obstetrics and Gynecology, 117,* 435–449.

Wickings, E. J., Zaidi, P., Brabant, G., & Nieschlag, E. (1981). Stimulation of pituitary and testicular functions with LH-RH agonist or pulsatile LH-RH treatment in the rhesus monkey during the non-breeding season. *Journal of Reproduction and Fertility, 63,* 129–136.

Wildt, L., Marshall, G., & Knobil, E. (1980). Experimental induction of puberty in the infantile female rhesus monkey. *Science, 207,* 1373–1375.

Wilson, M. E., Gordon, T. P., Blank, M. S., & Collins, D. C. (1984). Timing of sexual maturity in female rhesus monkeys *(Macaca mulatta)* housed outdoors. *Journal of Reproduction and Fertility, 70,* 625–633.

Winter, J. S. D., Faiman, C., Hobson, W. C., Prasad, A. V., & Reyes, F. I. (1975). Pituitary-gonadal relations in infancy. I. Patterns of serum gonadotropin concentrations from birth to four years of age in man and chimpanzee. *Journal of Clinical Endocrinology and Metabolism, 40,* 545–551.

Zgliczynski, S., Baranowska, B., Jeske, W., Niewiadomska, A., Rozbick, A. G., & Schally, A. V. (1974). The effect of D-Trp6-LRH upon secretion of gonadotropin—a possible therapeutic application in anorexia nervosa. *Acta Endocrinologica* (Copenhagen), *105,* 161–166.

2

The Onset of Human Puberty: Biological and Environmental Factors

Nancy J. Hopwood, Robert P. Kelch, Paula M. Hale, Tarina M. Mendes, Carol M. Foster, and Inese Z. Beitins

The human reproductive system undergoes a remarkable period of development and activity during fetal life (Kaplan, Grumbach, & Aubert, 1975) and early infancy, when there is transient secretion of increased gonadal steroids and gonadotropins (Kaplan et al., 1975; Sizonenko, 1978). However, an arrest of maturation occurs shortly thereafter, and the hypothalamic-pituitary-gonadal axis appears to be nearly dormant during early childhood (Conte et al., 1980). It has been postulated that this quiescent period is the result of central nervous system (CNS) restraint systems. Hypothalamic lesions in rodents (Donovan & van der Werff ten Bosch, 1956) and clinical observations in children with precocious puberty who have CNS lesions (Huseman et al., 1978) support the concept that there is an active restraint process of the hypothalamic-pituitary axis during early childhood. The mechanism by which this restraint operates is unknown, although it has been the subject of vigorous investigation.

During the quiescent phase, the prepubertal reproductive system is characterized by low follicle-stimulating hormone (FSH) and luteinizing-hormone (LH) secretion, with a high FSH: LH ratio, especially in girls (Kelch et al., 1980). During this period there is also enhanced sensitivity of the hypothalamic-pituitary axis to the feedback effects of gonadal steroids from the ovary or testis (Grumbach, Grave, & Mayer, 1974), so that the LH-secretory response to exogenously administered synthetic gonadotropin-releasing hormone (GnRH) is low (Grumbach et al., 1974; Kelch et al., 1980). The fact that low gonadotropin secretion is present in functional agonadal or surgically castrated individuals supports the hypothesis that the CNS restraint system cannot be due to sex steroid feedback alone.

In adults LH secretion is highly pulsatile during both day and night. The frequency of the pulse is 90–120 minutes, but this pulse frequency is greatly influenced by the varying hormonal milieu (Kelch et al., 1975; Huseman & Kelch, 1978, Marshall & Kelch, 1986). For example, the absence of gonadal steroids increases gonadotropin pulse frequency in adult agonadal individuals to nearly circhoral or hourly rates (Boyar et al., 1973b). The positive-feedback effects of estradiol (Fig. 2-1) in adult females cannot be demonstrated in young girls until midpubertal development has been achieved (Reiter, Kuling & Hamwood, 1974). The transition between the childhood or inhibitory stage and the adult stage is gradual, requiring a period of at least 4–5 years. It is believed by many investigators that the onset of puberty is heralded by the onset of episodic GnRH secretion, initially detected as episodic secretion of LH during sleep (Boyar et al., 1974a,b). There is now ample evidence that GnRH is secreted episodically in the prepubertal child long before physical signs of puberty appear (Jakacki et al., 1982). The onset of puberty therefore appears to be associated with an amplification of pulsatile gonadotropin secretion. The mechanisms by which this process occurs and the maturation of the process that ultimately leads to clinical pubertal changes have been the subject of many of our investigations described here.

Research Studies on Hypothalamic-Pituitary Regulation of Human Puberty

We have been able to learn a significant amount about the maturation of the hypothalamic-pituitary-gonadal axis by the pulsed administration of synthetic GnRH to individual children over time and by serial measurements of plasma gonadotropins both at night and during the day at varying ages and stages of pubertal development. Most of the children who have participated in our clinical projects have been referred to us because of short stature or delayed adolescence, and after thorough evaluation, have been considered "endocrinologically normal."

Longitudinal Studies: GnRH Responsiveness

A large cohort of children with presumed isolated growth hormone (GH) deficiency were studied serially to add to our understanding of the spontaneous maturation of the hypothalamic-pituitary axis in response to GnRH and to determine whether those children who would ultimately be found to have gonadotropin deficiency could be diag-

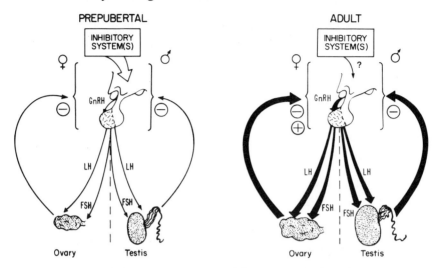

Figure 2–1. Hypothalamic-pituitary-gonadal axis. GnRH, Gonadotropin-releasing hormone; LH, luteinizing hormone; FSH, follicle-stimulating hormone; +, positive feedback; −, negative feedback. (Reprinted with permission from Bacon et al., 1982, p. 191.)

nosed prior to the normal age for puberty. Synthetic GnRH (Warner-Lambert/Parke-Davis) (2.5 μg/kg, IV bolus) was given as a standardized GnRH test (Kelch et al., 1975). A single test did not predict which children would ultimately become gonadotropin-deficient, but serial observations in individual children gave us a better understanding of the pattern of gonadotropin secretion over time. Although children with isolated GH deficiency have lower than normal responses to GnRH, their patterns closely parallel those of normal children (Kelch, Grumbach, & Kaplan, 1972; Sauder et al., 1981).

Figure 2-2 demonstrates serial gonadotropin responses in a young girl with isolated GH deficiency at a chronological age of 9 years and a bone age of 7 years, which is reflective of her physiological maturity. The prompt initial FSH rise is typical of prepubertal girls, with a relatively high FSH : LH ratio. Repeat studies at bone ages of 8 and 9 years indicate a decrease in FSH, but the responses remain prepubertal (FSH > LH). However, when her bone age reached 11 years—the average age at which the first physical signs of puberty appear in girls—the LH response was now greater than that of FSH, which is typical of puberty. This pubertal response to GnRH closely parallels the onset of breast budding (stage 2) (Kelch et al., 1972).

Similar studies are summarized in Figure 2-3 for a prepubertal boy at bone ages 6, 7, 9, and 11 years. FSH responses are low throughout,

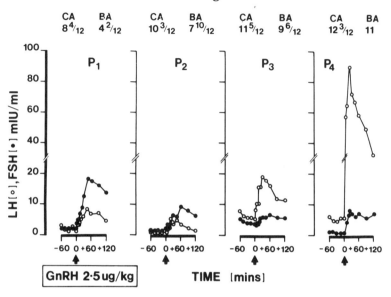

Figure 2–2. Serial gonadotropin responses to intravenous GnRH in a girl with isolated growth hormone (GH) deficiency. CA, Chronological age in years; BA, bone age in years; P_1–P_4, pubertal stages 1–4. (Reprinted with permission from Kelch et al., 1983, p. 233.)

but there is progressive LH responsiveness as pubertal stages progress. The first physical sign of puberty in boys is testicular enlargement, which heralds stage 2 (Kelch et al., 1972); it usually occurs in normal boys by a bone age of 12 years.

The onset of pubic hair growth in both boys and girls closely follows the first sign of puberty just described, and is initially the result of increased secretion of adrenal androgen. This process is commonly referred to as adrenarche. Although investigators have wondered whether adrenarche could play a role in triggering the onset of hypothalamic-pituitary-gonadal maturation, clinical observations in children with adrenal insufficiency have not supported this concept (Cutler & Loriaux, 1980).

It is also known that as puberty proceeds, and immunoreactive LH and FSH rise, there is an increase in biologically active LH as well (Lucky et al., 1980; Reiter et al., 1982; Burstein et al., 1985). Bioactive LH in humans is usually undetectable during the prepubertal years, then rises dramatically during pubertal maturation (Reiter et al., 1982). In adults the dissociation of immunoreactive and biologically active LH peaks is small (<25%) (Dufau et al., 1983), but in children more discordance is

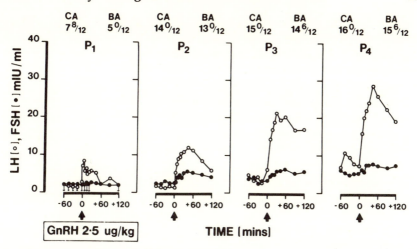

Figure 2–3. Serial gonadotropin responses to intravenous GnRH in a boy with isolated GH deficiency. Abbreviations as in Figure 2–2. (Reprinted with permission from Kelch et al., 1983, p. 234.)

present (Reiter et al., 1982), possibly related to qualitative changes in the LH molecule (Burstein et al., 1985; Reiter et al., 1984, 1989).

Pulsatile GnRH Secretion in Prepubertal Children

Considerable evidence supports the conclusion that GnRH secretion is low during childhood. As puberty approaches there is a sleep-entrained increase in LH secretion, and gradually, more episodic secretion of LH is easily demonstrable (Boyar et al., 1974b).

It has been unclear whether GnRH pulse frequency alone, GnRH amplitude alone, or both are decreased in the prepubertal child because of the difficulty of studying young children. Peripheral blood levels of LH are frequently at or near the lower limit of assay sensitivity. However, we have proposed the working hypothesis that GnRH pulse frequency plays a regulatory role in the development and function of the human reproductive system. A series of studies in prepubertal and early pubertal children were designed to document gonadotropin secretion, and by inference, GnRH secretory patterns during the transition period from childhood into adolescence, because endogenous GnRH cannot be measured in circulating peripheral blood.

Initially, it was important to document whether LH was secreted episodically during the quiescent (inhibitory) childhood stage of pubertal development. Gonadotropin secretory patterns of 22 sexually immature children whose skeletal ages were less than 12 years were studied during the day and night. We were able to demonstrate pulsatile secretion of LH in approximately half of the children. In addition, there was augmented LH secretion during the nighttime period, as reflected by both plasma LH concentrations and urinary excretion of gonadotropins during sleep (Jakacki et al., 1982).

Figure 2-4 illustrates the results of a typical study obtained from a 7-year-old boy with a bone age of 4 years. FSH and LH were low during the afternoon, with concentrations often below assay sensitivity, but at midnight, LH and FSH pulsations were detected and mean concentrations were increased. In response to a standard test dose of GnRH, the FSH and LH response patterns were low and of equal magnitude, typical of a prepubertal boy. In contrast, a similar study (Fig. 2-5) from a 14-year-old boy with no pubertal signs and a delayed bone age of 10 years, showed more enhancement of LH secretion during sleep, and greater LH response to synthetic GnRH administration with an increase in the LH : FSH ratio. The observation that prepubertal children secrete LH in a pulsatile manner well before physical evidence of sexual maturation is apparent was also demonstrated by other investigators (Levine & Cutler, 1982).

Figure 2–4. Day and night gonadotropin secretion in a typical early prepubertal boy. HA, Height age in years; other abbreviations as in Figure 2–2. Low gonadotropin secretion was present throughout the day, but at midnight (*) pulsatile LH and FSH were detected. Response to bolus GnRH is immature (i.e., FSH = LH). (Adapted with permission from Jakacki et al., 1982. Copyright by Williams & Wilkins, Baltimore.)

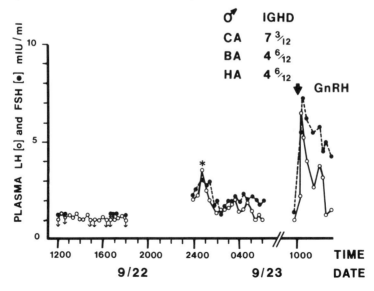

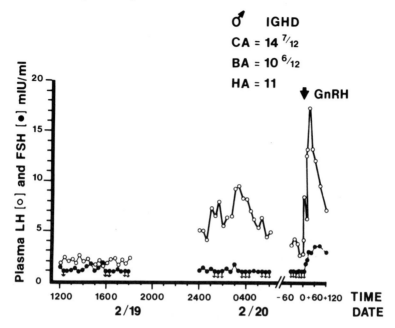

Figure 2–5. Day and night gonadotropin secretion in a typical late prepubertal boy. Abbreviations as in Figure 2–4. LH secretion is enhanced during sleep, and gonadotropin response to bolus intravenous GnRH shows a typical pattern for early puberty (LH > FSH).

Although we were able to demonstrate pulsatile secretion patterns of gonadotropins in some prepubertal children, the remarkably low amplitudes of the pulses made a precise estimate of the GnRH pulse frequency difficult, especially in the younger children. Priming some of the children with synthetic GnRH given in a pulsatile manner (24 ng/kg IV pulses of GnRH every 2 hours for 4 days) allowed us more easily to ascertain the pulsatile nature of the secretory pattern. A pulse frequency of approximately one pulse every 3–4 hours was present in prepubertal children (Kelch, Hopwood, & Marshall, 1979; Kelch et al., 1980; Jakacki et al., 1982).

Role of Endogenous Opiates

Endogenous opioid peptides have been shown to be important modulators of gonadotropin secretion in adult humans (Stubbs et al., 1978; Morley et al., 1980; Quigley & Yen, 1980). We wondered whether endogenous opiates could play a role in the suppression of gonadotropin secretion and in the day/night difference in gonadotropin secretion detected in the prepubertal child. To answer this question, daytime gonadotropin secretion was studied under the influence of opiate antagonism by naloxone in four children (two in late prepuberty and two in early puberty) who had low daytime but increased LH secretion at night. Naloxone had no effect on daytime gonadotropin secretion in the three youngest children but produced a slight but discernible increase in plasma LH in the most mature child, a boy at midpuberty. Naloxone produced a striking increase in mean plasma LH and in LH pulse frequency in amenorrheic women who had normal body weight. Thus, it does not appear that endogenous opiates play a role in suppression of gonadotropin levels in children, at least prior to midpuberty.

GnRH Pulse Frequency

We next speculated that gonadotropin and (by inference) GnRH pulse frequency change throughout the day in prepubertal and early pubertal children. Observations were derived from additional detailed studies in 32 children whose bone ages were between 11 and 14 years. (Kelch et al., 1989). These patients were studied over 6–24 hours with an average of 15 hours of continuous observation. Blood samples were withdrawn every 15–20 minutes in order to detect significant gonadotropin pulses.

A typical example was an early pubertal boy with a bone age of 12 years who showed an increase in LH pulse amplitude and frequency simultaneously with the onset of sleep. Between midnight and 3 to 4 a.m., gonadotropin pulses occurred on a nearly hourly basis; after this, LH pulse amplitude and frequency decreased. Serum testosterone rose two- to threefold from early evening until 4 a.m. The mean LH pulse frequency of 21 early pubertal boys was calculated and expressed as pulses per patient per hour (Kelch et al., 1987; Khoury et al., 1985). Before midnight, LH pulse frequency averaged approximately 0.3 pulses per patient hour or approximately 1 pulse every 3 hours. After midnight, however, pulse frequency more than doubled and remained high until 4 a.m.

These observations, as well as those in the prepubertal children, clearly demonstrated that LH pulse frequency is not constant throughout the day and increases at the onset of sleep. In the older children it was apparent that the rise in pulse frequency preceded the rise in LH amplitude. We then began to wonder about the role that sex steroids might play in the regulation of this nocturnal rise, since the LH pulse frequency began to fall when the serum testosterone level began to rise.

Role of Sex Steroids in GnRH Secretion

In order to examine the role that sex steroids might have in the nocturnal secretion of gonadotropins, we examined the effects of different doses of long-acting testosterone injections on pulsatile LH secretion in

10 boys in early to midpuberty whose bone ages were 11–14 years (Kelch et al., 1985). Blood samples were taken every 20 minutes for 20 consecutive hours over two consecutive weekends before and 6 days after testosterone enanthate was given IM (0, 25, 50, or 75 mg/m²). Figure 2-6 depicts results from an early pubertal boy whose chronological age was approximately 15 years and bone age 13 years. Note that during the control study he demonstrated an impressive sleep-entrained increase in LH and FSH secretion. Serum testosterone rose dramatically overnight. A synthetic GnRH bolus elicited a brisk LH response, typical of early puberty. One week later, when serum testosterone was constant as a result of the steady state brought about by the IM injection, LH and FSH secretion were severely suppressed to or below assay sensitivity, without alteration of pituitary responsiveness. We studied other boys with smaller doses of testosterone and showed that the pulsatile secretion of LH was very sensitive to all but the smallest doses

Figure 2–6. Gonadotropin secretory patterns in an early pubertal boy with constitutionally delayed adolescence (chronological age, 15.7 years; stage 3 puberty; bone age, 13.5 years), before and 6 days after initiation of testosterone enanthate (T) therapy (50 mg/m² IM). Maximum incremental LH responses to GnRH were not changed by therapy. (Reprinted with permission from Kelch et al., 1983, p. 251.)

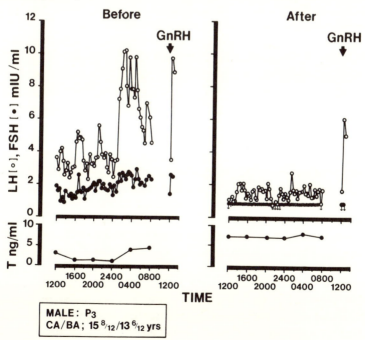

of testosterone (Kelch et al., 1985). These results indicate that, at this stage of pubertal development, sex steroids reduce gonadotropin secretion primarily by reduction of GnRH pulse amplitude at the hypothalamus. These studies did not answer the question whether testosterone was acting directly or indirectly via conversion to another metabolite such as estradiol.

In order to determine the sensitivity of the GnRH pulse generator to testosterone, acute testosterone infusions were given to early pubertal boys. The boys, who had a mean bone age of $12\frac{1}{2}$ years, were studied twice, once with an IV infusion of saline and once with testosterone (100 μg/hour). Blood samples were withdrawn every 10 minutes between 8 p.m. and 8 a.m., followed by boluses of GnRH to test pituitary responsiveness. During the night of the testosterone infusion, serum testosterone rose rapidly, then maintained a steady state. The artificially induced testosterone rise 3 hours before the usual onset of nocturnal LH amplification and testosterone rise did not prevent the sleep-entrained LH rise initially, but there appeared to be attenuation of LH pulse frequency and amplitude later in the night; this observation (Hale et al., 1988) is under further study. Pituitary responsiveness to GnRH was unaffected by the infusion of testosterone. These observations contrast significantly with the acute suppressive effects of testosterone infusions on nocturnal gonadotropin secretion in adult men (Santen, 1975), and suggest that, in early pubertal boys during the early hours of sleep, there may be refractoriness or relative insensitivity of the GnRH pulse generator to the acute effects of testosterone.

Summary of Neuroendocrine Effects Associated with the Onset of Puberty

These studies show that GnRH pulse frequency and amplitude are low during childhood, although GnRH secretion increases during sleep. As a result of low GnRH stimulation of pituitary gonadotropins, there is a low pituitary responsiveness to GnRH, a high ratio of FSH to LH in blood, and low gonadal steroid production. The onset of puberty is heralded by a striking amplification or reactivation of a previously established pulsatile and sleep-entrained increase in gonadotropin secretion. The amplification of LH secretion during sleep appears to be best explained by an increase in GnRH pulse frequency and amplitude, which gradually induces testicular and ovarian maturation (Marshall & Kelch, 1986). The control mechanism(s) for the low (almost dormant), gonadotropin secretion present during childhood, and the events that lead to changes in GnRH pulse frequency and amplitude ultimately responsible for stimulating sex steroid secretion remain to be further delineated. However, our studies suggest that the mechanisms involved are not endogenous opiates or acute feedback by sex steroids.

Timing of the Onset of Puberty

Specific mechanisms involved in the timing of the onset of the pubertal events are complex and poorly understood. Events that significantly alter the CNS regulation of GnRH secretion, such as destructive hypothalamic lesions seen in some children with isosexual central sexual precocity, have given us insight into the role of the CNS-inhibitory restraints normally delaying pubertal events until the end of the first decade of life in humans. Although it was formerly thought that the majority of cases of true isosexual precocity in girls were "idiopathic" in origin, improved cranial computerized tomography has shown that many young girls with sexual precocity do have anatomically discernible lesions in the hypothalamus, such as hamartomas of the tuber cinereum (Cacciari et al., 1983).

In children with central precocity, early activation of the hypothalamic-pituitary axis usually follows the sequence of normal puberty, often at a greatly accelerated rate. The hormonal profiles of these young children parallel those of normal pubertal maturation: increasing daytime and nocturnal pulsatile gonadotropin levels and sex steroid levels, pubertal LH responses to GnRH, and marked increases in LH bioactivity (Bidlingmaier, Butenandt, & Knorr, 1977; Boyar et al., 1973a; Reiter et al., 1975; Matthews et al., 1982; Lucky et al., 1980).

Until recently there had been no useful medical therapy that would stop the galloping linear growth and skeletal advancement in these rapidly maturing children. However, it is now possible to treat children with central precocity with daily injections of GnRH agonists after a brief period of pituitary gonadotropin augmentation (Crowley et al., 1981). Initial reports of decreased linear growth and skeletal maturation with this therapeutic modality are encouraging (Mansfield et al., 1983; Luder et al., 1984).

Figure 2-7 shows the typical gonadotropin responses present in a 5-year-old boy with central idiopathic precocity who had midpubertal development and a bone age of 13 years. The upper panel shows his overnight pulsatile LH secretion—a pattern that is typical of mid puberty. With GnRH analogue therapy (8 μg/kg SC once daily), mean LH levels were halved and pulses markedly blunted. Serum testosterone concentrations significantly decreased from 6 ng/ml to 0.2 ng/ml in the first 3 months of therapy, and social behavior improved. This therapy therefore effectively institutes a temporary reversible reduction in pituitary gonadotropin secretion. The primary or secondary effects of these GnRH analogues on other pituitary hormone secretion are currently under study (Mendes et al., 1987).

Pubertal events in normal children usually span 4 years, but there may be a wide range of timing for the onset of these events (Marshall

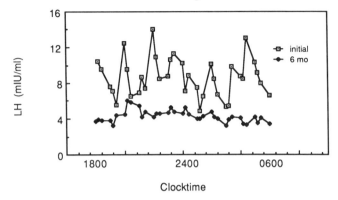

Figure 2–7. LH-secretory patterns in a boy with idiopathic precocious puberty (chronological age, 5 years; bone age, 13 years) before (▫) and 6 months after (●) therapy with GnRH analogue (D-His-A). Blood samples taken every 20 minutes over a 12-hour period (1800–0600 hours; 6 p.m. to 6 a.m.) were tested for LH. Dose of analogue was 8 μg/kg SC daily. Mean LH secretion was halved upon therapy, and serum testosterone levels fell into the prepubertal range.

and Tanner, 1969, 1970). Peak growth rate occurs in early puberty in girls associated with initiation of breast development (stage 2). In boys, peak growth velocity is later (midpuberty or stage 3–4) and is usually preceded by a period of decelerating growth velocity (stage 2). Menarche usually occurs $2\frac{1}{2}$–3 years after the onset of breast budding, but menstrual cycles usually remain irregular and may often be anovulatory for several years (Apter & Vihko, 1977). Thus, puberty is considered to be early if the first physical sign occurs prior to age 8 years in girls and age 9 in boys, and delayed if no physical sign has appeared prior to age 13 years in girls and age 14 in boys.

It is well known that geographic, ethnic, and genetic factors interact with socioeconomic status, health, nutrition, and emotions to determine the precise age of onset of puberty for any single individual. By far the most common cause of pubertal delay is a physiological or constitutional abnormality, which is often familial. Children in this group will enter puberty later than their peers and, since skeletal maturation is also delayed, they will reach a normal height for their respective families later than average. What is often difficult to understand clinically is the interplay of nutritional and emotional factors that also are known to delay pubertal onset or progression. Pubertal onset and progression parallel bone age closely, but skeletal advancement seems to be subject to the same biological and environmental factors as puberty itself.

The association of a minimal percentage of body fat with menarche and the initiation of the pubertal growth spurt has been widely debated (Frisch & Revelle, 1970; Fishman, 1980). The presence or development of a "critical" factor altering metabolic rate and hypothalamic function has also been hypothesized (Ojeda et al., 1980). Evidence that there is an association between nutritional factors and body composition on the one hand, and time of onset of puberty on the other, is provided by the earlier age of menarche in moderately obese girls (Zacharias et al., 1969), and by delayed maturation of children in varying states of malnutrition (Kulin et al., 1982, 1984). Low gonadotropin secretion is common in many states of chronic illness or low body weight, particularly when the illness or weight loss occurs prior to or during the pubertal process (Reiter, Stern, & Root, 1981).

Nutritional deficiencies associated with significant chronic illness (e.g., inflammatory bowel disease) delay linear growth, skeletal maturation, and pubertal onset (Tenore et al., 1977), but the precise mechanism is often poorly understood. Improvements in growth and onset of puberty usually do not accompany specific replacement of individual nutrients or minerals, but rather begin when body weight begins to normalize (Layden et al., 1976).

Other nutritional causes of pubertal delay have been related to a fear of obesity (Pugliese et al., 1983), food aversion in athletes (Smith, 1980), and anorexia nervosa (Irwin, 1981). In these conditions, studies of the hypothalamic-pituitary axis may reveal a reversion to a prepubertal pattern of gonadotropin secretion or maturational arrest (Boyar et al., 1974a; Hurd, Palumbo, & Gharib, 1977; Marshall & Kelch, 1979). Figure 2-8 shows the pulsatile LH secretory pattern in a woman with anorexia nervosa. The similarity to that of a prepubertal girl is striking. The gonadotropin secretion in this young woman who had been amenorrheic for about 10 years was studied while her body weight was low. Gonadotropin secretion during a 24-hour control day was very low, similar to that seen in prepubertal girls. Over 5 days she was given injections of GnRH every 2 hours. The initially high FSH : LH ratio, typical of the prepubertal girl, gradually converted to a pubertal pattern on the fifth day of therapy. There was a gradual rise of estradiol (Fig. 2-8, lower hatched bars), reflective of ovarian responsiveness. Prior to GnRH therapy, a GnRH bolus resulted in a prepubertal response (plasma FSH > LH). After 5 days of GnRH pulses, a standard GnRH test resulted in a pubertal response (plasma LH > FSH). These observations are reflective of a rapid hypothalamic-pituitary maturation without change in body weight (Marshall & Kelch, 1979).

Serial LH secretion patterns of younger girls with anorexia nervosa have been studied by Pirke et al. (1979) and clearly demonstrate the maturational effect on the hypothalamic-pituitary axis associated with refeeding. When a nutritionally recovered young girl lost 19% of her

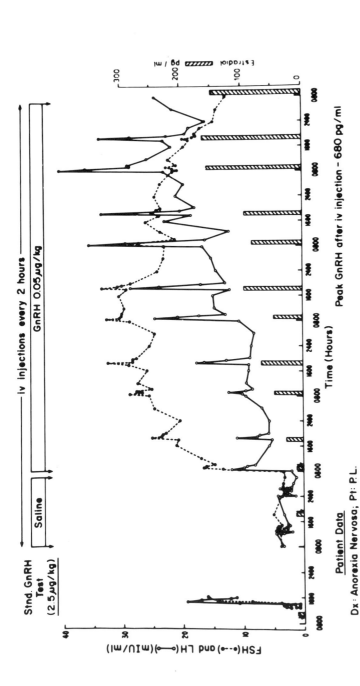

Figure 2–8. Gonadotropin responses to pulsatile intravenous administration of GnRH in a patient with anorexia nervosa. On day 1 of a 7-day study, LH and FSH responses to GnRH were equal and just within the early pubertal range. Bolus saline pulses (day 2) and GnRH pulses, 0.05 μg/kg, were given IV every 2 hours (days 3–7). Over the course of the week there was a reversal of the FSH : LH ratio in response to a constant albeit pulsatile GnRH stimulus. Bar graphs depict rising estradiol levels in response to this change. This reversal is very similar to the changes noted during early puberty in girls. (Reprinted with permission from Marshall & Kelch, 1979. Copyright by Williams & Wilkins, Baltimore.)

weight, there was prompt reversion to a prepubertal pattern, which again became pubertal with weight gain. Many of these young women, however, never return to normal menstrual cyclicity despite maintenance of normal body weight, suggesting that additional CNS influences other than nutrition are often important in the pathogenesis of the reproductive abnormality in patients with anorexia nervosa (Mecklenburg et al., 1974).

Intense dieting as a result of fear of obesity often leads young women to institute eating patterns that can dramatically affect physical growth and pubertal progression. Figure 2-9 shows growth data from a young girl who developed an aversion to food at age 11–12 years. At that time height and weight were appropriate. However, with the subsequent weight loss, linear growth arrest began and lasted for years. In addition, she began intense exercise to maintain her low body fat. Pubertal changes did not begin, however, until she stopped her diet and intense exercise at age 18 years. Menarche occurred at age 21 years, 3 years after pubertal onset. This young woman was therefore in a state of

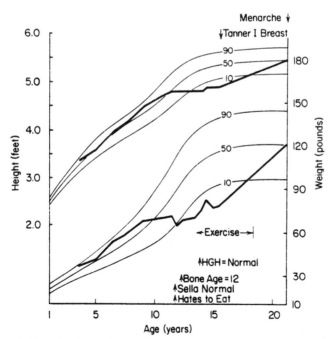

Figure 2–9. Growth chart of a young woman who had growth and pubertal arrest in response to intensive dieting initially, and then dieting and intense exercise. Only when both dieting and exercise ceased did pubertal progression begin.

pubertal arrest for 6 years, brought on by her low body weight, strenuous exercise, emotional state—or all three.

Female athletes whose training began before the usual age of menarche have been shown to have delayed onset of menarche; they are also more likely to show amenorrhea or have irregular periods during intense physical training than their peers who began their training later (Frisch et al., 1981). However, it is well known that menstrual dysfunction is frequent in female athletes (Bullen et al., 1985) and women undergoing any vigorous physical exertion (Warren, 1980) and is often correlated with lower body weight. It is probable that thinness and intense exercise act synergistically to produce metabolic effects that can alter the hypothalamic-pituitary axis (Vandenbroucke, van Laar, & Valkenburg, 1982).

Emotional stress with or without weight loss may also delay pubertal onset and progression. Dramatic arrest of growth and pubertal progression was shown in a 16-year-old boy described in detail by Magner, Rogol, and Gordon (1984) after he suffered a traumatic shock. Adolescent-aged children with psychosocial dwarfism can show marked physical stunting, skeletal delay, and delayed puberty (Hopwood & Becker, 1979; Bowden & Hopwood, 1982). These children may have increased caloric expenditures or poor caloric utilization to help explain, in part, their lack of weight gain despite large dietary intakes. Pituitary growth hormone secretion may also be low, presumably as a result of stress-related inhibition of the hypothalamic-pituitary axis (Powell, Hopwood, & Barratt, 1973; Powell et al., 1967). An improvement in the child's environment may lead to dramatic catch-up growth and rapid pubertal progression if the child is already of pubertal age.

It is likely that emotional factors could also have a role in an individual who has a very sluggish progression through puberty in more subtle ways. A fear of growing up can become manifest in the arrest of linear growth and pubertal progression (Hopwood & Schwartz, unpublished data). A prepubertal boy aged 17 years and 3 months, with a bone age of 14 years and height age of 12 years, had normal gonadotropin responses to bolus GnRH for a pubertal boy and borderline provocative but low spontaneous GH secretion while growing at a very slow rate (3.5 cm/year). Psychological evaluation revealed guilt about wishing his father would die, and when this later occurred, a fear of growing up, because, he said, "if you grow up you have to die." Further counselling and treatment with short-term low-dose anabolic steroids resulted in improvement in his growth velocity (8.5 cm/year) and normal progression through puberty. Thus, the adolescent with delayed pubertal progression deserves careful evaluation of psychosocial and nutritional as well as biological factors.

References

Apter, D., & Vihko, R. (1977). Serum pregnenolone, progesterone, 17-hydrox-yprogesterone, testerone and 5 α-dihydrotesterone during human puberty. *Journal of Clinical Endocrinology and Metabolism, 45*, 1039.

Bidlingmaier, F., Butenandt, O., & Knorr, D. (1977). Plasma gonadotropins and estrogens in girls with idiopathic precocious puberty. *Pediatric Research, 11*, 91.

Bowden, M. L., & Hopwood, N. J. (1982). Psychosocial dwarfism: Identification, intervention and planning. *Social Work in Health Care, 7*, 15.

Boyar, R. M., Finkelstein, J. W., David, R., Roffwarg, H., Kapen, S., Weitzman, E. D., & Hellman, L. (1973a). Twenty-four hour patterns of plasma luteinizing hormone and follicle-stimulating hormone in sexual precocity. *New England Journal of Medicine, 289*, 282.

Boyar, R. M., Finkelstein, J. W., Roffarg, H., Kapen, S., Weitzman, E. D., & Hellman, L. (1973b). Twenty-four hour luteinizing hormone and follicle-stimulating hormone secretory patterns in gonadal dysgenesis. *Journal of Clinical Endocrinology and Metabolism, 37*, 521.

Boyar, R. M., Katz, J., Finkelstein, J. W., Kapen, S., Weiner, H., Weitzman, E. D., & Hellman, L. (1974a). Anorexia nervosa. Immaturity of the 24-hour luteinizing hormone secretory pattern. *New England Journal of Medicine, 291*, 861.

Boyar, R. M., Rosenfeld, R. S., Kapen, S., Finkelstein, J. W., Roffwarg, H. P., Weitzman, E. D., & Hellman, L. (1974b). Human puberty: Simultaneous augmented secretion of luteinizing hormone and testosterone during sleep. *Journal of Clinical Investigation, 54*, 609.

Bullen, B. A., Skrinar, G. S., Beitins, I. Z., von Mering, G., Turnbull, B. A., & McArthur, J. W. (1985). Induction of menstrual disorders by strenuous exercise in untrained women. *New England Journal of Medicine, 312*, 1349.

Burstein, S., Schaff-Blass, E., Blass, J., & Rosenfield, R. L. (1985). The changing ratio of bioactive to immunoreactive luteinizing hormone (LH) through puberty principally reflects changing LH radioimmunoassay dose response chracteristics. *Journal of Clinical Endocrinology and Metabolism, 61*, 508.

Cacciari, E., Frèjaville, E., Cicognani, A., Pirazzoli, P., Frank, G., Galsamo, A., Tassinari, D., Zappulla, F., Bergamaschi, R., and Cristi, G. F. (1983). How many cases of true precocious puberty in girls are idiopathic? *Journal of Pediatrics, 102*, 357.

Conte, F. A., Grumbach, M. M., Kaplan, S. L., & Reiter, E. O. (1980). Correlation of luteinizing hormone-releasing factor-induced luteinizing hormone and follicle-stimulating hormone release from infancy to 19 years with the changing pattern of gonadotropin secretion in agonadal patients: Relation to the restraint of puberty. *Journal of Clinical Endocrinology and Metabolism, 50*, 163.

Crowley, W. F., Comite, F., Vale, W., Rivier, J., Loriaux, D. L., & Cutler, G. B., Jr. (1981). Therapeutic use of pituitary desensization with a long-acting LHRH agonist: A potential new treatment for idiopathic precocious puberty. *Journal of Clinical Endocrinology and Metabolism, 52*, 370.

Cutler, G. B., Jr., & Loriaux, D. L. (1980). Adrenarche and its relationship to the onset of puberty. *Federation Proceedings, 39*, 2384.

Donovan, B. T., & van der Werff ten Bosch, J. J. (1956). Precocious puberty in rats with hypothalamic lesions. *Nature, 178*, 745.

Dufau, M. L., Veldhuis, J. D., Fraiolo, F., Johnson, M. J., & Beitins, I. Z. (1983). Mode of secretion of bioactive LH in man. *Journal of Clinical Endocrinology and Metabolism, 57,* 993.

Fishman, J. (1980). Fatness, puberty and ovulation. *New England Journal of Medicine, 303,* 42.

Frisch, R. E., & Revelle, R. (1970). Height and weight at menarche and a hypothesis of critical body weights and adolescent events. *Science, 169,* 397.

Frisch, R. E., Gotz-Welbergen, A. V., McArthur, J. W., Albright, T., Witscho, J., Bullen, B., Birnholz, J., Reed, R. B., & Herman, H. (1981). Delayed menarche and amenorrhea of college athletes in relation to age of onset of training. *Journal of the American Medical Association 246,* 1559.

Grumbach, M. M., Grave, G. D., & Mayer, F. E. (Eds.) (1974). Hypothalamic-pituitary regulation of puberty in man: Evidence and concepts derived from clinical research. In *The control of the onset of puberty* (pp. 115–166). New York: Wiley.

Hale, P. M., Khoury, S., Foster, C. M., Beitins, I. Z., Hopwood, N. J., Marshall, J. C., and Kelch, R. P. (1988). Increased luteinizing hormone pulse frequency during sleep in early to mid-pubertal boys: Effects of testosterone infusion. *Journal of Clinical Endocrinology and Metabolism, 66,* 785.

Hopwood, N. J., & Becker, D. J. (1979). Psychosocial dwarfism: Detection, evaluation and management. *Child Abuse and Neglect, 3,* 439.

Hurd, H. P. II, Palumbo, P. J., & Gharib, H. (1977). Hypothalamic-endocrine dysfunction in anorexia nervosa. *Mayo Clinic Proceedings, 2,* 711.

Huseman, C. A., & Kelch, R. P. (1978). Gonadotropin responses and metabolism of synthetic gonatropin-releasing hormone (GnRH) during constant infusion of GnRH in men and boys with delayed adolescence. *Journal of Clinical Endocrinology and Metabolism, 47,* 1325.

Huseman, C. A., Kelch, R. P., Hopwood, N. J., & Zipf, W. B. (1978). Sexual precocity in association with septo-optic dysplasia and hypothalamic hypopituitarism. *Journal of Pediatrics, 92,* 748.

Irwin, M. (1981). Diagnosis of anorexia nervosa in children and the validity of DSM-III. *American Journal of Psychiatry, 138,* 1382.

Jakacki, R. I., Kelch, R. P., Sauder, S. E., Lloyd, J. S., Hopwood, N. J., & Marshall, J. C. (1982). Pulsatile secretion of luteinizing hormone in children. *Journal of Clinical Endocrinology and Metabolism, 55,* 453.

Kaplan, S. L., Grumbach, M. M., & Aubert, M. L. (1975). The ontogenesis of pituitary hormone and hypothalamic factors in the human fetus: Maturation of central nervous system regulation of anterior pituitary function. In R. O. Greep (Ed.), *Recent progress in hormone research,* Vol. 32 (p. 161). New York: Academic Press.

Kelch, R. P., Clemens, L. E., Markovs, M., Westhoff, M. H., & Hawkins, D. W. (1975). Metabolism and effects of synthetic gonadotropin releasing hormone (GnRH) during human sexual maturation. *Journal of Clinical Endocrinology and Metabolism, 40,* 53.

Kelch, R. P., Corley, K. P., Valk, T. W., & Marshall, J. C. (1980). Quantitative estimation of gonadotropin-releasing hormone (GnRH) secretion during human puberty. In E. Cacciari & A. Prader (Eds.), *Pathophysiology of puberty* (pp. 23–41). New York: Academic Press.

Kelch, R. P., Grumbach, M. M., & Kaplan, S. L. (1972). Studies on the mechanism of puberty in man. In B. B. Saxena, C. G. Belling, & H. M. Gandy (Eds.); *Gonadotropins* (pp. 524–534). New York: Wiley.

Kelch, R. P., Hopwood, N. J., & Marshall, J. C. (1979). Studies on the secretion of gonadotropin-releasing hormone (GnRH) during human sexual maturation. *University of Michigan Journal of Medicine, 45,* 60.

Kelch, R. P., Hopwood, N. J., Sauder, S. E., & Marshall, J. C. (1985). Evidence for decreased secretion of gonadotropin-releasing hormone (GnRH) in pubertal boys during short term testosterone treatment. *Pediatric Research, 19,* 112.

Kelch, R. P., Khoury, S. A., Hale, P. M., Hopwood, N. J., and Marshall, J. C. (1987). Pulsatile secretion of gonadotropins in children. In W. Crowley and J. Hofler (Eds.), *Episodic hormone secretion methods of analysis and normative data.* New York: Academic Press.

Kelch, R. P., Marshall, J. C., Sauder, S. E., Hopwood, N. J., & Reame, N. E. (1983). Gonadotropin regulation during human puberty. In R. L. Reid (Ed.), *Neuroendocrine aspects of reproduction* (pp. 229–256). New York: Academic Press.

Khoury, S. A., Sauder, S. E., Hale, P. M., Hopwood, N. J., Beitins, I. Z., Marshall, J. C., & Kelch, R. P. (1985). Acute and chronic effects of clonidine on growth hormone and gonadotropin secretion in adolescent boys. *Pediatric Research, 19,* 608A.

Kulin, H. E., Bwibo, N., Mutie, D., & Santner, S. J. (1982). The effect of chronic childhood malnutrition on pubertal growth and development. *American Journal of Clinical Nutrition, 36,* 527.

Kulin, H. E., Bwibo, N., Mutie, D., & Santner, S. J. (1984). Gonadotropin excretion during puberty in malnourished chilren. *Journal of Pediatrics, 105,* 325.

Layden, T., Rosenberg, J., Nemchusky, B., Elson, C., & Rosenberg, I. H. (1976). Reversal of growth arrest in adolescents with Crohn's disease after a parenteral alimentation. *Gastroenterology, 70,* 1017.

Levine, J. A., & Cutler, G. B., Jr. (1982). Developmental changes in neuroendocrine regulation of gonadotropin secretion in gonadal dysgenesis. In *Endocrine Society Program and Abstracts: 64th Annual Meeting* (p. 152).

Lucky, A. W., Rich, B. H., Rosenfield, R. L., Fang, V. S., & Roche-Bender, N. (1980). LH bioactivity increases more than immunoreactivity during puberty. *Journal of Pediatrics, 97,* 205.

Luder, A. S., Holland, F. J., Costigan, D. C., Jenner, M. R., Wielgosz, G., & Fazekas, A. T. A. (1984). Intranasal and subcutaneous treatment of central precocious puberty in both sexes with a long-acting analog of luteinizing hormone-releasing hormone. *Journal of Clinical Endocrinology and Metabolism, 58,* 966.

Magner, J. A., Rogol, A. D., & Gorden, P. (1984). Reversible growth hormone deficiency and delayed puberty triggered by a stressful experience in a young adult. *American Journal of Medicine, 76,* 737.

Mansfield, M. J., Beardsworth, D. E., Loughlin, J. S., Craword, J. D., Bode, H. H., Rivier, J., Vale, W., Kushner, D. C., Crigler, J. F., & Crowley, W. F. (1983). Long-term treatment of central precocious puberty with a long-acting analogue of luteinizing hormone-releasing hormone. Effects on somatic growth and skeletal maturation. *New England Journal of Medicine, 309,* 1286.

Marshall, J. C., & Kelch, R. P. (1979). Low dose pulsatile gonadotropin-releasing hormone in anorexia nervosa. *Journal of Clinical Endocrinology and Metabolism, 49,* 712.

Marshall, J. C., & Kelch, R. P. (1986). Gonadotropin-releasing hormone: Role of pulsatile secretion in the regulation of reproduction. *New England Journal of Medicine, 315,* 1459.

Marshall, W. A., & Tanner, J. M. (1969). Variations in patterns of pubertal changes in girls. *Archives of Disease in Childhood, 44,* 291.

Marshall, W. A., & Tanner, J. M. (1970). Variations in the pattern of pubertal changes in boys. *Archives of Disease in Childhood, 45,* 13.

Matthews, M. J., Parker, D. C., Rebar, R. W., Jones, K. L., Rossman, L., Carey, D. E., & Yen, S. S. (1982). Sleep-associated gonadotropin and oestradiol patterns in girls with precocious development. *Endocrinology, 17,* 601.

Mecklenburg, R. S., Loriaux, D. L., Thompson, R. H., Anderson, A. E., & Lipsett, M. B. (1974). Hypothalamic dysfunction in patients with anorexia nervosa. *Medicine, 53,* 147.

Mendes, T. M., Foster, C. M., Hopwood, N. J., Beitins, I. Z., & Kelch, R. P. (1987). Neuroendocrine changes with D-His GnRH analogue. *Pediatric Research, 22,* A.

Morley, J. E., Baranetsky, N. G., Wingert, T. D., Carlson, H. E., Hershman, J. M., Melmed, S., Levin, S. R., Jamison, K. R., Weitzman, R., Chang, R. J., & Varner, A. A. (1980). Endocrine effects of naloxone-induced opiate receptor blockage. *Journal of Clinical Endocrinology and Metabolism, 50,* 251.

Ojeda, S. R., Andrews, W. W., Advis, J. P., & White, S. S. (1980). Recent advances in the endocrinology of puberty. *Endocrine Reviews, 1,* 228.

Pirke, K. M., Fichter, M. M., Lund, R., & Doerr, P. (1979). Twenty-four hour sleep-wake pattern of plasma LH in patients with anorexia nervosa. *Acta Endocrinologica, 92,* 193.

Powell, G. F., Brasel, J. A., Raiti, S., & Blizzard, R. M. (1967). Emotional deprivation and growth retardation simulating idiopathic hypopituitarism II. Endocrinologic evaluation of the syndrome. *New England Journal of Medicine, 276,* 1279.

Powell, G. F., Hopwood, N. J., & Barratt, E. S. (1973). Growth hormone studies before and after catch up growth in a child with emotional deprivation and short stature. *Journal of Clinical Endocrinology and Metabolism, 37,* 674.

Pugliese, M. T., Lifshitz, F., Grad, G., Fort, P., & Marks-Katz, M. (1983). Fear of obesity. A cause of short stature and delayed puberty. *New England Journal of Medicine, 309,* 514.

Quigley, M. E., & Yen, S. S. C. (1980). The role of endogenous opiates on LH secretion during the menstrual cycle. *Journal of Clinical Endocrinology and Metabolism, 51,* 179.

Reiter, E. O., Beitins, I. Z., Ostrea, T., & Gutai, J. P. (1982). Bioassayable luteinizing hormone during childhood and adolescence and in patients with delayed pubertal development. *Journal of Clinical Encocrinology and Metabolism, 54,* 155.

Reiter, E. O., Biggs, D. E., Veldhuis, J. D., & Beitins, I. Z. (1989). Pulsatile release of bioactive luteinizing hormone in prepubertal girls: Discordance with immunoreactive luteinizing hormone pulses. *Pediatric Research, 21,* 409.

Reiter, E. O., Kaplin, S. L., Conte, F. A., & Grumbach, M. M. (1975). Responsitivity of pituitary gonadotropes to luteinizing hormone-releasing factor in idiopathic precocious puberty, precocious thelarche, precocious adrenarche, and in patients treated with medroxyprogesterone acetate. *Pediatric Research, 9,* 111.

Reiter, E. O., Kulin, H. E., & Hamwood, S. M. (1974). The absence of positive

feedback between estrogen and luteinizing hormone in sexually immature girls. *Pediatric Research, 8,* 740.

Reiter, E. O., Stern, R. C., & Root, A. W. (1981). The reproductive endocrine
system in cystic fibrosis. *American Journal of Diseases of Children, 135,* 422.

Reiter, E. O., Sizonenko, P. C., Witt, M. F., & Beitins, I. Z. (1984). Sex differences in detectability of bio (B) and immuno (I)-LH in early pubertal
development: a longitudinal study. *Pediatric Research 18,* 474A.

Santen, R. J. (1975). Is aromatization of testosterone to estradiol required for
inhibition of luteinizing hormone secretion in men? *Journal of Clinical
Investigation, 56,* 1555.

Sauder, S. E., Corley, K. P., Hopwood, N. J., & Kelch, R. P. (1981). Subnormal
gonadotropin responses to gonadotropin-releasing hormone persisting
into puberty in children with isolated growth hormone deficiency. *Journal of Clinical Endocrinology and Metabolism, 53,* 1186.

Sauder, S. E., Kelch, R. P., Hopwood, N. J., & Marshall, J. C. (1984). Comparison of the effects of opiate antagonism on gonadotropin secretion in
children and in women with hypothalamic amenorrhea. *Pediatric Research 18,* 322.

Sizonenko, P. C. (1978). Endocrinology in preadolescents and adolescents. I.
Hormonal changes during normal puberty. *American Journal of Diseases of
Children, 132,* 704.

Smith, N. J. (1980). Excessive weight loss and food aversion in athletes simulating anorexia nervosa. *Pediatrics, 66,* 139.

Stubbs, W. A., Delitala, G., Jones, A., Jeffcoate, W. J., Edwards, C. R. W.,
Ratter, S. J., Besser, G. M., Bloom, S. R., & Alberti, K. G. M. M. (1978).
Hormonal and metabolic responses to an enkephalin analogue in normal
man. *Lancet, 2,* 1225.

Tenore, A., Berman, W. F., Parks, J. S., & Bongiovanni, A. M. (1977). Basal
and stimulated serum growth hormone concentrations in inflammatory
bowel disease. *Journal of Clinical Endocrinology and Metabolism, 44,* 622.

Vandenbroucke, J. P., vanLaar, A., & Valkenburg, H. A. (1982). Synergy between thinness and intensive sports activity in delaying menarche. *British Medical Journal, 284,* 1907.

Warren, M. P. (1980). The effect of exercise on pubertal progression and reproductive function in girls. *Journal of Clinical Endocrinology and Metabolism,
51,* 1150.

Zacharias, L., & Wurtman, R. J. (1969). Age at menarche, genetic and environmental influences. *New England Journal of Medicine, 280,* 868.

3

Biological and Social Influences on the Endocrinology of Puberty: Some Additional Considerations

Stephanie A. Sanders and June M. Reinisch

The preceding chapters by Cameron and Hopwood address our current level of understanding about the potential regulatory mechanisms of puberty. They cite endocrinological, environmental, and psychosocial variables that can stimulate or inhibit the pubertal process. With the advances in assay techniques and the prospective studies reported by Nottelman, Chrousos, and colleagues (Chapter 6), it is clear that our understanding of the pubertal process is significantly more sophisticated than it was even a few years ago. Although pulsatile patterns of gonadotropin-releasing hormone (GnRH), beginning initially during sleep (see Chapters 1, Cameron: and 2, Hopwood), are believed to precede gonadal transition into reproductive functioning, we still have not determined what triggers the onset of puberty or, specifically, what stimulation occurs or what inhibition is lifted that initiates the onset of the pubertal GnRH pattern.

To gain insight into additional types of potential regulating mechanisms that might be involved in the setting and adjustment of the biological clock that controls pubertal onset, it may be helpful to broaden the perspective from which we view puberty to a developmental model of sex differences over the life span. This perspective highlights the interaction of biological and environmental factors in shaping the organism over time.

The Multiplier Effect Model

In order to illustrate this interactive approach, we have modified a concept developed by E. O. Wilson (1975), which is presented in Figure 3-1. The model addresses the interplay of biology and the social environment in shaping the development of sex differences. It begins at conception when the overlap between males and females is almost total. That is, the only difference resides in 1 of 46 chromosomes. Genetic material on this chromosome directs the differentiation of the male gonad into testes, providing a second difference. The testes, in turn, begin to synthesize testosterone. During gestational development, both the genitalia and the brain are sexually differentiated under hormonal influence (explained in more detail later). At birth, sex differences are small but relevant to (1) how the infant responds to the environment and (2) how the social environment responds to the infant. First, the sexes differ with respect to their perception of environmental stimuli (Gandelman, 1983; Reinisch, Gandelman, & Speigel, 1979). These perceptual differences could be the result of somatic sex differences of the central nervous system *(CNS)* or peripheral (sensory) receptors. It is likely that perceptual, cognitive, and temperamental differences lead to differential interpretation of, and response to, the environment. Second, most societies treat infants, children, and adults differently based on their sex as determined by their external genitalia. The successive interactions between the organism and environment alter the organism as it develops and augment differences between the sexes. Puberty is the second of two developmentally significant eras of hormonal impact that influence the physiology and behavior of the adult organism and increase sexual differentiation. The first occurs prenatally.

Prenatal Sexual Differentiation

The multidisciplinary nature of this volume and the need to contextualize puberty within this broader developmental perspective warrant a brief review of the prenatal aspects of the sexual differentiation process. Male and female conceptuses are virtually identical except at the chromosomal level: male zygotes have one X and one Y sex chromosome, whereas females have two X chromosomes. During the initial period of development the gonads are undifferentiated. At 6 weeks postconception, in a normal male the presence of H-Y antigen causes the gonadal tissue to begin to differentiate into testes. By 7–8 weeks, the fetal testes initiate the production of testosterone, which causes the subsequent differentiation of internal and external genitalia into the male phenotype. In the absence of H-Y antigen or its specific cellular receptor, the embryonic gonad will eventually develop into an ovary. It is the absence of masculinizing androgenic hormones (e.g., testosterone) that permits the female genital phenotype to be expressed. It is important to note that hormones, rather than genetics directly, are responsible for the differentiation of the internal and external genitalia into male and female types. Regardless of the composition of the sex chromo-

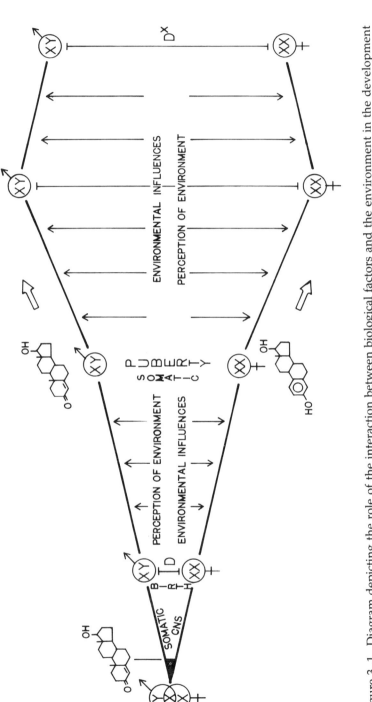

Figure 3–1. Diagram depicting the role of the interaction between biological factors and the environment in the development of sex differences, known as the multiplier effect. (Modified from Reinisch & Sanders, 1987.)

somes (i.e., XX or XY), it is the presence of androgenic hormones that induces the male phenotype and the absence of such stimulation that results in the female phenotype.

Parallel to genital dimorphism, there is now strong evidence of sexual dimorphism in brains of animals and humans on such dimensions as neural connections, volume of cell nuclei, dendritic field patterns, and size of brain nuclei, as well as oxidative metabolism, protein content, serotonin levels, RNA metabolism, and cholinesterase activity (De Vries et al., 1984; Gorski, 1987; Reinisch & Sanders, 1984). Data from laboratory animals indicate that exposure to androgenic hormones during early development directs differentiation of the male phenotype. Among the dimensions that can be affected during the process of sexual differentiation of the CNS in rodents is the hypothalamic regulation of the pituitary-gonadal axis controlling the timing of pubertal onset and subsequent fertility. Adult behavioral patterns including sexual and aggressive behavior are also altered by hormonal manipulation, presumably reflecting underlying differences in brain structure and function. Studies of humans exposed to sex-atypical prenatal hormonal environments as a result of genetic anomalies or medical treatment of their mothers during pregnancy with exogenous hormones or drugs have suggested similar effects on the sexual differentiation of the genitalia, the brain, or both (given that behavior may serve as a bioassay for sexual differentiation of the brain). Alterations of the prenatal hormonal milieu have been shown to affect personality, aggression, and cognitive abilities (for reviews see Ellis, 1982; Hines, 1982; Reinisch, 1974, 1976, 1983; Reinisch & Sanders, 1984, 1987, in press; Sanders & Reinisch, 1985).

Of particular relevance to this volume are the effects on the hypothalamic-pituitary-gonadal axis and on sexual behavior. Reviews of the pertinent animal experimental data on the effects of prenatal administration of hormones on puberty and behavior have been provided by Reinisch (1974, 1976, 1983), Gorski (1987) and Goy, Wolf, and Eisele (1977). Based on such data, the role of prenatal and neonatal hormones is conceptualized as organizing or sensitizing neural systems, with the role of pubertal hormones being understood as activational (Beach, 1945, 1971; Goy, 1968; Goy & McEwen, 1980; Harris, 1964; Phoenix et al., 1959; Young, Goy, & Phoenix, 1964).

Depending on the species, the type and amount of hormone, and the timing of exposure, it appears that the prenatal environment can alter both the timing of puberty and subsequent fertility. For example, exposure to androgens appears to delay the onset of menstruation in human females and rhesus monkeys. Similarly to testosterone-induced pseudohermaphroditism in rhesus monkeys (i.e., females genitally masculinized by prenatal exposure to testosterone; Goy, 1970), girls with adrenogenital syndrome (AGS) have been found to have delayed menarche (Money & Schwartz, 1977). AGS is due to a genetic abnormality that causes a deficiency in an enzyme necessary to the production of cortisol. As the adrenal glands attempt to synthesize the required amount of cortisol, androgenic by-products are accumulated (Williams, 1981). In this way, genetic females are exposed to abnormally high levels of androgens during development. In extreme cases, the genitalia are so masculinized that these infant females pass medical inspection as boys with undescended testicles. Surgery may be required to correct genital defects, and cortisone replacement therapy halts the production of adrenal androgens. AGS girls may show extreme delays in menarche even when they are well regulated on cortisone from early infancy. The degree of delay may be related to the amount of androgen produced by the adrenals during gestation or to the individual's sensitivity to that hormone exposure.

Steroid hormones are not the only substances that can alter the timing of puberty, fertility, and sexual behavior when present early in life. Another group of compounds that can affect sexual differentiation and development is the barbiturates. For example, female rats exposed to phenobarbital during gestational days 12–19 showed a significant delay in onset of puberty as determined by time of vaginal opening and appearance of first-estrus smear (Gupta et al., 1980). These animals also experienced higher rates of abnormal estrous cycles and infertility as compared to controls. Further studies revealed that prenatal phenobarbital exposure significantly affected plasma steroid hormone and gonadotropin concentrations and uterine cytoplasmic estrogen receptors (Gupta et al., 1980). Similar reproductive alterations, including delayed testicular descent, decreased fertility, and permanent reduction in both plasma and brain testosterone levels have been found in male rats exposed prenatally or neonatally to barbiturates (Gupta, Shapiro, & Yaffe, 1980; Gupta, Yaffe, & Shapiro, 1982).

When administered during gestation, barbiturates appear to have two modes of action relevant to brain differentiation (Reinisch & Sanders, 1982). They can directly influence the development and survival of CNS cells, and they can indirectly affect brain development by altering hepatic metabolism of the sex steroids, which in turn shifts the prenatal hormone environment. (Exposure to barbiturates induces hepatic microsomal enzymes, which metabolize both barbiturates and steroid hormones. In fact, barbiturates have been used as antiandrogens in animal experimentation.) Reviews of this literature may be found in Reinisch and Sanders (1982) and Fishman and Yanai (1983).

Thus, it appears that alteration of the prenatal milieu by exogenous hormones and certain drugs can have consequences that are not apparent until much later in development. Thus, prenatal events in mammals, including humans, can substantially alter pubertal events occurring many years later. It is possible that normally occurring differences in the prenatal hormone environment contribute not only to differences between the sexes in the hypothalamic-pituitary regulation of gonadal hormones and behavior, but also to timing differences in the onset of puberty between and within the sexes. Clearly, a number of interesting research questions can be asked about the relationship between prenatal hormones and the pubertal process.

The Role of Pheromones

Let us turn now to the pubertal era itself. Cameron (Chapter 1) and Hopwood (Chapter 2) have presented data from nonhuman primates and humans, respectively, that examine the hormonal events underlying pubertal onset as well as some of the factors that can interfere with this process. Given the interactionist perspective represented in our multiplier effect model (Fig. 3-1), it is of interest to identify some of the social or environmental influences that may interact with biological factors in the determination of pubertal onset. Others (Chapters 1, Cameron; and 2, Hopwood) have cited stress, excess exercise, and insufficient diet as causes of pubertal delay. However, another area that is of interest to our laboratory as possibly relevant to the endocrinology of puberty is pheromones, the chemical messengers that facilitate interaction among members of a species. Sexual attractants in insects were the first pheromones to be identified, and similarly acting substances have subsequently been identified in a number of mammalian species. Pheromones can affect sexual behavior, fertility, puberty (addressed later), aggression, and maternal behavior (see Albone, 1984; Vandenbergh, 1983a). In addition to the other variables that might influence pubertal onset and regulation, evidence is accumulating to support the possible role of chemical inputs from males and females in human reproductive and sexual functioning. In the following review we outline some of the relevant data.

Human Evidence

There is evidence that pheromonal communication may take place among humans. The phenomenon of menstrual synchrony has been fairly well documented (Graham & McGrew; 1980; McClintock, 1971; Quadagno et al., 1981; Russell, Switz, & Thompson, 1980). That is, women who spend considerable time together tend to develop synchronized menstrual cycles to a greater extent than would be expected by chance. Synchrony usually develops within 3–4 months after women begin spending time together, moving in as roomates in college, or working closely together. That pheromones may be involved in the development of menstrual synchrony has been suggested by a number of researchers (McClintock, 1971; Preti et al., 1986; Russell et al., 1980).

The first data that specifically tested the hypothesis of a pheromonal cause of menstrual synchrony were collected by Russell and co-workers (1980), who reported that perspiration from a donor woman induced a shift in the timing of menses in other women. Perspiration from the donor, who reported that other women's cycles had often shifted to become synchronized with hers, was mixed with alcohol and applied to the upper lips of five women four times per week. Six women comprising a control group were swabbed with alcohol alone. After 4 months of treatment, the experimental group's onset dates of menstrual flow had shifted so that they were only an average of 3.4 days different from the donor's, as compared to 9.2 days for the control group.

Preti and colleagues (1986) subsequently conducted a prospective, double-blind study testing the same hypothesis in a similar fashion. They used combined auxillary extract from a group of female donors. The subjects, women who reported their menstrual cycles to be normal (29.5 ± 3 days), were exposed to axillary extracts or plain ethanol rubbed on the upper lip of the subject three times a week for 10–13 weeks. At the end of the experiment, for the experimental group exposed to axillary extract, the number of days difference in menses onset relative to the "donor cycle" was significantly reduced from 8.3 to 3.9 days, whereas the control group showed no change. These two studies (Preti et al., 1986; Russell et al., 1980) provide more direct evidence supporting the hypothesis that pheromones may play a role in human reproductive functioning.

Recent data from our laboratory are consistent with the hypothesis that pheromones may contribute to the development of menstrual synchrony. Lesbian couples who were sexually exclusive and cohabiting (spending at least 4 nights a week together) were significantly more likely to have synchronized menstrual cycle onset dates than were those who either spent fewer nights together or had multiple female partners. Those in this latter group perhaps received competing pheromonal inputs from women other than their primary partners (Sanders, Ziemba-Davis, & Reinisch, 1987).

There are also two studies suggesting that pheromones produced by men may influence the occurrence of ovulation (Veith et al., 1983) as well as menstrual cycle length (Cutler et al., 1986) in women.

Although research is needed to explore further the possibility that pheromones can affect human menstrual cycle patterns and therefore hypothalamic-pituitary regulation of ovarian function, supportive evidence is accumulating.

Experiments with Mammals Other than Humans

Although we know of no published reports regarding the possibility of pheromonal regulators of human puberty, pheromones have been shown to influence puberty as well as cyclicity and fertility in a number of other mammalian species.

In general, pheromones produced by males accelerate female puberty (see Vandenbergh, 1983b). In the house mouse *Mus musculus*, vaginal opening and first estrus occurred 20 days earlier in females exposed to an adult male as compared to females isolated from males (Vandenberg, 1967). Soiled bedding transferred from a male's cage to a female's cage induced earlier puberty (Vandenberg, 1969). Exposure to male urine has the same effect, even at 100-fold dilutions (Vandenberg, 1983b). Exposure to adult males or their urine leads to luteinizing-hormone (LH) release within 20 minutes. The ability of males or their urine to accelerate female puberty appears to be androgen dependent. Urine from juvenile males does not produce the effect, nor does urine from males 10–15 days after castration (Drickamer & Murphy, 1978). Testosterone replacement can restore a castrated male's ability to accelerate female puberty (Lombardi, Vandenberg, & Whitsett, 1976). Even females injected with testosterone produce the pheromone in their urine and its malelike effect. Social factors affecting testosterone levels influence the ability to accelerate puberty: Only urine from dominant male mice will have this effect (Lombardi & Vandenberg, 1977).

Among saddle-backed tamarins, *Sanguinus fuscicollis*, juvenile females reared with adult males conceived at an average of 398 days of age as compared to 631 days when reared with male peers (Epple & Katz, 1980). Pigs (Brooks & Cole, 1970) and cows (Izard & Vandenbergh, 1982) also exhibit male-influenced acceleration of female puberty. In prairie voles (Dluzen et al., 1981), direct physical contact is needed. Within 1 hour of skin contact with male urine, the posterior half of the female olfactory bulb showed a 54% depletion of norepinephrine in conjunction with a 185% increase in LH-releasing hormone in the hypothalamus. This resulted in an increase in LH production by the pituitary gland, which stimulated increased estrogen production in the ovaries leading to increases in uterine weight.

Adult females, on the other hand, seem in general to inhibit pubertal onset in young conspecific females, with the exception that urine from pregnant or lactating female *mice* leads to pubertal acceleration (Vandenbergh, 1983b). For example, in the house mouse *M. musculus* the presence of other females (group v. single rearing) delays the onset of puberty (Vandenbergh, 1983b). This inhibition effect occurs whether or not a male is present. Soiled bedding from group-housed female mice inhibits puberty in isolated juvenile females (Drickamer, 1974). Externally collected urine from group-housed females inhibits puberty, but urine from isolated females has no effect (McIntosh & Drickamer, 1977). Pubertal inhibition is represented by a 4–5 day delay of first estrus. Although it is not known whether pheromones are involved, among marmosets *Callithrix jacchus* (Abbott & Hearn, 1978) and saddle-back tamarins *S. fuscicollis* (Katz & Epple, as cited in Vandenbergh, 1983b), only the dominant female becomes pregnant while ovulation is suppressed in subordinates. However, if a young female is removed and placed with a male, she will begin cycling while her peers who remain with the dominant female do not. The mother gerbil (Payman & Swanson, 1980) suppresses puberty of female offspring only while lactating or rearing a second litter. Nonpregnant mothers or mothers whose litters are removed are not effective.

In general, adult females inhibit female puberty and males accelerate it. Thus, in a number of mammalian species there is evidence suggesting that adult females and males produce pheromones that can influence the timing of pubertal onset in younger conspecific females.

There is also evidence that the timing of puberty in male mammals may be affected pheromonally. In general, females seem to stimulate or accelerate male pubertal development, whereas other males appear to delay or inhibit it (Vandenbergh, 1983b). Male mice reared with females when compared to isolated or group-reared males show more rapid growth of testes and epididymides at 37 days of age (Fox, 1968). The presence of adult males inhibits testicular and accessory-organ growth in young males (Vandenbergh, 1971). An older female can also inhibit male puberty if she dominates the young male in fights (Svare, Bartke, & Macrides, 1978). Other species such as the prairie deer mouse and common voles also show male inhibition of masculine puberty (Vandenbergh, 1983b).

Data on other species and evidence suggesting that humans may also produce pheromones that can influence reproductive cyclicity (e.g., menstrual synchrony) lead to the following questions: Are there pheromones that can accelerate or delay the onset of puberty in humans? If so, are there social and hormonal factors that influence their effectiveness? Does responsiveness to these pheromones vary developmentally or among individuals? Do prenatal events affect the responsivity to these and other socioenvironmental regulators of pubertal onset?

Summary

The multiplier effect model is a useful way of illustrating the biology–environment transactions that influence human sexual differentiation.

It particularly highlights the role of hormones during two important developmental eras, prenatal and pubertal. The prenatal environment—especially the prenatal hormonal milieu—is probably involved in setting the neural timing mechanism that underlies pubertal onset. This is part of the organizing or sensitizing effect of prenatal hormones. Depending on the brain differentiation that has occurred, developing children will respond differentially to environmental stimuli and also will elicit differential responses from the environment depending on their actions and physical characteristics. Through the developmental transaction of biology and environment, the responses of the organism to socioenvironmental and internal biological factors that may proximally regulate pubertal onset will be shaped. (We have suggested that one such proximate factor, in addition to those mentioned by Cameron in Chapter 1 and Hopwood in Chapter 2, may be pheromonal.) The onslaught of hormonal impact at puberty further differentiates the individual and socioenvironmental responses to that individual, all of which significantly influences adolescent and adult behavioral development, resulting in the period of greatest difference between the sexes—that is, the reproductive years.

Acknowledgments

This work was supported in part by National Institute of Child Health and Human Development grants HD17655 and HD20263 to J. M. Reinisch. We gratefully acknowledge the support of The Kinsey Institute staff.

References

Abbott, D. H., & Hearn, J. P. (1978). Physical, hormonal, and behavioral aspects of sexual development in the marmoset monkey. *Journal of Reproduction and Fertility, 53,* 155–166.

Albone, E. S. (1984). *Mammalian semiochemistry: The investigation of chemical signals between mammals.* Chichester: John Wiley & Sons Ltd.

Beach, F. A. (1945). Bisexual mating behavior in the male rat: Effects of castration and hormone administration. *Physiological Zoology, 18,* 390–402.

Beach, F. A. (1971). Hormonal factors controlling the differentiation, development, and display of copulatory behavior in the ramstergig and related species. In E. Tobach, L. R. Aronson, & E. Shaw (Eds.), *Biopsychology of development* (pp. 249–296). New York: Academic Press.

Brooks, P. H., & Cole, D. J. A. (1970). The effect of the presence of a boar on the attachment of puberty in gilts. *Journal of Reproduction and Fertility, 23,* 435–440.

Cutler, W. B., Preti, G., Krieger, A., Huggins, G. R., Garcia, C. R., & Hawley, H. J. (1986). Human axillary secretions influence women's menstrual cycles: The role of donor extract of men. *Hormones and Behavior, 20,* 463–473.

De Vries, G. J., De Bruin, J. P. C., Uylings, H. B. M., & Corner, M. A. (Eds.) (1984). *Progress in brain research*. Vol. 61; *Sex differences in the brain*. Amsterdam: Elsevier.

Drickamer, L. C. (1974). Sexual maturation of female house mice: Social inhibition. *Developmental Psychobiology, 7*, 257–265.

Drickamer, L. C., & Murphy, R. X., Jr. (1978). Female mouse maturation: Effects of excreted and bladder urine from juvenile and adult males. *Developmental Psychobiology, 11*, 63–72.

Dluzen, D. E., Ramirez, V. D., Carter, C. S., & Getz, L. L. (1981). Male vole urine changes luteinizing hormone-releasing hormone and norepinephrine in female olfactory bulb. *Science, 212*, 573–575.

Ellis, L. (1982). Developmental androgen fluctuations and the five dimensions of mammalian sex (with emphasis upon the behavioral dimension and the human species). *Ethology and Sociobiology, 3*, 171–197.

Epple, G., & Katz, Y. (1980). Social influences on first reproductive success and related behaviors in the saddle-back tamarin. *International Journal of Primatology, 1*, 171–183.

Fishman, R. H. B., & Yanai, J. (1983). Long-lasting effects of early barbiturates on central nervous system and behavior. *Neuroscience and Biobehavioral Reviews, 7*, 19–28.

Fox, K. A. (1968). Effects of prepubertal habitation conditions on the reproductive physiology of the male house mouse. *Journal of Reproduction and Fertility, 17*, 75–85.

Gandelman, R. (1983). Gonadal hormones and sensory function. *Neuroscience and Biobehavioral Reviews, 7*, 1–17.

Gorski, R. A. (1987). Sex differences in the rodent brain: Their nature and origin. In J. M. Reinisch, L. A. Rosenblum, & S. A. Sanders (Eds.), *Masculinity/femininity: Basic perspectives*. New York: Oxford University Press.

Goy, R. W. (1968). Organizing effects of androgens on the behaviour of rhesus monkeys. In R. P. Michael (Ed.), *Endocrinology and human behavior* (pp. 12–31). London: Oxford University Press.

Goy, R. W. (1970). Experimental control of psychosexuality. In G. W. Harris & R. G. Edwards (Eds.), *A discussion on the determination of sex*. London: Philosophical Transactions of the Royal Society, Series B, Vol. 259, 149–162.

Goy, R. W., & McEwen, B. S. (1980). *Sexual differentiation of the brain*. Cambridge, MA: MIT Press.

Goy, R. W., & Resko, J. A. (1972). Gonadal hormones and behavior of normal and pseudohermaphroditic nonhuman primates. In *Recent progress in hormone research, the proceedings of the 1971 Laurentian Hormone Conference* (Vol. 28, pp. 707–733). New York: Academic Press.

Goy, R. W., Wolf, J. E., & Eisele, S. G. (1977). Experimental female hermaphroditism in rhesus monkeys. In J. Money & H. Musaph (Eds.), *Handbook of sexology* (pp. 139–156). Amsterdam: Elsevier/North-Holland.

Graham, C. A., & McGrew, W. C. (1980). Menstrual synchrony in female undergraduates living on a coeducational campus. *Psychoneuroendocrinology, 5*, 245–252.

Gupta, C., Shapiro, B. H., & Yaffe, S. J. (1980). Reproductive dysfunction in male rats following prenatal exposure to phenobarbital. *Pediatric Pharmacology, 1*, 55–62.

Gupta, C., Sonawane, B. R., Yaffe, S. J., & Shapiro, B. H. (1980). Phenobarbital exposure in utero: Alterations in female reproductive function in rats. *Science, 208*, 508–510.

Gupta, C., Yaffe, S. J., & Shapiro, B. H. (1982). Prenatal exposure to phenobarbital permanently decreases testosterone and causes reproductive dysfunction. *Science, 216,* 640–641.

Harris, G. W. (1964). Sex hormones, brain development and brain function. *Endocrinology, 75*(4), 627–648.

Hines, M. (1982). Prenatal gonadal hormones and sex differences in human behavior. *Psychological Bulletin, 92*(1), 56–80.

Izard, M. K., & Vandenbergh, J. G. (1982). The effects of bull urine on puberty and calving date in crossbred beef heifers. *Journal of Animal Science, 55,* 1160–1168.

Lombardi, J. R., & Vandenbergh, J. G. (1977). Pheromonally induced sexual maturation in females: Regulation by the social environment of the male. *Science, 196,* 545–546.

Lombardi, J. R., Vandenbergh, J. G., & Whitsett, J. M. (1976). Androgen control of the sexual maturation pheromone in house mouse urine. *Biology of Reproduction 15,* 179–186.

McClintock, M. K. (1971). Menstrual synchrony and suppression. *Nature, 229,* 244–245.

McIntosh, T. K., & Drickamer, L. C. (1977). Excreted urine, bladder urine, and the delay of sexual maturation in female house mice. *Animal Behaviour, 25,* 999–1004.

Money, J., & Schwartz, M. (1977). Dating, romantic and nonromantic friendships, and sexuality in 17 early-treated adrenogenital females, aged 16–25. In P. A. Lee, L. P. Plotnick, A. A. Kowarski, & C. J. Migeon (Eds.), *Congenital Adrenal Hyperplasia* (pp. 419–431). Baltimore: University Park Press.

Payman, B. C., & Swanson, H. H. (1980). Social influence on sexual maturation and breeding in the female mongolian gerbil *(Meriones unguiculatus). Animal Behaviour, 28,* 528–535.

Phoenix, C. H., Goy, R. W., Gerall, A. A., & Young, W. C. (1959). Organizing action of prenatally administered testosterone propionate on the tissues mediating mating behavior in the female guinea pig. *Endocrinology, 65,* 369–382.

Preti, G., Cutler, W. B., Garcia, C. R., Huggins, G. R., & Lawley, H. J. (1986). Human axillary secretions influence women's menstrual cycles: The role of donor extract of females. *Hormones and Behavior, 20,* 474–482.

Quadagno, D. M., Shubeita, H. E., Deck, J., & Francoeur, D. (1981). Influence of male social contacts, exercise and all-female living conditions on the menstrual cycle. *Psychoneuroendocrinology, 6,* 239–244.

Reinisch, J. M. (1974). Fetal hormones, the brain, and human sex differences: A heuristic integrative review of the recent literature. *Archives of Sexual Behavior, 3,* 51–90.

Reinisch, J. M. (1976). Effects of prenatal hormone exposure on physical and psychological development in humans and animals: With a note on the state of the field. In E. J. Sacher (Ed.), *Hormones, behavior and psychopathology* (pp. 69–94). New York: Raven Press.

Reinisch, J. M. (1983). Influence of early exposure to steroid hormones on behavioral development. In W. Everaerd, C. B. Hindley, A. Bot, & J. J. van der Werff ten Bosch (Eds.), *Development in adolescence: Psychological, social and biological aspects* (pp. 63–113). Boston: Martinus Nijhoff.

Reinisch, J. M., Gandelman, R., & Speigel, F. S. (1979). Prenatal influences on cognitive abilities: Data from experimental animals and human genetic and endocrine syndromes. In M. A. Wittig & A. C. Petersen (Eds.), *Sex-related differences in cognitive functioning* (pp. 215–239). New York: Academic Press.

Reinisch, J. M., & Sanders, S. A. (1987). Behavioral influences of prenatal hormones. In C. B. Nemeroff & P. T. Loosen (Eds.), *Handbook of clinical psychoneuroendocrinology* (pp. 431–448). New York: Guilford Press.

Reinisch, J. M., & Sanders, S. A. (1982). Early barbiturate exposure: The brain, sexually dimorphic behavior, and learning. *Neuroscience and Biobehavioral Reviews, 6*(3), 311–319.

Reinisch, J. M., & Sanders, S. A. (1984). Prenatal gonadal steroidal influences on gender-related behavior. In G. J. De Vries, J. P. C. De Bruin, H. B. M. Uylings, & M. A. Corner (Eds.), *Progress in brain research.* Vol. 61, *Sex differences in the brain* (pp. 407–416). Amsterdam: Elsevier.

Reinisch, J. M., & Sanders, S. A. (in press) Prenatal hormonal contributions to sex differences in human cognitive and personality development. In H. Moltz, I. L. Ward, & A. A. Gerall (Eds.), *Handbook of Behavioral Neurobiology (Vol. 10), Sexual Differentiation: A Lifespan Approach.* New York: Plenum.

Russell, M. J., Switz, G. M., & Thompson, K. (1980). Olfactory influences on the human menstrual cycle. *Pharmacology, Biochemistry, and Behavior, 13*, 737–738.

Sanders, S. A., & Reinisch, J. M. (1985). Behavioral effects on humans of progesterone-related compounds during development and in the adult. In D. Ganten & D. Pfaff (Eds.), *Current topics in neuroendocrinology.* Vol. 5, *Actions of progesterone on the brain* (pp. 175–205). Berlin/Heidelberg: Springer-Verlag.

Sanders, S. A., Ziemba-Davis, M., & Reinisch, J. M. (1987). *Menstrual cycle patterns in lesbian couples.* Paper presented at the 7th conference of the Society. for Menstrual Cycle Research, Sexuality and the Menstrual Cycle: Clinical and Sociocultural Implications, June, Ann Arbor, MI.

Svare, B., Bartke, A., & Macrides, F. (1978). Juvenile male mice: An attempt to accelerate testis function by exposure to adult female stimuli. *Physiology and Behavior, 21*(6), 1009–1014.

Vandenbergh, J. G. (1967). Effect of the presence of a male on the sexual maturation of female mice. *Endocrinology, 81*, 345–349.

Vandenbergh, J. G. (1969). Male odor accelerates female sexual maturation in mice. *Endocrinology, 84*, 658–660.

Vandenbergh, J. G. (1971). The influence of social environment on sexual maturation in male mice. *Journal of Reproduction and Fertility, 24*, 383–390.

Vandenbergh, J. G. (1983a). *Pheromones and reproduction in mammals.* New York: Academic Press.

Vandenbergh, J. G. (1983b). Pheromonal regulation of puberty. In J. G. Vandenbergh (Ed.), *Pheromones and reproduction in mammals* (pp. 95–112). New York: Academic Press.

Veith, J., Buck, M., Gertzlaf, S., Van Dolfsen, P., Slade, A. (1983). Exposure to men influences the occurrence of ovulation in women. *Physiology & Behavior, 31*, 313–315.

Williams, R. H. (1981). *Textbook of endocrinology.* Philadelphia: Saunders.

Wilson, E. O. (1975). *Sociobiology: The new synthesis* (pp. 11–13). Cambridge, MA: Belknap Press, Harvard University.

Young, W. C., Goy, R. W., & Phoenix, C. H. (1964). Hormones and sexual behavior. *Science, 142*, 21–218.

4

A Comparative Primate Perspective on Adolescence

Leonard A. Rosenblum

> Since so many developments are involved, it is difficult to mark a
> single point at which an individual may be said to have begun
> adolescence.
>
> (Kinsey, Pomeroy, & Martin, 1948, p. 189)

As the Kinsey quote suggests, adolescence is neither a point in time
nor an event signaled by some particular behavioral or morphological
change. One may define puberty in specific neuroendocrinological terms,
but adolescence is, of its essence, a period of transitions rather than a
moment of attainment. It is the nature of those transitional processes
that concerns us. While we may recognize, indeed agonize over, the
diverse pathways followed by our own species during the stormy passage into maturity in human cultures, the march toward adulthood
would appear to involve many of the same basic elements within the
other primates. The role of this commentary is certainly not to provide
any sort of survey of the extensive animal literature on the behavioral
and morphological changes that culminate in reproductive and social
maturity. Rather it is an effort to provide a comparative framework
within which one may see parallel factors at work in shaping the form
of adult expression in both human and nonhuman primates.

First, the usual note of caution regarding terms. As already suggested, adolescence may best be understood as the pattern of changes
that occur across a period of time, and is not denoted by a particular
event, behavior, or physical achievement. Thus, the *adolescent period,*

rather than "adolescence" as a state of the individual, nor "adolescent" as a quality of particular behavior traits or physical features, should be used to define the topic of our discussion here. Although we often speak of adolescent or even infantile patterns in "full adults," or even aged humans (and this is true of nonhumans as well), these terms reflect an assumption of developmental origins or the relegation of the pattern to another, more "appropriate" period in the life cycle. Since behaviors rarely disappear overnight from the animal's repertoire, any more than they appear in full form and magnitude when they first emerge, our problems in defining the end of the adolescent period are as difficult as defining its beginning. It is most important that we carefully maintain the distinction between features carried over from earlier periods and remaining as part of the later repertoire, from our concern with the adolescent period itself. The primate begins life in a state of virtually absolute dependence for its survival on the constant attention, care, and nurturance of its primary caregiver—generally its mother. Even as the infant moves with increasing freedom around its physical environment and comes into contact with other members of its social group with increasing frequency, its behavior and the reactions it solicits from those around it, will reflect the considerable influence of its vigilant parent as well as the changing features that reflect its physical development. How it looks, how it behaves, and to whom it belongs will all help shape others' reactions to the developing infant. As one seeks to grasp the onset of this transitional period between infantile and mature status, under natural conditions, it may be impossible to separate the effects of the changing physiological state of the infant from the nature of the reactions of those around it.

An early example of this interactive process is the social effect of the "natal coat" with which the primate infant is generally born—that is, a coat of a different shade from that of the adult coat (Sugiyama, 1965). As the infant gradually gains motor ability and movement from the mother, the natal coat appears to elicit some degree of group solicitude and forbearance in this earliest phase of the infant's outward explorations. But, in many species, at around the 3-to 4-month point, the coat color shifts toward that of the adults. As the infant gains increasing size, skill, and capacity to move efficiently around the habitat, flee, and avoid predators, group reactions to the infant change as well. Adult members of the group become less solicitous and tolerant toward the infant; gradually they begin treating the new member the same as others in the group, albeit somewhat less harshly.

Perhaps a more relevant example of adolescent transitions to consider is the onset of sexual behavior in the male; rather than merely fragments of the adult pattern, one sees apparent sexual arousal, with full mounting and thrusting. Several years before the onset of the surge in gonadal androgens, well before active spermatogenesis, one may observe active sexual behavior in young males under certain specifiable circumstances (Rosenblum & Nadler, 1971). It is well known that male primates do not often copulate with females unless they are able to demonstrate some degree of dominance. In general then, a young male paired with a large adult female—even one in the periovulatory period of maximum sexual receptivity—will fail to show any apparent sexual interest in her. Indeed, avoidance, cringing, and fear may be the most prevalent of the male's behaviors (Rosenblum & Nadler, 1971). However, if that same pairing were to take place in the context of a social group within which the infant's mother was significantly dominant over the estrous female, the young male may be the subject of active solicitation from the female and may mount her vigorously.

Similarly, if the young male is directly paired with a receptive but small, and hence less dominant female, the young male may engage in very active copulations with her, and, as a reflection of his highly aroused state, will show very brief latencies between mounts. Indeed, intromission may be achieved and "orgastic" patterns will be observed. While most theorists would generally include the emergence of this type of sexual responsivity as a reflection of adolescent development, it is clear that only a portion of variance involved in the appearance of the pattern can be seen to lie in the physical development of the young animal. A significant source of this behavioral expression must also be attributed to the nature of the complex social configuration within which we observe these behaviors.

In light of these types of data, perhaps one perspective from which we can profitably view adolescence is to consider the question of response thresholds. As internal structures and events change, there may be a gradual change in the level of stimuli necessary to release a given pattern of behavior; sexually active adult males may respond to females in various stages of their reproductive cycles, and in many different situations, while younger (and perhaps more geriatric) males may need a more receptive female or one less potentially threatening for characteristic patterns to emerge. Nonetheless, in the absence of an understanding of the stimuli to which our subjects are being exposed, we cannot delineate the factors that must coalesce to elicit the patterns we label as adolescent.

Let us consider another aspect of adolescent development, the gradual shift from the peer groups of early life to the various assemblages of adult society. Here, too, one must look for the mixture of individual motivation to seek the company of adults and the nature of the adult reaction (i.e., acceptance or rejection). Consider the case of the Peruvian squirrel monkey. It is a feature of the social organization of this species that the male and female members of the large troop are "sexually segregated." That is, while males and females remain within what we have called "a sphere of potential interaction," females remain in close isosexual groupings while males remain very close to other males and generally avoid making a close contact with the females (Coe & Rosenblum, 1974; Rosenblum, Coe, & Bromley, 1975). As a consequence, when infants are born, their initial social experiences occur almost exclusively with the other females of the mother's group. Maturing fairly rapidly, these small primates initially move into mixed-sex peer groups that are differentiated sexually along various behavioral lines but not segregated regarding interactive patterns. By the time the subjects reach puberty, both males and females have joined their respective adult isosexual subgroups. How does this transition take place?

In a series of experiments we have shown that progress along this pathway reflects the combined roles of external stimuli and physical maturation of the young (Coe & Rosenblum, 1974; Rosenblum & Coe, 1977). When prepubertal, 2-year-old males and females are placed together in the absence of a segregated adult group, these youngsters maintain high levels of intersexual interaction. When, a group of adult males and females was added to these adolescents, there was a gradual breakup of the mixed-sex peer group as each sex shifted to increasing proximity with their adult isosexual counterparts. Observations indicated that each sex of adolescent was both more attracted to (i.e., approached more often) the adult members of their own sex, and was less likely to be rejected by their same-sex adult group members. Within 3 weeks of introduction of the male and female adult subgroups into the living area, interactions between the male and female adolescents dropped sharply, and their participation in the segregated social structure of their species moved toward completion. When the adults were removed, however, the segregation of the adolescents broke down and the mixed-sex peer group was reestablished. In spite of the maturational readiness of these 2-year-olds to respond to adults and the social structure they provided, the segregation could not be maintained in their absence at this point in development.

When, however, this same experiment was carried out with fully weaned 1-year-olds, a different pattern emerged. Once again the yearlings, in the absence of adults, failed to segregate. Interactions between males and females were at indistinguishable levels. However, unlike their more mature counterparts, the yearling group did not segregate sexually when adults were introduced. This did not appear to be the result of indiscriminate rejection by the adults, but rather seemed to reflect the lack of motivation on the part of the yearlings to approach their same-sex adult group members in any consistent fashion. This study therefore reflected that the shift from the early pattern of non-segregated peer groups to the adult structure of this species involved not only a physical, maturational change in these youngsters (unidentified as yet but occurring sometime during the second year of life) but also their responsivity to different classes of adult individuals as well as the reactions of those adults to them as they approached. Any effort to ascribe this fundamental shift to either internal or external factors alone would miss the critical transactional quality of these developments and fail thereby to identify correctly the nature of the adolescent transition taking place.

Lest we throw out the baby with the bathwater, it is important to bear in mind that some elements of the transitional changes occurring during the adolescent period may bear more heavily than others on internal changes or external influences. Clearly, the experiments on early deprivation of social experience in rhesus monkeys suggests that regardless of the relative normality of hormonal changes at puberty, and regardless of the normality of subsequent stimulus configurations, deprived males in particular may never perform even infantile sociosexual patterns (Sackett, Tripp, & Grady, 1982). They never make substantial progress toward psychological and behavioral maturity, regardless of their level of physical maturation. Thus, under some conditions at least, environmental conditions and experience may completely overwhelm the impact of physical changes taking place during what would ordinarily be the adolescent period. Indeed, one may question here even the use of the term adolescent, since in many ways these deprivation-reared subjects seem locked into a relatively infantile behavioral status.

Similarly, in an experiment performed in our laboratory some years ago, we demonstrated abrupt and quite dramatic behavioral changes that were entirely dependent on a shift in hormonal status and were completely reversible when the hormonal stimulation was changed (Rosenblum & Bromley, 1978). In this study, we examined the impact of high levels of sex-typical gonadal hormones on social behavior in a group of male and female bonnet macaques. All the subjects were more than 1 year under the average age of puberty during the study, that is, they were in what might be considered an early part of the adolescent period of development. While adult members of this species generally spend long periods of the day in close, contact huddling, younger animals initiate such contact relatively infrequently and maintain this behavior for relatively short periods. In contrast, high levels of social play of various types are characteristic of infants and adolescents but virtually absent in adults.

Following several weeks of baseline observations, in counterbalanced fashion, and blind to the observers, males were given either androgen or the vehicle, while females were given estrogen or the vehicle. Across the study, administration of the gonadal hormones caused a dramatic drop in play behavior and sharp increases in contact huddling in both the males and females. These changes were maintained so long as the gonadal hormones continued to be administered. Nonetheless, 3 weeks following cessation of hormone administration, the more age-typical patterns of frequent play and infrequent huddling reemerged. Thus, in this instance at least, the changes in behavior from those characteristic of an earlier developmental period to those more characteristic of adulthood seemed almost completely dependent on a specific hormonal shift. Of course these subjects had been maternally and socially reared prior to these manipulations, and it is conceivable that distortions in their prior experience might have blocked or altered these results, as was previously suggested. But clearly, given a base of appropriate experience, the physical alteration of hormonal status appeared to account for the most important changes in this case.

As we attempt to gain a grasp of the interplay of events that shape the course of, and perhaps determine, the outcome of the transitions of adolescence, these comparative examples highlight a number of foci of concern. Of course we must be attentive to the physical changes occurring in an individual during a given period of development. It is crucial that the emphasis here be placed on changes within a given individual; as with all other aspects of development, averages offer only a rough guide to individual attainments. Yet we must also consider the range of experiences that preceded the onset of the physical changes we seek to incorporate into our definition of adolescence. Existing data suggest that a variety of prior experiences, or the lack thereof, may either facilitate or retard the expression of particular patterns in any given situation. Similarly, measures of these physical changes in the absence of a defined setting within which behavior is to be expressed, leaves any understanding of adolescent development in a contextual vacuum. Therefore, as a last element of our investigative and conceptual efforts, we must seek to understand the nature of the stimuli to which our subjects are being exposed, in terms of both our subjects' reactions to the stimuli they confront and the responses that our subjects provoke from the world around them. This integrated, multidimensional approach, in which both internal and external changes and stimulus events—both past and present—are incorporated into our conceptualizations and empirical investigations, offers our best hope of understanding the complexities of the adolescent experience.

References

Coe, L. C., & Rosenblum, L. A. (1974). Sexual segregation and its ontogeny in squirrel monkey social structure. *Journal of Human Evolution, 3,* 551–561.

Kinsey, C. A., Pomeroy, W., & Martin, C. (1948). *Sexual behavior in the human male.* Philadelphia: Saunders.

Rosenblum, L. A., & Bromley, L. J. (1978). The effects of gonadal hormones on peer interactions. In D. Chivers & J. Herbert (Eds.), *Recent advances in primatology* (pp. 161–164). London: Academic Press.

Rosenblum, L. A., & Coe, C. (1977). Sexual segregation in squirrel monkeys. In B. Poirier & S. Chevalier-Skolnikoff (Eds.), *Socialization in primates* (pp. 479–500). New York: Aldine.

Rosenblum, L. A., Coe, C., & Bromley, L. (1975). Peer relations in monkeys: The influence of social structure, gender and familiarity. In M. Lewis & L. A. Rosenblum (Eds.), *The origins of behavior: Friendships and peer relations* (pp. 67–98). New York: Wiley.

Rosenblum, L. A., & Nadler, R. D. (1971). Ontogeny of male sexual behavior in bonnet macaques. In D. Ford (Ed.), *Influence of hormones on the nervous system* (pp. 388–400). Basel: Karger.

Sackett, G. P., Tripp, R., & Grady, B. (1982). Rhesus monkeys reared in isolation with added social, nonsocial and electrical brain stimulation. *Annali dell Instituto Superiore di Sanita, 18,* 203–213.

Sugiyama, Y. (1965). Behavioral development and social structure in two troops of Hanuman langurs *(Presbytis entellus). Primates* (Inuyama), *6,* 243–247.

5

Hormonal and Social Determinants of Adolescent Sexual Initiation

J. Richard Udry

The overall purpose of our study is to examine how biological and social factors interact to affect the development of sexuality in adolescence. Our model for adolescent sexual behavior postulates two sources for motivation for sexual behavior in adolescence. The source everyone but social scientists knows about is biological libido, resulting from hormones associated with puberty and adulthood. The second is socially generated motivation, in which social influences specify the rewards of sex and to whom they apply. But in the face of this motivation, there is a set of social controls to prevent adolescents from becoming sexually active. No adults approve of sex for the early adolescent. If the controls are universally effective, there is no sexual behavior. Inevitably some adolescents escape the controls—either because they experienced less effective control behavior on the part of adults, or because some characteristics of their own produced sexual motivation strong enough even to overcome the adult controls they experienced.

Motivation alone is not enough to lead to coitus: one must have a partner. Not all adolescents are equally attractive partners. Since in this "deviant behavior" the partner is not usually a victim but a willing participant, the ability to attract a partner must be a part of our overall theoretical model. As Figure 5-1 demonstrates this model postulates three categories of determinants for initiation of coitus: motivation, attractiveness, and social controls.

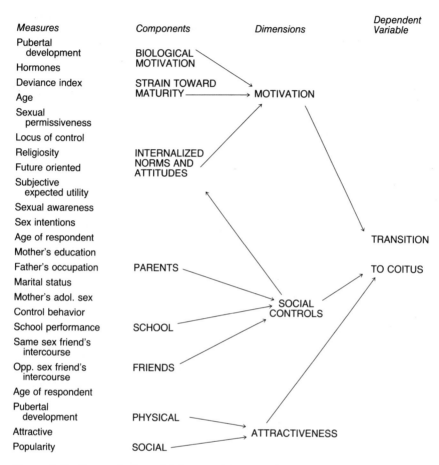

Figure 5-1. Conceptual model for transition to coitus.

A Panel Study of Transition to Coitus

Our overall approach to the problem of identifying the causes of adolescent sexual behavior has been to follow a panel of early adolescents, beginning in grades 7, 8, and 9 (ages 11–15), over a period of 2 years. We elected to study all the pupils in certain schools in a sunbelt city. This aspect of the design was dictated by our desire to identify the influence of friends on one another's sexual behavior. This was accomplished by having adolescents name their best friends of each sex. Since all the pupils in a school were potential respondents, this enabled us to match friends' questionnaires. We interviewed more than 1400 (75%

of those eligible) adolescents in 1980, and followed up more than 1100 of these 2 years later, (>90% of those still eligible). We used primarily self-administered questionnaires. We also administered a questionnaire to the mothers of most respondents at both time periods. All questionnaires were essentially the same at the two time periods. The adolescents provided certain family information, a self-assessment of pubertal development using multiple items, descriptions of their own attitudes and sexual behavior, and their perceptions of friends' attitudes and behavior.

Four features of our research design are significant improvements over most of the studies of adolescent sexual behavior. First, we measure all the determinants of sexual behavior before the initiation of coitus has occurred. The only previous study to use this design is by Jessor and Jessor (1975). Without this feature it is impossible to distinguish the causes from the consequences of sexual behavior. Second, we measure the behavior and attitudes of parents and friends by asking them rather than the index respondent to report. Direct parental responses have been used before (Thornton & Camburn, 1983), but there were obtained after the sexual behavior of interest had occurred. Direct friend responses have been used by Kandel (1978) but not for measuring sexual behavior. By actually interviewing parents and friends, we escape the distortion of interpersonal perception. Third, we specifically incorporate the dimensions of motivation and attractiveness. Nearly all previous studies have concentrated exclusively on social norms and social controls (e.g., Hogan & Kitagawa, 1985). Fourth, ours is the only study that incorporates measures of pubertal development and pubertal hormones among the determinants of adolescent sexual behavior. Nottelmann et al. (Chapter 6, this volume) measure pubertal development and hormones of adolescents for other behavioral relationships. Dornbusch et al. (1981) examine relationships between pubertal development and dating, but not sexual behavior.

Table 5-1 gives results of an analysis of the determinants of the inception of coitus between rounds for those who were virgins at the first interview. We used a logit multiple-regression model with stepwise addition of variables according to our theoretical model of the causal relationships among the independent variables. These data are reported in more detail in Udry and Billy (1987), where each variable is described and defined. Race–sex groups were analyzed separately because several variables had race or sex interactions or both.

The sources of social influence on white girls' initiation of coitus are many and strong. The sources of social influence for white boys are few and far between. The sources of social influence for black girls are nil. Black boys are not shown because most black boys were nonvirgin at the first interview, and the number making a transition to coitus was

Table 5-1
Hierarchical Logit Regression Coefficients for t_1 Variables Predicting Coitus by t_2 for t_1 Virgins

VARIABLES	WHITE MALES		WHITE FEMALES		BLACK FEMALES	
	Zero Order	At Entry	Zero Order	At Entry	Zero Order	At Entry
Pubertal Development			.48**	.48**	1.10**	1.10**
Age			.73**	.65**	.42*	.18
Attractiveness			.24	.13		
Both Parents			−.70*	−.60		
Same-Sex Friend Coitus			1.86**	1.71**		
Opposite-Sex Friend Coitus			1.30**	1.30**		
Popularity with Opposite Sex	.16**	.16**				
Grades			−.65**	−.60*		
Deviance	.25*	.20	.89**	.74**		
Sex Experience	.51**	.32	.94**	.69**		
Think About Sex			.27**	.10		
Turn On			.16**	.15		
Subjective Expected Utility	.02**	.01*	.02**	.02*	.02*	.02*
Sexual Permissiveness	.31**	.18	.42**	.19		
Premarital Index	.06*	.01	.10**	−.02		
Discount Rate			−.25*	−.17		
Locus of Control			−.21*	.02		
Future Sex	.21**	.09	.38**	.19	.21*	.19

Note: *Significant at .05 level; **significant at .01 level. "At entry" coefficients controlled for all variables entered higher in the table. Omitted variables were not significant at zero order.

too small for useful analysis. For black girls, the only variables predicting initiation of coitus were pubertal development and sexual intentions. Pubertal development was a very strong influence, with those 1 standard deviation above the mean ten times as likely to initiate intercourse as those 1 standard deviation below the mean. It appears that once a black girls gets to a certain stage of pubertal development, she begins coitus, with the other measured sources of potential influence playing no role.

There are relatively few sources of influence that differentiate who among the virgin white boys initiates coitus in the subsequent 2 years. The only variable of significant interest is popularity with members of the opposite sex. The more girls who named a boy as best friend at time 1 (t_1), the more likely the boy was to have sex in the next 2 years.

We cannot tell whether this is a true popularity effect; in other words, it is unclear whether girls are more willing to have sex with him because a lot of girls are his friends, or whether if a boy has several girls from which to choose, he is more likely to get one of them to have sex with him.

Social influence on a white girl's probability of sexual debut comes from everywhere. No dimension of the theoretical model fails to contribute a course of influence, and many of these predictors are quite strong. As an example, virgins who had a best boyfriend and a best girlfriend who had both had sex were 6 times as likely to debut as girls who had only one of the two who were experienced, and more than 20 times as likely to debut as the girl who had neither a best boyfriend or a best girlfriend who had had sex (Billy & Udry, 1985). Most of the sources of influence operate independently of one another: The inclusion of several other variables in the model does not reduce their coefficients in an important way. Notice that the friendship effects are missing from the other groups. Does this mean that only white girls experience "peer group effects"?

This analysis forces us to examine exactly what is meant by peer group effects. We imagine that there is a generally positive value on having had sex in the male peer group as expressed in male-only social interaction. One can suppose that this increases the level of sexual involvement in boys generally. But this explanation is in macro terms. At the micro level, the sexual behavior of boys is not differentially affected according to the behavior of those selected as friends. The opposite is true of white girls. We imagine that there is no generally positive value attributed to having had sex as expressed in female-only social interaction. Under these circumstances, the sexual behavior of one's best friend emerges as a major influence differentiating which girls will have sex.

Let us pay particular attention to the effects of pubertal development. In our original model, we saw two ways in which we thought pubertal development would have effects. The first is that it would be a social signal to the adolescent, friends, parents, and potential sex partners of the appropriateness of sexual interest. A closely related effect would be that the adolescent would be sexually attractive to partners. The second way in which pubertal development would be related to sexual behavior is that it would stand as a proxy for hormonal state. As a matter of fact, we found that by round two, for all groups but black males, those who were nonvirgins were significantly more developed than those who were virgins. This relationship was equally strong for white males and females, and about twice as strong for black females. When age is added to a logistic regression containing pubertal development to compare virgins and nonvirgins at t_2, it adds nothing to the fit of the model for white males, adds significantly about one-third to the χ^2 for black females, and doubles the χ^2 for white females. Thus, the relative importance of age (after purging it of pubertal development effects) and pubertal development differs dramatically for the race–sex groups.

Hormone Relationships to Adolescent Sexual Behavior

Are these pubertal development effects working through social interpretation processes, are they proxies for hormonal effects, or some combination of the two? Figure 5-2 displays the theoretical problem: Path 1 is noncontroversial and merely states that with age, hormones increase. Path 2 represents lagged effects of hormones on pubertal development. Path 3 is noncontroversial and merely states that pubertal development is caused by hormones. These three paths are taken for granted and are not further examined. A biological model states that hormones stimulate sexual behavior by increasing libido (path 4).

Lay and scientific thinking has long held that sexual behavior in adolescence is caused by increases in sex hormones, which activate the sex drive and a search for sexual activity (Reuben, 1969; Katchadourian, 1980). There is no previous empirical support for this idea except for the fact that increases in hormones and increases in sexual behavior occur at about the same ages in the population (Kinsey, Pomeroy, & Martin, 1948). It is well established that men and women who have subnormal androgen levels also have low libido, and that administration of exogenous testosterone usually increases sexual interest (Bancroft & Skakkebaek, 1978).

A sociological model states rather that hormones only cause pubertal development (path 3) and that pubertal development is socially interpreted as a signal for social encouragement of sexual behavior (path 5) (Gagnon & Simon, 1973; Hardy, 1964). This model would also expect

Figure 5–2. Theoretical path model.

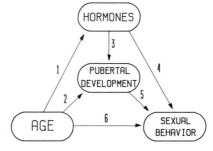

an age-graded normative effect net of the effect of pubertal development (path 6).

In order to get a first-stage answer to the theoretical problem, we did a cross-sectional hormone–behavior study. For a sample of about 100 males and 100 females from the same school population, drawn randomly from our grades 9 and 10 white t_2 respondents, and one third from a new randomly drawn sample of eighth-graders (ranging in age from 12 to 16), we studied the relationships between hormones and a wide range of sexual attitudes and behaviors (Udry et al., 1985; Udry, Talbert, & Morris, 1986). Blood samples were obtained from all subjects between 3 and 7 p.m. Three samples were drawn at 15-minute intervals using an indwelling catheter. Boys' samples were drawn on a random day. Girls' samples were drawn to represent the follicular and luteal phases of the menstrual cycle. One set of samples was drawn between menstrual cycle days 5–9, and another between cycle days 18 and 23. Premenarchial girls were removed from the sample at this point, since no cycle reference was available. Some other girls were removed because menstrual irregularity precluded identifying cycle phase. Since there is no correlation between luteal and follicular values of most hormones, nothing can be learned about hormone–behavior relationships in postmenarchal girls without cycle phase-specific hormone measures.

The three blood samples drawn on a given day were pooled. The serum was separated and both sexes were assayed for the following hormones: testosterone (T), androstenedione (AD), dehydroepiandrosterone (DHEA) and its sulfate (DHEAS), luteinizing hormone (LH), testosterone-binding globulin (TEBG), and an index of free testosterone (FTI), thought to be the best measure of unbound T available for action at the cellular level. For females, we also measured total estrogens (E) and progesterone (P). The first four are androgens, theoretically candidates for effects on sexual behavior, while the other hormones have less clear potential for sexual effects. Details of the hormone assay procedures are published elsewhere (Udry et al., 1985). Table 5-2 gives means and standard deviations of hormone values for each sex.

For males, the most theoretically relevant hormone for sexual behavior is the FTI. Table 5-3 shows the responses to several sexual variables according to FTI quartiles. The relationships are rather dramatic. As we developed multivariate regressions, once FTI was in the model, no other hormone added significantly to predicting any sexual variable. We then added pubertal development and then age to the FTI model to test for the paths in Figure 5-2. Neither age nor pubertal development contributed significantly to the models for any sexual behavior, while adding age or pubertal development had trivial effects on the coefficient for FTI. We conclude that all effects of FTI are direct, and do not work through age or pubertal development.

Table 5-2
Means and Standard Deviations of Hormone Values for Each Sex

| HORMONE | FEMALES (n = 81) | | | | MALES | |
| | Follicular | | Luteal | | | |
	Mean	SD	Mean	SD	Mean	SD
DHEAS (ng/ml)	1.32	0.646	1.30 (n = 80)	0.627	2.07 (n = 102)	0.935
Δ⁴-AD (ng/ml)	3.80	2.56	5.99 (n = 80	2.78	0.99 (n = 102)	0.610
DHEA (ng/ml)	6.24	6.51	3.20 (n = 80)	3.45	1.48 (n = 101)	1.03
LH (MIU/ml)	15.06	6.17	30.57 (n = 72)	17.60	10.75 (n = 102)	4.80
T (ng/ml)	0.604	0.418	0.737 (n = 77)	0.400	4.98 (n = 102)	2.56
TEBG (nmol/L)	57.85	21.70	67.41 (n = 79)	33.98	46.75 (n = 102)	13.70
FTI	0.044	0.041	0.048 (n = 77)	0.038	41.82 (n = 102)	26.67
P (ng/ml)	1.08	1.23	4.53 (n = 80)	5.73	—	—
E (ng/ml)	0.066	0.058	0.191 (n = 79)	0.104	—	—

For females, we constructed the most parsimonious hormone regression model by forward sequential entry and then backward deletion. After the most parsimonious hormone model was obtained, pubertal development and then age were added. By this procedure we were able to determine whether the effects on the sexual dependent variable were directly hormonal, or worked throughout pubertal development. The results are given in Table 5-4. In the females, we most often observe effects on sexual motivation and noncoital behavior from adrenal androgens, with some other curious effects. Except for masturbation, there were only direct hormone effects, with no effects through pubertal development. Pubertal development had an additional effect on masturbation, suggesting that both direct libidinal and indirect social effects through pubertal development are at work on this behavior. No hormone effects on coitus were found.

Summarizing the results of the panel analysis of the large sample, and the hormone analysis, we may draw the following conclusions:

Table 5-3
Sample Characteristics by FTI Quartile—Males

	FTI Quartile[a]			
	Low		High	
Sample Characteristics (%)	1	2	3	4
Ever Had Intercourse	16.0 (25)	20.0 (25)	32.0 (25)	69.2[b] (26)
Had Any Sexual Outlet in the Last Month	8.7 (23)	30.4 (23)	65.0 (20)	76.2[b] (21)
Not Intending to Have Intercourse in the Next Year	40.0 (25)	32.0 (25)	16.0 (25)	4.0[b] (25)
High on "Turn-on" Scale hi-low Dichotomy	30.8 (26)	40.0 (25)	64.0 (25)	57.7[c] (26)
Think about Sex Less Often Than Daily	57.7 (26)	48.0 (25)	24.0 (25)	26.9[c] (26)
Have Ever Masturbated	12.0 (25)	28.0 (25)	25.0 (24)	61.5[b] (26)

[a] Base numbers in parentheses; numbers do not always sum to 102 because of a few missing cases on some of the variables.
[b] Differences in percentages between low and high quartiles of FTI are significant at $p < .01$.
[c] Differences in percentages between low and high quartiles of FTI are significant at $p < .05$.

1. The sexual motivation, subjective sexual states, and noncoital sexual behavior of both males and females are androgen dependent.
2. The coital behavior of males is highly hormone dependent, and not much differentiated by social influences.
3. The coital behavior of girls is not hormone dependent, but is highly differentiated by social influence from diverse and independent sources.

These are not experimental data, and the design does not allow strong causal inference. But the causal inference is justified by other fully controlled experiments on adults. These results imply that the pubertal development effects observed for white males and females in our panel study described above need reappraisal and reinterpretation.

Pubertal Development and Sexual Behavior

The pubertal development effect observed in the larger study on white males and white females needs to be reconciled with the results from

Table 5-4
Best OLS Models Predicting Adolescent Female Sexual Variables

DEPENDENT VARIABLE	R^{2a}	n	B	BETA
Ever had intercourse (*no significant variables*)				
Ever masturbated	.19	73		
Follicular FTI			3.56	.34**
Follicular TEBG			.004	.22
Follicular P			−.09	−.25*
Pubertal Development			.19	.36**
Masturbated Last Month	.11	72		
Follicular FTI			2.23	.27*
Follicular TEBG			.003	.20
Age			.11	.24*
Sexual experience factor	.11	73		
Luteal DHEA			.11	.35**
Turn-on index	.05	78		
Follicular E			−.12	−.26*
Think about sex	.06	77		
Follicular T			.85	.27*
Future sex	.24	78		
Luteal DHEA			.25	.30**
Follicular Δ4-AD			.40	.35**
Follicular DHEAS			−1.38	−.31**
Follicular LH			−.12	−.25*
Follicular T			1.52	.22*

[a] Adjusted for degrees of freedom; *$p < .05$; **$p < .01$

the hormone study. Our measure of pubertal development is a factor score based on a set-specific factor analysis of several self-rated items on various aspects of pubertal development. Our method of separating age and pubertal development effects should be explained. One cannot develop without also getting older. If age is put first into a model, and then pubertal development, predicting sexual behavior, age will take some of the variance that should belong to pubertal development. If pubertal development is put into the model first, and age second, then the increase in explanatory power through adding age captures all aspects of age except what is specifically attributable to development. The additional effect of age is then attributable to social effects and learning. This logic explains why pubertal development should not be controlled by age or anything else to determine its net effects. We assume on theoretical grounds that none of the other variables we measured can affect pubertal development.

Table 5-5 presents zero-order relationships between pubertal development and coital experience at rounds one and two, and the relationship between round one pubertal development and transition to coitus between rounds for t_1 virgins. Every race–sex group shows a significant relationship at round one. Numerous colleagues have found this an unconvincing causal relationship, arguing that those already having had coitus will exaggerate their pubertal development. We have demonstrated to our satisfaction that this does not occur. Those who made the transition to coitus between rounds did not increase their reported pubertal development between rounds any more than those who remained virgins. Pubertal development at t_1 predicts transition to coitus for t_1 virgins by t_2, but only significantly for girls, and especially for black girls. By t_2, the pubertal development/ever had coitus coefficients are attenuated for white males, because pubertal development does not significantly predict transition between rounds for them. Thus, the t_2 correlation is a residual of the fact that the white males' early transitions were related to development, but the later transitions were not. There were not enough black male virgins by t_2 to make a transition analysis for them.

For black females, early transitions are only moderately related to pubertal development, but between-round transitions were strongly related to t_1 development, so that the t_2 development/coitus relationship is quite strong. Nevertheless, it appears justified from the entire set of relationships to conclude that pubertal development is a significant causal factor in initiation of coitus for all groups but black males. The reason we cannot make the case convincing for black males is that more than half of the original sample reported ages at first coitus that were prepubertal. Another reason for the attenuation of t_2 relationships is that by t_2 the sample was mainly 14, 15, and 16 years old, by which time the differences in pubertal development among members of the sample have been reduced. Among 16- to 18-year-olds, we would not expect

Table 5-5
Zero-Order Logit Coefficients Between Pubertal Development (PD) and Intercourse

	MALES		FEMALES	
	White	Black	White	Black
PD t_1 and Had Intercourse t_1 (All Respondents)	.72**	.64**	.57**	.41**
PD t_1 and Had Intercourse t_2 (T$_1$ Virgins)	.28	—	.48**	1.10**
PD t_2 and Had Intercourse t_2 (All Respondents)	.37**	—	.37**	.97**

Note: **Significant at .01 level. Blank cells indicate too few virgins to compute.

to find important relationships between pubertal development and coitus, since hardly anyone would still be at the early stages of development.

So far, everything makes sense for white males. Testosterone is related to pubertal development, and pubertal development is related to having had coitus in our hormone study. But we can show that when T is controlled, pubertal development does not predict coitus. This makes the effects of pubertal development spurious.

For white girls, things are not so clear. Because of the gradual rise in hormone levels both before and after puberty, in the age range of our sample, neither androgenic nor "female" hormones are related to pubertal development in our hormone sample. Nor are they related to coitus. But the hormones are related to other aspects of sexual motivation and behavior. Pubertal development is not related to having had coitus in our female hormone sample, but it is in our main sample, in all three comparisons offered in Table 5-5. Since in this age group, pubertal development is not related to female hormone levels, we must conclude that the pubertal development/coitus relationship shown in the main sample for girls is a true causal relationship. For females we reach the uncomfortable conclusion that hormones cause sexual motivation and noncoital sexual behavior, while pubertal development puts one at high risk of coitus independent of current hormone status.

Hormonal Effects on Personality and Nonsexual Behaviors

Is the effect of androgens limited to sexual behavior, or do hormones affect nonsexual behavior as well? An important third possibility is that hormones have some general effect on more global aspects of personality, which in turn facilitate sexual behavior. The following evidence should help us address the different possibilities. The first data set is a group of mixed sexual and nonsexual items derived from the hormone study described above. Table 5-6 shows zero-order correlation coefficients that reach the .05 level of significance, separately for male and female samples. These results are quite revealing. Males show androgen effects on nearly every variable, whether obviously sex related or not. Females show androgen relationships to only four of the variables, three of which are not sex related. The one that is sex related shows signs opposite to those for males. Girls' feminist attitudes are related to high androgen levels, while boys' attitudes on feminist items are not androgen related. Girls *and* boys have inverse relationships between androgen levels and religious behavior.

We asked respondents to tell us what was more important to them in members of the opposite sex they date: looks, personality, reputa-

tion, or popularity. This was coded 1 for looks and 0 for other responses. The importance of looks was directly related to androgens for
boys, but inversely related for girls. The significance of this result is
unclear, but it seems potentially important.

One final item. Our index of deviant behaviors, which asked whether
respondents had ever engaged in each of a list of behaviors ranging
from minor (smoked cigarettes) to major (scared someone into giving
you money). Androgens were very highly correlated with deviant behaviors for males, but showed no relationship at all to deviance for
females.

Overall, female androgen effects are quite specific and not sex related, while male androgen effects sweep across the variables in Table
5-6. Yet, we observe substantial effects of androgens on the females'
more specific sexual behavior.

There is another approach to answering the question of whether hormones have general personality effects or are specific to sexual behavior. We administered the Adjective Check List (ACL) to our hormone
study subjects, and correlated the hormone measures with the standard scored dimensions of the test. The number of relationships identified was below what would be expected by chance. We then conducted an exploratory factor analysis for personality factors that might
be related to each hormone. We did a correlation matrix of all hormones with all items. For each hormone, where there were significantly more items correlated at the .01 level than expected by chance,
a factor was constructed of the related adjectives, after reducing the list
of adjectives to around ten by eliminating those that were highly inter-
correlated with another item on the list. We discarded factors that had
eigenvalues (E) below 1.0.

For males, the only hormone that generated a significant personality
dimension was T. For females, significant dimensions were extracted
for both T and P. The factors are shown in Table 5-7. The factor dimensions for male and female T appear to tap a similar dimension of out-
going, confident dominance. Because of the face similarity of the male
and female T dimensions, we explored whether T has the same effects
on female personality as it has on males. When we use the female T
adjectives to create a male T factor, the eigenvalue of the factor is about
the same as that generated for females, and the correlation with male
T is nearly as high as that generated by the male T factor. Using this
as presumptive evidence of the existence of a common factor, we constructed a common factor by selecting the adjectives from both male
and female T factors that correlated at a significance level of at least .01
for one sex and at least .05 for the other. From this list, we deleted
adjectives that fewer than ten total respondents checked. Ten adjectives met these criteria. This list was subjected to principal-components

Table 5-6
Selected Hormone–Behavior Correlations

	MALES (n = 101)	FEMALES (n = 78)
Subjective Expected Utility of Coitus	DHEAS 23*; (LH 23*); T 30**; TEBG −31**; FTI 33**	—
Church Attendance	FTI −27; T −28	FolDHEA −22*
Importance of Religion	(LH −24); T −22; TEBG 26	FolDHEA −27*; FolAD −29*
Deviant Index	DHEAS 28*; (LH 28*); T41**; TEBG −39**; FTI 37**	—
Been in Love	—	—
Gone Steady	FTI 22*	—
Steady No. of Times	Δ⁴-AD 27; DHEA 49**	(LutLH 25*; LutE 25*)
Steady No. of Partners	DHEA 35**	—
Looks Important in a Date	DHEA 23*; T 21*; FTI 22*	FolDHEAS −23; LutFTI −26; LutDHEAS −25; LutT −28
Importance of College	DHEA −21*; FTI −19*	(LutE 23*; FolP −37**)
Go with Lots/with One	—	(FolLH −28*; LutP −31*)
Sexual Permissiveness	(LH 25*); T 23*; TEBG −31**; FTI 30	—
Premarital Sexual Liberal	(LH 23*); T30**; TEBG −28*; FTI 30**	—
Feminist Liberal	—	FolDHEA 22*; FolDHEA 27* (LutLH −26*); LutDHEAS 27*
TV Teaches Sex	(LH −22*); TEBG 29*; FTI −21*	(LutLH 28*)

Note: *Significant at .05 level; **significant at .01 level.
Fol = Follicular; Lut = Luteal

factor analysis for each sex. Only one significant factor was generated for each sex, with eigenvalues shown in Table 5-7, column 3. The correlations of this factor with T for each sex were only slightly lower than the sex-specific factor. The regression coefficient of the common T factor summative score on T was computed for each sex. The regression coefficient was five times as large for females as for males, indicating

Table 5-7
ACL Factors Generated by Hormone Analysis

MALES *Testosterone*	FEMALES *Follicular* *Testosterone*	COMMON *Testosterone*	FEMALE *Follicular* *Progesterone*
Ambitious	Charming	Cynical	Boastful
Cynical	Cynical	Dominant	Foresighted
Dominant	Discreet	Original	Obnoxious
Original	Disorderly	Outgoing	Quitting
Persistent	Dominant	Self-centered	Showoff
Pessimistic	Enterprising	Sensitive	Stern
Robust	Frivlous	Sexy	Tough
Sarcastic	Initiative	Understanding	Unrealistic
Severe	Original	Enterprising	
Showoff	Pleasant	Pleasant	
Spontaneous			
Stingy			
Temperamental			
Uninhibited			
		Males:	
$E = 3.88$	$E = 2.41$	$E = 2.49$	$E = 1.99$
$R = .49$	$r = .54$	$e = .45$	$r = .77$
		Females:	
		$E = 2.17$	
		$r = .48$	

that females are much more sensitive to T. But the standard deviation of T was five times as large for males as for females, and the male mean was eight times as high as for females. This means that T would have the same impact on personality in females as in males, in spite of the dramatically lower levels of T in females.

We conclude from this analysis that T has organizing effects on the personality of males and females that are essentially similar. Does T affect sexual responses through this effect on personality, or does it have direct effects, or both? The answer to this question for females is that any effects of T on personality are probably not related to sexual responsiveness. T is not the main androgen affecting female sexual behavior, and the androgens that are important for female sexual behavior do not produce a personality factor. The correlation of T with having had intercourse is not significant for females. But having had intercourse does generate a significant ACL factor for females, which correlates with the ACL T factor at $r = .84$, and contains several common adjectives. T correlates with the ACL I factor at $r = .33$. While these results are provocative, they do not offer unambiguous support for the idea that hormones work through personality change to encourage sexual behavior.

For boys, we can do a more formal path model to determine whether T works directly to produce sexual response, or whether it works by creating a personality dimension that predisposes the boy to coitus, or some of each. This path model shows that none of the effect of T on coitus is through the personality factor. In fact the ACL T factor does not significantly predict coitus. From the data so far available, it is not possible to conclude that androgens affect sexual behavior indirectly through effects on personality. At the same time, it is probably premature to abandon the hypothesis.

Discussion

There are still many unexplained findings, as well as contradictory findings. Our information with regard to blacks are so uninformative as to be frustrating. What they tell us so far is that the process of sexual initiation differs by race. The overwhelming importance of pubertal development in black females stands in contrast to its modest importance in whites. We have no hormone data on blacks, but the low correlation for white girls between hormone levels and pubertal development makes it impossible to explain the effects of pubertal development among black girls as a proxy for hormone effects. Furthermore, most aspects of pubertal development in girls are not androgen dependent. On the face of it, one might imagine that panel studies including hormones would help to clarify the issues. But the gradual rise of androgens in the period after menarche for girls makes an efficient research design difficult.

For boys, panel studies including hormones offer real promise of definitive results. A little-known yet well-established aspect of pubertal development is that T levels rise abruptly in pubertal boys, moving from prepubertal to adult levels in a period as short as 6 months or less on the average. Experiments on androgen-deficient adult males indicate that effects on internal sexual states and sexual behavior are observed within a few weeks after androgen replacement, while pubertal development proceeds at a more deliberate pace as the body responds with tissue growth. These results can be employed to distinguish hormone effects on different aspects of sexuality, and to separate these effects from those of social processes.

A study of 100 males is now being conducted by this writer, making use in the research design of the facts just described. The boys have been enrolled on the following basis: Their initial serum T levels were prepubertal, but their age and pubertal development criteria indicated that they were likely to experience their T surge within the next 2 years.

The boys are followed with weekly measures of T levels and various dimensions of behavior. Repeated personality tests over the 2 years will allow good measures of T effects on personality. By identifying the timing of changes and invoking known and theoretical lag times, we have a good chance of separating social and hormonal processes and their interrelationships. What we suppose we will observe is rather immediate responses of subjective states and perhaps autonomic sexual responses to the rather sudden tenfold increase in T, followed by changes in sexual behavior and personality. Presumably the boys won't know what hit them, but we will.

Conclusions

First, it can be seen that we have a lot to learn about the sexual behavior of adolescents and how pubertal development, hormones, and social processes affect it.

Second, increases in androgenic hormones at puberty contribute to explaining sexual motivation and internal sexual states as well as noncoital sexual behavior in both male and female adolescents, and to explaining the initiation of coitus in males. These effects are mostly directly biological and do not work through the social interpretation of pubertal development. Pubertal development and its social interpretation have additional effects in putting females at high risk of coitus.

Third, initiation of coitus in white males is strongly hormone dependent and only weakly influenced by the social sources we examined, while in white females initiation of coitus is strongly influenced by a wide variety of social sources and does not have identifiable hormonal predictors.

Fourth, the hormonal changes of puberty may exert strong influences on the personalities of adolescents. Preliminary analysis suggests that the personality effects of hormones may be independent of the sexual effects, and not an indirect route for hormone effects on sexual behavior.

When social controls on adolescent sex are very tight, there will be little sexual behavior in this age group to explain. When social controls are either only moderately strong or only moderately effective, we will obtain results like those discussed in this chapter. Today the social controls work through females. Now imagine a future in which all girls at puberty are touched with a magic contraceptive wand that renders them infertile until their twenty-first birthday. Suppose that everyone becomes indifferent to adolescent coitus. Under these circumstances, we would expect social controls to disappear. Pubertal development would become more predictive of the initiation of coitus, operation through social perception processes. The importance of androgenic hormones in predicting coital initiation should emerge for girls as a primary motivational factor released from social constraints.

References

Bancroft, J., & Skakkebaek, N. (1978). Androgens and human sexual behavior. In R. Porter & J. Whelan (Eds.), *Ciba Foundation Symposium* (new series) 62, 209–226. Amsterdam: Excerpta Medica.

Billy, J. O. G., & Udry, J. R. (1985). The influence of male and female best friends on adolescent behavior. *Adolescence, 20,* 21–32.

Dornbusch, S., Carlsmith, M., Gross, R., Jennings, D., Rosenberg, A., & Duke, P. (1981). Sexual development, age, and dating: A comparison of biological and social influences upon one set of behaviors. *Child Development, 52,* 178–185.

Gagnon, J. H., & Simon, W. (1973). *Sexual conduct: The social sources of human sexuality.* Chicago: Aldine.

Hardy, K. (1964). An appetitional theory of sexual motivation. *Psychological Review, 71,* 1–18.

Hogan, D. P., & Kitagawa, E. M. (1985). The impact of social status, family structure, and neighborhood on the fertility of black adolescents. *American Journal of Sociology, 90,* 825–855.

Jessor, S., & Jessor, R. (1975). Transition from virginity to nonvirginity among youth: A social-psychological study over time. *Developmental Psychology, 11,* 473–484.

Kandel, D. B. (1978). Homophily, selection, and socialization in adolescent friendships. *American Journal of Sociology, 84,* 427–436.

Katchadourian, H. H. (1980). Adolescent sexuality. *Pediatric Clinics in North America, 27,* 17–28.

Kinsey, A. C., Pomeroy, W. B., & Martin, C. (1948). *Sexual behavior in the human male.* Philadelphia: Saunders.

Reuben, D. (1969). *Everything you always wanted to know about sex.* New York: Bantam Books.

Thornton, A., & Camburn, D. (1983). The influence of the family on premarital sexual attitudes and behavior. Unpublished paper, Institute for Survey Research, University of Michigan, Ann Arbor.

Udry, J. R., & Billy, J. O. G. (1987). Initiation of coitus in early adolescence. *American Sociological Review, 52,* 841–855.

Udry, J. R., Billy, J. O. G., Morris, N. M., Groff, T. R., & Raj, M. H. (1985). Serum androgenic hormones motivate sexual behavior in adolescent boys. *Fertility and Sterility, 43,* 90–94.

Udry, J. R., Talbert, L. M., & Morris, N. M. (1986). Biosocial foundations for adolescent female sexuality. *Demography, 23,* 217–230.

6

Hormones and Behavior at Puberty

Editha D. Nottelmann,
Gale Inoff-Germain,
Elizabeth J. Susman, and
George P. Chrousos

Early adolescence (ages 10–14) is a period of important developmental transitions. Changes occur in cognitive, emotional, and social functioning and, most strikingly, with the onset of puberty, in physical stature and body contour. In recognition of accumulating evidence of the interrelatedness of psychological functioning and pubertal changes during early adolescence, researchers studying this period of development increasingly are examining psychological processes in relation to the processes of pubertal development. In particular, there is renewed interest in biological–psychosocial interactions (e.g., Lerner & Foch, 1987).

The role of pubertal hormones in these biological–psychosocial interactions has been a matter of speculation for many years. It is well known that hormones influence physical growth and pubertal maturation (e.g., Styne & Grumbach, 1978; also see Nottelmann et al., 1987b). Because changes in adolescent behavior appear to coincide temporally with the physical changes of puberty, there has been a tendency to attribute behavioral changes to hormonal influences as well—especially the emergence of problem behavior. However, very little is actually known about hormone–behavior relations in normal adolescents. The few studies that have examined hormone–behavior relations are of relatively recent origin, have been concerned primarily with aggression, and have focused on males and a single hormone, testosterone (e.g.,

Mattsson et al., 1980; Olweus et al., 1980). Assumptions about hormonal influences on behavior in pubertal-aged adolescents are based largely on extrapolation from studies of adults, young children, and clinical or atypical populations, as well as on extrapolation from studies using animal models.

Normal pubertal development in humans involves two distinct processes: "adrenarche" (i.e., maturation of adrenal androgen secretion), involving the hypothalamic-pituitary-adrenal (HPA) axis; and "gonadarche," reactivation of the hypothalamic-pituitary-gonadal (HPG) axis and maturation of gonadal sex steroid secretion. Adrenarche usually occurs at ages 6–8. Adrenal androgen secretion increases gradually, continues to rise through puberty, and reaches asymptote in late adolescence. No physiological role has been ascribed as yet to adrenal androgens, other than stimulation of growth of small amounts of pubic hair. Gonadarche usually occurs at ages 9–13. Gonadotropin levels rise first, followed by gonadal sex steroids, the levels of which rise more steeply than adrenal androgens and reach asymptote around midadolescence. The gonadal sex steroids are responsible for the development of secondary sex characteristics. Testosterone and its active metabolite 5-dihydrotestosterone masculinize boys, and estradiol is the hormone primarily responsible for feminizing girls.

The collaborative National Institute of Mental Health/National Institute of Child Health and Human Development (NIMH–NICHD) study on which we are reporting in this chapter focuses on these two processes by examining adrenal and gonadal axis hormones. The study represents a first effort to investigate the role of a large complement of hormones in biological–psychosocial interactions in early adolescence. We examined adrenal androgens, gonadotropins, and sex steroids in relation to a wide spectrum of behavioral measures. The purpose of the study was (a) to explore whether there are relations between hormones and behavior in a sample of boys and girls representing all stages of pubertal development and whose hormone levels and behavior fall into the normal range; and (b) if there are such relations, to describe them and generate causal hypotheses and questions for further research.

We begin with a survey of related research on normal adolescent psychosocial functioning in relation to physical pubertal status and on hormone–behavior relations in general, together with an outline of the implications of this research for hormone–behavior relations in early adolescence. Next, we describe our study and present some of our current findings.[1] We conclude with a discussion of what we have learned so far about hormone–behavior relations.

Survey of Related Research

The Influences of Physical Pubertal Status on Psychosocial Functioning

PHYSICAL PUBERTAL STATUS

The evidence of biological–psychosocial interactions in early adolescence comes primarily from studies that examine psychosocial adjustment in relation to pubertal status based on the development of secondary sex characteristics (Hill & Moenks, 1977; Lerner & Foch, 1987). Such studies indicate, for example, that the body image of boys tends to improve with pubertal development (Petersen, Tobin-Richards, & Boxer, 1983), that postmenarchial girls (later stages of pubertal development) tend to report more problems but have a better overall self-concept (Garwood & Allen, 1979), and that the dominance hierarchy in same-sex groups of 12- to 14-year-olds tends to be related to their pubertal status (Savin-Williams, 1979). More mature pubertal status also is associated with reports of ˙higher levels of heterosocial interactions (Crockett & Dorn, 1987). Recent findings indicate that as pubertal-age boys and girls mature, they increasingly tend to have conflict with their mothers, but that for boys such conflict decreases when they reach the later stages of pubertal development (Hill et al., 1985; Steinberg, 1987). It has been suggested that conflict in parent–child relations during the pubertal years may represent temporary perturbations that are most marked around midpuberty (Hill et al., 1985; Hill & Holmbeck, 1987).

TIMING OF PHYSICAL MATURATION

The most significant findings on the impact of puberty involve timing of physical maturation (Gross & Duke, 1980). The effects of timing on psychosocial functioning are particularly strong: The normal range of pubertal development encompasses large age differences for the onset of puberty (ages 9.5–13.5 for boys and ages 8–13 for girls) and for attainment of sexual maturity (ages 13.5–17 for boys and ages 13–18 for girls) (Marshall & Tanner, 1969, 1970). This wide age variation in physical pubertal development means that relatively early and relatively late maturers will have a conspicuously different appearance from that of their peers. This impact of being "early" or "late" is magnified because the process occurs at a time when many adolescents are caught up in social comparisons (Seltzer, 1982) and quite concerned about *not* being different in any respect from their peers. Girls tend to be sensitive about relatively early pubertal development. As girls, on average, enter puberty 12–18 months earlier than boys, early-maturing girls are among the first in their peer group to show signs of sexual maturation (i.e., ahead of almost all boys and most girls in the same grade in school).

In contrast, boys tend to be sensitive about relatively late pubertal development. Late-maturing boys are likely to feel awkward because they are among the last in their peer group to lose their childlike appearance (i.e., after most boys and almost all girls in their peer group have begun to undergo pubertal change). They also may have trouble coping with lagging physical stature and strength gains, which are so important for many of the athletic activities in which adolescent male peer relations tend to thrive. For boys, later maturation generally has been reported to have adverse effects (e.g., Mussen & Cover, 1957). For girls, findings include adverse effects of earlier as well as later maturation (e.g., Jones & Mussen, 1958; Faust, 1960).

PHYSICAL STATURE

Studies focusing specifically on physical stature similarly indicate that height and weight relative to same-age or same-grade peers has important implications for self-esteem and self-concept in general during the pubertal years (Stolz & Stolz, 1944; Blyth et al., 1981; Nottelmann, 1982; Nottelmann & Welsh, 1986), but the findings are mixed and dependent on social environments. For example, girls who are taller than most of their classmates (and probably pubescent) are likely to have negative feelings about their bodies if they are still in elementary school, where they stand out, but not if they are in secondary school, where many other students are taller (Nottelmann & Welsh, 1986). For boys, being relatively tall generally is likely to have positive implications; being tall and quite heavy, however, is not (Blyth et al., 1981).

Relative physical maturity, moreover, has social stimulus value not only for the adolescents themselves, but also for others who interact with them (Hill & Moenks, 1977; Lerner & Foch, 1987). For example, adults may accord higher social status to physically more mature individuals while expecting more responsible behavior from them than they do from same-age peers who are less physically mature. Conversely, the less mature individuals may experience less pressure for responsible behavior but have to cope with being treated like younger children, by peers as well as adults (e.g., Wilson et al., 1984). Thus, adolescents' relative physical maturity status may elicit interactive behavior from others that, in turn, may enhance their positive or negative feelings about their pubertal status based on self-comparison with peers.

IMPLICATIONS FOR HORMONE–BEHAVIOR RELATIONS

The physical changes of puberty appear gradually over the course of months to years, and some time after the onset of the hormone level changes that are responsible for them. Although it is not clear whether physical and hormonal pubertal changes have similar effects on behavior, it is expected that hormonal influences should manifest themselves earlier than physical maturity influences.

In a general puberty-related developmental model for psychosocial functioning in early adolescence (i.e., one that includes all pubertal stages and interdependencies among puberty-related developmental markers), some similarity in relations of physical and hormonal status to behavior may be observed nevertheless. Physical pubertal status influences could be expected to be due in part to associated cumulative hormone level effects; hormone level effects, in turn, could be attributed in part to pubertal development generally as reflected, though in lagged fashion, in both physical and endocrine status.

Thus, given the mixed findings for the effects of physical maturity status on psychosocial functioning, the rise in hormone levels in pubertal-age adolescents could be expected to have positive or negative effects, depending on the behavior under consideration. In line with timing of physical maturation findings, hormone–behavior relations also could be expected to be stronger when examined jointly with chronological age. Moreover, if one were to adopt the perturbation hypothesis for hormone–behavior relations, predicting increasingly stronger effects following the initial pubertal rise in hormone levels until midpuberty and decreasing effects thereafter, one would also expect hormone–behavior relations to be stronger if quadratic hormone–behavior relations were examined in addition to linear relations.

Still, there are reasons why hormone–behavior relations could differ from relations between physical puberty status and behavior. One is that hormone levels in themselves have no social stimulus value. Another, more important reason is that hormone levels may have direct effects on behavior through neuroendocrine mechanisms (Ellis, 1982; Nyborg, 1983).

Hormone–Behavior Relations

According to recent interdisciplinary investigations, androgens and estrogens are among the large number of neurochemicals identified as neuroregulators (i.e., neurotransmitters and neuromodulators) that are believed to have a critical role in central nervous system (CNS) functioning (Alpert et al., 1981). Thus, the dramatic rise in androgen and estrogen levels during puberty may effect changes in CNS activity and orchestration of neuroregulators that, in turn, have consequences for mood and behavior regulation (de Wied & van Keep, 1980; Hamilton, 1984; Eriksson & Modigh, 1984; Siris et al., 1980).

GONADOTROPINS

One major thrust in the study of hormone influences on behavioral functioning has been the search for hormonal factors that may be associated with the presence of psychiatric illness or alterations in mood. Biochemical disturbances involving neuroregulators have been implicated in depressive conditions and schizophrenia (Hamburg, Elliott, & Parron, 1982; Akiskal & McKinney, 1975). Investigations involving links between these conditions and gonadotropins as well as their releasing hormones are reported (e.g., Brambilla et al., 1978; Amsterdam et al., 1982; Gil-Ad et al., 1981; Cantalamessa et al., 1985; Ferrier et al., 1982), but many studies of HPG axis functioning in psychiatric disturbance are flawed methodologically and should be interpreted cautiously (Tolis & Stefanis, 1983). It is noteworthy nevertheless that attenuated gonadotropin production commonly is associated with depressive disorders (Tolis & Stefanis, 1983).

SEX STEROIDS

In relations between gonadal steroids and psychiatric and behavioral disturbance, the associations usually have been between estrogens and depressive affect on the one hand, and between androgens and aggression on the other.

Studies of estrogen and depressive affect typically involve women and focus on hormonal fluctuations that are associated with the menstrual cycle and menopause. There are reports of fluctuations in mood with phase of the menstrual cycle (e.g., Smith, 1975; Bardwick, 1976), with self-esteem high at the time of ovulation (Bardwick, 1976). Increases in estradiol level have been found to improve depressive symptomatology for many women with low estrogen levels (Montgomery et al., 1987), but relations are not always linear (de Lignieres & Vincens, 1982). The role of hormones also has been examined in depression and/or irritability associated with the premenstrual phase of the menstrual cycle, but the degree to which menstrual cycle-related hormone changes are responsible for alterations in affect in women with a "diagnosis" of "premenstrual syndrome" has been questioned (Rubinow & Roy-Byrne, 1984).

Hormone levels and aggression have been studied extensively in animals and less extensively, but with increasing interest, in humans. Both sets of literature have tended to focus on males. Most research linking hormone levels to aggression also has focused on the influence of androgens, primarily that of testosterone. The animal literature indicates that higher levels of testosterone are related to higher degrees of aggression in most species (e.g., Eleftheriou & Sprott, 1975; Bouissou, 1983). In most cases, these findings involve rank-related aggression (Eleftheriou & Sprott, 1975). In adult males, individual differences in testosterone level have been linked to traits of aggression, assertiveness, or impulsivity, especially where provocation or threat are involved (Ehrenkranz, Bliss, & Sheard, 1974; Doering et al., 1975; Houser,

1979; Persky, Smith, & Basu, 1971; Scaramella & Brown, 1978; Wilson, Prange, & Lara, 1974). Similar findings, however, also have been interpreted in terms of influences on degree of fearfulness (see Bouissou, 1983) or influences on degree of irritability, negative affect, or mood (Doering et al., 1975; Mazur & Lamb, 1980). For adolescent boys in the later stages of puberty, higher testosterone levels also have been associated with higher degrees of aggression (Mattsson et al., 1980; Olweus et al., 1980).

The effect of sex steroids on sexual behavior has been examined largely in connection with mating behavior in lower animals and sexual dysfunction in humans. The classic paper by Phoenix and colleagues (1959), describing organizing actions of testosterone, dealt with mating behavior in the female guinea pig. Many studies of hormonal influences on sexual behavior in animals (e.g., Eberhart, Keverne, & Mueller, 1980) have included a focus on aggressive behavior as well, because of the frequently found link between dominance behavior and sexual activity. However, there has been increasing interest in how various hormones and endocrine-related events affect sexual behavior in normal human adolescents and adults. Udry and colleagues (Udry et al., 1985; Chapter 5, this volume), for example, reported recently that sexual motivation and sexual behavior are related to testosterone levels in normal male adolescents. Whereas hormone levels (primarily adrenal androgens) also were related to sexual motivation and some aspects of sexuality in normal female adolescents, sexual intercourse was found to be influenced predominantly by social processes (Udry, Talbert, & Morris, 1986). These findings for adolescents appear to be consistent with those of studies of adult men and women (for a review, see Bancroft, 1987); in other words, hormone influences on behavior are highly predictable in men but variable in women.

ADRENAL ANDROGENS

Although disturbances in HPA axis functioning are being examined systematically by a variety of investigators (e.g., Gold et al., 1986a, b; Cutler et al., 1979; Albertson et al., 1984; Counts et al., 1987), few studies include adrenal androgens as a focus (examples of exceptions are Hansen, Kroll, & MacKensie, 1982; Tourney & Hatfield, 1973; Erb, Kadane, & Tourney, 1981; Brophy, Rush, & Crowley, 1983; Barrett-Connor, Khaw, & Yen, 1986; Parker et al., 1985; Parker, Levin, & Lifrak, 1985). The scant evidence suggests that dehydroepiandrosterone (DHEA) may be lowered or DHEA diurnal rhythms may be altered in schizophrenia (Erb, Kadane, & Tourney, 1981) and that DHEAS (DHEA sulfate) and/or DHEA levels may be lower in victims of cardiovascular accidents and in critically ill patients (Barrett-Connor, Khaw, & Yen, 1986; Parker, Levin, & Lifrak, 1985).

Implications for Hormone–Behavior Relations in Early Adolescence

In summary, what is known about links between hormones and behavior indicates that there are relations between hormone levels and psychosocial functioning and that these relations generally tend to be linear. The surveyed studies also suggest that such relations may emerge while the endocrine system is undergoing change in early adolescence. As sex steroid levels rise most dramatically during puberty, sex steroids should figure prominently in hormone–behavior relations: for boys, testosterone in relation to externalizing behaviors; for girls, estradiol in relation to internalizing behaviors. The gonadotropins, as an integral part of the gonadal (HPG) axis, may be similarly related to psychological adjustment and behavior. It is not clear whether their role in behavior is causal or merely due to their linkage to the sex steroids. As far as adrenal androgens are concerned, it is conceivable that they are related to adolescent psychosocial functioning similar to testosterone (a much more potent androgen of gonadal origin). In early adolescence, of course, hormone–behavior relations should reflect predominantly developmental rather than individual differences in hormone levels. Therefore, this pattern of prediction rests on the assumption of a developmental model of increasingly strong hormone–behavior relations during the pubertal rise in hormone levels.

Studies of disturbances in HPA functioning suggest, however, that potential effects of adrenal androgens may complement and interact with potential effects of gonadal hormones rather than show parallel effects. General HPA axis functioning is stress responsive. HPA axis activation, as evidenced in mild hypercortisolism (higher levels of cortisol), is associated with psychological and physical stress (e.g., Parker et al., 1985; Gold et al., 1986a, b; Luger et al., 1987; Parker, Levin, & Lifrak, 1985; Villanueva et al., 1986); and there is evidence that HPA axis activation suppresses HPG axis functioning by suppressing luteinizing hormone-releasing hormone (LHRH) secretion (Plant, 1986), gonadotropin secretion (Sakamura, Takebe, & Nakagawa, 1975; Sowers, Rice, & Blanchard, 1979; Vierhapper, Waldhaeusl, & Nowotny, 1981, 1982), as well as sex steroid secretion (Bambino & Hsu, 1981; Cumming, Quigley, & Yen, 1983; Schaison, Durand, & Mowszowicz, 1978). Moreover, HPG axis sensitivity to stress is evident in attenuated gonadotropin secretion in depression (Tolis & Stefanis, 1983) and altered testosterone levels in response to psychological stress (see van de Poll et al., 1982; Leshner, 1983; Rose, 1980). Severe psychological stress also has been found to retard physical growth and maturation (Powell et al., 1967). In support of the hormonal aspects of a stress model for early adolescence, there are findings of delayed onset of puberty and regression from pubertal to prepubertal hormone levels (suppression of the gonadal system) in highly trained ballet dancers and anorexics (Frisch, Wyashak & Vincent, 1980; Warren, 1980; Warren et al., 1986). HPA axis activation (high cortisol levels) is known to be associated with chronic intensive exercise (Luger et al., 1987; Villanueva et al., 1986) and anorexia nervosa (Gold et al., 1986a). To a lesser degree, there may very well be interrelations among adjustment and behavior problems, HPA axis activation, and suppression of HPG axis hormone levels in normal adolescents.

The adrenal androgen that would be most telling is Δ_4-androstenedione (Δ_4-A). Although Δ_4-A follows the same maturational pattern as the other adrenal androgens, its secretion, as shown in Figure 6-1, is more closely linked to cortisol than the Δ_5 adrenal androgens, DHEA and DHEAS. Evidence of dissociation of Δ_4- from Δ_5-adrenal androgens (Counts et al., 1987) suggests further that elevated Δ_4-A levels, like elevated cortisol levels—possibly in conjunction with relatively low Δ_5 adrenal androgen levels (and perhaps also with relatively low gonadotropin or sex steroid levels)—may reflect stress associated with adjustment problems.

It is of note that stress-associated elevations of plasma cortisol may

Figure 6–1. A schematic representation of the regulation of adrenal adrogen secretion. Generally, all adrenal androgens, regardless of their configuration (Δ_4 or Δ_5), are dependent on adrenocorticotropic hormone (ACTH) stimulation of the adrenal *zona reticularis*. Development of this zone occurs between 4–5 and 20 years of age. A putative hormone, namely adrenal androgen-stimulating factor (AASF), has been proposed as regulator of *zona reticularis* growth. Alternatively, programmed development of *zona reticularis* cells can explain its age-dependent growth. The dependence of Δ_4-androstenedione (Δ_4-A) on ACTH is greater than that of Δ_5 adrenal androgens (bold arrow). This has been suggested by the findings that Δ_4-A is closely linked to cortisol secretion. Chronic stress is associated with increases in cortisol and androstenedione secretion at the expense of (decreased) secretion of Δ_5 adrenal androgens (see text). CRH, corticotropin-releasing hormone.

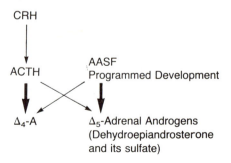

be accompanied by concurrent decreases of Δ_5-adrenal androgen secretion (Parker et al., 1985; Parker, Levin, & Lifrak, 1985). This is probably a result of redirection within the steroidogenesis pathway during chronic stress. Steroid precursors are processed into cortisol (a Δ_4 compound) rather than into DHEA or DHEAS (Δ_5 compounds). This mechanism may explain the negative correlation reported recently of plasma DHEAS concentrations with cardiovascular morbidity and mortality in a large sample (Barrett-Connor, Khaw, & Yen, 1986).

The two neuroendocrine axes and paths of stimulation and possible paths of inhibition in such a stress model for hormone–behavior relations in early adolescence are shown in Figure 6-2.

NIMH–NICHD Collaborative Study

The participants in our study were 108 healthy adolescents—56 boys and 52 girls—and their parents. The majority of the families were white and middle to upper middle class. The adolescents were enrolled by age and pubertal stage (Tanner criteria: for boys, genital stage; for girls, breast stage [Marshall & Tanner, 1969, 1970]). The initial age range was 10–14 years for boys and 9–14 years for girls, and all five stages of pubertal development were represented (see Table 6-1). Of the 52 girls, 18 (35%) were postmenarchial.

The adolescents were seen three times across a 1-year period, at 6-month intervals, for assessments of physical maturity, endocrine status, and psychological functioning. In this chapter, we are reporting cross-sectional findings from our first assessments.

Biological Assessments

Physical Maturity and Growth Measures

In addition to pubertal stage based on genital and breast stage for boys and girls, respectively, the pubertal stage measures used to enroll participants, our physical maturity measures included pubic hair stage (Tanner criteria), height, weight, height for age (Hamill et al., 1979), and weight for age (Hamill et al., 1979) for both boys and girls; and, additionally, for boys, testicular volume (see Nottelmann et al., 1987b). (Not used in most of our analyses were pubic hair stage and testicular volume, measures highly related to our primary pubertal stage measures.)

HORMONE MEASURES

The hormone measures included serum hormone level determinations for hormones of the HPA and HPG axes (see Nottelmann et al., 1987b). For the HPA axis, three adrenal androgens were assessed: DHEA, its

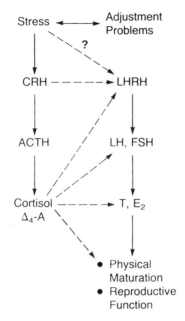

Figure 6–2. A schematic representation of the two neuroendocrine axes that change during pubertal development. The hypothalamic-pituitary-adrenal (HPA) axis (left), which is activated during physical or emotional stress, is responsible for the secretion of cortisol and adrenal androgens, such as Δ_4-androstenedione (Δ_4-A). Although both cortisol and adrenal androgens are dependent on the secretion of hypothalamic corticotropin-releasing hormone (CRH) and therefore pituitary adrenocorticotropic hormone (ACTH), only the secretion of adrenal androgens changes developmentally. The hypothalamic-pituitary-gonadal (HPG) axis (right), which changes developmentally, is responsible for the secretion of the sex steroids testosterone (T) in boys and estradiol (E_2) in girls. The sex steroids bring about the physical maturation of puberty and are responsible for sustaining reproductive function. Solid lines indicate stimulation; interrupted lines indicate inhibition. FSH, follicle-stimulating hormone; LH, luteinizing hormone.

sulfate DHEAS, and Δ_4-A. For the HPG axis, we assessed the gonadotropins, luteinizing hormone (LH) and follicle-stimulating hormone (FSH), and two sex steroids, testosterone (T) and estradiol (E_2). We also computed the testosterone/estradiol ratio (T: E_2).[2]

In our examination of hormone–behavior relations, we used mean hormone values based on separate radioimmunoassays of three blood samples between 8 and 10 a.m., drawn at 20-minute intervals in order to minimize measurement error that may be introduced by circadian rhythms and pulsatile fluctuations. Some measurement error may have

Table 6-1
Sample of Boys and Girls by Pubertal Stage

	NUMBER OF SUBJECTS	
PUBERTAL STAGE[a]	Boys	Girls
1	12	10
2	14	10
3	10	13
4	7	10
5	13	9
TOTAL	56	52

[a]Pubertal stage represents genital stage for boys, breast stage for girls.

been introduced into the hormone values of girls, because the blood of postmenarchial girls was drawn without regard to the menstrual cycle. As a result, potential relations between hormones and behavior may be attenuated. However, menstrual cycle-related variation in our sample should be minimal. By chance, nine of the eighteen postmenarchial girls were in the follicular phase when blood was drawn. Follicular-phase assessments are roughly comparably to anovulatory-cycle assessments (Apter & Vihko, 1985). Moreover, the relatively low gynecological age of the postmenarchial girls (mean time since menarche = 1.23 years) made it very likely that their cycles were anovulatory (<1 year, $p = .85$; <2 years, $p = .66$) (Apter & Vihko, 1985), further increasing the probability of follicular-phase hormone profiles.

The hormone values for our sample, plotted against pubertal stage (for boys, genital stage; for girls, breast stage) are shown in Figures 6-3, 6-4, and 6-5 (Nottelmann et al., 1987b). They suggest that there is a two- to threefold increase in the level of the three adrenal androgens DHEA, DHEAS, and Δ_4-A (see Fig. 6-3) and the gonadotropins LH and FSH (see Fig. 6-4); and, for the sex steroids, an eighteenfold increase in T levels for boys and an eightfold increase in E_2 levels for girls (see Fig.6-5).

INTERRELATIONS OF PHYSICAL MATURITY AND HORMONE MEASURES

Pubertal changes at the physical and hormonal levels are developmentally interrelated. Specifically, our sample yielded the following results. First, the various indices of physical maturity were moderately to highly correlated. Second, hormone level intercorrelations generally were moderate, with only a few correlation coefficients exceeding .60. Strongest were correlations within each hormone group: the adrenal

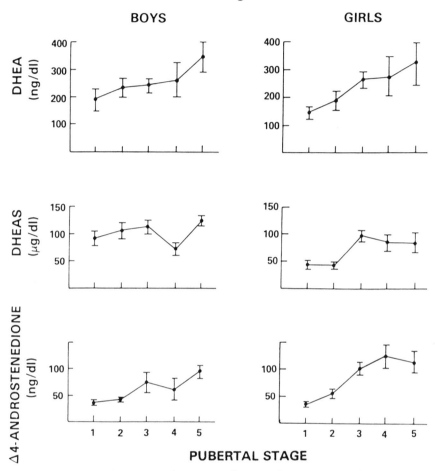

Figure 6–3. Mean and standard error of dehydroepiandrosterone (DHEA), dehydroepiandrosterone sulfate (DHEAS), and Δ_4-androstenedione levels for boys and girls by pubertal stage (genital and breast stage, respectively). (From Nottelmann et al., 1987b.)

androgens, the gonadotropins, and the sex steroids. Finally, hormone levels generally were moderately correlated with the physical maturity measures and with chronological age (Nottelmann et al., 1987b).

Behavior Assessments

The behavioral measures included in the study are based on adolescent self-report, parent report, and observational data. They were collected within a mean of 2.3 days of biological assessments. We focus here on

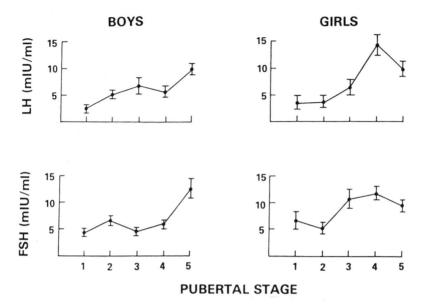

Figure 6–4. Mean and standard error of serum luteinizing hormone (LH) and follicle-stimulating hormone (FSH) levels for boys and girls by pubertal stage (genital and breast stage, respectively). (From Nottelmann et al., 1987b.)

two sets of measures of adolescent psychosocial functioning: adjustment problems and behavior problems.

The adjustment problem measures are based on adolescent self-report on ten scales of the Offer Self-Image Questionnaire for Adolescents (Ostrov, Offer, & Hartlage, 1984; Offer, Ostrov, & Howard, 1977, 1984), which have distinguished reliably among normal, disturbed, and delinquent adolescents (Offer, Ostrov, & Howard, 1977). On a six-point scale, adolescents indicate how well each of 113 items describes them. The ten scales (areas of adjustment) are shown in Table 6-2 with mean scores and standard deviations for our sample, separately for boys and girls. High scores indicate poor adjustment and low scores, good adjustment. There were virtually no sex differences. The internal consistency coefficients (alphas) for the scales in our sample ranged from .64 to .88. In general, the scores for our sample were more similar to those reported previously for normal than for delinquent adolescents (Offer, Ostrov, & Howard, 1977).

The other set of findings is based on parent report on the Child Behavior Checklist (Achenbach & Edelbrock, 1981, 1983). Although individual behavior scales differ somewhat for boys and girls, both sets of scales include comparable internalizing and externalizing problems. For

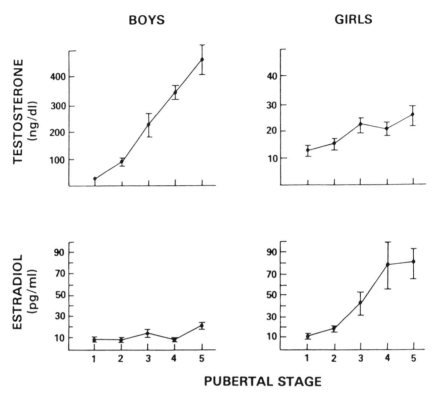

Figure 6–5. Mean and standard error of serum testosterone and estradiol levels for boys and girls by pubertal stage (genital and breast stage, respectively). (From Nottelmann et al., 1987b.)

boys, internalizing scales include Somatic Complaints, Schizoid, Uncommunicative, and Obsessive-Compulsive; externalizing scales include Delinquent (acting out), Aggressive, and Hyperactive. An additional scale is Hostile Withdrawal. For girls, internalizing scales include Anxious/Obsessive, Somatic Complaints, Schizoid, Depressive Withdrawal; externalizing scales include Delinquent (acting out), Aggressive, and Cruel. An additional scale is Immature/Hyperactive. These scales also have been shown to be reliable and valid behavior problem measures (Achenbach & Edelbrock, 1983). On the 120 items of the Child Behavior Checklist, the number of significant sex differences (six) did not exceed chance level. Therefore, for problem behaviors, there were virtually no sex differences either.[3]

Hormone–Behavior Relations

Although it is an empirical question whether hormone levels and behavior are likely to be related in a linear or quadratic fashion in early

Table 6-2
**Means and Standard Deviations by Sex for Areas of Adjustment on the
Offer Self-Image Questionnaire for Adolescents**

	Boys		Girls	
ADJUSTMENT AREA	M	SD	M	SD
Impulse Control	2.86	.68	2.91	.57
Emotional Tone	2.22	.68	2.22	.73
Body and Self-Image	2.47	.77	2.51	.68
Social Relationships	2.24	.80	2.19	.70
Morals[a]	2.64	.69	2.30	.57
Family Relations	2.23	.64	2.19	.63
Mastery of the External World	2.47	.63	2.47	.62
Vocational-Educational Goals	2.08	.69	2.01	.55
Psychopathology	2.53	.65	2.58	.60

[a]The Morals scale scores were significantly different ($p < .01$) for boys and girls.

adolescence, we have been expecting hormone–behavior relations during this developmental period to be primarily linear and, based on previous hormone–behavior relations studies, negative, with increases in hormone levels accompanied by increasingly poor psychosocial functioning. Therefore, our initial explorations and first reports on hormone–behavior relations have concentrated on linear relations (Nottelmann et al., 1987a, c; Susman et al., 1985, 1987). In one of our studies we consulted scatter plots but found no evidence of curvilinear relations (Inoff-Germain et al., 1988). We have since begun to examine quadratic hormone–behavior relations systematically, separately for each hormone in relation to measures of psychosocial functioning, by entering quadratic terms into regression analyses at the second step, after partialing out the linear terms at the first step. There were no significant quadratic findings to support a perturbation hypothesis for hormone–behavior relations for the measures of psychosocial functioning examined so far, including those discussed in this chapter (unpublished observation). Therefore, in this chapter we continue to discuss linear hormone–behavior relations only.

For the examination of linear relations between hormones and behavior, multiple-regression forward entry analysis was used, in which all hormone values were potential "predictors" and measures of psychosocial functioning and behavior were "outcome" variables (in a statistical sense, not to imply causality). Although individual and developmental differences in hormone levels are confounded during puberty, we were interested in exploring whether hormone levels that are high in relation to stage of pubertal development may be more strongly as-

sociated with adjustment and behavior problems than hormone level—
or relative developmental endocrine status—per se. Therefore, these
relations also were examined with hormone levels controlled for pubertal stage (forced entry at the first step) and, further, in order to take
into account possible hormone-related timing of maturation effects, in
relation to hormone levels controlled for chronological age and for both
chronological age and pubertal stage. In the process, we expected to
begin to explore the usefulness of a general puberty-related developmental model by examining how much hormone level variation in relation to psychosocial functioning is shared with chronological age and
physical pubertal stage and with physical growth measures of height,
weight, height for age, and weight for age. All analyses were done
separately for boys and girls.

HORMONE CORRELATES OF ADOLESCENT PSYCHOSOCIAL FUNCTIONING:
SELF-REPORT ON THE OFFER SELF-IMAGE QUESTIONNAIRE FOR
ADOLESCENTS

Hormone–behavior relations based on adolescent self-ratings on the
Offer Self-Image Questionnaire for Adolescents were examined in two
steps: (1) for overall psychosocial functioning (mean total scale score)
and (2) for specific areas of psychosocial functioning (mean individual
scale scores). The results are presented in that order, first for boys and
then for girls.

Table 6-3 shows the hormone–behavior relations for overall psychosocial functioning. These relations indicate that the significant hormone
correlates were HPA and HPG axis hormones for boys and HPG axis
hormone only for girls.

For boys, a profile of higher Δ_4-A levels (HPA axis) and either lower
T levels or a lower T: E_2 ratio (also reflective of relatively low T levels)
(HPG axis) was associated with a higher degree of adjustment problems. These associations held when hormone levels were controlled for
chronological age, pubertal stage or both. Moreover, when hormone
levels were controlled for chronological age, hormone–behavior relations were stronger because of a third hormone correlate, E_2. Chronological age was the only developmental marker significantly related to
adjustment; and the findings involving chronological age suggest that
older boys who also had the hormone profile of higher Δ_4-A and lower
sex steroid levels were especially likely to have adjustment problems.
The relations between hormones and behavior held also when hormone levels were controlled for age-referenced physical growth measures (i.e., height for age and weight for age) that indirectly assess
timing of maturation; but only higher Δ_4-A levels continued to be significantly associated with adjustment when hormone levels were controlled simultaneously for height for age and weight for age. In contrast, control for straight physical growth measures, variation in height,

or weight across all ages and pubertal stages represented in the study, rendered hormone–behavior relations nonsignificant.

For girls, hormone–behavior relations were relatively weak. However, higher FSH levels (HPG axis) were associated with higher degrees of adjustment problems; also associated with higher degrees of adjustment problems were higher FSH levels controlled for pubertal stage, chronological age and pubertal stage simultaneously, height and weight simultaneously, or weight for age. However, control for developmental markers not as closely allied to puberty (i.e., chronological age, height, weight, or height for age and weight for age simultaneously) rendered the hormone correlation nonsignificant.

A breakdown of hormone–behavior relations by area of adjustment that underlie these overall findings is presented in Table 6-4.

For boys, the findings for Social Relationships and Mastery of the External World generally reflect overall findings, in that correlations with hormones for these areas of adjustment were significant, whether or not hormone levels were controlled for other developmental markers. The pattern across all areas of adjustment revealed, however, that hormone–behavior relations were dependent, more often than not, on chronological age or pubertal stage, or on measures of physical growth. For three areas of adjustment, for instance, height as well as chronological age was a significant correlate: Not only older boys, but also taller boys who also had a lower T:E_2 ratio (reflective or relatively low T levels and lower stages of pubertal development) had higher degrees of adjustment problems related to Emotional Tone, Body and Self-Image, and Social Relationships. Height for age was a significant correlate, too, indicating that boys relatively short for their age had higher degrees of adjustment problems related to Family Relationships and Morals. In addition, hormone correlates were rendered nonsignificant by control for pubertal stage (e.g., Body and Self-Image, Psychopathology, Superior Adjustment) or by control for measures of physical growth, especially for weight (e.g., Emotional Tone, Body and Self-Image, Education, Superior Adjustment), which suggest that developmental variation in hormone levels shared with these developmental markers is related to these areas of adjustment rather than developmental variation that is unique to hormone levels. This is not surprising, as T levels are responsible for the pubertal change and physical growth of boys and, in our sample, highly correlated with these developmental markers (Nottelmann et al., 1987a). Finally, it is interesting to note that there was an instance of dissociation between Δ_4- and Δ_5-adrenal androgens, which is associated with stress, in relation to adjustment problems in our sample of normal adolescent boys: A profile of higher Δ_4-A and lower DHEAS levels, together with lower T levels, was associated with higher degrees of problems related to Superior Adjustment.

For girls, as overall findings suggest, the breakdown by area of adjustment revealed chronological age and pubertal stage to be factors in hormone–behavior relations involving gonadotropins. Except for Social Relationships, control for chronological age generally rendered these relations nonsignificant, indicating that gonadotropin correlates tend to reflect developmental variation shared with chronological age in our sample of girls rather than developmental variation that is unique to gonadotropin levels. For other areas of adjustment, HPA axis hormone correlates emerged that generally were dependent on pubertal stage; that is, higher Δ_4-A levels (HPA axis) controlled for pubertal stage were associated with higher degrees of adjustment problems as reflected in

Table 6-3
Multiple Regression of Hormone Levels on Adolescent Psychosocial Adjustment Problems: Self-Ratings

PREDICTORS[a]	SIGNIFICANT CORRELATES	R	R^2	R^2 CHANGE	BETA[b]
Boys					
HL	Δ_4-A	.31*	.10	.10	.54**
	T	.46**	.21	.11	−.41*
HL controlled for CA	CA	.31*	.10	.10	.58***
	T:E_2	.51**	.26	.16	−.68***
	Δ_4-A	.59***	.35	.09	.52***
	E_2	.67***	.44	.09	−.36*
HL controlled for PS	PS	.06	.00	.00	.26
	Δ_4-A	.34	.12	.12	.50**
	T	.48*	.23	.11	−.60*
HL Controlled for CA and PS	PS				−.10
	CA	.38*	.14	.14	.61***
	Δ_4-A	.53**	.28	.14	.54**
	T:E_2	.62***	.39	.11	−.63**
	E_2	.67***	.45	.06	−.38*
HL Controlled for HT	HT	.12	.01	.01	.12
HL controlled for WT	WT	.14	.02	.02	.14
HL Controlled for HT and WT	WT				.12
	HT	.14	.02	.02	.02
HL Controlled for HT%	HT%	.12	.01	.01	−.11
	Δ_4-A	.38*	.14	.13	.55**
	T	.47*	.22	.09	−.36*
HL Controlled for WT%	WT%	.01	.00	.00	−.02
	Δ_4-A	.32	.10	.10	.55**
	T	.46*	.21	.11	−.40*
HL Controlled for HT% and WT%	WT%				.16
	HT%	.16	.03	.03	−.34
	Δ_4-A	.39	.15	.12	.37*

Table 6-3 (continued)

PREDICTORS[a]	SIGNIFICANT CORRELATES	R	R^2	R^2 CHANGE	BETA[b]
Girls					
HL	FSH	.29*	.08	.08	.29*
HL Controlled for CA	CA	.09	.01	.01	.09
HL Controlled for PS	PS	.06	.00	.00	−.19
	FSH	.34	.11	.11	.36*
HL Controlled for CA and PS	PS				−.47
	CA	.25	.04	.04	.35
	FSH	.39	.15	.11	.32*
HL Controlled for HT	HT	.06	.00	.00	.06
HT Controlled for WT	WT	.08	.01	.01	.08
HT Controlled for HT and WT	WT				.21
	HT	.09	.01	.01	−.21
	FSH	.31	.09	.08	.31*
HL Controlled for HT%	HT%	.08	.01	.01	−.08
HL Controlled for WT%	WT%	.02	.00	.00	.01
	FSH	.29	.08	.08	.29*
HL Controlled for HT% and WT%	WT%				.08
	HT%	.10	.01	.01	−.14

[a] CA, chronological age; HL, hormone level; HT, height; HT%, height for age; PS, pubertal stage; WT, weight; WT%, weight for age.
[b] The beta weights shown represent the relative contribution of variables to the final equation.
*p < .05; **p < .01; ***p < .001.

Family Relationships, Mastery of the External World, and Psychopathology.

HORMONE CORRELATES OF ADOLESCENT PSYCHOSOCIAL FUNCTIONING: PARENT REPORT ON THE CHILD BEHAVIOR CHECKLIST

Overall hormone–behavior relations for adolescent psychosocial functioning based on parent-reported behavior problems on the Child Behavior Checklist were examined across internalizing scales, externalizing scales, and across all scales for total number of behavior problems. Hormones were significantly related to the total number of behavior problems in boys, but in girls the relationship was significant only for internalizing behavior problems. The results are presented in Table 6-5. The only significant hormone correlates were HPA axis hormones.

For boys, higher Δ_4-A levels were associated with more behavior problems. These associations held when hormone levels were controlled for other developmental markers directly or indirectly assessing

Table 6-4
Significant Relations between Adolescent Psychosocial Adjustment and Hormone Levels

Adjustment Area	HL	HL(CA)	HL(PS)	HL(CA,PS)	HL(HT)	HL(WT)	HL(HT,WT)	HL(HT%)	HL(WT%)	HL(HT%,WT%)
Boys										
Emotional Tone		.61*** CA .60*** T:E₂ -.56** Δ₄-A .29*	.37* PS .50* T:E₂ -.45*	.56** PS .14 CA -.59** T:E₂ .54**	.44* HT .51** T:E₂ -.39*		.44* WT -.11 HT .61* T:E₂ -.40*			
Body and Self-Image		.57*** CA .68*** T:E₂ -.49**		.57*** PS .03 CA .67*** T:E₂ -.50**	.29* HT .51** T:E₂ -.39*		.30* WT .05 HT .46 T:E₂ -.38*			
Social Relationships	.48** Δ₄-A .50** T:E₂ -.32*	.63*** CA .51** T:E₂ -.57*** Δ₄-A .42*	.51** PS .29 T:E₂ -.48* Δ₄-A .39*	.63*** PS -.06 CA .53** T:E₂ -.55** Δ₄-A .43*	.56** HT .38* T:E₂ -.48** Δ₄-A .39*	.54* WT .29 Δ₄-A .43* T:E₂ -.40*	.56** WT .05 HT .33 T:E₂ -.48* Δ₄-A .39*	.48* HT% .01 Δ₄-A .50** T:E₂ -.32*	.48* WT% .03 Δ₄-A .49** T:E₂ -.32*	.39 WT% .13 HT% -.13 Δ₄-A -.38*
Family Relationships								.40* HT% -.36* Δ₄-A .30*		.42* WT% -.21 HT% -.20 Δ₄-A .31*
Morals				.50* PS -.66** CA .61** Δ₄-A .37*				.43* HT% -.40** Δ₄-A .31*		.44* WT% .16 HT% -.52* Δ₄-A .31*
Mastery of the External World	.45* Δ₄-A .56** T -.38*		.39* PS -.24 Δ₄-A .48*	.51** PS -.59** CA .47* Δ₄-A .52*	.47* HT .14 Δ₄-A .55** T -.47*	.49* WT .24 Δ₄-A .56** T -.53	.50* WT .33 HT -.14 Δ₄-A .57** T -.49*	.41* HT% -.24 Δ₄-A .41*	.46* WT% .03 Δ₄-A .55** T -.38*	.44* WT% .28 HT% -.45* Δ₄-A .40*
Education		.54** CA .39* T:E₂ -.55** Δ₄-A .51** E₂ -.33*	.49** PS .42 T -.72** Δ₄-A .45*	.52* PS .23 CA .23 T -.69** Δ₄-A .46*				.44* HT% .00 Δ₄-A .52** T -.42*		

Psychopathology		.56**; CA .38*, $T{:}E_2$ -.55**, Δ_4-A .52**, E_2 -.39*						
Superior Adjustment		.72***; CA .30*, $T{:}E_2$ -.25, DHEAS -.40**, Δ_4-A .54***, T -.81***, FSH .47**	.69***; HT .22, T -.99***, Δ_4-A .55**, DHEAS -.41*, FSH .49**		.68***; WT -.07, HT .28, T -.99***, Δ_4-A .54**, DHEAS -.40**, FSH .48**			
Girls								
Impulse Control	.33*; LH .33*	.46**; CA .26, FSH .29*	.33*; HT -.02, LH .33*	.38; WT .02, LH .32*				.36; WT% .24, HT% -.29, $T{:}E_2$ -.32*
Body and Self-Image	.29*; FSH .29*						.31; WT% .10, FSH .30*	
Social Relationships	.41*; LH .41*	.58***; PS -.37, CA .64**, LH .43**, DHEAS -.34*	.41*; HT -.01, LH .42*	.42*; WT .13, FSH .38**	.42*; WT .25, HT -.15, FSH .40*	.48**; HT% -.25, LH .43**	.43*; WT% -.12, LH .44**	.49**; WT% .14, HT% .35, LH .42**
Family Relationships	.37*; PS -.33, Δ_4-A .44*	.39; PS -.52*, CA .26, Δ_4-A .39*						
Mastery of the External World	.37*; PS -.44*, Δ_4-A .35*							
Psychopathology	.35*; Δ_4-A .35*	.37*; PS -.14, Δ_4-A .43*	.36*; HT -.09, Δ_4-A .40*	.35*; WT .00, Δ_4-A .35*	.37; WT .21, HT -.27, Δ_4-A .39*	.41*; HT% -.21, Δ_4-A .38**	.38*; WT% -.14, Δ_4-A .38*	.41; WT% .05, HT% -.24, Δ_4-A .37**

Note: HL, Hormone levels; HL(CA), hormone levels controlled for chronological age; HL(PS), HL controlled for pubertal stage; HL(CA,PS), HL controlled for CA and PS; HL(HT), HL controlled for height; HL(WT), HL controlled for weight; HL(HT,WT), HL controlled for HT and WT; HL(HT%), HL controlled for height for age; HL(WT%), HL controlled for weight for age; HL(HT%,WT%), HL controlled for HT% and WT%. Multiple correlation coefficients and final solution beta weights by area of adjustment.

$*p < .05;\ **p < .01;\ ***p < .001.$

Table 6-5
**Multiple Regression of Hormone Levels on Adolescent Psychosocial
Adjustment Problems: Parent Ratings**

Predictors[a]	Significant Correlates	R	R^2	R^2 Change	Beta[b]
Boys					
HL	Δ_4-A	.33*	.11	.11	.33*
HL Controlled for CA	CA	.18	.03	.03	.18
HL Controlled for PS	PS	.13	.02	.02	−.11
	Δ_4-A	.35	.12	.10	.40*
HL Controlled for CA and PS	PS				−.29
	CA	.18	.03	.03	.22
	Δ_4-A	.38	.14	.11	.42*
HL Controlled for HT	HT	.23	.05	.05	.23
HL Controlled for WT	WT	.32*	.10	.10	.32*
HL Controlled for HT and WT	WT				.45
	HT	.33	.11	.11	−.16
HL Controlled for HT%	HT%	.08	.01	.01	.09
	Δ_4-A	.33	.11	.10	.48**
	E_2	.44	.20	.09	−.36*
HL Controlled for WT%	WT%	.26	.07	.07	.26
HL Controlled for HT% and WT%	WT%				.44*
	HT%	.31	.10	.10	−.35
	Δ_4-A	.44	.19	.09	.32*
Girls					
HL	—				
HL Controlled for CA	CA	.03	.00	.00	.21
	DHEAS	.32	.10	.10	−.37*
HL Controlled for PS	PS	.06	.00	.00	−.06
HL Controlled for CA and PS	PS				−.26
	CA	.16	.03	.03	.43
	DHEAS	.35	.12	.09	−.37*
HL Controlled for HT	HT	.07	.00	.00	−.07
HL Controlled for WT	WT	.04	.00	.00	−.04
HL Controlled for HT and WT	WT				.06
	HT	.07	.01	.01	−.12
HL Controlled for HT%	HT%	.18	.03	.03	−.18
HL Controlled for WT%	WT%	.21	.05	.05	−.21
HL Controlled for HT% and WT%	WT%				−.18
	HT%	.21	.05	.05	−.05

Note: For boys, adjustment is based on both internalizing and externalizing
behavior problems; for girls, on internalizing behavior problems only.
[a] CA, chronological age; HL, hormone level; HT, height; HT%, height for age;
PS, pubertal stage; WT, weight; WT%, weight for age.
[b] The beta weights shown represent the relative contribution of variables to the
final equation.
*p < .05; **p < .01

timing of maturation (i.e., pubertal stage, chronological age and pubertal stage simultaneously, height for age, or height for age and weight for age simultaneously). However, control for chronological age, height, weight, and weight for age rendered these hormone–behavior relations nonsignificant. Of these other developmental markers, only weight was a significant correlate, suggesting that heavier boys were likely to have more behavior problems.

For girls, hormone–behavior relations were relatively weak. The only significant hormone correlates were dependent on chronological age; that is, lower DHEAS level controlled for chronological age, or for chronological age and puberty stage simultaneously, were associated with internalizing problem behavior.

A breakdown of hormone–behavior relations by individual behavior problem scales (all scales for boys, internalizing scales for girls) is presented in Table 6-6. For both boys and girls, hormone–behavior relations analyzed by individual scale generally reflected overall findings (i.e., based on the total number of problems for boys and internalizing problems for girls). For boys, however, relations were stronger for the few scales with significant hormone correlates; and, in addition to higher Δ_4-A levels, lower gonadal sex steroid and lower DHEAS levels were associated with higher degrees of problem behavior—lower T levels with Obsessive-Compulsive behaviors, lower E_2 levels with Delinquent (acting-out) behaviors, and lower DHEAS levels with Hyperactive behaviors. Control for other developmental markers had virtually no effect on the hormone correlates of Obsessive-Compulsive and Delinquent (acting-out) behaviors, but all except height for age rendered the hormone correlates of Hyperactive behaviors nonsignificant. The hormone correlates for Hyperactive behaviors, which show the dissociation pattern between Δ_4- and Δ_5-adrenal androgens, therefore, appear to reflect developmental variation shared with the other developmental markers rather than developmental variation that is unique to hormone levels. The overall finding of associations between weight and problem behaviors was evident only for somatic complaints, without hormone correlates.

For girls, lower DHEAS levels, as well as lower DHEAS levels controlled for chronological age, pubertal stage, or both, were associated with internalizing behavior problems. However, control for physical growth measures generally rendered this correlation nonsignificant, suggesting that the DHEAS level variation that is related to internalizing problem behavior is not a developmental variation unique to hormone levels. Although there were no significant correlations between hormones and externalizing behaviors, it is noteworthy that weight for age was significantly correlated; that is, low weight for age was associated with problem behaviors reflected in the scales labeled Delinquent ($R = .38$), Aggressive ($R = .33$), and Cruel ($R = .29$).

Table 6-6
Significant Relations between Parent-Reported Adolescent Behavior Problems and Hormone Levels

Type of Behavior	HL	HL(CA)	HL(PS)	HL(CA,PS)	HL(HT)	HL(WT)	HL(HT,WT)	HL(HT%)	HL(WT%)	HL(HT%,WT%)
Boys										
Internalizing Behavior										
Obsessive-Compulsive	.47** Δ_4-A .58** T −.36*	.40** CA −.17 Δ_4-A .44**	.49** PS −.39* Δ_4-A .61***	.49** PS −.48* CA .11 Δ_4-A .61***	.39* HT −.12 Δ_4-A .43*	.54** WT .36* Δ_4-A .58** T −.58**	.58** WT .63* HT −.41 Δ_4-A .61** T −.48*	.47* HT% .03 Δ_4-A .58** T −.37	.52** WT% .25 Δ_4-A .56** T −.43*	.56** WT% .55** HT% −.51* Δ_4-A .59* T −.36*
Externalizing Behavior										
Delinquent	.58** Δ_4-A .65*** E_2 −.44**	.58*** CA .06 Δ_4-A .63*** E_2 −.44**	.58*** PS .02 Δ_4-A .64*** E_2 −.44**	.57*** PS −.05 CA .09 Δ_4-A .65*** E_2 −.43**	.59*** HT .13 Δ_4-A .61*** E_2 −.48**	.60*** WT .16 Δ_4-A .61*** E_2 −.48**	.68*** WT .18 HT −.03 Δ_4-A .62*** E_2 −.47**	.58*** HT% .02 Δ_4-A .65*** E_2 −.44**	.60*** WT% .14 Δ_4-A .63*** E_2 −.47**	.61*** WT% .28 HT% −.20 Δ_4-A .63*** E_2 −.42**
Hyperactive	.42* Δ_4-A .52** DHEAS −.38*							.43* HT% −.08 Δ_4-A .55** DHEA −.39*		.34 WT% .51* HT% −.35
Girls										
Internalizing Behavior										
Depressed Withdrawal	.32* DHEAS −.32*	.34 CA .13 DHEAS −.39*	.33 PS −.01 DHEAS −.32*	.38 PS −.27 CA .35 DHEAS −.38*		.33 WT .09 DHEAS −.37				

Note: HL, Hormone levels; HL(CA), HL controlled for chronological age; HL(PS), HL controlled for pubertal stage; HL(CA,PS), HL controlled for CA and PS; HL(HT), HL controlled for height; HL(WT), HL controlled for weight; HL(HL,WT), HL controlled for HT and WT; HL(HT%), HL controlled for height for age; HL(WT%), HL controlled for weight for age; HL(HT%,WT%), HL controlled for HT% and WT%. Multiple correlation coefficients and final solution beta weights by behavior problem scales.
*p < .05; **p < .01; ***p < .001.

Conclusions

We outlined two interrelated models for hormone–behavior relations in early adolescence, a "developmental model" and a "stress model." The pattern of findings reviewed in this chapter offer support for both models.

Beginning with the developmental model, our cross-sectional findings suggest that the rise in gonadal (HPG) axis hormone levels has different developmental implications for boys and girls. For boys, there appear to be positive implications. Higher rather than lower sex steroid levels were associated with lower degrees of adjustment and behavior problems. The hormone correlates of adjustment problems, however, more often than not were dependent on other developmental markers like chronological age and therefore also reflect timing of maturation influences. Although the HPG axis hormone correlates that emerged when pubertal stage was held constant suggest that individual as well as developmental differences may be contributing to hormone–behavior relations, we have some evidence that within-stage hormone level differences reflect rate of maturation (Nottelmann et al., 1987d). In addition to later maturation (timing of maturation), a slower *rate* of maturation may be associated with adjustment and behavior problems. For girls, the findings were relatively weak, but they do suggest that the rise in HPG axis hormone levels has negative implications. Higher levels of gonadotropins were associated with higher degrees of adjustment problems.

The related findings for adrenal (HPA) axis hormones offer support for a stress model, again more strongly for boys than for girls. Higher Δ_4-A levels quite consistently were associated with higher degrees of adjustment and behavior problems: For boys this was usually in conjunction with lower T levels, frequently in conjunction with higher age, and sometimes in conjunction with lower pubertal stage or lower height for age; for girls, in a few instances it was in conjunction with earlier pubertal stage. For boys more so than girls, then, there was an indication that HPA axis activation during early adolescence, as reflected in higher Δ_4-A levels, may have subtle suppressive effects on the HPG axis (i.e., T levels), affecting either the onset of puberty or the rate of pubertal maturation, as suggested in Figure 6-6. Furthermore, for boys, the pattern of stress-related dissociation in adrenal androgens, higher Δ_4-A and lower DHEAS levels, in relation to adjustment and behavior problems was observed twice. For girls, in keeping with reported associations for DHEAS levels (e.g., Parker et al., 1985), whenever DHEAS levels were related to psychosocial functioning, lower DHEAS levels were associated with higher degrees of adjustment and behavior problems. Nevertheless, a stress model based on Δ_4-A levels may be less appropriate for girls than for boys. In girls, Δ_4-A levels may be of ovarian as well as adrenal origin, following HPG axis activation. Moreover,

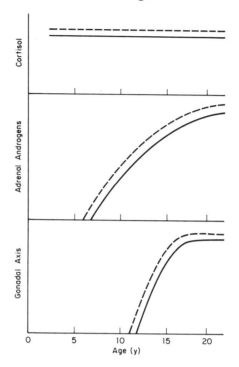

Figure 6–6. A schematic representation of the relative activity of the hypothalamic-pituitary-adrenal (HPA) and hypothalamic-pituitary-gonadal (HPG) axes during development. Cortisol secretion remains relatively constant during development (top panel). Adrenal androgen secretion starts at 6 years and reaches peak levels at 20 years of age (middle panel). Gonadal steroid secretion starts at 11 years and reaches peak levels at 16 years of age (bottom panel). The solid lines represent individuals with low levels of chronic stress. The interrupted lines represent individuals with higher levels of chronic stress.

in our sample, Δ_4-A levels were correlated significantly with cortisol levels for boys ($r = .53$), but not for girls.

Obviously, a stress model based on cross-sectional data spanning a period of rapid developmental change must be entertained with caution. For boys, relations between HPG axis hormone levels and adjustment and behavior problems suggest that the early pubertal stages are likely to be more difficult and perhaps more stressful than the later pubertal stages. The findings also suggest that the early pubertal stages are likely to be especially difficult for later maturing boys (but well within the normal range in our sample of 10- to 14-year-old boys). As the developmental pattern for Δ_4-A, as well as for T, is one of change from lower to higher levels, it seems plausible that relatively high Δ_4-A levels in conjunction with relatively low HPG axis hormone levels reflect HPA axis activation in response to stress and some delay in HPG axis activation. It is equally possible, however, that such an endocrine profile reflects normative development—that is, relative HPA axis predominance (higher Δ_4-A and lower T levels) in the earlier pubertal stages and, in the later pubertal stages, ascendance and predominance of the HPG axis (lower Δ_4-A and higher T levels). In other words, perhaps Δ_4-A levels, which begin to rise at adrenarche (several years prior to gonadarche), should be predominant when HPG axis hormones are at low levels or just beginning to rise and should remain predominant until the dramatic rise in gonadal sex steroid levels is well under way (our cross-sectional findings suggest an eighteenfold increase in T levels compared to a two- to threefold increase in Δ_4-A levels). T levels should become predominant during the later stages of pubertal development. Inspection of individual standardized hormone profiles of the boys in our sample indeed revealed many cases with relatively high Δ_4-A and low T levels at earlier stages and, vice versa, many cases of relatively low Δ_4-A and high T levels at later stages of pubertal development. Thus, for boys, hormone levels rather than physical maturity status may be significant correlates of adjustment and behavior simply because hormone levels provide a more sensitive index of general pubertal status.

Giving full recognition to these developmental considerations, we propose an integrated developmental stress model for hormone–behavior relations in early adolescence. The incidence of pathological adrenal hypersecretion and a long period of HPG axis suppression and delay in maturation (as, for example, in anorexia nervosa) probably is relatively low. Normative development, at the other end of the spectrum, may include a transitional period of somewhat increased HPA axis function at the time of expected gonadarche, with negligible suppressive effects. However, in some individuals the transitional period may be somewhat prolonged, though still within the normal range. Excessive sensitivity of the HPG axis to changes of the HPA axis or a predisposition to high biological reactivity to stressful events in the social environment may result in the combination of high HPA axis function and low HPG axis function. In the general population, between 10 and 20% of children and adolescents are estimated to have psychological or psychiatric problems of sufficiently severe nature to benefit from clinical intervention (Petersen & Craighead, 1986). Thus, even in our small sample, the findings may reflect influences of relatively poor psychosocial functioning on the endocrine system and, therefore, on timing of maturation. Of course, the degree to which poor psychosocial functioning may influence the endocrine system, or alternately, the degree to which the endocrine system may influence adjustment and behavior, has to be addressed in longitudinal research that begins with pre-pubertal assessments of adjustment and behavior, and involves follow-up assessments throughout the pubertal years. Ideally, such an intensive investigation of hormone–behavior relations should be done in a fairly large cohort or in a sample of children identified for their poor psychosocial functioning, as well as with children whose adjustment and behavior is well within the normal range.

Major support for the two interrelated models for hormone–behavior relations in early adolescence emerged in the findings for boys, which were not only stronger but also more consistent and generalized than the findings for girls. There were no marked sex differences in adjustment and behavior problems. Therefore, it seems that there are sex-related differences in hormone influences on behavior. One factor in such hormone influence differences may be the increasing male/female divergence in hormone profiles during HPG axis maturation that is due primarily to changes in gonadal sex steroid levels. Although T and E_2 levels change in both males and females, the major changes are in T levels for males and in E_2 levels for females, resulting in exponentially higher T levels in males than females and in increasingly higher E_2 levels in females than males. Hormone influences on behavior could be due to potentially different direct effects of T and E_2 levels or indirect effects of relative T and E_2 levels through changes in neuroendocrine system functioning. Sex differences in hormone–behavior relations also have been attributed to prenatal organizational influences of sex steroids in males that are activated during puberty and dispose males and females to respond differently to the rise in gonadal sex steroids (e.g., Marcus et al., 1985; Nyborg, 1983; Susman et al., 1987). Although we cannot rule out that the weaker findings for girls may be due in part to measurement error introduced by menstrual cycle-related variation in hormone levels, as explained earlier, we expected this to be a minimal problem. Moreover, in an observational study of a sub-sample of these adolescents, we did find relatively strong and consistent relations between hormone levels and the behavior of girls in interaction with their parents, but few significant relations for boys (Inoff-Germain et al., 1988). We speculated that, for girls, more so than for boys, the expression of hormone-mediated behaviors may be dependent on the social context. Another factor in sex-related differences in hormone influences on behavior, then, may be that socialization influences are more important modulators of hormone-mediated behaviors for girls than for boys.

Finally, it is clear that our findings favor a general puberty-related developmental model for psychosocial functioning during early adolescence. Also, instead of revealing redundancies in the interdependencies of included puberty-related indices, the findings generally suggest complementarity. That is, the findings suggest not only that it is useful to examine more than one group of hormones in a study of hormone–behavior relations in early adolescence (i.e., adrenal as well as gonadal axis hormones); they also suggest that it is important to examine such relations in the context of other developmental markers such as chronological age and pubertal stage.

References

Achenbach, T. M., & Edelbrock, C. S. (1981). Behavioral problems and competencies reported by parents of normal and disturbed children aged four through sixteen. *Monographs of the Society for Research in Child Development, 46* (1), 1–82.

Achenbach, T. M., & Edelbrock, C. S. (1983). *Manual for the child behavior checklist and the revised child behavior profile.* Department of Psychiatry, University of Vermont, Burlington.

Akiskal, H. S., & McKinney, W. T., Jr. (1975). Overview of recent research in depression. *Archives of General Psychiatry, 32,* 285–305.

Albertson, B. D., Hobson, W. C., Burnett, B. S., Turner, P. T., Clark, R. V., Schiebinger, R. J., Loriaux, D. L., & Cutler, G. B., Jr. (1984). Dissociation of cortisol and adrenal androgen secretion in the hypophysectomized, adrenocorticotropin-replaced chimpanzee. *Journal of Clinical Endocrinology and Metabolism, 59,* 13–18.

Alpert, J. E., Cohen, D. J., Shayvitz, B. A., & Piccirillo, M. (1981). Neurochemical and behavioral organization: Disorders of attention, activity, and aggression. In D. O. Lewis (Ed.), *Vulnerabilities to delinquency* (pp. 109–171). New York: Spectrum Publications.

Amsterdam, J. D., Winokur, A., Lucki, I., Snyder, P., Harris, R. I., Caroff, S., & Rickels, K. (1982). Growth hormone, prolactin, and thyrotropin responses to gonadotropin-releasing hormone in depressed patients and healthy volunteers. *Psychoneuroendocrinology, 7,* 177–184.

Apter, D., & Vihko, R. (1985). Hormonal patterns of the first menstrual cycles. In S. Venturoli, C. Flamigni, & J. R. Givens (Eds.), *Adolescence in females* (pp. 215–238). Chicago: Year Book Medical Publishers.

Bambino, T. H., & Hsu, A. J. W. (1981). Direct inhibitory effect of glucocorticoids upon testicular luteinizing hormone receptor and steroidogenesis *in vivo* and *in vitro. Endocrinology, 108,* 2142–2148.

Bancroft, J. (1987). A physiological approach. In J. Geer and W. T. O'Donohue (Eds.), *Theories of human sexuality* (pp. 411–421). New York: Plenum.

Bardwick, J. M. (1976). Psychological correlates of the menstrual cycle and oral contraceptive medication. In E. J. Sachar (Ed.), *Hormones, behavior, and psychopathology* (pp. 95–103). New York: Raven.

Barrett-Connor, E., Khaw, K.-T., & Yen, S. S. C. (1986). A prospective study of dehydroepiandrosterone sulfate, mortality, and cardiovascular disease. *New England Journal of Medicine, 315,* 1519–1524.

Blyth, D. A., Simmons, R. G., Bulcroft, R., Felt, D., Van Cleave, E. F., & Bush, D. M. (1981). The effects of physical development on self-image and satisfaction with body-image for early adolescent males. *Research in Community Health, 2,* 43–73.

Bouissou, M. F. (1983). Androgens, aggressive behavior and social relationships in higher mammals. *Hormone Research, 18,* 43–61.

Brambilla, F., Smeraldi, E., Sacchetti, E., Negri, F., Cocchi, D., & Muller, E. E. (1978). Deranged anterior pituitary responsiveness to hypothalamic hormones in depressed patients. *Archives of General Psychiatry, 35,* 1231–1238.

Brooks-Gunn, J. (1987). Pubertal processes and girls' psychological adaptation. In R. M. Lerner & T. T. Foch (Eds.), *Biological-psychological interactions in early adolescence* (pp. 123–153). Hillsdale, NJ: Erlbaum.

Brophy, M. H., Rush, A. J., & Crowley, G. (1983). Cortisol, estradiol, and androgens in acutely ill paranoid schizophrenia. *Biological Psychiatry, 18,* 583–590.

Cantalamessa, L., Catania, A., Silva, A., Orsatti, A., Motta, P., & Cazzullo, C. L. (1985). Gonadotropin-releasing hormone elicits abnormal hormone response in schizophrenia. *Psychoneuroendocrinology, 10,* 481–484.

Collu, R., Gibb, W., & Ducharme, J. R. (1984). Effects of stress on the gonadal function. *Journal of Endocrinological Investigation, 7,* 529–537.

Counts, D. R., Pescovitz, O. H., Barnes, K. M., Hench, K. D., Chrousos, G. P., Sherrins, R. J., Comite, F., Loriaux, D. L., & Cutler, G. B., Jr. (1987). Dissociation of adrenarche and gonadarche in precocious puberty and in hypogonadotropic hypogonadism. *Journal of Clinical Endocrinology and Metabolism, 64,* 1174–1178.

Crockett, L. J., & Dorn, L. (1987). *Young adolescents' pubertal status and reported heterosocial interaction.* Paper presented at the biennial meeting of the Society for Research in Child Development, Baltimore, April.

Cumming, D. C., Quigley, M. E., & Yen, S. S. C. (1983). Acute suppression of circulating testosterone levels by cortisol in men. *Journal of Clinical Endocrinology and Metabolism, 57,* 671–673.

Cutler, G. B., Jr., Davies, S. E., Johnsonbough, R. E., & Loriaux, D. L. (1979). Dissociation of cortisol and adrenal androgen secretion in patients with secondary adrenal insufficiency. *Journal of Clinical Endocrinology and Metabolism, 49,* 604–609.

de Lignieres, B., & Vincens, M. (1982). Differential effects of exogenous oestradiol and progesterone on mood in postmenopausal women: Individual dose/effect relationships. *Maturitas, 4,* 67–72.

de Wied, D., & van Keep, P. A. (1980). *Hormones and the brain.* Baltimore: University Park Press.

Doering, C. H., Brodie, K. H., Kraemer, H. C., Moos, R. H., Becker, H. B., & Hamburg, D. A. (1975). Negative affect and plasma testosterone: A longitudinal human study. *Psychosomatic Medicine, 37,* 484–491.

Eberhart, J. A., Keverne, E. B., & Mueller, R. E. (1980). Social influences on plasma testosterone levels in male Talapoin monkeys. *Hormones and Behavior, 14,* 247–266.

Ehrenkranz, J., Bliss, E., & Sheard, M. H. (1974). Plasma testosterone: Correlations with aggressive behavior and social dominance in man. *Psychosomatic Medicine, 36,* 469–475.

Eleftheriou, B. E., & Sprott, R. L. (1975). *Hormonal correlates of behavior.* Vol. 1 *A lifespan view.* New York: Plenum.

Ellis, L. (1982). Developmental androgen fluctuations and the five dimensions of mammalian sex (with emphasis upon the behavioral dimension and the human species). *Ethology and Sociobiology, 3,* 171–197.

Erb, J. L., Kadane, J. B., & Tourney, G. (1981). Discrimination between schizophrenic and control subjects by means of plasma dehydroepiandrosterone measurements. *Journal of Clinical Endocrinology and Metabolism, 52,* 181–186.

Eriksson, E., & Modigh, K. (1984). Depression, α_2-receptors and sex hormones: Neuroendocrine studies in rat. *Advances in Biochemical Psychopharmacology, 39*, 161–178.

Faust, M. S. (1960). Developmental maturity as a determinant of prestige in adolescent girls. *Child Development, 31*, 173–184.

Ferrier, I. N., Cotes, P. M., Crow, T. J., & Johnstone, E. C. (1982). Gonadotropin secretion abnormalities in chronic schizophrenia. *Psychological Medicine, 12*, 263–273.

Frisch, R. E., Wyashak, G., & Vincent, L. (1980). Delayed menarche and amenorrhea and ballet dancers. *New England Journal of Medicine, 303*, 18–19.

Garwood, S. G., & Allen, L. (1979). Self-concept and identified problem differences between pre and postmenarchial adolescents. *Journal of Clinical Psychology, 35*, 528–537.

Gil-Ad, I., Dickerman, Z., Weizman, R., Weizman, A., Tyano, S., & Laron, Z. (1981). Abnormal growth hormone response to LRH and TRH in adolescent schizophrenic boys. *American Journal of Psychiatry, 138*, 357–360.

Gold, P. W., Gwirtsman, H., Averginos, P. C., Nieman, L. K., Galluci, W. T., Kaye, W., Jimerson, D., Ebert, M., Rittmaster, R., Loriaux, D. L., & Chrousos, G. P. (1986a). Abnormal hypothalamic-pituitary-adrenal function in anorexia nervosa. *New England Journal of Medicine, 314*, 1335–1342.

Gold, P. W., Loriaux, D. L., Roy, A., Kling, M. A., Calabrese, J. R., Kellmer, C. H., Nieman, L. K., Post, R. M., Pickar, D., Gallucci, W., Averginos, P., Paul, S., Oldfield, E. H., Cutler, G. B., & Chrousos, G. P. (1986b). Responses to corticotropin-releasing hormone in the hypercortisolism of depression and Cushing's disease. *New England Journal of Medicine, 314*, 1329–1335.

Gross, R. T., & Duke, P. M. (1980). The effect of early versus late physical maturity on adolescent behavior. *Pediatric Clinics of North America, 27*, 71–77.

Hamburg, D. A., Elliott, G. R., & Parron, D. L. (1982). *Health and behavior: Frontiers of research in the behavioral sciences.* Institute of Medicine, National Academy of Sciences. Washington, DC: National Academy Press.

Hamill, P. V. V., Drizd, T. A., Johnson, C. L., Reed, R. B., Roche, A. F., & Moore, W. M. (1979). Physical growth. National Center of Health Statistics percentiles. *American Journal of Clinical Nutrition, 32*, 607–629.

Hamilton, J. A. (1984). Psychobiology in context: Reproductive-related events in men's and women's lives. *Contemporary Psychiatry, 3*, 325–328.

Hansen, C. R., Kroll, J., & MacKensie, T. B. (1982). Dehydroepiandrosterone and affective disorders. *American Journal of Psychiatry, 139*, 386–387.

Hill, J. P., & Holmbeck, G. N. (1987). Familial adaptation to biological change during adolescence. In R. M. Lerner & T. T. Foch (Eds.), *Biological–psychosocial interactions in early adolescence* (pp. 207–223). Hillsdale, NJ: Erlbaum.

Hill, J. P., Holmbeck, G. N., Marlow, L., Green, T. M., & Lynch, M. E. (1985). Pubertal status and parent–child relations in families of seventh-grade boys. *Journal of Early Adolescence, 5*, 31–44.

Hill, J. P., & Moenks, F. J. (1977). Some perspectives on adolescence in modern societies. In J. P. Hill & F. J. Moenks (Eds.), *Adolescence and youth in prospect* (pp. 28–78). Guilford, England: IPC Science and Technology Press.

Houser, B. B. (1979). An investigation of the correlation between hormone levels in males and mood, behavior, and physical discomfort. *Hormones and Behavior, 12*, 185–197.

Inoff-Germain, G., Arnold, G. S., Nottelmann, E. D., Susman, E. J., Cutler, G. B., Jr., & Chrousos, G. P. (1988). Relations between hormone levels and observational measures of aggressive behavior of young adolescents in family interactions. *Developmental Psychology, 24,* 129–139.

Jones, M. C., & Mussen, P. H. (1958). Self-conceptions, motivations, and interpersonal attitudes of early- and late-maturing girls. *Child Development, 29,* 491–501.

Lerner, R. M., & Foch, T. T. (Eds.) (1987). *Biological-psychosocial interactions in early adolescence.* Hillsdale, NJ: Erlbaum.

Leshner, A. I. (1983). Pituitary-adrenocortical effects on intermale agonistic behavior. In B. B. Svare (Ed.), *Hormones and aggressive behavior* (pp. 27–38). New York: Plenum.

Luger, A., Deuster, P. A., Kyle, S. B., Gallucci, B. S., Montgomery, L. C., Gold, P. W., Loriaux, D. L., & Chrousos, G. P. (1987). Acute hypothalamic-pituitary-adrenal responses to the stress of treadmill exercise: Physiologic adaptations to physical training. *New England Journal of Medicine, 316,* 1309–1315.

Marcus, J., Maccoby, E. E., Jacklin, C. E., & Doering, C. H. (1985). Individual differences in mood in early childhood: Their relation to gender and neonatal sex steroids. *Developmental Psychobiology, 18,* 327–340.

Marshall, W. A., & Tanner, J. M. (1969). Variations in the pattern of pubertal changes in girls. *Archives of Diseases in Childhood, 44,* 291–303.

Marshall, W. A., & Tanner, J. M. (1970). Variations in the pattern of pubertal changes in boys. *Archives of Diseases in Childhood, 45,* 13–23.

Mattsson, A., Schalling, D., Olweus, D., Low, H., & Svensson, J. (1980). Plasma testosterone, aggressive behavior, and personality dimensions in young male delinquents. *Journal of the American Academy of Child Psychiatry, 19,* 476–490.

Mazur, A., & Lamb, T. A. (1980). Testosterone status and mood in human males. *Hormones and Behavior, 14,* 236–246.

Montgomery, J. C., Brincat, M., Tapp, A., Appleby, L., Versi, E., Fenwick, P. B. C., & Studd, J. W. W. (1987). Effect of oestrogen and testosterone implants on psychological disorders in the climacteric. *The Lancet, 7,* 297–299.

Mussen, P. H., & Cover, M. C. (1957). Self-conceptions, motivations and interpersonal attitudes of late- and early-maturing boys. *Child Development, 28,* 243–256.

Nottelmann, E. D. (1982). Children's adjustment in school: The interaction of physical maturity and school transition. In Bruce Mackenzie-Haslam (Chair), *Individual differences and school structures affecting the school transitions of early adolescents.* Symposium conducted at the annual meeting of the American Educational Research Association, New York, March. ERIC Document Reproduction Service No. PS012808.

Nottelmann, E. D., Susman, E. J., Blue, J. H., Inoff-Germain, G., Dorn, L. D., Loriaux, D. L., Cutler, G. B., Jr., & Chrousos, G. P. (1987a). Gonadal and adrenal hormone correlates of adjustment in early adolescence. In R. M. Lerner & T. T. Foch (Eds.), *Biological–psychosocial interactions in early adolescence: A life-span perspective* (pp. 303–323). Hillsdale, NJ: Erlbaum.

Nottelmann, E. D., Susman, E. J., Dorn, L. D., Inoff-Germain, G., Loriaux, D. L., Cutler, G. B., Jr., & Chrousos, G. P. (1987b). Developmental processes in early adolescence: Relations among chronologic age, pubertal stage, height, weight, and serum levels of gonadotropins, sex steroids, and adrenal androgens. *Journal of Adolescent Health Care, 8,* 246–260.

Nottelmann, E. D., Susman, E. J., Inoff-Germain, G., Cutler, G. B., Jr., Loriaux, D. L., & Chrousos, G. P. (1987c). Developmental processes in early
adolescence: Relations between adolescent adjustment problems and
chronologic age, pubertal stage, and puberty-related serum hormone
levels. *Journal of Pediatrics, 110,* 473–480.

Nottelmann, E. D., Susman, E. J., Inoff-Germain, G., & Chrousos, G. P. (1987d).
*Concurrent and predictive relations between hormone levels and social-emotional
functioning in early adolescence.* Paper presented at the biennial meeting of
the Society for Research in Child Development, Baltimore, April. ERIC
Document Reproduction Service No. PS016606.

Nottelmann, E. D., & Welsh, C. J. (1986). The long and the short of physical stature in early adolescence. *Journal of Early Adolescence, 6,* 15–
27.

Nyborg, H. (1983). Spatial ability in men and women: Review and new theory.
Advances in Behavioral Research and Therapy, 5, 89–140.

Offer, D., Ostrov, E., & Howard, K. I. (1977). *The Offer Self-Image Questionnaire
for Adolescents: A manual.* Chicago: Michael Reese Hospital.

Offer, D., Ostrov, E., & Howard, K. I. (1984). The self-image of normal adolescents. *New Directions in Mental Health Services, 22* (June), 5–17.

Olweus, D., Mattsson, A., Schalling, D., & Low, H. (1980). Testosterone,
aggression, physical, and personality dimensions in normal adolescent
males. *Psychosomatic Medicine, 42,* 253–269.

Ostrov, E., Offer, D., Hartlage, S. (1984). The quietly disturbed adolescent.
New Directions in Mental Health Services, 22 (June), 73–81.

Parker, L., Eugene, J., Farber, D., Lifrak, E., Lai, M., & Juler, G. (1985). Dissociation of adrenal androgen and cortisol levels in acute stress. *Hormone
and Metabolic Research, 17,* 209–212.

Parker, L. N., Levin, E. R., & Lifrak, E. T. (1985). Evidence for adrenocortical
adaptation to severe illness. *Journal of Clinical Endocrinology and Metabolism, 60,* 947–952.

Persky, H., Smith, K. D., & Basu, G. K. (1971). Relation of physiologic measures of aggression and hostility to testosterone production in man. *Psychosomatic Medicine, 33,* 265–277.

Petersen, A. C., & Craighead, W. E. (1986). Emotional and personality devel-
opment in normal adolescents and young adults. In G. Klerman (Ed.),
Suicide and depression among adolescents and young adults (pp. 19–52). New
York: American Psychiatric Press.

Petersen, A. C., Tobin-Richards, M., & Boxer, A. (1983). Puberty: Its measurement and its meaning. *Journal of Early Adolescence, 3,* 47–62.

Phoenix, C. H., Goy, R. W., Gerall, A. A., & Young, W. C. (1959). Organizing
action of prenatally administered testosterone propionate on the tissues
mediating mating behavior in the female guinea pig. *Journal of Endocrinology, 65,* 369–382.

Plant, T. M. (1986). Gonadal regulation of hypothalamic gonadotropin-releasing
hormone release in primates. *Endocrine Reviews, 7,* 75–88.

Powell, G. F., Brasel, J. A., Raiti, A., & Blizzard, R. M. (1967). Emotional de-
privation and growth retardation simulating idiopathic hypopituitarism:
II. Endocrinologic evaluation of the syndrome. *New England Journal of
Medicine, 276,* 1279–1283.

Rivier, C., Rivier, J. & Vale, W. (1986). Stress-induced inhibition of reproductive functions: Role of endogenous corticotropin-releasing factor. *Science,
231,* 607–609.

Rose, R. M. (1980). Androgens and behavior. In D. de Wied and P. A. van

Keep (Eds.), *Hormones and the brain* (pp. 175–203). Baltimore: University Park Press.

Rubinow, D. R., & Roy-Byrne, P. (1984). Premenstrual syndrome: Overview from a methodologic perspective. *American Journal of Psychiatry, 141,* 163–172.

Sakamura, M., Takebe, K., & Nakagawa, S. (1975). Inhibition of luteinizing hormone secretion induced by synthetic LRH by long-term treatment with glucocorticoids in human subjects. *Journal of Clinical Endocrinology and Metabolism, 40,* 774–779.

Savin-Williams, R. C. (1979). Dominance hierarchies in groups of early adolescents. *Child Development, 50,* 923–935.

Scaramella, T. J., & Brown, W. A. (1978). Serum testosterone and aggressiveness in hockey players. *Psychosomatic Medicine, 40,* 262–265.

Schaison, G., Durand, F., & Mowszowicz, I. (1978). Effect of glucocorticoids on plasma testosterone in men. *Acta Endocrinologica, 89,* 126–131.

Seltzer, V. C. (1982). *Adolescent social development: Dynamic functional interaction.* Lexington, MA: Lexington Books.

Siris, S. G., Siris, E. S., Van Kamman, D. P., Docherty, J. R., Alexander, P. E., & Bunner, W. E., Jr. (1980). Effects of dopamine blockade on gonadotropins and testosterone in men. *American Journal of Psychiatry, 137,* 211–214.

Smith, S. L. (1975). Mood and the menstrual cycle. In E. J. Sachar (Ed.), *Topics in psychoendocrinology* (pp. 19–58). New York: Grune & Stratton.

Sowers, J. R., Rice, B. F., & Blanchard, S. (1979). Effect of dexamethasone on luteinizing hormone and follicle-stimulating hormone responses to LHRH and to clomiphene in the follicular phase of women with normal menstrual cycles. *Hormone Metabolism Research, 11,* 478–480.

Steinberg, L. (1987). Impact of puberty on family relations: Effects of pubertal status and pubertal timing. *Developmental Psychology, 23,* 451–460.

Stolz, H. R., & Stolz, L. M. (1944). Adolescent problems related to somatic variation. In H. B. Henry (Ed.), *The 43rd Yearbook of the National Society for the Study of Education: Part I: Adolescence.* Chicago: University of Chicago Press.

Styne, D. M., & Grumbach, M. M. (1978). Puberty in the male and female: Its physiology and disorders. In S. S. C. Yen & R. B. Jaffe (Eds.), *Reproductive endocrinology: Physiology, pathophysiology, and clinical management* (pp. 189–240). Philadelphia: Saunders.

Susman, E. J., Inoff-Germain, G., Nottelmann, E. D., Cutler, G. B., Jr., & Chrousos, G. P. (1987). Hormones, emotional dispositions, and aggressive attributes in young adolescents. *Child Development, 58,* 1114–1134.

Susman, E. J., Nottelmann, E. D., Inoff, G. E., Dorn, L. D., Cutler, G. B., Jr., Loriaux, D. L., & Chrousos, G. P. (1985). The relation of relative hormone levels and physical development and social-emotional behavior in young adolescents. *Journal of Youth and Adolescence, 14,* 245–264.

Tolis, G., & Stefanis, C. (1983). Depression: Biological and neuroendocrine aspects. *Biomedicine and Pharmacotherapy, 37,* 316–322.

Tourney, G., & Hatfield, L. M. (1973). Androgen metabolism in schizophrenics, homosexuals, and normal controls. *Biological Psychiatry, 6,* 23–36.

Udry, J. R., Billy, J. O. G., Morris, N. M., Groff, T. R., & Raj, M. H. (1985). Serum androgenic hormones motivate sexual behavior in adolescent boys. *Fertility and Sterility, 43,* 90–94.

Udry, J. R., Talbert, L. M., & Morris, N. M. (1986). Biosocial foundations for adolescent female sexuality. *Demography, 23,* 217–227.

van de Poll, N. E., Smeets, J., van Oyen, H. G., & van der Zwan, S. M. (1982).

Behavior consequences of agonistic experience in rats: Sex differences and the effects of testosterone. *Journal of Comparative and Physiological Psychology, 96,* 893–903.

Vierhapper, H., Waldhaeusl, W., & Nowotny, P. (1982). Corticotropin-secretion in adrenocortical insufficiency: Impact of glucocorticoid substitution. *Acta Endocrinologica, 101,* 580–585.

Vierhapper, H., Waldhaeusl, W., & Nowotny, P. (1981). Suppression of luteinizing hormone induced by adrenocorticotropin in healthy women. *Journal of Endocrinology, 91,* 399–403.

Villanueva, A. L., Schlosser, C., Hopper, B., Liu, J. H., Hoffman, D. I., & Rebar, R. W. (1986). Increased cortisol production in women runners. *Journal of Endocrinology and Metabolism 63,* 133–136.

Warren, M. P. (1980). The effects of exercise on pubertal progression and reproductive function in girls. *Journal of Clinical Endocrinology and Metabolism 51,* 1150–1157.

Warren, M. P., Brooks-Gunn, J., Hamilton, L. H., Hamilton, W. G., & Warren, L. F. (1986). Scoliosis and fractures in young ballet dancers: Relationship to delayed menarchial age and secondary amenorrhea. *New England Journal of Medicine, 314,* 1348–1353.

Wilson, D. M., Duke, P. M., Dornbusch, S. M., Ritter, P. L., Carlsmith, J. M., Hintz, R. L., Gross, R. T., & Rosenfeld, R. G. (1984). *Height and intellectual development.* Paper presented at the annual meeting of the Society for Pediatric Research, San Francisco, May.

Wilson, I. C., Prange, A. J., Jr., & Lara, P. P. (1974). Methyltestosterone with imipramine in men: Conversion of depression to paranoid reaction. *American Journal of Psychiatry, 131,* 21–24.

Notes

1. The hormone–behavior relations data discussed in this chapter have been reported in part in previous reports, in simplified form (see Nottelmann et al., 1987a, c).

2. Two additional related measures, testosterone–estradiol binding globulin (TeBG) and cortisol (F), were obtained but not used in these analyses. TeBG was excluded because of missing t_1 data for a substantial number of cases. Cortisol was not included because our focus was on hormone levels that undergo developmental change during puberty.

3. According to parent report, boys were more likely than girls to show off/ clown, swear/use obscene language, and have trouble concentrating; and girls were more likely than boys to behave like the opposite sex, cry a lot, and complain about physical problems.

7

Changing Patterns of Psychiatric Disorders During Adolescence

Michael Rutter

For many years it was generally thought, following the views of G. Stanley Hall (1904), that adolescence was a time of "storm and stress" characterized by emotional turmoil and psychic disturbance. It is now clear that this stereotypical view of the teenage years is mistaken (Rutter et al., 1976; Rutter, 1980; Graham & Rutter, 1985). Most young people pass through adolescence without developing any form of significant mental disturbance. Nevertheless, adolescence is an age period during which there are striking changes in both the frequency and form of psychiatric disorder. It is not so much that there is any general increase in overall prevalence but, rather, that there are substantial alterations in pattern.

Epidemiological data on age changes in overall prevalence are decidedly sparse and there are no investigations in which directly comparable methods of measurement have been used across the age span extending from childhood through adolescence to early adult life. Perhaps the nearest approach is provided by the findings from the Isle of Wight study (Graham & Rutter, 1973, Rutter et al., 1976). When like was compared with like, it appeared that psychiatric disorders were slightly commoner in adolescence than in middle childhood, but in all probability the rates were fairly similar in adolescence to those in adult life. Psychiatric clinical referral rates are broadly in keeping with the epidemiological findings suggesting some rise in referrals between childhood and adolescence (Baldwin, 1968; Rosen et al., 1965; Wing & Fryers, 1976). However, the data are contradictory on whether the peak is reached in adolescence or in early adult life. Instead of discussing possible meanings of these rather minor age trends in overall prevalence of mental disorders, it is more fruitful to focus on the far more impressive age trends for changes in the frequency of specific types of psychiatric disorder during adolescence.

Changes in Pattern of Specific Psychiatric Conditions

Affective Disorders

Most types of affective disorder appear to increase markedly in frequency during adolescence. This is most obvious, and best documented, for completed suicide. Thus, U.S. statistics show that suicide before the age of 12 years is exceedingly rare (with a rate of 0.06 per million), that there is a 100-fold increase over the next 4 years and an additional 10-fold increase to a rate of 76 per million at 16- to 19-year-olds (Eisenberg, 1980; Shaffer & Fisher, 1981). British statistics show much the same picture (Shaffer, 1974). The stigma attached to suicide, together with the complex procedures that lead to official certification, may lead to systematic underreporting. It seems likely that this tendency may be greater among young children and adolescents, but possible underreporting biases could not possibly account for the massive age trends that are apparent in all sets of data (Shaffer, 1986). Nevertheless, it would be quite wrong to regard suicide as an adolescent phenomenon, because the rate continues to rise throughout life to reach a peak in old age.

Attempted suicide or parasuicide is also relatively infrequent before puberty and shows the same massive increase during middle and later adolescence (Hawton, 1986). However, unlike completed suicide, the peak is at 15–19 years with a progressive decline thereafter (Kreitman, 1977). It is also apparent that whereas suicide is much more frequent in males, attempted suicide is far commoner in females. Probably, too, attempted suicide is less likely than completed suicide to be associated with an overt depressive disorder (Hawton et al., 1982). It seems that the increase in suicide over the adolescent age period is not entirely a function of an increase in depressive disorders because, within a psychiatric clinic sample, Carlson and Cantwell (1982) found that suicide ideation increased over the same age period.

During recent years there has been a growing appreciation that major depressive conditions can and do sometimes arise in preadolescent children (Cantwell & Carlson, 1983; Rutter, Izard, & Read, 1986; Puig-Antich & Gittelman, 1982). However, although serious affective disturbances can occur in middle childhood, psychiatric clinic data are consistent in showing that their frequency increases substantially over the years of adolescence. For example, J. Pearce (1978; personal communication, 1982), in an investigation of children attending the Maudsley hospital, found that whereas only one in nine prepubertal children showed depressive syndromes, about one quarter of postpubertal children did so; this was a more than twofold increase in rate. There was also a change of sex ratio in age. Among the prepubertal children depressive syndromes were twice as common in boys, whereas after puberty they were twice as common in girls. It is particularly striking that mania and bipolar affective disorders are especially uncommon before puberty, although again they can occur in younger children (Carlson, 1983).

General population studies have shown broadly similar age trends. Thus, in the Isle of Wight study there were only three cases of depressive disorder in a sample of some two thousand children at age 10 years. In sharp contrast, 4–5 years later there were nine cases of "pure" depressive disorder and a further twenty-six cases of mixed affective disorder—a huge increase (Rutter, 1980; Rutter et al., 1976). Until very recently, however, the epidemiological age trends have had a question mark over them because the instruments used for children of different ages have not been directly comparable. The recent findings from Weissman and her colleagues (1987), using structured interviews with parents and children in a comparative study of children of depressed and normal parents, have shown that the findings are not likely to be an artifact of errors of measurement. They found very few cases of depression under the age of 10 years and a marked increase during the next 5 years with a further increase up to age 20. Interestingly, the age of onset was somewhat earlier in the high-risk group of children of depressed parents. The data from Akiskal et al. (1985) on the offspring and siblings of adult bipolar patients confirmed that, even in this high-risk group, full-blown bipolar psychosis did not appear before puberty.

The few data that are available also suggest that immediate grief reactions following bereavement are both milder and of shorter duration in young children compared with those in adolescents or adults (Bowlby, 1980; Kliman, 1968; Rutter, 1966; van Eerdewegh et al., 1982).

Against this overall pattern of an increase in the rate of affective disturbance during adolescence must be set the evidence that this pattern does not apply to all forms of negative mood state. Thus, crying is most prevalent in infancy and irritability shows little change in frequency over the 5- to 15-year age span (Shepherd, Oppenheim, & Mitchell, 1971). Also the picture of "protest" followed by "despair" as a consequence of separation and disruption of caregiving relationships is mainly a feature of the preschool years (Bowlby, 1969–82). It is evident that children of all ages can and do experience misery and unhappiness. It is not the suffering of negative mood as such that increases over the teenage years, but rather the experience of negative mood states with cognitive and vegetative components of depression, with suicidal ideation, and with pervasive and persistent social impairment.

Nondepressive Disorders

The overall rate of nondepressive emotional disorders probably does not change greatly over the adolescent age period, although there seem to be some changes in pattern (Rutter & Garmezy, 1983). Thus, it appears that whereas emotional disorders in earlier childhood tend to be somewhat diffuse in form, those arising in adolescence are more likely to be differentiated in their symptomatology with a closer resemblance to adult neurotic conditions. Clear-cut hysterical reactions and obsessive compulsive disorders, though occurring in young children, become more common during adolescence. There are also alterations in the focus of phobic states. Animal phobias, which are very common in preschool children, rarely arise for the first time during the teenage years. In contrast, social phobias and agoraphobia, which are rare before puberty, begin to assume importance during adolescence (Abe & Masui, 1981). Little is known about age trends and sex ratio, but one study (Caplan, 1970) showed that with hysterical reactions the male/female ratio was almost equal before puberty, whereas after puberty there was a marked female preponderance.

Anorexia Nervosa

Of all psychiatric disorders, anorexia nervosa is possibly the one that is most characteristically associated with an onset during adolescence. Typically, the disorder is first manifest some time between 14 and 17 years of age (Russell, 1985). Thus, the syndrome usually begins during the few years immediately after puberty, although prepubertal cases are not uncommon (Jacobs & Isaacs, 1986). In these cases the disorder usually begins in the period immediately leading up to puberty. Thus, in the Jacobs and Isaacs (1986) study, the mean age of onset for prepubertal anorexia nervosa was 11.2 years, with a range extending from 7 to 14 years. Anorexia nervosa is very much commoner in girls than in boys, although the sex difference may be less marked in prepubertal cases. As with depression, the age trends in the clinical disorder seem to be paralleled by closely comparable trends in similar behaviors in the general population. Thus, severe dieting is very much a general adolescent phenomenon; it is largely seen in adolescent girls, who characteristically tend to be dissatisfied with the body changes at puberty, especially with the increased deposition of fat (Rutter & Sandberg, 1985). The question arises whether the severe dieting in "normal" girls constitutes a subclinical form of anorexia nervosa as seen in psychiatric clinics. Abraham and colleagues (1983) found that some 15%

of young women had fulfilled the criteria for anorexia or bulimia nervosa at some time, and about half this number had used laxatives or diuretics in order to lose weight. However, none had engaged in the self-induced vomiting that is so often seen in anorexia nervosa. Similarly, Garner and co-workers (1984) noted that the morbid fear of becoming fat and the severe dieting common among ballet dancers often was not accompanied by other psychological features of anorexia nervosa. Szmukler and co-workers (1985) also showed that anorexic-like states in ballet dancers do not have the poor prognosis usually associated with anorexia nervosa. There appear to be both continuities and discontinuities between clinic and community cases.

Substance Abuse

Almost all forms of substance abuse, including alcoholism, first become a common problem during late adolescence and earlier adult life (Rutter, 1980). For example, Magnusson, Stattin, and Allen (1986) found in their Swedish longitudinal study that the proportion of girls who had been drunk more than ten times rose from 6% at age $14\frac{1}{2}$ to 26% at age 16 years. Similarly, over the same age period the proportion smoking hashish rose from 3% to 12%. The American national surveys indicate that for most drugs the rate of usage rises steeply during the middle teens to reach a peak in the 18- to 21-year age group with a steep falloff thereafter (U.S. Commission on Marijuana and Drug Abuse, 1973). The pattern found with sedatives and stimulants was somewhat different in that the increase in usage occurred somewhat later and there was a continuing high rate of usage, especially of sedatives, into middle adulthood. The one exception to these age trends is provided by glue sniffing, the only form of drug abuse practiced by a significant proportion of preadolescent children (Watson, 1980). Alcohol abuse also differs in that, although it increases markedly in frequency during adolescent years, it continues to rise in frequency throughout life to reach a peak in middle life.

Conduct Disturbances

It is generally held that delinquency is a typically adolescent phenomenon. The official crime statistics certainly appear to confirm this impression (Rutter, 1980; Rutter & Giller, 1983). Thus, in England and Wales, indictable offenses increase fourfold between 10 and 15 years, followed by an equally steep decline in the early twenties (Home Office, 1977). The age trends in other countries are broadly similar. Nevertheless, epidemiological data show that the impression of delinquency as a largely adolescent phenomenon is somewhat misleading. Both self-reports and teacher ratings show that most delinquent individuals already show some form of antisocial behavior during middle childhood or preadolescence (Robins, 1978; Farrington, 1979; Cline, 1980). Prosecutions usually do not begin until later, because young children cannot, by law, be convicted, and because police are less likely to prosecute young first offenders. Socially disruptive behaviour (such as rebelliousness, destructiveness, cruelty, and aggression) does not alter greatly in rate over the 8- to 15-year age period (Rutter, 1980; Rutter & Giller, 1983). There is an increase during adolescence in the extent to which this takes the form of frankly delinquent activities (such as theft and serious vandalism). However, the increase in the number of *individuals* engaged in delinquency is less than the increase in the amount and range of delinquent *activities* by those who are delinquent. In particular, there is a rise during the teenage years in the rate of offenses involving personal assault or breaking into property. Violent crime shows its greatest increase during late adolescence. The apparent fall in delinquent activities during early adult life is also not as straightforward as it seems at first sight (Farrington, 1986). There is indeed a drop in the overall level of delinquent activities in the population at large, but there is not much fall in the rate of delinquent activities by persistent offenders.

Schizophrenia

Although schizophrenia can occur in prepubertal children, taking a form similar to that seen in adult life (Eggers, 1978, 1982), it remains a rather rare disorder until the middle teens. Community psychiatric register data show a steady increase in the number of cases between 12 and 18 years of age (Weiner & Del Gaudio, 1976). Nevertheless, although the onset of psychotic manifestations of schizophrenia is usually in late adolescence or early adult life, in about half the cases there have been nonpsychotic behavioral precursors in childhood (Offord & Cross, 1969; Rutter & Garmezy, 1983). The prepsychotic behavioral abnormalities in childhood do not constitute an easily recognizable pattern. However, usually they take the form of abnormalities in interpersonal relationships as shown by odd unpredictable behavior, social isolation, and rejection by peers. In addition, in males there may also be solitary antisocial behavior in the home (but not group delinquency). Frequently these behavioral features are accompanied by neurodevelopmental immaturities in the form of clumsiness, visuospatial difficulties, and verbal impairment, together with attentional deficits characterized by poor signal–noise discrimination. In addition to the adolescent onset of classic schizophrenia, the late teens is also the age period when schizophreniform psychoses may arise in individuals who have shown developmental disorders, perhaps particularly involving language, in early childhood (Rutter, 1988a). For example, Lewis and Mezey (1985) reported six cases of psychoses arising in adolescence in individuals who had shown childhood disturbance, including developmental delay, and whose computed axial tomographic (CAT) scans had shown septum pellucidum cavities.

Autism

Infantile autism, of course, is a pervasive developmental disorder that has been present from infancy onward. It does not usually show marked remissions or relapses, nevertheless, certain changes not infrequently occur during the adolescent years. Most strikingly, about a quarter of autistic individuals show an onset of epileptic seizures during this age period (Rutter, 1970; Deykin & MacMahon, 1979). Those who develop seizures at this time have usually not shown neurological abnormalities earlier. The onset in adolescence stands out as different from the more usual earlier childhood onset that is found both in mentally retarded individuals and in the general population. In addition, a small proportion of autistic individuals show a behavioral deterioration in adolescence, sometimes accompanied by an apparent intellectual decline (Rutter, Tizard, & Whitmore, 1970; Gillberg & Steffenburg, 1987).

Developmental Disorders

There are no psychiatric conditions that show a marked fall in frequency that is specific to the adolescent age period. However, the disorders that involve a delay in maturational functioning are characterized by a continuing improvement, and hence a fall in prevalence through middle childhood and adolescence. The most marked drop occurs in earlier childhood, but the tail of the falling rates extends into adolescence. This is so, for example, with developmental language disorders (Yule & Rutter, 1987). Frequently, however, the language impairment is followed by reading and spelling difficulties as well as emotional and social problems. Nocturnal enuresis, too, becomes increasingly less common so that by the age of 14 years only about 1% of children are regularly enuretic (Rutter, Yule & Graham, 1973). Curiously, the rate of decline for wetting does not alter between 4 and 10 years of age (Oppel, Harper & Rider, 1968; Rutter, 1988a); adequate data for later age periods are not available. The prevalence of enuresis in adults is not known but a small minority of childhood enuretics do continue wetting into adult life (Forsythe & Redmond, 1974).

Changing Correlates According to Age of Onset

Surprisingly little attention has been paid to the possibility that age of onset may constitute a useful and meaningful criterion by which to subdivide psychiatric disorders. The very limited data that are available suggest that the possibility warrants further study. Thus, in the Isle of Wight study (Rutter et al., 1976; Rutter, 1980) the total-population epidemiological study at age 15 years was based on the same population that had been studied previously at age 10 years. This allowed the group of psychiatric disorders at 15 to be subdivided into those that had already been present at age 10 and those that had arisen de novo during early adolescence. Three main differences according to age of onset were found. First, the disorders beginning before age 10 occurred predominantly in boys whereas those arising in adolescence had a sex ratio nearer unity. Second, the earlier onset conditions were strongly associated with indicators of family psychopathology such as marital discord and parental mental disorder, whereas this was very much less the case with new disorders during adolescence. To an important extent this appeared to be a function of chronicity, as family psychopathology was also not very strongly associated with psychiatric disorder arising before age 10 but not persisting to age 15 years. However, chronicity did not account for the third difference, namely that with reading retardation. Children with psychiatric disorders persisting from earlier childhood had a rate of specific reading retardation that was several times higher than that in the general population; the difference was even more marked with respect to reading difficulties at age 14. The picture with new disorders was quite different; these showed no association with reading difficulties at either age 10 or 14. Very few other studies have made this comparison but, where they have, the results appear generally similar (Robins & Hill, 1966; Werner & Smith, 1977).

It may also be the case that the effects of age of onset vary by diagnosis. For example, it seems that school refusal arising in adolescence has a substantially worse prognosis than that with an onset in earlier childhood (Rodriguez, Rodriguez, & Eisenberg, 1959). The reverse, however, applies with delinquency (Loeber, 1982; Rutter & Giller, 1983). Recidivism and persistence into adult life is much more likely with delinquency beginning in early or middle childhood than with that which starts during adolescence. The meaning of these patterns remains somewhat obscure at the moment. However, it may be that the significant feature is whether or not the onset is at a time when the phenomenon, or at least a lesser variant of it, normally occurs in the general population. Thus, separation anxiety is a normal phenomenon in early childhood but is abnormal in adolescence. It may be, therefore, that the syndrome of school refusal in adolescence has a somewhat different meaning from that arising during the earlier school years. The possibility warrants further exploration.

Meaning of Age Trends

Thus far in the chapter we have considered the findings on age trends in the pattern of psychiatric disorder without considering their meaning. It is evident that there are many ambiguities involved in the interpretation of the meaning of age differences (Rutter, 1989). In part, the difficulties stem from a variety of methodological problems. For example, in recent years investigators have paid increasing attention to the possibility that the same phenomenon may be manifest in different ways at different phases of development. There are several examples of psychological phenomena showing heterotypic continuity (Moss & Susman, 1980). Thus, it seems that the temperamental feature of behavioral inhibition is shown by somewhat different characteristics at 6 years of age than in infancy (Kagan, Resnick, & Snidman, 1986). The same could apply to several of the psychiatric disorders considered here. For example, is the rarity of mania in the years before puberty a consequence of this disorder not occurring before adolescence or, rather, is it a function of mania exhibiting itself in a somewhat different form in earlier life? Similarly, is the relative infrequency of major depressive conditions in earlier childhood a consequence of young children being less able to describe the feelings of guilt, self-depreciation, and hopelessness that make up the picture of major depression in adult life? It seems rather unlikely that such methodological features account for the major age trends that have been discussed, but it has to be said that the matter has not yet been adequately investigated.

Methodological problems aside, several quite different meanings of age need to be considered when examining age trends, including biological maturity, mental age or cognitive maturity, duration and type of experiences, and social age or stage.

Biological Maturity

Biological maturity, of course, is far from synonymous with chronological age. There is huge individual variation, for example, in the age when children reach puberty, with the normal range extending over a 5-year age span (Rutter, 1980). There is also a marked sex difference, with girls reaching puberty some 2 years earlier than boys. These interindividual and sex differences in biological maturity are most obvious in adolescence but they are present throughout the whole period of development. Their existence is methodologically important in allowing investigators to separate the effects of biological maturity from other meanings of chronological age. Surprisingly, however, until recently most investigations into the psychological changes during adolescence did not report whether their subjects were prepubertal or postpubertal. As a consequence we lack knowledge on which changes are, and which are not, a function of biological maturity. It should be added that biological maturity is by no means a single phenomenon. The development of different body systems do not run in parallel (Tanner, 1962, 1970). Thus, for example, brain development is at its peak in infancy with relatively little change evident during the adolescent years. This is in sharp contrast to the reproductive system where the main development occurs during the period of puberty.

Because testosterone is known to have an important (but far from exclusive) controlling function over sex drive in both sexes, and because it also has some effect on aggressivity, it might be thought that the hormonal changes associated with puberty might play a part in the increase in delinquent activities during adolescence. There is very little relevant evidence on this issue and, in particular, it is not known whether such age trends as there are in delinquency are a function of chronological age or puberty. Two studies examining the correlates of individual variations in testosterone level within males have shown a weak association with aggressivity and disinhibition, though not with delinquency as such (Olweus, 1986; Daitzman & Zuckerman, 1980). Olweus concluded that there was a modest tendency for a higher level of testosterone to be associated with an increased readiness to respond vigorously and assertively to provocations and threat. In addition, there was a more indirect effect by which a high level of testosterone seemed to be accompanied by impatience and irritability, which increased the boys' readiness to engage in aggressive behavior of the unprovoked type. The data are too meager to allow any strong conclusions and it is obvious that the role played by hormones is merely one among many. Nevertheless, it is possible that sex hormones play some role in the increase in aggressive behavior during adolescence, though not, to any appreciable extent, to age trends in delinquency as a whole.

The possibility that hormonal effects might play a part in the rise in depressive feelings and disorders during adolescence was examined in the Isle of Wight study (Rutter, 1980). It was found that depressive features in 15-year-old boys were much more frequent in those who had reached puberty than in those who had not, with pubescent boys intermediate. It was not possible to make the same comparison in girls, as virtually all girls had reached puberty by that age. The finding in boys was somewhat surprising and it is important that it be tested on other groups as well as in females. The finding raises the possibility that hormonal factors may play a part in the rise in depression that is characteristic of adolescence, but it should be borne in mind that the mechanism may reside in young people's reaction to pubertal change, rather than in the hormonal effects per se.

Indirect effects associated with sexual maturity were evident in the findings from the Stockholm longitudinal study. As already noted, Magnusson, Stattin, and Allen (1986) found a rise in alcohol consumption and smoking of hashish between $14\frac{1}{2}$ and 16 years of age. Both behaviors were more prevalent in those who had reached puberty early than in those who had a late menarche. Thus, less than 2% of girls who reached puberty after 13 years had been drunk more than 10 times compared with nearly 17% of those who reached puberty before 11 years. Norm-breaking generally was more frequent among the early maturers. However, further analyses showed that this was a function of associating with older girls. The early-maturing girls who did *not* form part of an older social group did *not* show a higher level of norm-breaking. In other words, it seemed that the appreciation that they were more mature than their peers led the early-maturing girls to seek the company of an older age group, with whose norms they then conformed (rather than those of their own age group). The stimulus was physically induced, but the mechanism was social. The finding that it is the association with older girls that is relevant in this connection leaves open the question of why the behavior, attitudes, and social norms of the population as a whole should change with age during adolescence. Is that a consequence of hormonal changes, of cognitive level, or of altered social circumstances? We do not know.

Because of the evidence of an important genetic component to schizophrenia, it might be supposed that the rise in prevalence during late adolescence was likely to be a function of some aspect of brain maturation. Indeed that might well be the case, but we lack data to test the possibility adequately, and such data as are available raise some awkward questions. For example, boys generally mature some 2 years later than girls, but the mean age of first admission for males with schizophrenia is about 5 years earlier than that of females (Zigler & Levine, 1981). Of course, it is quite possible that the explanation for the sex difference is different from that for the age trend. It may be pertinent that studies of schizophrenia arising in adolescence have shown a male preponderance (Kolvin, 1971) that is not evident in cases with an onset in adult life. Seeman (1982) suggested that being female conferred a degree of protection and that, although females show the same susceptibility to schizophrenia in later decades, males remain more at risk for a severe and chronic illness.

The same expectations of a biological explanation apply to the development of epileptic seizures in autistic individuals during adolescence. After all, there is very strong evidence that autism is likely to be due to an organic deficit of one kind or another (Rutter, 1988b). However, the phenomenon has been little studied up to now, and alternative explanations need to be considered. For example, behavior sometimes worsens during adolescence and it is possible that the use of psychotropic drugs to control behavior may reduce the threshold for seizures. That did not seem to be an adequate explanation in the series studied by Rutter (1970), but further systematic study is required.

The association between the timing of the onset of anorexia nervosa and puberty, together with the very marked sex difference, raises the possibility of hormonal influences. However, it seems more probable that the timing is associated with psychological reactions to puberty, rather than with hormonal effects as such. For boys, all the pubertal changes (such as growth of facial and body hair, breaking of voice, increased masculinity, and altered physique) tend to have unambiguously positive connotations, which are accompanied by positive self-perceptions. Perhaps because of this early maturing, boys may have a slight advantage in personality. The data mostly derive from early American longitudinal studies with relatively weak measures, but the findings are reasonably consistent in showing that late maturers tend to feel less adequate, less confident, and more anxious (McCandless, 1960; Clausen, 1975). The pattern in girls is quite different. The course of physical maturation in females does not give rise to the same unequivocal positive social response (Tobin-Richards, Boxer, & Peterson, 1982). Thus, the greater maturity associated with the menarche may have positive personal significance, but the positive impact is reduced by negative attitudes to menstruation (Grief & Ulman, 1982) as reflected in the terms used for it (such as the "curse"). Moreover, unlike the situation in boys, puberty in girls is accompanied by a steady increase in body fat. At least in modern Western cultures this increase in fat is generally not welcomed by girls, and adolescence is accompanied by a marked increased in dieting. It is tempting to see anorexia nervosa as an exaggeration of these "normal" social trends. However, as already noted, there are both similarities and dissimilarities between anorexia nervosa and normal dieting. Moreover, the dieting seen in so many adolescents (as well as that found in many ballet dancers to a more severe degree; Szmukler et al., 1985) tends to have a good prognosis, whereas anorexia nervosa is one of the few psychiatric conditions in childhood that carries with it a significant mortality (Isager et al., 1986).

It must also be borne in mind that genetic effects may become manifest for the first time during adolescence. Heredity is influential throughout the life span; heritability for many characteristics tends to increase during the course of development, and genes produce change as well as continuity in development (Plomin, 1986). These general principles apply to polygenic influences, but it is also the case that single-gene effects may not be apparent until late in the life span. This is most obvious with Huntington's chorea when dementia is not usually apparent until middle life. However, it could also be the case with other conditions. For example, might genetic factors responsible for bipolar affective disorders not become operative until the adolescent years? In that connection, it may be relevant that there is some evidence suggesting that affective disorders with an onset before 20 years of age tend to have a higher genetic loading (Weissman et al., 1984), and that depressive disorders in the offspring of depressed parents tend to have an earlier onset than those found in the general population (Weissman et al., 1987).

Cognitive Maturity

The possibility that cognitive maturity plays a role in susceptibility to psychiatric disorder arises most obviously in the case of depression. Because the concept of a depressive disorder involves cognitive ideations such as guilt, helplessness in the face of task failure, and hopelessness about the future, it could be that young children are relatively protected from depression because they lack the ability to experience such cognitions. This is unlikely to be a sufficient explanation in that severe depressive disorders of an adult type do occasionally occur in younger children. Nevertheless, it is certainly possible that children's cognitive immaturity might protect them from developing depressive disorders in relation to negative life events.

Very little is known on the developmental changes that directly apply to depressive ideation, but there are some findings on the broader aspects of cognitive processes that might be linked with depression or with susceptibility for depression. For example, young children tend to have an overoptimistic view of their own competence, and it is only during the early years of schooling that they begin to adjust their self-perceptions as a consequence of task failure (Dweck & Elliott, 1983). Perhaps this tendency accounts for the finding of Rholes and colleagues (1980) that young children are less likely to show learned helplessness in response to repeated, experimentally induced task failure. It seems that it is not until 8 years or so that most children begin to talk about being proud or ashamed of themselves (Harter, 1983); self-awareness in the form of marked self-consciousness also seems to increase during adolescence (Rosenberg, 1979). Anxieties about the future may also increase during the teenage period (Coleman, 1974, Coleman, Herzberg, & Morris, 1977). Young children tend not to think much about the long-term future, nor do they conceptualize actions in terms of distant consequences. Probably it is only during later childhood and earlier adolescence that future perspectives come to the fore. It is possible that such perspectives might be important in the development of feelings of hopelessness about the rest of life. There are scarcely any data to test the role of cognitive factors in susceptibility to depression. However, Carlson, Asarnow, and Orbach (1987), in their study of a psychiatric inpatient sample, found that suicidal ideation was less frequent in children performing below grade level at school, although grade level was not associated with the likelihood of showing depression. Further research into age trends in social cognition (i.e., the thought processes referred to above), together with their relationship with depression, is much needed.

Duration and Type of Experiences

Because chronological age and experiences tend to be closely associated within any one subculture, few investigators have attempted to separate the two. However, this is where comparisons across societies or across time periods may be most informative. For example, Hirschi and Gottfredson (1983) argued that there was an invariant relationship between age and crime, and hence, that age had a direct causal affect on criminal behavior. Farrington (1986) has used historical trends to show that this is a somewhat misleading oversimplification. Thus, in England, the peak crime rate for males was 13 years in 1938, 14 in 1961, and 15 in 1983. American statistics for 1982 show a later peak than that in England, at 17 years for nonviolent crimes and 18 years for violent offenses. The secular changes and age trends suggest that the peak is more a function of the age when compulsory schooling ceases than of chronological age as such. The secular trends for females show, however, that this explanation does not account for the pattern in girls. The peak was at 19 years in 1938, but by 1983 it had dropped to 14 years. Doubtless, in both sexes the age–crime curve is a result of multiple influences. The cessation of schooling is one effect in adolescence, but the reduction of parental controls, the changing characteristics of the peer group with employment and marriage, changing opportunities and economic factors, together with altered sex hormone levels are others.

Research in adults has shown that negative life events that carry long-term contextual threat are associated with an increased likelihood of the onset of depressive disorders (Brown & Harris, 1978), and also that emotional support from close, confiding relationships serves a protective function (Cohen & Syme, 1985). This raises the question of whether the rise in the rate of depression in adolescence might be a function of either an increase in stressful life events or a diminution in emotional support. Unfortunately, not only do we lack adequate data on whether or not there are age trends in frequency of life events or adequacy of social support, but we also do not know whether variations in either link with susceptibility to depression in childhood and adolescence. Nevertheless, there are reasons for supposing that such factors might play some role. Adolescence tends to be accompanied by the making of children's first sexual love relationships and also with the breaking of such relationships. The adult data suggest that the loss of a love relationship is one of the most important precipitants of depression. In addition, of course, adolescence is the time of exams, leaving school, career choice, and generally widening social experiences. Also, although most adolescents retain good relationships with their parents (Rutter, 1980), they ordinarily seek to become more autonomous and less reliant on their parents for immediate support. All these, and other changes might conceivably play a part in increasing susceptibility to depression. Whether in fact they do is unknown in the absence of relevant data.

In examining these matters, it will be important to take account of individual differences in young people's life experiences and circumstances. It is unfortunate that most studies of psychological changes associated with adolescence have tended to consider these in age terms without reference to individual variations. For example, in the United Kingdom during the late teenage years, young people may still be involved in full-time education; of those in education some will be repeating examinations in an attempt to compensate for earlier educational failure whereas others will be continuing to experience academic success. Other young people will be working full time, but an increasingly high proportion will be experiencing chronic unemployment. Some teenagers will still be living in their parents' home, some will be in hostels or lodgings of various kinds, and just a few will have set up their own homes. There is substantial evidence that low scholastic attainment is associated with an increased rate of behavioral difficulties (Rutter & Giller, 1983), that attempted suicides are commoner in those who are unemployed (Platt, 1986), and that psychiatric disorder is more frequent among those who are at university and living away from home (Rimmer et al., 1978; McMichael & Hetzel, 1974). It would seem reasonable to suppose that psychological changes in adolescence are likely to be influenced by the social circumstances of young people at each age. More use should be made of these social variations in examining adolescent development.

A related point is that the social transitions cannot be considered as if they have the same meaning for everyone. For example, criminologists have failed to find a consistent association between marriage and changes in delinquent behavior (Rutter & Giller, 1983). However, West (1982) found that the effects of marriage on crime depended on whether or not the spouse was delinquent. The men who married nondelinquent women tended to have a decline in offending; if the spouse was delinquent, however, offending tended to increase slightly. Similar considerations apply to many other circumstances. For example, for low-achieving disenchanted adolescents, dropping out of school tends to be associated with a reduction in delinquent activities (Elliot & Voss, 1974). The supposition is that the change of peer group to one in which the social mores are nondelinquent played a major part in this reduction. But, would this be the same if leaving school meant joining an alienated group of unemployed teenagers? Alternatively, would the same be found for high-achieving adolescents leaving schools where the rate of delinquency was low and law-abiding behavior was the norm? It is evident that the role of experiences in accounting for changes in sociopsychological functioning with age cannot be considered by treating these social transitions as if they have the same meaning and effect for everyone.

Social Stage

Petersen (1987; Petersen & Crockett, 1985) has argued that a further dimension of age is provided by the set of norms that apply when people reach a certain social stage as defined by society. For example, many privileges and responsibilities in school are defined as available in terms of the particular year or grade in school reached. This may play a part in the finding that the transition to secondary school is sometimes accompanied by a decrease in self-esteem (Simmons, Rosenberg, & Rosenberg, 1973; Harter & Connell, 1982). We lack data on the generality of this phenomenon, and the move to secondary school is also accompanied by a marked change in school environment. Nevertheless, surprisingly little use has been made of the existing variations in both the timing of school transitions and the extent to which transitions involve marked social changes. Thus we have yet another aspect of age trends that needs to be studied further!

Conclusions

Of all age periods, adolescence is the one with the most striking and interesting changing patterns of psychiatric disorder. At one time there was a general view that the psychiatric disorders of this age period were a direct consequence of the psychological hurdles of adolescence and that their meaning was therefore quite different from those of phenomenologically similar disorders arising either earlier or later in life. That view has been consistently contradicted by empirical research findings (Rutter, 1980). Nevertheless, those negative findings in no way diminish interest in this age period. Although it is clear that the disorders that arise during the teenage years are not different in kind for the most part, the serious question remains why the rates of specific psychiatric conditions change so markedly during this age period. Of course it is most unlikely that the same explanation will be found for each of the trends with different disorders. The crucial point is that age is an ambiguous phenomenon with many different meanings. Some of the changing patterns of disorder may be a consequence of different aspects of biological maturation, while others may be a reflection of variations in cognitive maturity. Some are likely to be a consequence of variations in life experiences, and yet others may reflect social stages as defined by society. At present, we have no more than encouraging leads on a few hypotheses regarding possible explanations. Their further study should constitute an important item on the research agenda of the future. The issues are potentially of wide-ranging importance. An understanding of the processes involved in the age trends in changing patterns of psychiatric disorders in adolescents should be informative on the mechanisms involved in both the genesis and the persistence of a range of psychiatric conditions.

Acknowledgments

This work was supported in part by the John D. and Catherine T. MacArthur Foundation Mental Health Research Network on Risk and Protective Factors in the Major Mental Disorder.

References

Abe, K., & Masui, T. (1981). Age–sex trends of phobic and anxiety symptoms in adolescents. *British Journal of Psychiatry, 138,* 297–302.

Abraham, S. F., Mira, M., Beumont, P. J. V., Sowerbutts, T. D., & Llewellyn-Jones, D. (1983). Eating behaviours among young women. *Medical Journal of Australia, 2,* 225–228.

Akiskal, H. A., Downs, J., Jordan, P., Watson, S., Daugherty, D., & Pruitt, D. B. (1985). Affective disorders in referred children and younger siblings of manic-depressives: Mode of onset and prospective coures. *Archives of General Psychiatry, 42,* 996–1003.

Baldwin, J. A. (1968). Psychiatric illness from birth to maturity: An epidemiological study. *Acta Psychiatrica Scandinavica, 44,* 313–333.

Bowlby, J. (1969/82). *Attachment and loss I. Attachment.* London: Hogarth Press.

Bowlby, J. (1980). *Attachment and loss III. Loss, sadness and depression.* New York: Basic Books.

Brown, G. W., & Harris, T. (1978). *Social origins of depression.* London: Tavistock.

Cantwell, D. P., & Carlson, G. A. (Eds.) (1983). *Affective disorders in childhood and adolescence: An update.* New York: Spectrum Publications.

Caplan, H. L. (1970). Hysterical "conversion" syndrome in childhood (M. Phil dissertation, University of London).

Carlson, G. A. (1983). Bipolar affective disorders in childhood and adolescence. In D. P. Cantwell & G. A. Carlson (Eds.), *Affective disorders in childhood and adolescence: An update.* New York: Spectrum Publications.

Carlson, G. A., Asarnow, J. R., & Orbach, I. (1987). Developmental aspects of suicidal behavior in children—I. *Journal of the American Academy of Child and Adolescent Psychiatry, 26,* 186–192.

Carlson, G. A., & Cantwell, D. P. (1982). Suicidal behavior and depression in children and adolescents. *Journal of the American Academy of Child Psychiatry, 21,* 361–368.

Clausen, J. A. (1975). The social meaning of differential physical and sexual maturation. In S. E. Dragastin & G. H. Elder (Eds.), *Adolescence in the life cycle: Psychosocial change and social context* (pp. 25–48). London: Halsted Press.

Cline, H. F. (1980). Criminal behavior over the life span. In O. G. Brim & J. Kagan (Eds.), *Constancy and change in human development.* Cambridge, MA: Harvard University Press.

Cohen, S., & Syme, S. L. (Eds.) (1985). *Social support and health.* New York: Academic Press.

Coleman, J. C. (1974). *Relationships in adolescence.* London: Routledge & Kegan Paul.

Coleman, J. C., Herzberg, J., & Morris, M. (1977). Identity in adolescence: Present and future self-concepts. *Journal of Youth and Adolescence, 6,* 63–75.

Daitzman, R., & Zuckerman, M. (1980). Disinhibitory sensation seeking, personality and gonadal hormones. *Personality and Individual Differences, 1,* 103–110.

Deykin, E. Y., & MacMahon, B. (1979). The incidence of seizures among children with autistic symptoms. *American Journal of Psychiatry, 136,* 1310–1312.

Dweck, C. S., & Elliott, E. S. (1983). Achievement motivation. In E. M. Hetherington (Ed.), *Socialization, personality and social development.* Vol 4, *Mussen's handbook of child psychology* (4th ed., pp. 654–691). New York: Wiley.

Eggers, C. (1978). Course and prognosis of childhood schizophrenia. *Journal of Autism and Childhood Schizophrenia, 8,* 21–36.

Eggers, C. (1982). Psychoses in childhood and adolescence. *Acta Paedopsychiatrica, 48,* 81–98.

Eisenberg, L. (1980). Adolescent suicide: On taking arms against a sea of troubles. *Pediatrics, 66,* 315–320.

Elliot, D. S., & Voss, H. L. (1974). *Delinquency and dropout.* Toronto: Lexington Books.

Farrington, D. P. (1979). Longitudinal research on crime and delinquency. In N. Morris & M. Tonry (Eds.), *Criminal justice: An annual review of research* (Vol. 1, pp. 289–348). Chicago: University of Chicago Press.

Farrington, D. P. (1986). Age and crime. In M. Tonry & N. Morris (Eds.), *Crime and justice* (Vol. 7). Chicago: University of Chicago Press.

Forsythe, W. I., & Redmond, A. (1974). Enuresis and spontaneous cure rate. A study of 1129 enuretics. *Archives of Disorders of Childhood, 49,* 259–263.

Garner, D. M., Olmsted, M. P., Polivy, J., & Garfinkel, E. P. (1984). Comparison between weight-preoccupied women and anorexia nervosa. *Psychosomatic Medicine, 46,* 255–266.

Gillberg, C., & Steffenburg, S. (1987). Outcome and prognostic factors in infantile autism and similar conditions: A population-based study of 46 cases followed through puberty. *Journal of Autism and Developmental Disorders, 17,* 273–287.

Graham, P., & Rutter, M. (1973). Psychiatric disorder in the young adolescent. A follow-up study. *Proceedings of the Royal Society of Medicine, 66,* 1226–1229.

Graham, P., & Rutter, M. (1985). Adolescent disorders. In M. Rutter & L. Hersov (Eds.), *Child and adolescent psychiatry: Modern approaches* (2nd ed.). Oxford: Blackwell Scientific.

Grief, E. B., & Ulman, K. J. (1982). The psychological impact of menarche on early adolescent females: A review of the literature. *Child Development, 53,* 1413–1430.

Hall, G. S. (1904). *Adolescence: Its psychology and its relation to physiology, anthropology, sociology, sex, crime, religion and education.* New York: Appleton.

Harter, S. (1983). Developmental perspectives on the self system. In E. M. Hetherington (Ed.), *Socialization, personality and social development.* Vol. 4, *Mussen's handbook of child psychology* (4th ed., pp. 275–385). New York: Wiley.

Harter, S., & Connell, J. P. (1982). A comparison of alternative models of the relationships between academic achievement and children's perceptions of competence. In J. Nicholls (Ed.), *The development of achievement-related cognitions and behaviors*. Greenwich, CT: J A I Press.

Hawton, K. (1986). Suicide and attempted suicide among children and adolescents. *Developmental Clinical Psychology and Psychiatry* (Vol. 5). Beverly Hills, CA: Sage Publications.

Hawton, K., & Rose, N. C. (1986). Unemployment and attempted suicide among men in Oxford. *Health Trends, 18*, 29–31.

Hawton, K., O'Grady, J., Osborn, M., & Cole, D. (1982). Adolescents who take overdoses: Their characteristics, problems and contacts with helping agencies. *British Journal of Psychiatry, 140*, 118–123.

Hirschi, T., & Gottfredson, M. (1983). Age and the explanation of crime. *American Journal of Sociology, 89*, 552–584.

Home Office. (1977). *Criminal statistics England and Wales, 1976*. London: HMSO.

Isager, T., Brinch, M., Kreiner, S., & Tolstrup, K. (1986). Death and relapse in anorexia nervosa: Survival analysis of 151 cases. *Journal of Psychiatric Research, 19*, 515–521.

Jacobs, B. W., & Isaacs, S. (1986). Prepubertal anorexia nervosa: A retrospective control study. *Journal of Child Psychology and Psychiatry, 27*, 237–250.

Kagan, J., Reznick, J. A., & Snidman, N. (1986). Temperamental inhibition in early childhood. In R. Plomin & J. Dunn (Eds.), *The study of temperament: Changes, continuities and challenges* (pp. 53–66). Hillsdale, NJ: Erlbaum.

Klimₙn, G. W. (1968). *Psychological emergencies of childhood*. New York: Grune & Stratton.

Kolvin, I. (1971). Psychoses in childhood—a comparative study. In M. Rutter (Ed.), *Infantile autism: Concepts, characteristics and treatment* (pp. 7–26). London: Churchill-Livingstone.

Kreitman, N. (Ed.) (1977). *Parasuicide*. London: Wiley.

Lewis, S. W., & Mezey, G. C. (1985). Clinical correlates of septum pellucidum cavities: An unusual association with psychosis. *Psychological Medicine, 15*, 43–54.

Loeber, R. (1982). The stability of antisocial and delinquent child behavior: A review. *Child Development, 53*, 1431–1446.

Magnusson, D., Stattin, H., & Allen, V. (1986). Differential maturation among girls and its relation to social adjustment: A longitudinal perspective. In D. Featherman & R. M. Lerner (Eds.), *Life span and development* (Vol. 7, pp. 135–172). New York: Academic Press.

McCandless, B. R. (1960). Rate of development, body build and personality. *Psychiatric Research Reports, 13*, 42–57.

McMichael, A. J., & Hetzel, B. S. (1974). An epidemiological study of the mental health of Australian University students. *International Journal of Epidemiology, 3*, 126–134.

Moss, H. A., & Susman, E. J. (1980). Longitudinal study of personality development. In O. G. Brim & J. J. Kagan (Eds.), *Constancy and change in human development* (pp. 530–595). Cambridge, MA: Harvard University Press.

Offord, D. R., & Cross, L. A. (1969). Behavioral antecedents of adult schizophrenia. *Archives of General Psychiatry, 21*, 267–283.

Olweus, D. (1986). Aggression and hormones: Behavioural relationship with testosterone and adrenaline. In D. Olweus, J. Block & M. Radke-Yarrow (Eds.), *Development of antisocial and prosocial behavior: Research, theories, and issues* (pp. 51–72). New York: Academic Press.

Oppel, W. C., Harper, P. A., & Rider, R. V. (1968). The age of attaining bladder control. *Pediatrics, 42*, 614–626.

Pearce, J. (1978). The recognition of depressive disorder in children. *Journal of the Royal Society of Medicine, 71*, 494–500.

Pearce, J. (1982). Personal communication.

Petersen, A. C. (1987). The nature of biological–psychosocial interactions: The sample case of early adolescence. In R. M. Lerner & T. T. Foch (Eds.), *Biological–psychosocial interactions in early adolescence: A life span perspective.* Hillsdale, NJ: Erlbaum.

Petersen, A. C., & Crockett, C. (1985). Pubertal timing and grade effects on adjustment. *Journal of Youth and Adolescence, 14*, 191–206.

Platt, S. (1986). Parasuicide and unemployment. *British Journal of Psychiatry, 149*, 401–405.

Plomin, R. (1986). *Development, genetics and psychology,* Hillsdale, NJ: Erlbaum.

Puig-Antich, J., & Gittelman, R. (1982). Depression in childhood and adolescence. In E. S. Paykel (Ed.), *Handbook of affective disorders* (pp. 379–392). London: Churchill-Livingstone.

Rholes, W. S., Blackwell, J., Jordan, C., & Walters, C. (1980). A developmental study of learned helplessness. *Developmental Psychology, 16*, 616–624.

Rimmer, J. D., Halikas, J. A., Schuckit, M. A., & McClure, J. N. (1978). A systematic study of psychiatric illness in freshman college students. *Comprehensive Psychiatry, 19*, 249–251.

Robins, L. (1978). Sturdy childhood predictors of adult antisocial behaviour: Replications from longitudinal studies. *Psychological Medicine, 8*, 611–622.

Robins, L., & Hill, S. Y. (1966). Assessing the contributions of family structure, class and peer groups to juvenile delinquency. *Journal of Criminal Law, Criminology and Police Science, 57*, 325–334.

Rodriguez, A., Rodriguez, M., & Eisenberg, L. (1959). The outcome of school phobia: A follow-up study based on 41 cases. *American Journal of Psychiatry, 116*, 540–544.

Rosen, B. M., Bahn, A. K., Shellow, R., & Bower, E. M. (1965). Adolescent patients served in outpatient psychiatric clinics. *American Journal of Public Health, 55*, 1563–1577.

Rosenberg, M. (1979). *Conceiving the self.* New York: Basic Books.

Russell, G. F. M. (1985). Anorexia and bulimia nervosa. In M. Rutter & L. Hersov (Eds.), *Child and adolescent psychiatry: Modern Approaches* (2nd ed., pp. 625–637). Oxford: Blackwell Scientific.

Rutter, M. (1966). *Children of sick parents: An environmental and psychiatric study.* Institute of Psychiatry/Maudsley Monograph No. 16. London: Oxford University Press.

Rutter, M. (1970). Psychological development: Predictions from infancy. *Journal of Child Psychology and Psychiatry, 11*, 49–62.

Rutter, M. (1980). *Changing youth in a changing society: Patterns of adolescent development and disorder.* London: Cambridge, MA: Harvard University Press (Originally published, London: Nuffield Provincial Hospitals Trust, 1979.)

Rutter, M. (1988a). Epidemiological approaches to developmental psychopathology. *Archives of General Psychiatry, 45*, 486–500.

Rutter, M. (1988b). Biological basis of autism: Implications for intervention. In F. J. Menolascino & J. A. Stark (Eds.), *Preventive and Curative Intervention in Mental Retardation* (pp. 265–294). Baltimore: Paul H. Brookes Publishing.

Rutter, M. (1989). Age as an ambiguous variable in developmental research: Some epidemiological considerations from psychopathology. *International Journal of Behavioral Development, 12*, 1–34.

Rutter, M., & Garmezy, N. (1983). Developmental psychopathology. In E. M. Hetherington (Ed.), *Socialization, personality and social development.* Vol. 4,

Mussen's handbook of child psychology (4th ed., pp. 775–911). New York: Wiley.

Rutter, M., & Giller, H. (1983). *Juvenile delinquency: Trends and perspectives*. Harmondsworth, England: Penguin Books.

Rutter, M., Graham, P., Chadwick, O., & Yule, W. (1976). Adolescent turmoil: Fact or friction? *Journal of Child Psychology and Psychiatry, 17*, 35–36.

Rutter, M., Izard, C. E., & Read, P. B. (Eds.) (1986). *Depression in young people: Clinical and developmental perspectives*. New York: Guildord Press.

Rutter, M., & Sandberg, S. (1985). Epidemiology of child psychiatric disorder: Methodological issues and some substantive findings. *Child Psychiatry and Human Development, 15*, 209–233.

Rutter, M., Tizard, J., & Whitmore, K. (Eds.) (1970). *Education health and behaviour*. London: Longman (Reprinted 1981: Melbourne, FL: Krieger).

Rutter, M., Yule, W., & Graham, P. (1973). Enuresis and behavioural deviance: Some epidemiological considerations. In I. Kolvin, R. MacKeith, & S. R. Meadow (Eds.), *Bladder control and enuresis: Clinics in developmental medicine, 48–49* (pp. 137–147). London: Heinemann/Spastics International Medical Publications.

Seeman, M. V. (1982). Gender differences in schizophrenia. *Canadian Journal of Psychiatry, 27*, 107–112.

Shaffer, D. (1974). Suicide in childhood and early adolescence. *Journal of Child Psychology and Psychiatry, 15*, 275–292.

Shaffer, D. (1986). Developmental factors in child and adolescent suicide. In M. Rutter, C. E. Izard, & P. Read (Eds.), *Depression in young people: Clinical and developmental perspectives* (pp. 383–396). New York: Guilford Press.

Shaffer, D., & Fisher, P. (1981). The epidemiology of suicide in children and young adolescents. *Journal of the American Academy of Child Psychiatry, 20*, 545–565.

Shepherd, M., Oppenheim, B., & Mitchell, S. (1971). *Childhood behaviour and mental health*. London: University of London Press.

Simmons, R. G., Rosenberg, R., & Rosenberg, M. (1973). Disturbances in the self image at adolescence. *American Sociological Review, 38*, 553–568.

Szmukler, G. I., Eisler, I., Gillies, C., & Hayward, M. E. (1985). The implications of anorexia nervosa in a ballet school. *Journal of Psychiatric Research, 19*, 177–181.

Tanner, J. M. (1962). *Growth at adolescence* (2nd ed.). Oxford: Blackwell Scientific.

Tanner, J. M. (1970). Physical growth. In P. H. Mussen (Ed.), *Carmichael's manual of child psychology* (3rd ed., pp. 77–155). New York: Wiley.

Tobin-Richards, M. H., Boxer, A. M., & Peterson, A. C. (1982). The psychological significance of pubertal change: Sex differences in perceptions of self during early adolescence. In J. Brooks-Gunn & A. C. Peterson (Eds.), *Girls at puberty: Biological and psychological perspectives* (pp. 127–154). New York: Plenum.

U.S. Commission on Marijuana and Drug Abuse (1973). *Drug use in America: Problems of perspective* (Second Report of the commission). Washington, DC: U.S. Government Printing Office.

van Eerdewegh, M. M., Bieri, M. D., Parilla, R. H., & Clayton, P. (1982). The bereaved child. *British Journal of Psychiatry, 140*, 23–29.

Watson, J. M. (1980). Solvent abuse by children and young adults. *British Journal of Addiction, 75*, 27–36.

Weiner, I. B., & Del Gaudio, A. C. D. (1976). Psychopathology in adolescence: An epidemiological study. *Archives of General Psychiatry, 33*, 187–193.

Weissman, M. M., Gammon, G. D., John, K., Merikangas, K. R., Warner, V.,

Prusoff, B. A., & Sholomskas, D. (1987). Children of depressed parents: Increased psychopathology and early onset of major depression. *Archives of General Psychiatry, 44,* 747–753.

Weissman, M. M., Wickramaratne, P., Merikangas, K. R., Leckman, J., Prusoff, B. A., Caruso, K. A., Kidd, K. K., & Gammon, G. D. (1984). Onset of major depression in early adulthood: Increased familial loading and specificity. *Archives of General Psychiatry, 41,* 1136–1143.

Werner, E. E., & Smith, R. S. (1977). *Kauai's children come of age.* Honolulu: University Press of Hawaii.

West, D. J. (1982). *Delinquency: Its roots, careers and prospects.* London: Heinemann (Cambridge, MA: Harvard University Press).

Wing, J. K., & Fryers, T. (1976). *Psychiatric services in Camberwell and Salford: Statistics from the Camberwell and Salford psychiatric registers 1954–1974.* London: Institute of Psychiatry.

Yule, W., & Rutter, M. (Eds.) (1987). *Language development and disorders. Clinics in developmental medicine* (No. 101/102). London: MacKeith/Blackwell Scientific.

Zigler, E., & Levine, J. (1981). Age of first hospitalization of schizophrenics. *Journal of Abnormal Psychology, 90,* 458–467.

8

Mood Changes During Adolescence

Robert T. Rubin

The contribution by Dr. Nottelmann and colleagues (chapter 6) is both an overview of hormone–behavior relations in adolescence and the description of a specific research study that attempted to relate behavioral measures in normal adolescents to Tanner pubertal stage and to circulating gonadotropin and adrenal and gonadal steroid hormone concentrations. Professor Rutter's contribution (Chapter 7) is a survey of the development of different psychiatric disorders during adolescence, with attention to methodological issues such as the confounding effects of age and pubertal status. In this chapter I will recapitulate and attempt to integrate the conclusions of these two presentations, and will indicate some issues of methodology and directions for future research.

Based on a thorough literature review as well as his own landmark Isle of Wight study (Rutter et al., 1976), Professor Rutter has pointed out that different types of psychiatric illness have very different life courses, from infancy and childhood, through adolescence, to adulthood and senescence (Rutter, 1980, 1985, 1986a). For example, adult obsessional traits often were manifested in childhood, thus exhibiting a continuity of presence throughout the life cycle. Other disorders are prevalent in childhood but show a sharply declining rate toward adolescence; one example is enuresis. However, the psychiatric disorders that make up the bulk of adult psychiatric morbidity are relatively uncommon in childhood, at least in their adult form, and do not have their onset until adolescence and later years. Examples of these illnesses are alcohol and other drug abuse, anorexia nervosa, schizophrenia, and major depression, including suicidal behavior. There are several putative causes of each of these disorders, ranging from sociocultural to psychobiological. Alcohol and drug abuse, for example, may include a genetic predisposition (Grove & Cadoret, 1983), but adolescent peer group sanctions and opportunities play an important role. Anorexia nervosa, while a disorder of biology, may have its early psychological roots in distorted parent–child relations (Bruch, 1973). Schizophrenia remains an etiological enigma: Genetic and neurochemical factors are believed to be very important, but the specific mechanisms are unknown. Also remaining largely unknown are the psychological precipitants, childhood antecedents, and specific reasons for the marked increase in the onset of schizophrenia in the late teenage and early adult period. Finally, there is the issue of depression, which shows not only a sharply increased rate of occurrence during adolescence but also a change in sex ratio, from being preponderant in prepubertal boys to being much more common in late adolescent and adult females.

As Professor Rutter and others have pointed out, adolescence is a time of rapid change in every area of life—physical growth and sexual maturation, increasing psychological independence from family and concomitant sociocultural attachment to peer group, and new and different educational challenges—all within a handful of years. So, there are correlations between the increased incidence of schizophrenia, depression, and other psychiatric illnesses during adolescence and all the sociopsychobiological changes of this period. The question is, of course, what are the cause-and-effect relationships, if any, between the adolescent changes and illness onset?

Now we encounter issues of methodology. Although we all use them, correlative data do have their limitations. For example, Rutter (1986b) has elaborated many of the factors that render age an ambiguous correlate of psychiatric illness in adolescence, including the clearly imperfect relationship between age and pubertal staging. Other confounders of age include duration and type of personal experiences, and secular societal trends such as length of compulsory schooling, ascent and decline of the so-called drug culture, and economic swings.

One of the most intriguing aspects of adolescence is the phenomenon of puberty, which indeed is a neuroendocrine tour de force, as has been presented in detail in other chapters. Rather than being related primarily to age, the sharp increase in depressive illness in adolescent boys correlates better with pubertal stage. Thus, we may reasonably speculate that hormonal changes have something to do with the onset of depression—but what? Hormones, of course, influence brain function, and the sharp increases in growth hormone, gonadotropins, and gonadal steroids during puberty might have important psychopathological consequences in at least two ways. The first is that they might directly affect brain function by altering the balances among those central nervous system (CNS) neurotransmitters believed to be important in depression, including norepinephrine, serotonin, and acetylcholine (Charney, Menkes, & Heninger, 1981). Receptors for both male and female gonadal steroids are present in several areas of the CNS. The second, to quote Professor Rutter (1986b), is that "the mechanism may reside in young people's reaction to physical change, rather than in the hormonal effects per se." How might we approach this question experimentally? One important preliminary consideration is to recapitulate exactly which biological phenomena constitute puberty.

Puberty, "the period of accelerated reproductive development that culminates in functional fertility" (Bronson & Rissman, 1986), varies greatly across species in terms of when in the life cycle it occurs and which factors trigger its onset. While seasonal factors such as day length and other external factors such as pheromones are important in many species, in humans the main influences are genetic, nutritional, and, to a lesser extent, emotional (Bronson & Rissman, 1986). From a genetic standpoint, human beings are still hunter–gatherers, with only a few hundred generations having occurred since the dawn of civilization (Short, 1976). Only in about the last two hundred years have peoples in many areas of the world had an ample or even adequate food supply. This has been reflected in the larger size and weight of individuals in several countries, and, particularly, in the secular decline in the average age of menarche (onset of menses) in developed countries, from about 16.5 years in 1860 to about 13.5 years in 1960 (Short, 1976). Thus, with the exception of special groups such as adolescent ballet dancers and other athletes who remain so lean that they lack the stored energy reserves necessary for sexual maturation, the main influences on the pubertal process in the Western world are genetic and emotional. Leaving aside the genetic disorders that produce pathological alterations in sexual development, both accelerated and delayed, there still is a wide variation in the timing of normal pubertal staging in both boys and girls (Short, 1976), which reflects the genetic influence.

Another important background concept is that puberty is a multistage process. The early manifestations may be produced by an increase in adrenal androgen secretion around ages 6–8, followed by increases in gonadotropins and gonadal steroids, initially during the hours of sleep. Breast budding in girls, genital development and spermatogenesis in boys, growth of pubic hair, and general body growth come next, with menarche in girls occurring, as mentioned, around 13.5–14 years. Ovulation generally does not occur until 2–3 years after menarche. Secondary sex characteristics such as distribution of body hair and breast development continue to mature for several more years.

Promoting these changes are the hormonal secretory changes, including the nocturnal surges of growth hormone, the gonadotropins, and gonadal steroids, and the estrogen positive-feedback mechanism on luteinizing hormone secretion that triggers ovulation. So, if one wishes to elucidate specific relationships between puberty and adolescent psychopathology, one must go beyond global pubertal staging to the delineation of specific hormonal secretion patterns and their relation to (for example) depressive symptomatology. Longitudinal, prospective studies of adolescents are one very expensive and time-consuming way of approaching this issue. Another way might be to assess psychopathology in relation to measures of puberty in adolescent cohorts who have suffered delayed puberty because of nutritional restrictions (e.g., refugee populations). However, here the confounding nature of the nutritional disturbance itself might be overwhelming.

Investigators already have attempted to relate specific hormone measures to psychological and behavioral attributes of pubertal adolescents, which brings us to a consideration of Chapter 6 by Dr. Nottelmann and colleagues. These investigators studied fifty-six boys and fifty-two girls in early adolescence. The psychological measures were a self-image questionnaire rated by the subjects themselves and a behavior checklist rated by the parents. This is an important complementary approach to behavioral and attitudinal assessment; the perspectives of the subject and of significant others may or may not coincide. The physiological measures were not only pubertal stage but also serum concentrations of gonadotropins, gonadal sex steroids, and adrenal androgens. Importantly, the blood samples were taken between 8 and 10 a.m., in order to minimize any circadian or 24-hour changes in hormonal concentrations, and three blood samples were taken at 20-minute intervals, in order to provide an integrated measure of hormones that are normally secreted in pulses. Finally, in an attempt to relate the behavioral to the hormonal measures more directly, the effects of age and pubertal stage were partialed out of the statistical analyses.

While there were a number of specific relationships discerned, which differed somewhat between boys and girls, in general the findings indicated that in both sexes discordance between different aspects of development (e.g., delayed puberty relative to chronological age) was related to self-image disturbances and behavior problems. Also, in both sexes increased androstenedione, an adrenal androgenic or male hormone, was associated with self-image and behavior problems. From these data, Dr. Nottelmann and co-workers offered one hypothesis, restated here in oversimplified form: Chronic psychosocial adjustment problems may be chronically stressful, resulting in heightened activity of the hypothalamic-pituitary-adrenal (HPA) axis, with increased androstenedione and cortisol secretion. In turn, chronic increases in circulating cortisol could suppress the secretion of gonadal steroids, leading to maturational delay.

There are some difficulties in relating the findings of this study to the "big picture" presented by Professor Rutter. First, this study was performed on clinically normal adolescents, so that differences among subjects along the psychological dimensions measured had a certain constriction of variance compared to adolescents with clinically evident psychiatric illness. Similarly, the hormone measures were not taken at the time when differences among pubertal subjects should be greatest—that is, at night. Second, the psychological and behavioral measures were analyzed according to specific dimensions of emotional tone, self-image, social and family relationships, and so on. Unless it has been shown that these dimensions are orthogonal (i.e., uncorrelated), they probably should be analyzed in a multivariate paradigm, for example by canonical correlation with the hormone measures. Third, many multiple-regression analyses were performed for the boys' and the girls' data: Multiple testing of the same variables can distort the true significance levels of the analyses. Finally, Dr. Nottelmann and colleagues base their interesting causal hypothesis on correlative data—data that just as easily could support an alternative hypothesis. This they also have acknowledged, namely that the adolescents' perceived maturational delay is the primary stressor, and the increased adrenal stress hormone secretion is an epiphenomenon with little physiological import.

These methodological issues aside, with regard to the fundamental aim of this study, it should be pointed out that attempts by others to develop psychohormonal relationships in normal subjects have met with varying success. For example, studies relating testosterone secretion to measures of hostility, aggressive behavior, and dominance in men have included those in which psychological rating scales were used to quantify hostility in otherwise normal subjects, as well as those in which indices of overtly aggressive and violent acts in antisocial individuals, mainly prisoners, were used (Rubin, Reinisch, & Haskett, 1981; Rubin, 1982). In the former group of studies, done on normal volunteers such as male college students, older men, and athletes, the results have been variable. In these subjects there has been no consistent correlation between circulating testosterone and various measures of hostility or aggression. In contrast, studies of plasma testosterone in overtly aggressive, assaultive, and violent male prisoners have been more consistent in demonstrating a relation between such behaviors and increased circulating testosterone. This suggests that we are more likely to be able to discern psychohormonal relationships in adolescents with extreme variations in psychological state than in normal adolescents.

So, we must face the question of how to design research studies of psychohormonal relationships in adolescents. We seem to have two choices. If we are casting a wide net—for example, attempting to relate the various aspects of puberty to the onset of psychopathology—then large-cohort, prospective, longitudinal studies are in order. As mentioned, such studies are costly, labor-intensive, and also slow in producing results. Also, in order to develop a large cohort, several study sites often must be used, which necessitates the establishment of comparable techniques and approaches to assessment among all investigators and sites. The alternative is to ask very specific questions, to test very specific hypotheses. For example, to test the hypothesis that chronic psychosocial adjustment difficulties in some adolescents result in increased HPA axis activity, other tests of HPA axis function could be done. The simplest would be to analyze the samples from the Nottelmann et al. study for cortisol, the classic adrenocortical stress-responsive hormone. If cortisol concentrations were not elevated into the stress range, along with androstenedione, the hypothesis would be severely weakened.

Other important considerations in research design are worth mentioning. As noted previously, one cannot infer causality from correlative data. So, we attempt to discern which event occurred first. For example, does weight loss or amenorrhea occur first in adolescents with anorexia nervosa? This is not a trivial issue for understanding the etiology and treatment of the disease: If weight loss comes first, then we are dealing with starvation amenorrhea and the primary treatment would be refeeding, whereas if amenorrhea comes first, we may be dealing with a CNS neurotransmitter disturbance that could require pharmacotherapy. As we might expect, stating the alternatives is far easier than testing them. Many studies of anorexic adolescents have been conducted, and both refeeding regimens and psychopharmacological management have met with some success.

From the psychological standpoint, we need to develop both categorical and dimensional data on our subjects. Categorical data include specific psychiatric diagnoses. It should be mentioned that the *DSM-III* diagnostic system (American Psychiatric Association, 1980), the system currently used in the United States, has recently undergone an in-depth revision. Thus, secular changes in our categorical data may be another vexing confounder when comparing results across studies. Dimensional data are most often developed in the form of psychological rating scales, as in the Nottelmann et al. study. Assuming reasonable validity, reliability, and so on for a given scale, important issues are the number of items on the scale, their intercorrelations, and whether they can be reduced by factoring to fewer and more stable dimensions. In general, neither categorical nor dimensional data can substitute for the other.

From the hormonal standpoint, another methodological concern is whether we are dealing with state or trait phenomena. State abnormalities are those that are related to an illness episode, such as increased adrenocortical activity during a bout of depression. When the depression is fully resolved, adrenocortical activity returns to normal. Other hormone changes may be trait related; that is, they are present before illness onset, and they persist after the illness has remitted. State markers may be useful for the differential diagnosis of a particular illness, for the monitoring of treatment effectiveness, and possibly for the prediction of relapse in persons who are already ill. In contrast, trait markers may offer insights into the genetics of the illness, especially if they correlate with familial loading for the illness. They also may identify currently healthy individuals who are at particular risk for developing the illness at a later time. Both state and trait hormone changes have been reported in depressed children, and these are different in some ways from the hormone changes of depressed adults (Rubin & Marder, 1983; Puig-Antich, 1986). Patterns of these hormones in depressed adolescents at different stages of puberty have not yet been clearly elucidated. The limited studies of late adolescents who have completed puberty indicate that they do have adult-type hormone changes.

In conclusion, a clear general message from the two chapters under consideration is that there is great variation among adolescents—in timing of puberty, amount of stress experienced, and types and rates of behavioral disturbance. Multiple factors, both physiological and psychosocial, may interact and lead to psychiatric morbidity. And, as a corollary, adolescents by and large are both physiologically and psychologically resilient; not only do the majority of adolescents remain psychologically healthy, but the healing process in the disturbed adolescent is a powerful one. These principles should be kept in mind by mental health professionals working with adolescents: Rarely does a single traumatic event lead to psychopathology, and very often therapeutic interventions are helpful, even though the results may not be evident until the adolescent becomes older and further maturation provides an additional corrective influence.

Acknowledgment

This work was supported by National Institute of Mental Health Research Scientist Award MH47363 and grant MH28380.

References

American Psychiatric Association (APA) (1980). *Diagnostic and statistical manual of mental disorders* (3rd ed.). Washington, DC: APA.
Bronson, F. H., & Rissman, E. F. (1986). The biology of puberty. *Biological Reviews, 61,* 157–195.

Bruch, H. (1973). *Eating disorders: Obesity, anorexia nervosa, and the person within.* New York: Basic Books.

Charney, D. S., Menkes, D. B., & Heninger, G. R. (1981). Receptor sensitivity and the mechanism of action of antidepressant treatment: Implications for the etiology and therapy of depression. *Archives of General Psychiatry, 38,* 1160–1180.

Grove, W. M., & Cadoret, R. J. (1983). Genetic factors in alcoholism. In B. Kissin & H. Begleiter (Eds.), *The biology of alcoholism* (Vol. 7), *The pathogenesis of alcoholism: Biological factors* (pp. 31–56). New York: Plenum.

Puig-Antich, J. (1986). Psychobiological markers: Effects of age and puberty. In M. Rutter, C. E. Izard, & P. B. Read (Eds.), *Depression in young people: Developmental and clinical perspectives* (pp. 341–381). New York: Guilford Press.

Rubin, R. T. (1982). Testosterone and aggression in men. In P. J. V. Beaumont & G. Burrows (Eds.), *Handbook of psychiatry and endocrinology* (pp. 355–366). Amsterdam: Elsevier.

Rubin, R. T., & Marder, S. R. (1983). Biological markers in affective and schizophrenic disorders: A review of contemporary research. In M. R. Zales (Ed.), *Affective and schizophrenic disorders: New approaches to diagnosis and treatment* (pp. 53–100). New York: Brunner/Mazel.

Rubin, R. T., Reinisch, J. M., & Haskett, R. F. (1981). Postnatal gonadal steroid effects on human behavior. *Science, 211,* 1318–1324.

Rutter, M. (1980). *Changing youth in a changing society: Patterns of adolescent development and disorder.* Cambridge, MA: Harvard University Press.

Rutter, M. (1985). Psychopathology and development: Links between childhood and adult life. In M. Rutter & L. Hersov (Eds.), *Child and adolescent psychiatry: Modern approaches* (2nd ed., pp. 720–739). Oxford: Blackwell Scientific.

Rutter, M. (1986a). The developmental psychopathology of depression: Issues and perspectives. In M. Rutter, C. E. Izard, & P. B. Read (Eds.), *Depression in young people: Developmental and clinical perspectives* (pp. 3–30). New York: Guilford Press.

Rutter, M. (1986b) *Age as an ambiguous variable in developmental research.* Paper presented at the Conference on Development: European Perspectives, Rome, September.

Rutter, M., Tizard, J., Yule, W., Graham, P., & Whitmore, K. (1976). Isle of Wight studies: 1964–1974. *Psychological Medicine, 6,* 313–332.

Short, R. V. (1976). The evolution of human reproduction. *Proceedings of the Royal Society (London), B195,* 3–24.

II

SOCIAL AND CULTURAL ASPECTS OF ADOLESCENT SEXUALITY

9

Emerging and Submerging Adolescent Sexuality: Culture and Sexual Orientation

Mary E. Hotvedt

A 15-year-old unmarried woman becomes pregnant. If she is a rural Iraqi peasant girl, her father may kill her. If she is a Kalahari bushwoman, she may marry quickly and comfortably. If she is a middle-class U.S. high school student, she might stay unmarried and attend a special class for expectant mothers. These responses to the same scenario—only one of several aspects of adolescent sexuality to be discussed—are not simply random reactions due to geographic or linguistic differences or to parental whim. Each outcome is part of an integrated cultural pattern in which the reproductive capacity and sexuality of the girl, as well as the disposition of her infant, have different economic and social portent.

The primary theoretical position of this chapter is that emergence and expression of sexual behavior in each culture are shaped by that culture to multiple purposes. When a child begins to mature and shows secondary sexual characteristics, the culture, through a variety of means, steps up its "shaping" of that individual into acceptable adult roles. A culture is a system of shared beliefs and meanings, institutions, and behaviors. Moreover, it is a system of ecological adaptation by which humans exploit an environment for their survival and continuance. Fundamentally, a culture—a people—seeks to continue itself through a system of food production and biological reproduction.

Sex education, then, in each culture is aimed not at merely teaching biological facts of reproduction to maturing individuals. Ethnographies and anecdotes from our own lives are sufficient to remind us that prepubescent children have a reasonably good grasp of the basics. In the introduction to their 1980 edited volume, *Sexual Meanings,* Ortner and Whitehead (1981) point out that a culture elaborates the biological givens of male and female to ends that meet needs of the group and also the needs of each individual actor. Sex education in all cultures also has to do with role training to be husband, wife, worker, parent, and lover. Each adolescent is trained and directed into a set of gender roles that meet these two major and related cultural tasks of production and reproduction. This is not a lockstep procedure, in most instances, but is one modulated by what Simon and Gagnon (1986) refer to as interpersonal and intrapsychic factors. Overall, however, the degree of personal freedom the society condones in sexual expression is related to the cultural expectations of the individual at that point in the life span, as both an economic and a reproductive part of the group.

The purposes of this chapter are multiple. The nonanthropologist reader is introduced to a brief typology and description of preindustrial societies, the traditional bailiwick of anthropology. The degrees to which sexual freedoms are allowed in certain types of preindustrial societies is discussed. Then, attention is given to specific kinds of cultural institutions that delineate and direct adolescent gender role behavior as well as sexual behavior. Courtship and marriage patterns are covered. Finally, one anthropological view of modern adolescent sexual behavior is offered.

Conceptually, the material of this chapter fits behind the primate behavior section and before the current surveys on adolescent sexual conduct. Picture primates and their intense interactions: the small close to their mothers, the young juveniles playing fiercely, the older ones practicing more adult behaviors. Imagine the grooming behavior, the dominance displays, presenting and mounting, the challenge to established authority, and the response to that challenge. Humans are primates, unique in many aspects, but evolving their behavior patterns from similar biological material. Remember also the intensity of emotions felt when young: see the almost crackling energy of a teen dance, the preening self-concern of the beauties, the shyness of the others, the frantic movement of the dancers, the class clowns laughing from the side, the embraces of the "steadies," the stern eyes of the chaperones. That same color, that energy comes through in every ethnographic description of youth, but may be harder to preserve in a comparative study such as this, for which the author apologizes.

Cross-cultural materials used here include theoretical works, ethnographies, historical reconstructions, and statistical surveys based on the Human Relations Area Files (HRAF). Some caveats need to be made regarding ethnographic material. By the very essence of human culture, this paper is a historical one. Much of the ethnographic evidence is time-limited in its veracity because of rapid cultural change within the century, more rapidly increasing with each decade. Another problem in an undertaking such as this is that cultural anthropology, on the whole, is more descriptive than quantitative in approach, so that the ethnographer's biases simply must be accepted. Bias can be caused by the anthropologist's sex, age, and marital status, by informant's response to these variables, by a theoretical viewpoint, and by sheer limitations in language ability and field resources. Finally, we must make note that, historically, anthropologists have not been well trained in pursuing sexual information. They bring to the field too often—at least in the past—their own sexual prejudices and concerns (Gebhard, 1971).

We need to redefine "adolescence" in cross-cultural perspective. To paraphrase Cohen (1964, pp. 22–23), adolescence, or nascent adulthood, is a variable period anywhere from late prepubescence to full biological maturation in which the individual learns to be socially responsible for oneself and one's actions. In some cultures, such as our own, adolescence is a long period, almost a decade, in which the individual has responsibilities and privileges different from those of childhood or full adulthood. In other societies, this special period may be viewed as lasting a few months to a few brief years, from the recognition of puberty (a biological event) to marriage and childbearing, the usual hallmarks of adult status. Fried and Fried (1980, p. 59) note that while adolescence may have no meaning or recognition in a culture, the fact of puberty is usually noted.

Typology of Cultures

Anthropologists have found that the greatest understanding of patterns of human behavior is achieved by studying cultures on the basis of their subsistence patterns, or their systems of production. Strongly related to each subsistence pattern is a degree of social complexity. Simple subsistence patterns are accompanied by more egalitarian social structures, for example. At the core of social structure is a system of reproduction, a way the culture replicates itself by giving birth to children and training them to become men and women who will fit into the production system as well as contribute to the reproductive system in their turn. Even the most technologically simple, egalitarian system differentiates between male and female roles in both production and reproduction in the domestic economy of the group (see Harris, 1979). The reproductive and productive systems impinge on each other and provide a set of parameters for elaboration of other aspects of behavior. Thus, despite geographic or linguistic differences, we can find similarities in many aspects of life among disparate cultures that share economic systems and are under similar reproductive constraints. Likewise, change to a different system of production or a major shift in reproductive strategy brings about predictable change in other aspects of social behavior. This latter point is demonstrated frequently by the process of modernization in technologically less complex systems. Several different types of cultures are discussed in this chapter: hunting and gathering systems; horticultural systems, and intensive agricultural systems.

Hunting and Gathering Systems

These are nonagricultural systems with simple technology for finding food. While relatively few hunter–gatherer cultures remain, they, in part, interest anthropologists because they may most closely resemble the earliest and longest surviving form of human culture. Some cultures (e.g., the Eskimos) derive the majority of their calories from animal protein and fat. Others are mainly dependent on the harvesting of wild plants. Fishing economies are also included.

Social organization is characterized by nuclear families and bands, the latter being small residential groups of kin that cooperate in economic and ceremonial activity. The band divides during times of food scarcity to allow greater exploitation of an area, and rejoins or combines with other bands when food is plentiful. Bands share a loose ownership of territory and all band members have equal environmental rights. Reciprocal arrangements such as marriage exchanges take place with neighboring bands (Harris, 1974, p. 260).

Hunters and gatherers have classless societies. Decision making is usually egalitarian, with age and expertise being respected. Headmen are spokesmen but not kings. Shamans perform medical, spiritual, magic, and judicial roles. Leaders, secular and shamanistic, are kept from becoming too powerful by social controls.

Each adult and adolescent takes part in basic subsistence work according to their mental and physical abilities. While each sex has its particular and distinct economic tasks, within each sex group there is very little work specialization. Individual talents, such as creating beautiful needlework, hunt planning, or storytelling, are honored, but these gifts are used for family and band benefit rather than individual accrual of wealth or power.

Reproductive strategies require enough children to keep band size constant but not so many as to deplete resources. Geriatric suicide has been reported in times of hardship in some hunting and gathering cultures.

Horticultural Systems

Horticulturalists raise crops without the use of the plough or irrigation. Domestication of animals is also part of the system. Pastoralists, peoples whose chief food source is herded domesticated animals, are one variation. Hunting, gathering, and fishing all play a part in horticultur-alists' food production as well.

The majority of tribal cultures still viable today are part of this cate-gory. Archaeology indicates that plant and animal domestication ex-isted in the Middle East by or before 9000 B.C., and in the Americas by or before 8000 B.C. (Harris, 1979, pp. 190, 214).

Horticulturism is distinguished from hunter–gatherer culture by an intensification and elaboration of the sexual division of labor, of rights and use of specific property, of rituals, and of population pressure. A spectrum exists. On one end are horticultural groups that are still quite similar to hunting and gathering cultures in their village size, social organization, and economic profile. On the other end are small nations or kingdoms of pastoralists or farmers numbering three hundred thou-sand or more. The elaborations or intensification over band society can be summarized as follows:

1. Authority increases within the descent group, sometimes with one lineage becoming "royal" or gaining ascendancy over other lineages of the tribe.
2. Warfare between economically competing groups increases; militarily successful males are rewarded with prestige, wealth, and marriages.
3. Economic surplus develops; wealth may accrue to a single lin-eage, and there is a decrease in egalitarianism.

Intensive Agriculture

The use of ploughs, draft animals, and irrigation marked a dramatic shift in social organization as well as food production wherever it ap-peared geographically. Economic surplus, for the first time, could al-low a part of the population to work without any direct input into food production. Urbanization occurred, along with new labor specializa-tions in trading, manufacturing, the military, and religion. The food producers themselves underwent a powerful role transformation: "With the intensification of production and the rise in population density, economic organization fell increasingly under state-administered insti-tutions that set production quotas and carried out lopsided distribu-tions. . . . They obliged people to increase their work input not merely by promising them prestige but by threatening them with socially im-posed material sanctions . . . leading ultimately to physical annihila-tion" (Harris, 1979, p. 297).

Land, then, is no longer under the total control of kinship groups whose members have access to and the right to it. Whole kin groups could and can be evicted. Peasants are "food producing farmers in preindustrial and underdeveloped societies, subject to exploitative obligations in the form of rent, taxes, tribute, [and] forced labor service" (Harris, 1974, p. 665).

In peasant societies, kinship groups serve as conservators of their resources in order to maintain position against competing groups and more powerful classes. Access to land is through familial inheritance, and it becomes important that title to the land be undisputed or dispossession can occur. This has strong implications for gender roles and sexuality, particularly for women.

Sexual Permissiveness in Preindustrial Cultures

Several researchers have used the Human Relations Area Files (HRAF), a detailed compilation of historical and ethnographic materials, to draw conclusions about the frequency of premarital sexual behavior as well as factors that influence or indicate permissiveness versus restrictiveness in postpubescent sexual behavior. Broude and Green (1980) used the 186 cultures in the Basic Standardized Sample of the HRAF (Murdock & White, 1980) to detail the percentage of cultures in which certain sexual acts are permissible. Reducing the sample to 141 cultures for which data on premarital sex were available, in 21% of the sample, premarital sex was rated as expected and approved. Of the total, 75% viewed premarital sex for females as not a particularly serious issue, whereas 25% of the totals sampled regarded premarital sex with strong disapproval and sanctions. Of the 114 cultures for which data on frequency of sexual activity were available, in 49% of that sample it was reported that the frequency of female premarital sex was common, whereas in 20% it was thought to occur rarely or never. Of 107 ethnographies, 60% reported that male premarital sexual activity was universal and that in only 12% of the sample was it uncommon or rare. Of 34 cultures in which initiation of premarital sexuality was discussed, 35% indicated that males were the initiators of premarital sex and in 18% of the sample, females initiated sex. Homosexuality was also surveyed, although this behavior was not reported exclusively for adolescents. Strong disapproval of homosexuality was reported for 41% of 42 cultures; it was accepted or ignored by 21%, and 12% reported no such concept. Of 70 ethnographies, 59% reported homosexuality absent or rare in frequency and 41% reported it present or not uncommon.

Adolescence, however brief, is also a time in which individuals with atypical gender roles or homosexual preferences are noted and sometimes accommodated by the culture. Cases of transvestic homosexuality occur frequently in the anthropological literature (see Carrier, 1980). Whitam (1983) has argued that exclusive homosexual behavior appears as a constant and significant subpattern of sexuality across cultures.

Homosexual activity has also been tolerated or encouraged in social cultures where premarital chastity between the sexes is strongly emphasized (Money and Erhardt, 1972; Schiefflin, 1976).

Levinson and Malone (1980), using the same HRAF sample of preindustrial societies, reported that the best predictors of sexual restrictiveness appeared to be cultural and social complexities. That is, large-scale societies tended more than small-scale societies to repress sexual expression. Features associated with limitations on premarital sexuality included state societies, those with major religions, those that were politically or technologically complex, those with the presence of a class system, larger community size, and where economic exchange at marriage was significant. Barry and Schlegel (1986) also used the standard sample of 186 societies (Murdock & White, 1980). Employing a statistical measure of sexual freedom developed in an earlier study, and recategorizing the cultures in the standard sample into categories based on subsistence patterns as we have done earlier in this chapter, they were able to generate correlations between sexual freedom and cultural complexity. Their sexual freedom scale includes ratings on scales of sexual nonrestraint and sexual expression:

> Sexual expression refers to encouragement of sexual behavior, taking into account the frequency, emotional intensity, importance, and variety, also the range of partners permitted. Heterosexual intercourse is usually the principal criterion. Other types of behavior taken into account include heterosexual foreplay, masturbation, homosexuality, sexual jokes, and exposing the genitals. Sexual restraint refers to taboos or restrictions on heterosexual intercourse and on other erotic behavior, including heterosexual play, masturbation and homosexuality. The information taken into account includes a high degree of modesty (keeping the genitals constantly covered in public) and widely extended incest taboos (Barry & Schlegel, 1986).

Barry and Schlegel's findings generally support those of Levinson and Moore (1980). Most notably, sexual freedom is lowest in the most technologically complex and class-stratified agricultural societies. Among hunters and gatherers, the absence of a puberty ritual for girls and the presence of monogamy were both correlated with sexual freedom. Among horticultural societies matrilineal descent (tracing kinship through the mother) was associated with sexual freedom. Among intensive agricultural groups who are not highly stratified, the presence of a puberty ritual for both males and females and a pattern of exogamy (marriage outside the local group) were tied to greater sexual freedom.

Institutions Involving Direction and Control of Adolescent Sexuality

Preindustrial cultures mark the transition from child to adult in a number of special ways, each designed to train the young person for adult roles and to remind him or her of membership and loyalty. One of the most common of these particular institutions is the puberty ritual or initiation rite.

Puberty rituals are ceremonies marking a change in status from childhood to either adolescence or adulthood. They are usually properties of less technologically complex cultures in which kin or tribal affiliations are primary. The ceremony is usually sponsored by a kin-based group, and very specific kin positions hold ceremonial importance. Schlegel and Barry (1980) used the HRAF Standard Sample of 186 societies (Murdock & White, 1980) to analyze the presence, forms, and features of puberty rituals. Information on presence or lack of boys' puberty rituals was available for 182 societies and on girls for 183 societies. They found ceremonies more common for girls than for boys (46% vs. 36%). Of those societies with rituals, there were marked differences for boys' and girls' ceremonies. Girls more often go through initiation alone (87%), whereas in 43% of the male rituals, boys were part of a large cohort. Girls' ceremonies more commonly involved only the immediate family (48%) or the local group (35%); boys' rites included the local group (41%) and the large group (48%). Most commonly, participation by adults is limited to the same sex (54–55%), or partially limited to the same sex (28–33%). Timing of these rituals varies from culture to culture, although most occur for girls at the time of genital maturation—and menses. For boys, rituals may take place from an earlier, prepubescent period, with the majority (87%) having occurred as long as 1 year after genital maturation (Schlegel & Barry, 1980).

Meanings of the ceremonies differ. For boys, rituals involve emphasis on group cohesion (team spirit, as it were) and on achievement. Tasks, hardships, or vision quests may precede or be part of the ceremony. Symbols of the culture may be shared with the initiates. Genital operations, such as circumcision, subincision, or superincision, are performed in 32% of the sample, and other types of pain may also be inflicted (Schlegel & Barry, 1980).

For girls, emphasis is more on relational roles than on achievement. Menstrual taboos and seclusion coupled with instructions from women, followed by purification, are a common form of ritual.

Landes (1971) contrasts the rituals of Ojibwa boys with those of girls. The Ojibwa are a Canadian-based tribe, originally exclusive hunters and gatherers:

Every few years the parents of the village decide that their pubescent boys should be sent on an isolated and prolonged fast for visions. Each family talks to its boys, urges upon them the significance of this trial, teaches them how to work up a vision, and how to recognize and reject an "evil" vision. . . .

So the boys are sent out to a neighboring island or to an isolated spot in the woods, without food or drink and each with a worn blanket to lie on. Some boys lie on the rough ground, others on rocks, some build themselves a "nest" in the tree. The fast lasts four to ten days. . . . The household is informed tacitly about the success of the vision-seeker when he is noticed going through some arbitrary behavior as tabooing certain foods, preparing a sweat tent, offering sacrifices, collecting, or making strange objects as mementos.

The girl goes through her ceremonial fast at the time of her first menstruation. But no parties of adults are convened to discuss it, even when it occurs during the months of village life, and the girl is put through no training preparatory to it. Her vision pursuit is neglected in the face of a greater portent, the blood discharge. . . .

She is hurried by her mother or grandmother out of the family lodge into a tiny isolated one built for her in the forest. She is dressed poorly, soot is smeared about her eyes, her gaze is downwards and she must not look at any living thing. Indeed, "she lives poorly", and is supposed to sit quietly and meditate during the period of the flow. None should approach her but women who are past the menopause, and girls in a condition similar to hers. . . . To begin with, this new view of themselves is startling. They see their brothers and fathers in a new light; also, derivatively, the weapons, clothing, and other objects belonging to males. They experiment with the ideas of strewing leaves in warning, and of shrinking away from the path of a man. . . . Instead of brooding upon the supernatural, at least to the extent determined by a hungry stomach, "new" women visit one another in their isolated lodges. They discuss their newly acquired sexual eligibility, and their general coming into adult importance. Older women visit them and discuss their new state with them and teach them sewing skills so that they will be desired in marriage (Landes, 1971).

Genital surgery occurs in only 8% of girls' rituals (Schlegel & Barry, 1980). Female surgery such as clitoridectomy and infibulation, where it is performed, is more often done while the girl is prepubescent. She may still go through a seclusion ritual at menarche (Abdollah, 1982). Tattooing or scarification, for either sex, can also be part of or separate from puberty rituals. These marks can show membership, bravery, or power, or they can enhance desirability.

Dormitories

The dormitory as an institution for youth takes interesting forms in preindustrial society. Here, two forms of dormitory will be contrasted to give a sense of how differently the same institution is used to further culturally appropriate training of its young members. All dormitories share certain features: a degree of isolation of adolescents from their nuclear families; and a large part of the training—both social and sexual—of the younger initiates carried out by the older ones. In these senses, preindustrial dormitories are very similar to those in industrial societies.

In his 1968 ethnography, Elwin describes the Munda as they were in the 1930s and 1940s. The Munda were at that time a population of six million, divided into several related groups, in northeast India. They were simple agriculturalists, non-Hindus, with little sex segregation or warfare. They were organized in patrilineal clans and preferred to marry outside the clan to related clans (preferred cross-cousin marriage). At a certain point in late childhood—though it might be as early as 7 years, the Munda would send their children to sleep in the *ghotul,* or dormitory, of the village. If children were reluctant to go, ghotul members would fetch them as their reluctance became apparent to the community.

The Sambia is a pseudonym for a Papuan New Guinea Highland people. Herdt (1981) describes the Sambia as a horticultural society of a few thousand, similar to surrounding tribes. Sambian society is highly sexually segregated and sexually antagonistic; there is a heavy emphasis on warfare. Clan structure is also patrilineal, with preferred marriage outside the clan. At around the age of 7, boys are sent by their fathers to the dormitory, the clubhouse, as the first phase of a six-stage initiation to full Sambian manhood (at ages 20–30).

Likewise, the Munda leave the ghotul as they achieve full adult status, although the age is earlier than for the Sambia (between 13 and 15). Munda initiation has two phases. In the early phase, the young initiates of both sexes learn the Munda rules of kinship, etiquette, and authority by obeying their "pledgemasters," doing favors for them, and referring to them by ritualized ghotul names, which also imply their social responsibilities and relationships. During the daytime, ghotul members work alongside their parents; but at day's end their loyalty must revert to the ghotul. As the initiate physically matures and becomes fluent in the policies of the ghotul, he or she is given one of the ritual names and is heterosexually initiated by an older member. Elwin (1968) reports two types of ghotul. One type practices exclusive "marriage" with an in-ghotul ceremony. While members are free to choose their mate on sentiment, they must respect incest taboos in their choices. The second type insists on rotation of sexual partners so that group cohesiveness is emphasized.

Sambia also practice sexual initiation. Boys are transformed into men by semen, the male essence. Young initiates are trained to fellate the older youths, to ingest their strength to add to their own masculinity. At the same time, all social contact with women is avoided. In the third stage of initiation, around ages 14–16, the fellators become the sexually dominant bachelors, who, in turn will be fellated by younger boys. Marriage follows shortly thereafter, but the older initiates are still involved with the sexual rituals of the clubhouse while they begin heterosexual contact. Newlywed men still sleep in the clubhouse. Marital sex begins with several months of heterosexual fellatio, and later, intercourse is attempted. At first, these relations are tense and fearful. While marital sex continues to be brief, by the last initiation phase, the majority of adult men are expected to be exclusively heterosexual (Herdt, 1981).

There are other parallels between the Munda and Sambia dormitories. Munda parents pretend not to know what the ghotul children do, even though they also were in the ghotul. Sambia women also pretend not to know what the clubhouse rituals are about. In both communities, the dormitory acts as a powerful unit. The ghotul can punish members for misconduct and fine parents for interfering with ghotul policy. Their greatest power is their right to boycott weddings. If a ghotul feels itself, as a group, offended, they will not attend wedding feasts. Their presence is considered essential for blessing, beauty, entertainment, and social acceptability. Sambia clubhouse members have power, too—over women, children, and of course, younger initiates. The noninitiated must flee from the sound of the sacred flutes controlled by the men of the clubhouse.

Both dormitories emphasize achievement rather than social position. Socialization within the dormitory is meant to shape the type of person who embodies the cultural ideal, regardless of birthright. Also, the adolescent sexual experiences provide powerful erotic imagery that continues beyond marriage in both these preindustrial societies.

In the dormitory experience, older youths are the sex educators of the young. In most other puberty rituals, adult relatives, more so than parents, provide sexual information and role training. In our own culture, we often debate whether parents or schools should provide sex education. The anthropological literature suggests that only rarely do parents perform this role. It is as if a taboo exists against parental involvement, and other members of the society are considered as more appropriate providers of postpubescent training.

Courtship, Marriage, and Premarital Pregnancy

In preindustrial societies, all social relationships are based on kinship, economic units are kin-based, and marriage is an alliance of families. It is difficult for those of us from postindustrial cultures to imagine a life ruled almost solely by such familial ties.

The subject of marriage alliances is a lengthy one, requiring descriptions of types of descent, residence after marriage, authority patterns, and wealth distribution. Our purpose here is to understand better the channeling of adolescent sexuality, and so these marriage alliance issues will be touched on only briefly.

All cultures have some system of courtship for the young. Forms and outcomes vary greatly. In hunter–gatherer groups, where there is little accrued wealth or population pressure, such as the Ojibwa, individual attraction or romantic love between the young may be encouraged (Landes, 1971). Premarital chastity then is not required of either sex, and pregnancy leads to marriage to one's choice. Among the Tiwi of Melville Island, off Northern Australia, girls may have several flirtations and love affairs during adolescence, but, before puberty, are married to older men with whom their parents have made contracts. Pregnancy returns her to her husband (Goodale, 1971). Thus, courtship does not lead to marriage, pregnancy does. Ghotul members leave for marriage with their prearranged partners because of pregnancy that resulted from sex in their ghotul (Elwin, 1968).

In Polynesian Mangaia, as in some other cultures, courtship and premarital sex are carried on at night in the family home, with a suitor slipping into his girlfriend's bed. If he is too clumsy and is caught, he might be beaten by her parents, but otherwise no one pays much attention (Marshall, 1971). Mangaian parents hope their daughters will not become pregnant until they meet with the right man, so they encourage their girls to see many suitors. It is thought that multiple sexual experiences prevent pregnancy (Marshall, 1971). Ghotul members also believe this, if they ascribe to the nonmonogamous form of ghotul (Elwin, 1968). The infrequency with which early adolescent pregnancy occurs in several sexually active populations suggests a high degree of adolescent sterility, perhaps due to diet. Abortifacient herbs and treatments may also account for the low number of marriages that must take place. Girls in such courtship situations are seldom anxious to marry and give up the freedom of the courtship period (Goodale, 1971).

Premarital chastity for girls is most emphasized, as was discussed earlier, in more stratified societies where more wealth is exchanged at marriage, and where patrilineage—the father's line of descent and inheritance—must be absolutely clear. Thus peasant groups with strong lineages are most likely to insist on virginity for brides. To ensure this, girls are isolated from unsupervised contact with nonfamily males or are heavily chaperoned. It is more their family than they themselves who are courted, and marriages for girls may be early—even prepubescent. Wolf (1972) reported that in rural Taiwan, marriages are arranged by families, now with the agreement of the youths. Love marriages are discouraged by parents, although adolescents fantasize about it. If a couple shows even mild interest in each other, their friends urge it to the point that they are almost as trapped as they are in a parentally approved relationship.

Required wealth and the availability of mates can also affect age at first marriage. Herlihy (1985) has charted changes in marriage age in Roman times and medieval Europe as associated with the prevalence of bride price and dowry. In such agrarian systems, premarital pregnancy is a major disruption to family alliances. It can result in disgrace for the girl and the child, her family, a less satisfactory marriage, or no marriage at all. In some areas, her death is the only redemption for the family's honor.

Modernization and Adolescent Sexuality

Thus far we have discussed preindustrial societies, the traditional domain of cultural anthropology. Anthropologists look at modernized systems also as a cultural type, having cohesive productive and reproductive systems. The puzzles are these: If, in all other types of cultures, greater technological complexity and social stratification are correlated with stricter controls on adolescent sexuality, why do modernized societies have less restrictive sexual behavior, much more like those of egalitarian band societies?

In anthropological terms, a modernized society is one characterized by high technological accomplishment, so that a small percentage of people produce food for a large population of highly specialized, mainly urbanized workers. Authority is in the government rather than in the kinship line. Ownership of property is largely individualized or in the state. Labor is mostly service oriented or in the production of goods—both areas where either gender can work. Emphasis is on a long training period for complex jobs, for which there is competition due to population pressures. The reproductive strategy is to have only enough children to have them trained well to place themselves advantageously in the work force. Technological advances in birth control allow people to limit births despite good diets that promote fertility. Ideally, parents prefer that children delay marriage or pregnancy until the children themselves can work and have sufficient wealth. Ideal marriage is one based on companionship and romantic love, ideas that gained cultural ascendancy with increased urbanization and industrialization (Stone, 1977). Marital alliances between families, except for the very wealthy, are largely pro forma or affectional rather than classic kinship alliances. Marriage is brittle because either male or female parents can raise and afford to pay for training of their young, and there is little or no extended-family economic involvement in the issue. Marriage is also unnecessary to achieve full adult status.

Adolescence in such a system is long, usually lasting until training is nearly completed or economic independence is established. The state, moreover, sets ages by which certain rights are obtained by the adolescent or young adult. Training (e.g., high school) is largely coeducational with large groups of adolescents and few adults; and time away from school allows a large population of age-mates to court and socialize with each other. Pressure for premarital chastity is familial or religious but can seldom be strictly enforced. Fear about one's reputation, sexually transmitted diseases, unwanted pregnancy, or abandonment by a fickle partner might delay sexual activity or decrease numbers of partners, but might not prevent sexual behavior. All of these factors combined make sexuality a personalized domain, less under the control of the family. This is consistent with the findings of Barry and Schlegel (1986) that sexual freedom for adolescents in preindustrial societies is correlated with descent through the mother's line, monogamy, and marriage outside the local group. Conflicts over adolescent sexual activity occur, even though the phenomenon is common. The problem may be in the clash between agrarian values and the exigencies of modernized society.

The U.S. population, for example, is an amalgam of ethnic groups, among which some cultures other than the dominant culture remain intact. Intact cultures are here defined as those that maintain an economic system other than the dominant one or use the dominant system for the means of the group, and that still have strong control over marriage within the culture (endogamy). Examples of intact cultures within the United States are the Amish, Hassidic communities, and several Native American communities, such as the Hopi and Navajo.

Ethnic groups are remnants of once intact cultures. They are no longer pure cultures because they no longer control a separate economy nor can they maintain boundaries by marriage within the group. The progression from "culture" to "ethnic group" is usually multigenerational; it may begin with emigration, slavery, conquest, or sheer swamping by the predominant technology and population (see McGoldrick, 1982).

As members of ethnic groups, we maintain social, familial, and religious values that we attempt to pass on to our young, while still training them to compete in American society. Since most of our cultural antecedents (i.e., the bases of our ethnicity) were in European, Asian, or Latin peasantries, or in highly stratified African tribes, our familial and sexual values may continue to reflect these sources (Hotvedt, 1983a) while we are trying also to impart the wisdom gained during our own American youth. A complete sexual message emerges: "Don't have sex now. But if you do, be careful." I believe the ambivalence of this message is influential in adolescents being sexual without birth control, or in a mother taking her daughter to get contraceptives without informing the father.

Forms of human sexual behavior, including adolescent sexual behavior, are evolving, and will most likely continue to do so as economic and reproductive systems are affected and different human responses are necessary to those conditions. It is hoped that this chapter make a valuable contribution to understanding the wide variation that occurs among cultures in response to emerging adolescent sexuality. It is also the author's wish that the reader has caught even a glimmer of the multitude of other cultures in their intensities and beauty. Robin Fox (1973) stated it well:

> Unlike poets, we "objective" scientists like to affect that only our brains lie in our less than lyrical studies of men and women—the real people who make up those awful abstractions like "social structure," "kinship system," "cultural unit," and "breeding population." But even if, for professional purposes, we are able to recollect our data in tranquillity, at least some of us are not so self-deceived as to believe that we are dispassionate about our material. Reason is, and ought to be, the slave of the passions; Hume was right in this. If the only motive for doing anthropology is that bleak professionalism that sees human beings as useful objects of study, the discipline has lost its connection with both its origins and its purpose. There is enough exploitation in the world without our adding intellectual exploitation. Our hearts, as well as our brains, should be with our men and women.

References

Abdollah, R. H. D. (1982). *Sisters in affliction*. London: Zed Press.

Barry III, H., & Schlegel, A. (1986). Cultural customs that influence sexual freedom in adolescence. *Ethnology, 25,* 151–162.

Broude, G. J., & Green, S. J. (1980). Cross-cultural codes on twenty sexual attitudes and practices. In H. Barry III & A. Schlegel (Eds.), *Cross-cultural samples and codes* (pp. 313–334). Pittsburgh, PA: University of Pittsburgh Press.

Carrier, J. M. (1980). Homosexual behavior in cross-cultural perspective. In J. Marmor (Ed.), *Homosexual behavior*. New York: Basic Books.

Cohen, A. (1964). *The transition from childhood to adolescence*. Chicago: Aldine.

Elwin, V. (1968). *The kingdom of the young*. Oxford: Oxford University Press.

Fox, R. (1973). *Encounter with anthropology*. New York: Harcourt, Brace & Jovanovich.

Fried, M. N., & Fried, M. H. (1980). *Transitions: Four rituals in eight cultures*. New York: Norton.

Gebhard, P. (1971). Introduction. In D. S. Marshall & R. C. Suggs (Eds.), *Human sexual behavior* (pp. xi–xv). New York: Basic Books.

Goodale, J. (1971). *Tiwi wives*. Seattle: University of Washington Press.

Harris, M. (1974). *Cows, pigs, wars & witches: The riddle of culture*. New York: Vintage Books.

Harris, M. (1979). *Cultural materialism: The struggle for a science of culture*. New York: Random House.

Herlihy, D. (1985). *Medieval households*. Cambridge, MA: Harvard University Press.

Herdt, G. H. (1981). *Guardians of the flutes*. New York: McGraw-Hill.

Hotvedt, M. (1983a). The cross-cultural and historical context. In R. Weg (Ed.), *Sexuality in the later years*. New York: Academic Press.

Hotvedt, M. (1983b). Gender identity and sexual orientation: The anthropological perspective. In M. Schwartz, A. Moraczewski, & J. A. Monteleone (Eds.), *Sex and gender*. St. Louis, MO: Pope John Center.

Landes, R. (1971). *The Ojibwa woman*. New York: Norton.

Levinson, D., & Malone, M. J. (1980). *Toward explaining human culture: A critical review of the findings of worldwide cross-cultural research*. New Haven, CT: HRAF Press.

Marshall, D. S. (1971). Sexual behavior in Mangaia. In D. S. Marshall & R. C. Suggs (Eds.), *Human sexual behavior*. New York: Basic Books.

McGoldrick, M. (1982). Ethnicity and family therapy: An overview. In M. McGoldrick, J. K. Pearce, & J. Giordano (Eds.), *Ethnicity and family therapy*. New York: Guilford Press.

Money, J., & Erhardt, A. (1972). *Man and woman, boy and girl*. Baltimore: Johns Hopkins University Press.

Murdock, G. P., & White, D. R. (1980). Standard cross-cultural sample. In H. Barry III & A. Schlegel (Eds.), *Cross-cultural samples and codes* (pp. 3–43). Pittsburgh, PA: University of Pittsburgh Press.

Ortner, S. B., & Whitehead, H. (Eds.) (1981). *Sexual meanings: The cultural construction of gender and sexuality*. Cambridge, MA: Cambridge University Press.

Schiefflin, E. (1976). *The sorrow of the lonely and the burning of the dancers*. Queensland, Australia: St. Martin's Press.

Schlegel, A., & Barry III, H. (1980). Adolescent initiation ceremonies: A cross-cultural code. In H. Barry III & A. Schlegel, (Eds.), *Cross-cultural codes and samples* (pp. 227–288). Pittsburgh, PA: University of Pittsburgh Press.

Simon, W., & Gagnon, J. H. (1986). Sexual scripts: Permanence and change. *Archives of Sexual Behavior, 15*(2), 97–120.

Stone, L. (1977). *The family, sex and marriage in England 1500–1800*. New York: Harper & Row.

Whitam, F. (1983). Culturally invariable properties of male homosexuality: Tentative conclusions from cross-cultural research. *Archives of Sexual Behavior, 12*(3), 207–226.

Wolf, M. (1972). *Women and the family in rural Taiwan*. Stanford, CA: Stanford University Press.

10

Social Support and Pressure and Their Impact on Adolescent Sexual Behavior

Jan E. Trost

Social support and social pressure—that is, social control—are significant for human society. We belong to groups and to society with all their norms, to which we are more or less obedient. Subsystems and their various norms can contradict each other or they can be congruent. It seems obvious that adolescents today live under a system that is infinitely more complex than adolescents of a few centuries ago. To simplify, we can say that earlier there were clear rites de passage, indicating when a child changed into an adult. For example, in some Christian societies the confirmation ceremony acted as such a rite of passage. Nowadays, at least in many Western societies, there is no such rite. The adolescent may be counted as a child until 20 years of age when it comes to buying liquor, but as an adult at 12 years of age when traveling by bus or train. Many are not considered adults until they have a college or university education or have married and had children. This is a confusing state of affairs.

In the debate about teenagers and their sexuality, parents are assumed, especially by some conservatives, to provide the norms in the family group. Parents ought to teach the youngsters social, sexual, and moral values—conveying societal norms. This presumes not only that the parents are both willing and able to do so, but also that these transmitted societal norms will be received accordingly and that the teenager in the family will value membership in the family so highly as to abide by these norms. Other social groups to which the teenager belongs (e.g., peer groups) might be sending conflicting messages and, more importantly, the teenager might receive these conflicting norms as more compelling and as more significant. If so, there would be social pressure upon the individual not to follow parental norms but to follow peer group norms.

One reason why the received norms from peer groups might be more compelling concerns the probability of sanctions. If we disregard internalized social norms—the person's own conscience—it seems obvious that sanctions from parents are less likely to be felt than sanctions from the peer group when the matter is sexuality. The parents will be seen as less likely than the peer group to know about the behavior, especially since communication about sex between parents and teenagers is inhibited, as many studies have demonstrated.

An indication of the lack of parental influence—at least with regard to sex information—is found in the American National Survey of Family Growth Cycle III from 1982 (Loewen & Leigh, 1986). When an interview sample consisting solely of females 15–17 years of age was asked where they had received information on pregnancy, 68% answered that parents had been the source. But, when they were asked what time during the month they were at greatest risk for a pregnancy, less than one third knew the correct answer. Thus, the messages from parents either were wrong or did not get through. In any case, this is an illustration of or indicator about the relative lack of importance to adolescents of their parents as a source of norms and information.

Nathanson and Becker (1986) show that, when the issue is parental and peer influence on decisions about contraception, the young women seem to obtain support from either parents or peers, representing alternative (rather than complementary) sources for the support. Their data also suggest that when parents are perceived as approving of a family planning visit, their active involvement is more likely and peer involvement less likely.

Miller et al. (1986) studied parental control and adolescent sexual behavior. They found that with very few parental rules proscribing sexual behavior, the adolescents' sexual permissiveness was high and they had more sexual intercourse than when the parental rules were more moderate. When the parental rules were perceived to be very strict, the attitudes and the behavior fell somewhere in between.

We also know that most teenagers in the United States perceive their parents as attaching a high value to premarital virginity. Yet we also know that very few youths are virgins by the time they reach 20 years of age. One indicator is that almost 20% of teenager girls in the United States will have had an abortion before reaching 20 years of age and that more than 20% have given birth before reaching that age. These figures are based on the most recently available birth and abortion statistics. If miscarriages and spontaneous abortions are included, we find that at least 50% of American girls have been pregnant by the time they reach the age of 20 years. So, the behavior does not at all fit the norms "officially" provided by the parental generation.

The age of majority in the United States is 18, and if we examine the cumulative abortion rates and birthrates for teenage girls younger than 18, we find that about 17% have had an abortion or have given birth to a child before their eighteenth birthday (Trost, 1987). Then, of course, many more (how many is not known) have had sexual intercourse and are therefore not virgins at that age.

However, as Lewin and Helmius (1986) argue, it is not helpful to concentrate on whether it is parents or peers who have the greatest influence; what is of great importance is *how* they exert their influence. Furthermore, teachers and siblings should not be forgotten, nor the influence of the mass media.

In today's complicated society, we can claim that the peer groups probably have a much higher influence than they had in earlier times. The school and the family are in many societies fairly isolated from each other.

Among the norms transmitted about contraceptive use is an indication that a girl should not use contraceptives unless she has an ongoing, steady sexual relationship. Otherwise, she would be looked upon as promiscuous or, even worse, to have planned for sexual intercourse. According to Planned Parenthood, it has become unfashionable for males to carry condoms in their wallets, to be "prepared"; however, this may change with education about the human immunodeficiency virus (HIV).

There are strong received social norms among teenage girls on the value of having a steady boyfriend. If the boyfriend wants to have sexual intercourse, and the girl does not, she might consent so as not to lose him (Trost, 1985). This, in combination with the previously mentioned social norms about contraceptives, increases the likelihood that the girl will become pregnant. Thus, we could argue that this pregnancy is not specifically a result of sexual intercourse without contraceptives, but a result of the existing received social norms within the social group of the adolescent.

In a study in the Netherlands in 1981, Nimwegen & Moors (1986) found that more than 80% of teenage boys and girls used contraception during their first sexual intercourse if this was within a stable and intimate relationship. Of those not in stable and intimate relationships, only 63% of the boys and 45% of the girls used contraceptives at the first sexual intercourse.

These data can be interpreted as relating to membership or nonmembership of the social group of the "stable dyad." Group membership, "going steady," includes more care and consideration than nonmembership does, and also more planning. In the Netherlands as well as in some other countries the social norms about contraception are un-equivocal and clear: Contraceptives should be used when pregnancy is not wanted. Contraceptives are also easily available there in contrast to some other countries. This can be illustrated by the fact that the teen-age abortion rates and birthrates are very low in the Netherlands com-pared to, for example, the United States (see Forrest, Chapter 14). Yet, we still see this pattern of contraceptive use tied to group membership. Thompson and Spanier (1978) found after path analysis of data col-lected among college students that discussion and sharing knowledge about contraception with the sexual partner fosters effective use of birth control. In their study, parents and peers did not emerge as significant contributors to contraceptive use. It should, however, be noticed that they only measured the perceived influence.

A study in the Flemish-speaking part of Belgium in 1983/84 (Geer-aert, 1986) showed that the best predictors of teenage contraceptive use were the individual's own internalized norms combined with the re-ceived norms from the partner. The influence of the peer group seemed to have very low predictive value, in contrast to some American stud-ies (Jorgenson & Sonstegard, 1984; Herold & McNamee, 1982) in which the received norms from the peer group seem to be more important. Contraceptives are more easily available and used in Belgium than in the United States. This discrepancy could be explained by the clear and strong social norm in Belgium that pregnancy should be prevented when the couple does not want a child, and that teenagers should not have children.

We assume that easy availability of contraceptives is in effect rein-forcing received social norms in favor of contraceptive use together with the sex education in schools and a relative openness toward sexuality, despite the strong influence of Catholicism in Flemish-speaking Bel-gium. The teenage birthrates are much lower in that part of the world than, for example, in the United States. No abortion rates are available in Belgium, since induced abortions are strictly prohibited; illegal abor-tion rates are not available, for obvious reasons.

It is not surprising that teenagers as well as adults some years ago overestimated the "promiscuity" among their own age group. Thus, normality in a statistical sense was misperceived. People thought that "all teenagers" had a lot of sex. Studies showed that they did not. But, according to the theorem of Thomas and Thomas (1928), what we per-ceive as real is real in its consequences; it does not matter if the percep-tion is wrong, because people act in accordance with their perceptions and not in accordance with the "objective" facts. In cases like this the perceived normality easily creates a feeling of being abnormal if one is not behaving in accordance with normality; thus the normality be-comes a received social norm to behave as normals do. A vicious circle occurs and people obey the norms, or more commonly, they pretend to do so.

We find the same with regard to condoms. Everyone "knows" that, for example, teenagers find condoms repugnant. In fact quite a few sex educators share this belief about teenagers, which makes them avoid promoting condom use. If we do not argue for condoms, the lack of recommendation acts as a received social norm enhancing the negative attitudes against condoms. We thus reinforce myths instead of fighting against them.

A more positive social norm of condom use can be conveyed in many ways. Since quite a few Swedish teenagers travel across Europe during the summertime, some regions in Sweden decided in the summer of 1986 that all those buying Eurorail cards would get a package of condoms for free when they picked up their tickets. Almost no debate followed this decision. Thus, we might claim that society tried to send a social norm to the teenager that they should protect themselves against pregnancy and against sexually transmitted diseases (STDs) if they had sexual intercourse.

The same idea is followed by RSFU, a Swedish organization similar to SIECUS or Planned Parenthood, arguing that if you want children sometime in the future, use condoms. Proper use of condoms decreases the risk for STDs, which can easily cause sterility. In 1986 the RSFU also distributed a brochure containing information about STD prevention, together with a packet of condoms, to all 18- to 24-year-old men and women in the three biggest cities of Sweden. Once again a strong positive procondom social norm was conveyed.

In the United States as we all know, sexual intercourse is shown or hinted at in many of the more popular movies and TV programs for adolescents as well as for adults. The heroes have sexual intercourse and we identify with them. So, the received message is that it is OK to have sex, even in casual relationships. At the same time, the heroes never use any contraceptives or at least they do not show any concern about protection. Thus, it is not only OK to have sexual intercourse in casual relationships, but to do so without any concern about prevention.

In Sweden, for example, many of the movies and TV programs are imported from the United States; however, this is counterbalanced by heavy advertising for contraceptives and also against unthoughtful sex in casual relationships—especially among adolescents. Commercials are shown before the regular movies at the movie theaters; none appear on TV or the radio, however. Often one of these commercials is released by the RFSU, itself one of the biggest condom sellers in Sweden.

Some time ago, I visited a Swedish movie theater with my 13-year-old daughter. One of the commercials showed a beautiful female adolescent. She played with a condom and said that she and her boyfriend had been going steady for a long time and now both wanted to have sexual intercourse. But he had to use a condom. Otherwise, she said, while blowing up the condom, he could "blow away," as she let the condom blow away. Of course, the audience laughed.

Why mention this? This is an example of how the adult society can try to implant and influence social norms among adolescents (and adults, too) about contraceptive use when having sexual intercourse and not wishing a pregnancy.

Some might interpret these messages as encouraging adolescents to have sexual intercourse or as suggesting that promiscuity is the norm. Yet such an interpretation is incorrect. We all know, unless we are ostriches, that most adolescents have sex before their teenage years are over, regardless of the society's norm with regard to abstinence (see the data shown above and also evidence presented in Chapter 14 by Forrest).

Adult society might transmit social norms against premarital sexual intercourse, but often the received message is a utopian norm, saying what should ideally happen or not happen. The behavioral norm as received can be quite different and is likely to be perceived by adolescents as adult hypocrisy.

We often hear about the "generation gap," yet among the values of adolescents and their parents are many similarities. They both highly value the dyad and reject promiscuity (see, for example, Lewin & Helmius, 1986). Youngsters as well as adults are inclined toward love and sexuality in combination and in dyadic relationships. The peer group frequently reflects the same values as the adult society does. Much of the social pressure or support—the social control—occurs among the adolescents themselves and builds upon the societal values present also among the adults.

Is the social pressure on adolescents concerning their sexuality and the support provided them in any way systematic? Maybe, maybe not. It seems, however, from data presented above that teachers, physicians, and other professionals are efficient in transmitting knowledge (when they are able and allowed to do so) but that they do not efficiently transmit values or attitudes that influence behavior.

Many studies seem to indicate that parents are similar to teachers and physicians in these respects. For example, it seems unlikely that parents, who watch and enjoy soap operas involving lots of premarital and extramarital sex, would be taken seriously when they provide their adolescent children with sexually restrictive norms.

The mass media, as hinted at earlier, also play an important role, although we should not assume that mass media by themselves are powerful in directing sexual behavior and values. What is printed, what is said on the radio, what is shown on TV are all "truths," especially when discussed and combined with the social reality; others (parents, friends, etc.) read, listen, and look.

Norms transmitted by negatively associated out-groups, real or fictitious, are likely to be either not received or not obeyed. Norms sent by valued in-groups, fictitious or real, are likely to be received correctly and also obeyed. Therefore, in societies or subsocieties with consistent social norms, obedience will be more extensive than when there is a lack of consistency or consensus. In the Netherlands it is accepted that adolescents have a sexual life, sex education is relatively prevalent, and contraceptives are easily available; and the teenage birthrates and abortion rates are very low.

The types of groups to which adolescents belong are numerous. Among the more important ones, with regard to norms, are probably peer groups, parent–child groups, and sibling groups. As mentioned earlier, the society at large also provides many norms. These various groups can provide similar norms, congruent norms, or conflicting norms.

It is trivial but not banal to stress that the male and the female, while being members of a dyad, also belong to separate parent–child groups, sibling groups, and often separate peer groups. Thus, the male and the female each can easily be exposed to different sets of norms. It is also important that these other groups are almost never physically present during the intimate meetings of the female and the male in the dyad, especially in circumstances suitable for sexual intercourse. Thus, the other groups can only indirectly "control" the behavior of the two in the dyad.

Traditionally we look at norms as directing or controlling attitudes and behavior. However, when it comes to these elements we should recognize that attitudes build on cognitions and that we also have sexual drives. It is often assumed that there is a direct link between cognition, attitudes, and behavior, but this connection is seldom perfect.

Let us take condoms as an example. As mentioned earlier, a common belief about condoms is that they reduce erotic sensitivity and that they have a high failure rate. An often quoted figure for the failure rate of condoms is about 10%. The basis for this figure is the Pearl index, which states that for 100 women during 1 year using condoms, there will be ten pregnancies. The 10% figure is outdated, stemming as it does from the 1940s when condoms were much lower in quality than they are now; yet this is the figure quoted in most scientific as well as journalistic publications. With a consistent and skillful use of condoms, the Pearl index should be much lower. Since the cognition or the belief is that there is a high failure rate, the attitude toward condoms is steered in a negative direction. With this negative attitude toward condoms, the likelihood for using them is further lowered.

Even if the attitude toward condoms is positive and the social cognition is that they are safe, both protecting against unwanted pregnancies and STDs, the behavior can be inconsistent. One reason is that the sex drive can overwhelm in a specific situation. Another one is that the two members of the couple might have different attitudes—one being positive toward condom use and the other negative. Even if society argues for abstinence among adolescents, it is unlikely that abstinence will be the result. The sex drive still exists, and if the cognition is that there is very little likelihood of pregnancy or transmission of STDs, the sex drive may well take over—especially if the norms of society and (for example) peer groups conflict, and the norms might steer the attitude in a sex-positive direction.

Finally, it seems reasonable to conclude that if society's aim is abstinence, the norms should consistently counteract the effects of the sex drive. History shows, however, that attempts in that direction fail. Furthermore, we do not know of any society in modern times in which all the efforts pull in the same direction; the case of TV soap operas is one glaring example. If society realizes that the sex drive is strong and cannot be inhibited by social influences, the norms have to be directed at careful behavior—that is, encouraging use of safe and effective contraception. The current concern about the acquired immune deficiency syndrome (AIDS) increases the likelihood that society's efforts will be directed toward advocating safe sex and condom use as well as abstinence and monogamy. This message, aimed by the mass media at the general population, will inevitably be received by adolescents.

References

Geraert, A. (1988). Prediction factors of contraceptive behaviour of single girls aged 15–19. In H. Moors and J. Schoorl (Eds.), *Lifestyles, Contraception, and Parenthood*. Brussels: NIDI/CBGS.

Herold, E. S., & McNamee, J. E. (1982). An explanatory model of contraceptive use among young single women. *The Journal of Sex Research, 18*, 289–304.

Jorgenson, S. R., and Sonstegard, J. S. (1984). Predicting adolescent sexual and contraceptive behavior: An application and test of the Fishbein model. *Journal of Marriage and the Family, 46*, 43–55.

Lewin, B., & Helmius, G. (1986). Ungdom, karlek och sex. Stockholm: Norstedts.

Loewen, I. R., & Leigh, G. K. (1986). Timing of transition to sexual intercourse: A multivariate analysis of white adolescent females ages 15–17. Paper presented at the annual meeting of the Society for the Scientific Study of Sex, St. Louis, MO.

Miller, B. C., McCoy, J. K., Olson, T. D., & Wallace, C. M. (1986). Parental discipline and control attempts in relation to adolescent sexual behavior and attitudes. *Journal of Marriage and the Family, 48*, 503–512.

Nathanson, C. A., & Becker, M. H. (1986). Family and peer influence on obtaining a method of contraception. *Journal of Marriage and the Family, 48*, 513–525.

Nimwegen, N. and Moors, H. (1988). The social context of sexual and contraceptive behaviour of adolescents in the Netherlands. In H. Moors and J. Schoorl (Eds.), *Lifestyles, Contraception, and Parenthood*. Brussels: NIDI/CBGS.

Thomas, W. I., & Thomas, D. S. (1928). *The child in America*. New York: A. A. Knopf.

Thompson, L., & Spanier, G. B. (1978). Influence of parents, peers, and partners on the contraceptive use of college men and women. *Journal of Marriage and the Family, 40*, 481–492.

Trost, J. (1985). Contraception for teenagers; Swedish solutions. *Transaction/Society, 23*, 44–48.

Trost, J. (1987). Tonarsgraviditerer och aggregerade data. *Nordisk Sexologi, 5*, 71–74.

11

Changing Influences on Adolescent Sexuality over the Past Forty Years

Gail Elizabeth Wyatt

I don't think anyone with a rational mind is going to say that as of a given date there will be no more teen-age sexual activity.

(Faye Wattleton, 1986)

Faye Wattleton, the president of Planned Parenthood Federation of America, appears to have a realistic appraisal of adolescent sexual behavior. Indeed, according to U.S. statistics for 1982, almost half of unmarried female adolescents 15–19 years old were reported to be sexually active (NSFG, 1984). Similarly, as of 1978, slightly over half of U.S. unmarried males 15–19 years old were sexually active (Alan Guttmacher Institute, 1981). There appears to be growing acceptance of the idea that sexuality will begin in adolescence (Caplow, 1982; Elliott & Morse, 1985; Robinson, King, & Balswick, 1972; Sorenson, 1973; Wyatt, 1989a).

The increasing numbers of sexually active adolescents give credit to the fact that adolescent sexuality is not a phenomenon of the 1980s. One has only to read selected writings of William Shakespeare, biblical stories, or folklore to be reminded of the trials and tribulations of adolescents and their love interests over the centuries. However, historically, marriage often occurred at earlier ages than it does today. According to the U.S. Census Bureau, the mean age of marriage is 23 years, and the age is slightly greater for some ethnic groups. For example, the mean ages for white and black females are 23 years and 25 years of age, respectively.[1] Mean ages for white and black males are 25 to 27 years, respectively (National Center for Health Statistics, unpublished data, 1983). Consequently, our society appears to be at a loss to understand how to cope with adolescent sexuality and the accompanying problems of early pregnancy outside marriage. While North America's predominant moral and religious principles do not condone sex outside of marriage, we also recognize that adolescents have not yet had the time to complete the level of education necessary to maintain a life-style in a technological society. Furthermore, they often lack the emotional maturity to assume parenting and committed relationship responsibilities. Apart from and sometimes even with their families' support, they do not have the financial resources to sustain themselves until they complete their training or educational goals and mature into individuals who are ready to assume the responsibilities that adulthood requires.

Thus, we are faced with the challenge of educating our society about adolescent sexuality, with the purpose of identifying the aspects of our families and environment that place adolescents at risk for even *earlier* sexual activity than would be desired. Research has demonstrated that adolescents are beginning their sexual activity earlier now than was the case with those who reached adolescence after World War II (Wyatt, Peters, & Guthrie, 1988a,b). With these realities facing us, social scientists and policymakers need to understand the influences on adolescent sexual activity to determine if these influences are having a greater impact on our youth than they once did.

In order to examine if and where changes exist, the first task is to determine what we already know about adolescent sexuality.

Research on Adolescent Sexuality

Black and white females are the most common subjects in research on adolescents. Although some research with Latino women has been conducted (Becerra & Felder, 1985; Darabi & Ortiz, 1987), it primarily concerns their reproductive behavior. Males are less frequently subjects in sex research because of difficulties in recruiting samples representing a range across demographic characteristics that may influence male sexual socialization and sexual behavior (Kinsey, Pomeroy, & Martin, 1948). Although sex research has ethnic and gender biases, the disproportionate numbers of studies that focus on black and white females is at least a beginning attempt to understand some of the pressures that adolescents face today regarding sexual activity.

In this chapter we review the current knowledge regarding adolescent sexual activity, including the limitations of existing research and the methodologies used to obtain data, as well as some of the factors known to influence sexual activity, such as the social environment of adolescents and their families, the decision-making process that adolescents use at the time of sexual activity, and their sexual abuse histories. Evidence from the literature on these issues is compared with that obtained from a recent study by the author.

The Wyatt Study

This chapter differs from others that discuss other aspects and consequences of adolescent sexual activity based on national surveys (see Chapters 13, Hofferth; and 14, Forrest). Much of the information in this chapter is drawn from the recent epidemiological study involving a sample of black and white women whose demographic characteristics varied in income level, education, and marital status, but were comparable across ethnic groups. The sample was stratified by age (18–36 years) in order to recruit women whose mothers reached adolescence at varying times in our society, when premarital virginity was both more and less of a social requirement. Additionally, the age criteria excluded women who required parental consent to discuss their sexual experiences. Los Angeles County was the geographic target area from which participants would be selected because black and white women showing the desired range of demographic characteristics resided there. In order to ensure that women's early socialization experiences would have occurred in the United States, women who had spent more than half of their first 12 years of life in another country were excluded. Women also identified their own ethnicity.[1] The actual quotas were based on the population of African-American women in Los Angeles County, ranging in education, marital status, and the presence of children.

Subjects were obtained by random-digit dialing of telephone prefixes in Los Angeles County combined with four randomly generated numbers. While 11,834 telephone numbers were generated, 6562 were found to be unusable numbers. The remaining 5272 gave access to 1348 households in which a woman resided. Of the women who met the demographic criteria, 709 women agreed to participate and 266 refused. There were 335 women who terminated telephone contact before information regarding their demographic characteristics could be obtained. Excluding those women, there was a 27% refusal rate.[2] Although the latter refusal rate is higher than studies including nonprobability samples, the strength of this sample rests on its comparable demographic characteristics, which allow for meaningful cross-ethnic group comparisons. In order to meet the desired quotas of women by demographic characteristics described above, the first 248 women were interviewed: 126 African-American women and 122 white American women. Because of the discrepancy between median incomes for blacks and whites (U.S. Bureau of the Census, 1980), it was not possible to match both samples on the income level. However, the range extended from less than $5000 to more than $50,000 per year, with comparability between groups except at the very low income levels. Of those women reporting less than $5000 per year, 80% were African-American and 20% were white women. However, these discrepancies between groups were also found in Los Angeles County statistics for income, by ethnic group.

The numbers of interviewed women in the quota categories were compared by the same demographic characteristics with 1980 census data for Afro-American women in Los Angeles County, using a chi-square (x^2) test as a measure of agreement. The results, together with the randomness of the random-digit dialing method of selection, support the general representativeness of the sample based on the quotas.

In order to allow for both within- and across-ethnic group comparisons, the quotas set for white women were selected to match those for Afro-American women. However, as a consequence, the sample of white women did not match the population distribution of these characteristics for white women in Los Angeles County as well as they did for their Afro-American peers. However, when weighted estimates were made, adjusting for the discrepancies, the moderation distortions could be adjusted for, with little loss of efficiency in estimating population averages based on quotas for white women.

When subjects agreed to participate, they were interviewed face to face by one of four highly trained and experienced women who matched the subject's ethnicity. Interrater reliability was established throughout data collection and averaged .90.

While other ethnic groups are represented in the national samples described in the Hofferth and Forrest chapters (Chapters 13 and 14), their demographic characteristics are often not comparable enough to differentiate the influence of ethnicity from critical variables such as income, number of parents in the home, or women's educational background—all of which might influence sexual practices. Similarly, most research on women's sexual experiences rarely delineates those that are consensual from those that occurred as a result of sexual abuse. This chapter covers a range of environmental, socializing, experiential, and individual decision-making variables that may influence adolescent sexual activity.

In a structured interview, women in the Wyatt sample were asked a series of questions about their family background, sexual socialization, sexual behaviors, and decisions to become sexually active. Their retrospective recollections about the circumstances of their first intercourse allow us to discuss this experience at a time in their lives (adulthood) when it is socially more acceptable to discuss their adolescent sexual activity. Adolescent subjects are often reticent to discuss their sexuality because of parental influences, and these concerns can sometimes interfere with a full disclosure of sexual attitudes and behaviors. The most powerful argument for use of adult women's retrospective recollections of their adolescent sexual activity is that it facilitates the examination of the long-term outcomes of early sexual activity with respect to women's sexual and psychological functioning (Wyatt, 1989b). Far too often the results of cross-sectional studies identify a problem but fail to reexamine its long-range effects. If our concern as researchers, clinicians, and policymakers is that adolescent sexual activity has pervasive long-range effects on women, then perhaps the use of adult samples will be helpful in developing models from which we can better understand youngsters who are currently adolescents and offer prevention programs to offset problems identified with adult samples. Limitations in retrospective data have been noted (Garobalo & Hindelang, 1977). Techniques were utilized to minimize response pattern biases (Schuman & Presser, 1981) and the demand characteristics of face-to-face interview procedures (Gelles, 1978), in order to minimize the inaccurate location of events in time (Huizinga & Elliott, 1984). The use of anchor points to delineate a specific time period also facilitated the recall of retrospective data (Loftus & Marburger, 1983). Sex research on women has identified ethnic differences in the onset of and preference for sexual behaviors (Kinsey et al., 1953; Wyatt, 1989b; Zelnik & Kantner, 1972, 1980). The data from Afro-American and white women, with comparable demographic characteristics, will allow for a reexamination of some of the findings of previous research (Wyatt, 1985). Thus, it is possible to contrast the two groups and to examine why ethnic differences occur when they do, as well as to examine the group as a whole.

What We Know About Adolescent Sexual Activity

Kinsey et al. (1953) were first to provide empirical documentation regarding premarital intercourse. They found that nearly 50% of their white, middle-class sample of women had intercourse before age 20. Gebhard et al. (1958) used the Kinsey data to show that a stratified sample of black females engaged in intercourse earlier than whites. By age 20, 82% of single black women reportedly had had premarital intercourse. Hunt (1974) and others (Fox & Inazu, 1980) confirmed this finding years later. However, some studies describe black adolescents as disapproving of premarital sex (Zelnik, Kantner, & Ford, 1981; Yankelovich, 1974). Others specifically describe black adolescents as disapproving of premarital sex before age 18 (Furstenberg, 1976). The reasons for these discrepant findings between attitudes and behavior may be due to the variation in the samples selected, the age of the subjects, and methods of data collection.

As mentioned earlier, more recent research suggests that premarital intercourse is occurring at younger ages (Caplow, 1982; Elliott & Morse,

1985; Robinson, King, & Balswick, 1972; Sorenson, 1973; Zelnik & Kantner, 1972) and differs by ethnic group. In their most recent study, Zelnik & Kantner (1980) found the average age of first intercourse to be 16.4 for white adolescents and 15.5 for black adolescents. As of 1971, 75% of never-married black teens reportedly had had intercourse before age 18, as compared to 40% of white teens.

However, while the trend toward earlier sexual intercourse appears to continue into the 1980s, ethnic differences are diminishing. For example, differences in the initial ages of onset of intercourse reported for 1971 had lessened by 1974. Sexual activity appears to be on the rise for white teenagers (Chilman, 1976), and virtually all of the increase in sexual intercourse between 1976 and 1979 was attributable to the statistics for never-married white adolescents (Zelnik & Kantner, 1980). Other evidence is confirming the reality of this pattern of increasingly early sexual activity among adolescents (Fox & Inazu, 1980; Elliott & Morse, 1985; Wyatt, 1987).

However, it is difficult to draw conclusions about ethnic differences from most of the research that has been conducted. When comparisons of sexual behaviors are made by ethnic groups, critical information about the demographic comparability of black and white samples is often not included (Belcastro, 1985; Kinsey et al., 1953; Gebhard et al., 1958; Reiss, 1967, 1971; Weis, 1983). Consequently, some of the results may be due less to ethnicity and more to factors such as the socioeconomic status (SES), marital status of the parents of origin (Wyatt, 1989b), or other regional or urban/rural differences. There is a need to control for the demographic characteristics of samples that have been identified as influencing sexual activity, as the Wyatt study has attempted to do.

Age of First Coitus in the Wyatt Sample

For this research, age of first coitus was examined in two ways: by mean differences between groups and by individual ages of onset (Wyatt, 1989a). First coitus as a result of a rape or other form of sexual abuse was not included, and only women's age of voluntary coitus was reported for the 245 sexually active women in the sample (for further discussion see Wyatt, 1989a). Afro-American women's mean age of first coitus was 16.7, white women's mean was 17.2, and the overall mean across ethnicity for the group was 16.9 years. No significant difference between ethnic groups was noted ($p > .05$).

It was also possible to examine age of first coitus by year, and Table 11-1 presents the cumulative percentages. In this sample, age of first coitus ranged from 10 to 27 years of age.

It was apparent that there were marginal numbers of women who reported first intercourse before age 13, and about 13% of both ethnic groups reported first intercourse at 14 or younger. Beginning at 15 years

Table 11-1
Cumulative Percentages of Age of First Voluntary Intercourse for
Afro-American and White Women

| | CUMULATIVE PERCENTAGE | | | |
| | AFRO-AMERICANS ($n = 121$) | | WHITES ($n = 116$) | |
AGE OF FIRST INTERCOURSE	Number	Percentage	Number	Percentage
10	1	0.8	0	
11	0	0.8	0	
12	2	0.2	1	0.9
13	4	6	4	0.4
14	9	13	11	14
15	22	31	11	23
16	20	48	18	39
17	23	67	15	52
18	18	82	31	79
19	11	91	14	91
20	3	93	2	92
21	5	98	7	98
22	1	98	0	98
23	1	99	0	98
24	0	99	0	98
25	1	100	0	98
26	0	100	1	99
27	0	100	1	100

of age, the proportion of women who had experienced first intercourse began to differ for the two ethnic groups. While for African-American women, 31% reported having intercourse at 15 or younger, only 23% of the white women reported intercourse during the same period—a span of 8 percentage points. At age 16, the gap is maintained; almost half of the Afro-American women (48%) experienced intercourse as compared to only 39% of white women. It was at age 17 or younger that about half of the white women reported first intercourse (52%), while 67% of Afro-American women had reported first sex. Beginning at age 18, the gap began to narrow for both groups of women, with almost 80% of both Afro-Americans and whites reporting first intercourse. By age 19, 91% of both groups had experienced first sex.

Table 11-2 compares other available statistics regarding age at first coitus to those found in our study. At first inspection, the differences noted confirm that adolescent sexual activity appears to be occurring at younger ages. However, some caution should be exercised in interpreting these differences. The women in our sample were adolescents

Table 11-2
A Comparison of Three Studies Reporting the Age of First Coitus with the Wyatt Study

AGE	PERCENTAGE FIRST COITUS			
	KINSEY ET AL. (1953) GEBHARD ET AL. (1958)		WYATT	
	White	*Black*	*White*	*Black*
Before Age 20	50	82	92	93
	ZELNIK & KANTNER (1972, 1980)		WYATT	
	White	*Black*	*White*	*Black*
At or Before Age 18	40	75	78	82
	NSFG (1984) *Adolescents*[a]		WYATT *Adolescents*[a]	
Age 15–19	50		75	

[a]No ethnic breakdown.

during the years between the 1960s and the 1980s. Other studies, such as National Survey of Family Growth (1984), include adolescents who were interviewed in the mid-1980s. Thus, if the age at first coitus were decreasing, one would expect that rates of first coitus for adolescents in the NSFG study would be higher than those for this study. One possible explanation for the apparently younger age of onset in our study is that the three other studies cited in Table 11-2 all obtained national samples, albeit some were highly stratified (Kinsey et al., 1953; Gebhard et al., 1958). Our study included a random stratified sample of two ethnic groups, 18–36 years of age, in Los Angeles County. It is always possible that Californians may begin sexual activity at younger ages, but there are no data to support this notion. There are obviously a variety of methodological variations between studies, regional and age differences, as well as the inclusion of a wide range of ethnic groups in the samples, which may account for differences in sexual activity.

In summary, the age of first coitus, which is considered to establish reinforcement contingencies for future sexual experiences (Byrne, 1977), appears to be occurring at earlier ages and ethnic differences appear to be diminishing. These trends suggest that factors other than ethnicity may be more helpful in predicting the early onset of sexual behaviors.

Other Aspects of Adolescent Sexual Behavior

The preferences for and frequency of sexual behaviors have also received some attention in research with the two ethnic groups of concern here (Kinsey et al., 1953; Hunt, 1974). Zelnik and Kantner's study (1972, 1980) of 15- to 19-year-old adolescents revealed that (1) blacks have intercourse less frequently per month than whites; (2) more blacks than whites report not having intercourse in the month prior to the interview; (3) fewer blacks than whites report having sexual relations six or more times per month (7.6% versus 16.1%); and (4) 16% of white adolescents have had four or more sexual partners, as compared with 11% of black adolescents. The variation in frequency of sexual contact was also confirmed in more recent research (Belcastro, 1985; Elliott & Morse, 1985).

Interestingly, these ethnic differences in the frequency of coitus and numbers of sexual partners have received less attention than age at first coitus. In the Wyatt study the numbers of sexual partners that women recall averaged eight but ranged from one to over three hundred during adolescence. There were significantly fewer Afro-American women (65%) who recalled having more than one sexual partner during adolescence, as compared to 34% of their white peers ($\chi^2 = 12.34$; df 4; $n = 151$; $p < .02$). Similarly, the length of these sexual relationships ranged from one long-term relationship lasting a year or more to numerous brief, onetime encounters. Of those women who reported brief encounters with their sexual partners, 70% were white as compared to 30% of Afro-Americans ($\chi^2 = 12.73$; df 3; $n = 148$; $p < .01$). These findings confirm previous reports that there may be a more moderate rate of sexual activity among black than among white women during adolescence. More research needs to be conducted on the rate of adolescent sexual activity to determine its effects on other sexual or psychological outcomes.

Family and Behavioral Factors Influencing Sexual Activity

In this section, family and environmental factors that have been identified as contributing to early sexual activity will be reviewed.

Some of the differences in the early sexual activity of adolescents reported by Zelnik and Kantner (1972) have been related to the following family characteristics: (1) Black teens younger than age 18 in families of low SES are more likely to have sexual experience than higher SES blacks; and (2) 50% of adolescents whose fathers have only an elementary-school education have had some sexual experience. When the father was college educated, this proportion was only 37%. The relationship was not as consistent for mother's education. Interestingly, as the age of the subject (between 15 and 19) increased for blacks, adolescents tended to have fewer sexual experiences, but the inverse relationship was true for their white peers.

Some of the literature (e.g., Kinsey et al., 1953; Zelnik & Kantner, 1972) has described the family constellation of women who engaged in early sexual activity, with apparently contradictory findings. Single parents tend to offer more information about sex education and to be more permissive about the sexual behavior of their children (Fox, 1981). Additionally, other studies have found that women who grew up in single-parent (female-headed) families are more likely to be sexually experienced and to become pregnant (Akpom, Akpom, & Davis, 1976; Barglow et al., 1968; Zelnik & Kantner, 1972). The relationship between educational information conveyed by single parents and the sexual behavior of adolescents is unclear. Another area of investigation that may need to be explored is the sexual behavior of single parents. The frequency and nature of dating and coital patterns that youngsters may observe in single-parent homes may have more impact than the verbal information that is conveyed.

The differences found in sexual behavior are not accounted for totally by examining ethnicity, SES, what parents teach their children or about sex, family interactions, or structure. In studies examining these factors, the populations studied range from college students to clinic and community samples (Akpom, Akpom, & Davis, 1976; Barglow et al., 1968; Zelnik & Kantner, 1972, 1980). More than likely the black samples included in these studies are either the well educated or at or below the poverty level (Fox, 1981; Fox & Inazu, 1980; Staples, 1973). Consequently, the effects of these family variables were reexamined in our study, in order to confirm the above-noted findings employing a more diverse sample with regard to education and income.

Socioeconomic Status and Family Characteristics—the Wyatt Study

First, the Hollingshead and Redlich Two Factor Index of Social Position (1957), used to obtain SES for the family of origin of both ethnic groups, was found to be significantly associated with age of first intercourse (analysis of variance [ANOVA], $F. = 2.28$; df 9,209; $p < .05$). Daughters of professional and semiprofessional families categorized by the Hollingshead and Redlich SES classification tended to be older when first experiencing voluntary intercourse (means ranging from 18.3 to 18.8 years) than those from families at the lower end of the classification system, in the skilled and unskilled professions (where means of first coitus ranged from 16.4 to 17.3 years). This finding supports that of Zelnik and Kantner (1972), but for *both* ethnic groups.

In an attempt to replicate some of these findings relating to family constellation, the number of parenting figures and the consistency of their presence in the home of origin were examined.

No relationship was found between the number or sex of parenting figures that women reported in their home of origin at or prior to age 12, and the age at first coitus. However, the relationship between number of parenting figures during adolescence and age of first coitus was significant ($F = 2.76$; df 7,229; $p < .01$). Women who lived with either biological or stepparents during adolescence (13–17 years) experienced first coitus 1 year later (mean age, 17.2 years) than those women who lived with single- or multiple-parent (i.e., one biological parent and other relatives) families ($F = 3.36$; df 3,229; $p < .05$), whose mean age at first coitus was 16 years.

When we consider consistency of parenting, we found 159 women whose single-parent, two-parent, or multiple-parenting figures were consistently in the home of origin prior to age 18, and 78 women whose parenting figures changed during those years. Consistent parenting, regardless of the *number* of parents, was also found to delay significantly first intercourse from age 16 to 17 years ($F = 4.90$; df 3,233; $p < .001$).

These findings suggest that homes with consistent parenting as well as those with two adults may provide more supervision of adolescent activities than those in which parenting figures were changing at such a critical time in women's sexual development. The lack of ethnic differences noted in analyses involving the number or consistency of parenting figures suggests that parental supervision may be important in delaying adolescent sexual activity, regardless of ethnicity.

The Influence of Prior Sexual Behaviors on First Coitus

What effect do other sexual behaviors have on the occurrence of first intercourse? These prior behaviors, and the feelings that emanate from them, may motivate adolescents to experience further sexual activity, including coitus (Weis, 1983).

Subjects were divided into three groups according to the age of necking (defined as kissing and touching from the neck up), those who began necking at age 13 or younger, at 14 and 15, and at 16 or older. Age of necking and ethnicity were independent variables and age of first coitus was the dependent variable in an ANOVA. It was anticipated that early onset of necking would be associated with early onset of intercourse, and that was found to be true ($F = 5.09$; df 5,231; $p < .001$). However, ethnic differences were not established. The mean ages of first coitus for those who engaged in necking at age 13 and younger, as well as those at 14 and 15 years (16.5 and 16.7 years, respectively), were significantly younger than for those who began necking at 16 or older (18.2 years) $p < .0001$). When adjusted for multiple comparisons (Miller, 1984), the significance was maintained.

Age of onset of petting, defined as kissing and touching breasts and genitals, was divided into 15 and younger and 16 and older. The AN-OVA was highly significant ($F = 8.39$; df 3,233; $p < .001$) because of differences in age of petting ($F = 22.73$; df 1,233; $p < .0001$). The means of age at first intercourse for the two petting groups were as follows: 16.4 years for women who began petting at age 15 or younger; and 17.8 years for women who began petting at age 16 or older ($p < .0001$). Once again, no ethnic differences were noted. The relationship between age of petting and onset of intercourse showed similar patterns when examined within each ethnic group.

Early necking and petting behavior therefore seems to contribute to early intercourse. While all of the factors reviewed have been found to influence the age of coitus, more research with African-American and white females with varying demographic characteristics needs to be conducted, in order to identify which factors, family or behavioral experiences contribute most to age of first coitus. Interestingly, when family and behavioral aspects of women's lives are examined, they tend to diminish differences between ethnic groups. This trend suggests that similar contributing factors appear to be influencing adolescent sexual behavior, regardless of ethnicity.

Adolescent Decision-Making About Sexual Activity

In spite of family influences, there are still a variety of individual decisions that have to be made prior to the onset of sexual activity. We asked the women in our sample about their expectations of their first sexual experience, whether or not coitus met those expectations, and finally, the reason that women engaged in first intercourse. For purposes of examining the influence of age on sexual decision-making, subjects were divided into two groups according to their age at first coitus: those who became sexually active before and after age 18, the age of legal status in the United States. The dichotomy of age reveals some interesting differences in decision-making prior to first coitus.

WOMEN WHO HAD FIRST COITUS BEFORE AGE 18

There were 151 women who had intercourse before age 18. They were asked if, before having intercourse for the first time, they had ever considered it and decided against it. If so, they were asked what their most influential reason was for *not* having intercourse at that time. For those women who recalled an experience of that kind (47% of the total), some interesting ethnic differences emerged. Fear of parental disapproval about becoming sexually active or fear of pregnancy was expressed significantly more often by African-American women (66%) than their white peers (34%) $\chi^2 = 11.38$; df 5; $n = 243$; $p < 0.4$). One Afro-American woman recalled: "I was afraid of getting pregnant. How could you explain it [pregnancy] to your mother after having promised you wouldn't do that [have sex before marriage]?"

Other reasons for thinking about and deferring coitus included acknowledgment of religious and social proscriptions, personal reasons, such as "I wasn't mature enough to assume the consequences of sex," or a lack of knowledge about sex.

Women were asked: "Before having intercourse, what did you think it would be like?" Over 45% of all women anticipated that the experience would be pleasant and enjoyable. Of those who anticipated an unpleasant experience, significantly more were Afro-American women (75%) than white (25%). However, the finding only reached marginal significance ($\chi^2 = 7.74$; df 3; $n = 151$; $p < .05$]. It is interesting that although at least one half of women had negative expectations of first coitus, they nevertheless became sexually active before the age of 18.

When women who experienced first sex before age 18 were asked if their first time met their expectations, just over 71% of both groups of women responded "no." In order to clarify the relationship between expectations of first coitus and their subjective rating of the experience after coitus occurred, responses to both of these questions were examined in relation to one another. For those who anticipated pleasure, 56% of Afro-American women (Fisher's Exact Test, $p < .05$) and 80% of their white peers (Fisher's Exact Test, $p < .009$) responded that intercourse did not meet those expectations. Of all responses to this question, 23% of Afro-American women and 17% of white women anticipated and experienced an unpleasant and/or painful first coitus. Although African-American women may have been slightly more realistic about what to expect, this finding also suggests that women who become sexually active prior to age 18 may not have realistic expectations of what first intercourse is like.

Finally, women were asked the reasons for having intercourse for the first time. Significantly more (79%) Afro-American women responded that they were "curious" about intercourse as opposed to 21% of their white peers ($\chi^2 = 11.7$; df 4; $p < .02$]. The three other most common responses to this question were partner or peer pressure to have sex, being in love, and feeling "old enough'" or ready to relinquish one's virginity (see Table 11-3). Although curiosity was rated as the most influential reason for first sex among Afro-American women, it was fourth among white women. Peer and partner pressure was rated as most influential for white women. One reason for these women endorsing curiosity and pressure by peers or the first partner as the main reasons for first sex may have been the lack of information about sex-

Table 11-3
Reasons for First Voluntary Intercourse Before Age 18

	PERCENTAGES OF TOP FOUR REASONS					
	AFRICAN-AMERICAN WOMEN			WHITE AMERICAN WOMEN		
REASONS	Number	Percentage	Order	Number	Percentage	Order
Curiosity— "I wondered what it was like."	31	39	1	8	13	4
Partner or Peer Pressure	20	25	2	19	32	1
"I loved him."	13	16	3	13	22	2
"I wanted to have sex."	11	14	4	12	20	3

uality that they received. In this sample, fewer than 37% received pro-hibitive information before age 12 from their parents about premarital sex, and only 60% received comparable information during adoles-cence. Consequently, those who were sexually active at or before age 18 seemed less influenced by parental opposition than by pressure from someone else or by curiosity about the experience. Individual readiness was almost the last reason for first sex for both ethnic groups.

WOMEN WHO HAD FIRST COITUS AT OR AFTER AGE 18

There were ninety-seven women who had first coitus at or after age 18. Both ethnic groups responded in a similar fashion. Interestingly, when asked if they had ever considered intercourse and decided against it, only three women answered "yes." In other words, when consid-ering having sex, the majority of this sample did so. Perhaps at age 18 or older, women are more definitive about the fact that if placed in the proper situation, they were going to be sexually active.

In response to what they thought the experience would be like, over half (57%) reported that they expected first coitus to be pleasant (10% more than the group having coitus before age 18). Those anticipating a negative experience decreased 10% in the older group, as compared to the earlier onset group.

When asked, "Did first intercourse meet your expectations?", 60% of the women responded negatively, in a similar fashion to their younger sexually active peers. We examined the expectations of first coitus with perceptions of the experience itself, but, in contrast to women who were sexually active at an earlier age, those who anticipated pleasure or pain usually experienced just those feelings. These findings suggest that when women 18 years or older have first sex, their experiences more closely meet their expectations.

Finally, the reasons for first intercourse were more evenly distributed among curiosity (26%), being in love (28%), and being ready to experience coitus (29%). However, more white women (79%) were in love with their first partners than their African-American peers (21%) [$x^2 = 14.99$; df 4; $n = 86$; $p < .005$].

In summary, women who considered having first coitus before age 18, but decided not to, tended to be more strongly inhibited by fear of pregnancy or parental disapproval as a deterrent to sex, than women who had coitus at or after age 18. When the older group of women considered first coitus, they were more likely to experience it. Both age groups anticipated that intercourse would be painful, especially women who were younger and those who were Afro-American. However, first intercourse appeared to be more of a disappointment to women whose first coitus occurred before age 18. Women who were older apparently experienced what they expected. Perhaps, as women mature, and are exposed to more factual information about first coitus, they become more aware of what the first experience entails. Afro-American women appeared to be slightly more realistic about intercourse and the discomfort that is sometimes experienced the first time.

In spite of their realism or lack of it, curiosity was the most common reason for experimenting with first coitus for young African-American women. Apparently, expectations of pain or discomfort did not outweigh other reasons for engaging in the first experience. For white women, pressure from girlfriends or from a partner to have sex was the most influential reason for first coitus (see Udry, Chapter 5). However, regardless of ethnicity, women who were at least 18 years old or older appeared to be influenced more by their own feelings or readiness to have sex than younger women. These findings suggest that younger women's sexual decision-making may be more affected by external reasons (e.g., lack of information or partner/peer pressure) than such decision-making by women who are at least age 18 when they experience first sex.

Sexual Abuse as It Influences Adolescent Sexual Activity

Finally, not all sexual experiences of adolescents, and particularly those initiating them into sex, are by their own consent. There are two reasons why sexual abuse experienced before age 18 is being included in this review of factors that have influenced adolescent sexuality. First, some research has suggested that black women may be more at risk for child sexual abuse than white women (Katz & Mazur, 1979). Second, the research that links sexual abuse experienced before age 18 and its relationship to later sexual patterns and problems is fairly well established (Benward & Densen-Gerber, 1975; Briere, 1984; Brown, 1979; Courtois, 1979; DeYoung, 1982; Herman, 1981; James & Meyerding, 1977; Jehu, Gazan, & Klassen, 1984/85; Meiselman, 1978; Silbert & Pines, 1981; Tsai & Wagner, 1978).

Thus, it is also important to review what we have learned about ethnic differences in child sexual abuse and the influence of these traumatic experiences on adolescent sexual functioning. Most of this research has had many methodological and sampling limitations (Wyatt, 1989b); and until recently, there have been questions regarding whether the sexual patterns, prostitution, or dysfunctional problems reported were in fact related to some of the traumatic sexual experiences or to a myriad of other family and psychological problems that these female victims also reported. Additionally, few of the studies cited above specifically isolate sexual activity during adolescence. They usually focus instead on sexual patterns established during adulthood (age 18 or older), without any mention of whether the patterns began during adolescence.

Some recent studies (Finkelhor, 1979; Russell, 1983, 1986; Wyatt, 1985) have used control groups consisting of other subjects in the sample who do not report child sexual abuse histories before age 18. This is one attempt to examine more carefully the relationship of sexual abuse and later sexual functioning. Some of these studies also avoid using nonprobability or clinical samples, which would increase the likelihood of the sample having major psychological problems that would not also be found in the control group (Russell, 1983, 1986; Wyatt, 1985).

Before we discuss the prevalence of child victimization and its effects, it is important to provide a definition of sexual abuse. Although there are a variety of definitions used, and a range of opinion about which one has the most utility for research (Wyatt, Peters, & Guthrie, 1988a,b; Peters, Wyatt, & Finkelhor, 1986), the five-component definition used in the Wyatt study (1985) will be described as follows:

Types of behavior. Sexual abuse required contacts of a sexual nature, ranging from those involving nonphysical contact such as solicitations to engage in sexual behavior and exhibitionism, to those involving body contact such as fondling, frottage, intercourse, and oral sex.

Age of subject. Childhood sexual abuse experiences had to occur prior to age 18, the age at which adult status is attained.

Age of perpetrator. An experience was defined as abuse if the perpetrator was 5 years older than the subject. If the age difference between a subject and the perpetrator was less than 5 years, only situations that were not wanted by the subject and that involved some degree of coercion were included (termed peer abuse). An example of such an experience was the rape of a 14-year-old female by a 16-year-old classmate.

Relationship of perpetrator to subject. Experiences could involve all types of perpetrators: family members, acquaintances, or strangers.

Willingness of the subject to participate. Experiences were considered as abuse depending on the perpetrator's age and the willingness of the victim to participate. If the victim was 12 or younger, experiences were included if the perpetrator was older, even if she willingly participated, the reason being that children do not understand what they are consenting to and are not really free to say no to an authority figure (Finkelhor, 1984). If the victim was 13 to 17 years old, experiences were considered abusive if the perpetrator was older and if the experiences were unwanted. If the perpetrator was an age peer, regardless of the age of the victim, the experiences had to be unwanted. Consensual, exploratory sexual behaviors between minors were not included in the definition of abuse.

Such a multifaceted definition differed from that of Finkelhor (1979) in that the age range between the victim and perpetrator was not used as a criterion for the exclusion of incidents. Whereas Russell (1983) examined only attempted or completed rapes of victims 14 to 17 years old by nonfamily perpetrators, our definition included a range of sexual behaviors with all perpetrators, regardless of their relationship to the victim. Finally, in addition to including incidents involving the procurement of children under age 14 only for "lewd or lascivious acts," as is specified in the California Penal Code 11165–11174 (pp. 512–513), incidents involving these acts for children under age 18 are also included.

The importance of defining sexual abuse is best illustrated by examining one of the first studies that reported prevalence figures for black and white females. Kinsey and colleagues (1953) asked female subjects if an adult male had ever approached them about sex or had sex with them at or before 12 years of age. Obviously, the ages of the victim, the perpetrator, and the type of abuse that occurred tended to limit the definition, and subsequently the data obtained. Additionally, this was the only question asked of subjects regarding what is now termed sexual victimization. These experiences were termed "prepubertal sexual experiences with an adult male" (Kinsey et al., 1953). Research has since identified the number and type of questions asked as key to limiting or enhancing the amount of information recalled by subjects, in relation to a particular sex-related event (Peters, Wyatt, & Finkelhor, 1986; Wyatt & Peters, 1986a,b). These criticisms of the definition and question structure notwithstanding, Kinsey and colleagues identified what was later known as one of the most troubling problems to child mental health and well-being—sexual abuse. Kinsey et al. (1953) reported that one in four women was sexually abused at or before age 12—a statistic that is still reported today, in spite of more recent prevalence rates.

Recently, the prevalence of child sexual abuse, or the proportion of women reporting at least one incident of sexual abuse within a specific time period (in this case, prior to puberty), in Kinsey's sample of women who were between the ages of 18 and 36 at the time they were interviewed, was compared to that found in our sample (Wyatt, Peters, & Guthrie, 1988a,b). In order to make a meaningful comparison, we modified our definition to fit Kinsey's. The prevalence of prepubertal abuse in the white women in Wyatt's sample was 45% as compared to only 23% of Kinsey's women. Likewise, there was a 10-point difference between the prevalence in Kinsey's black sample (29%) as compared to ours (39%). This difference might suggest an increase in abuse in the sample most recently collected. However, when prevalence rates were examined by successive age groups, no increasing trend was evident for either ethnic group. Similarly, other studies have not found an increase in the prevalence of child sexual abuse (Peters, Wyatt, & Finkelhor, 1986). These findings suggest that child sexual abuse that occurs before age 13 with adult male perpetrators has been continuing at a consistent rate for the past 33 years. And yet, the results do not fully address the question of whether more child sexual abuse is occurring. Because of the definition and question structure of Kinsey's study, cases of sexual abuse occurring when victims were between the ages of 13 and 17, as well as cases perpetrated by males younger than 18, were deleted from the Wyatt–Kinsey comparisons. If we broaden the definition to include (1) the ages of victim and perpetrator, and (2) multiple, behaviorally oriented questions that are asked of each subject, the prevalence of child victimization increases in Wyatt's study to 62% for the sample, overall. Similar to the findings of the Kinsey–Wyatt comparisons, no ethnic difference was found (Wyatt, 1985). Until researchers consistently use the same definition of child sexual abuse in research and samples with similar demographic characteristics in a variety of regions across the United States, the question of whether child sexual abuse is on the increase may be left unanswered.

In an attempt to examine the effect of child sexual abuse on sexual functioning, several procedures were undertaken. First, the mean ages of first coitus for both ethnic groups that occurred as a result of a rape or an incestuous or clearly involuntary act of sexual abuse (for twenty women) were deleted, and these women's age of *consensual* coitus was substituted. Second, a series of analyses were conducted to examine several aspects of women's abuse experiences and their adolescent sexual activity. We found that women who experienced at least one incident of contact sexual abuse (fondling, frottage, attempted or completed oral or vaginal intercourse) had consensual intercourse 15 months earlier on the average than women in the nonabuse group (Wyatt, 1989b). The mean age of first coitus was almost identical for both ethnic groups. Third, ages of first abuse and first coitus were examined to establish a temporal relationship between the two events. In 64% of cases for white women and 69% for Afro-American women, all contact abuse incidents occurred before the age of first coitus. In 65% of cases for white women and 80% of cases for their Afro-American peers, all noncontact incidents (exhibitionism or masturbators) occurred before first intercourse, strongly suggesting that child sexual abuse, the behaviors learned from it, and its psychological sequelae may influence the age of first coitus.

Women who experienced contact sexual abuse were also found to begin necking and petting earlier than nonabused women, to have more sexual partners between 13 and 17 years of age, and to have these sexual relationships on a more short-term basis (Wyatt, 1989b). These findings confirm results from other nonclinical studies regarding the effects or patterns of sexual behavior among women with sexual abuse histories (Behward & Densen-Gerber, 1975; Fromuth, 1983; Seidner & Calhoun, 1984; Tsai, Feldman-Summers, & Edgar, 1978).

In summary, in only one case was there an ethnic difference in sexual patterns. White women had significantly more adolescent sexual partners and briefer relationships than their black peers. This finding has also been confirmed in other studies (Belcastro, 1985; Elliott and Morse, 1985).

In those women experiencing sexual abuse before the age of 18, the abuse appeared to be more influential than ethnicity on their age at first coitus and subsequent sexual activity.

Discussion

This chapter has reviewed sex research on African-American and white adolescents (the two groups on which most studies have been conducted), aspects of their sexual behavior, and some of the factors influencing changes in research findings over the last 40 years.

One of the difficulties of reviewing previous research findings regarding adolescent sexuality is that the demographic characteristics of samples have been so different that comparisons across studies have not been useful. In these studies, one wonders why ethnicity was selected as the variable for comparison, when actually the samples frequently differed drastically on measures such as income or education of the parents of origin and family structure. In some cases, even though samples were representative of larger populations, their demographic incomparability only serves to confuse rather than to clarify differences noted when ethnic comparisons are made.

For example, one issue that emerged from recent research is the diminishing difference between black and white adolescents in the age of onset of coitus. Are ethnic differences truly diminishing? Perhaps so, but because previous research has included samples that were so discrepant, it is difficult to answer that question. We do find that research conducted in the 1980s demonstrated fewer ethnic differences in variables such as age of onset of coitus and the prevalence of child sexual abuse, but such differences in the preferences and frequency of sexual behavior appear to remain (Zelnik & Kantner, 1972).

Some of the findings regarding factors influencing adolescent sexual activity may be limited by the manner in which variables are coded. For example, family constellation is a very common variable in most social science research. However, most research designs conceptualize two-parent families as the optimum and most normative constellation. However, alternative family constellations in black families, such as the single-parent home, are becoming as predominant as two-parent households (U.S. Bureau of the Census, 1980). Therefore, research on the influence of single- and two-parent families needs to incorporate variables that tap other aspects of extended-family involvement (Billingsley, 1968). In our study the consistent presence of the parent in the home—regardless of whether there was one or two—as well as the presence of two parents was found to delay first coitus.

In spite of methodological limitations of sex research, we can conclude from the evidence that adolescents are at risk for the early onset of sexual behavior. It follows that the extension of the period of premarital sexual activity is increasing the likelihood that an unplanned pregnancy will occur. Black women are particularly at risk for unplanned pregnancies, partly because they tend to marry later than whites, or not at all (U.S. Bureau of the Census, 1980). Recent statistics also indicate that the opportunity for marriage is based on the available pool of men, which is smaller as women grow older (U.S. Bureau of the Census, 1980). However, another significant component to this issue is that marriage does not offer the same rewards to all segments of America. Indeed, rising unemployment among black males severely limits their attractiveness as potential breadwinners in black families. Consequently, as the premarital period extends, our society could be faced with increasingly more adolescents and young adults who may not be able to afford their children born out of marriage.

There are additional risks involved in regard to adolescent sexual activity. Although age of onset of sex has received attention, we do not know enough about preferences for sexual behaviors among the sexually active. If adolescents who have multiple partners are at more risk for spreading sexually transmitted diseases, then the frequency of sexual activity and its consequences needs to be incorporated into research and into education about sexuality as well.

As we concentrate on adolescent sexual activity and its consequences such as unplanned pregnancies and births out of marriage, we need to continue to study the impact of child sexual abuse on initial and later sexual patterns. The concepts of traumatic sexualization or altered perceptions of and knowledge about sex, as well as feelings of powerlessness, described by Finkelhor and Browne (1985), capture some of the dynamics of sexual abuse that may be found to influence the decision-making and sexuality of the adolescents about which we are concerned today.

Are we at a point in history where adolescent sexuality is inevitable? It appears so. Can intercourse be prohibited? Fear of parental disapproval or of pregnancy is probably as common today as ever. However, curiosity or pressure to experience sex appear to be as strong a motivator as fear is an inhibitor. Reasons for engaging in sex may differ between ethnic groups, and this should be taken into consideration when preparing educational information that is distributed to adolescents who seek information about sexuality.

It appears that the period from 15 to 17 years of age carries the greatest risk for the onset of early sexual activity, and particularly so for black adolescents. However, variables such as low parental income seems to increase that risk. Additionally, the likelihood of adolescents from impoverished backgrounds becoming sexually active at early ages may increase the risk of their continuing to live in poverty. This is an alarming trend, in light of today's economy.

In conclusion, the occurrence of adolescent sexual behavior hasn't changed, but the age of onset has. We have begun to refine the contributors to early onset and have found that ethnicity as a variable is less significant than SES, the presence and consistency of parents in the home, women's sexual abuse histories, and the age of onset of sexual behaviors that precede intercourse. These findings also highlight the value of educating children about the advantages of delaying coitus and offering them a realistic appraisal of the consequences of sexual activity. Adolescents are not likely to refrain from sex, but the more their decision-making is based on their own desire for sex, the more likely they may be to accept the responsibility that comes with being sexually active.

Notes

1. The terms Afro-American, African-American, and black are used interchangeably in reference to the Wyatt study. They refer to women of African

descent whose parentage also includes a variety of other ethnic and racial groups found in America. White women were of Caucasian descent, whose parentage included women of Jewish heritage as well. In other research cited, it is not possible to determine whether these distinctions were made in classifying women as black or white.

2. If the demographic characteristics of any woman who could not be contacted (i.e., no answers) was estimated, the rate of refusal, including those whose terminated phone contact, was 33%. However, the rate of refusal increases to 45% if those 335 women are all considered to be refusals.

References

Akpom, A., Akpom, K. L., & Davis, M. (1976). Prior sexual behavior of teenagers attending rap sessions for the first time. *Family Planning Perspectives, 8,* 203–260.

Alan Guttmacher Institute (1981). *Fact book on teenage pregnancy tables and references for teenage pregnancy: The problem that hasn't gone away.* New York: Alan Guttmacher Institute.

Barglow, P. Bornstein, M., Exum, D. B., Wright, M. K., & Visotsky, H. M. (1968). Some psychiatric aspects of illegitimate pregnancy in early adolescence. *American Journal of Orthopsychiatry, 38,* 672–687.

Becerra, R., & Felder, E. (1985). Adolescent attitudes and Behavior. *ISSR Quarterly, 1,* 4–7.

Belcastro, P. A. (1985). Sexual behavior differences between Black and White students. *The Journal of Sex Research, 21*(1), 56–67.

Benward, J., & Densen-Gerber, J. (1975). Incest as a causative factor in antisocial behavior: An exploratory study. *Contemporary Drug Problems, 4,* 323–340.

Billingsley, A. (1968). *Black families in white America.* Englewood Cliffs, NJ: Prentice-Hall.

Briere, J. (1984). *The effects of childhood sexual abuse on later psychological functioning: Defining a "post sexual abuse syndrome."* Paper presented at the Third National Conference on Sexual Victimization of Children, Washington, DC.

Brown, M. E. (1979). Teenage prostitution. *Adolescence, 14,* 665–680.

Byrne, D. (1977). Social psychology and the study of sexual behavior. *Personality and Social Psychology Bulletin, 3,* 3–30.

Caplow, T. (1982). Decades of public opinion: Comparing NORC and Middletown data. *Public Opinion,* Oct./Nov., 30–36.

Chilman, C. S. (1976). *Possible factors associated with high rates of out-of-marriage births among adolescents.* Paper presented at the University of Wisconsin, Milwaukee, WI.

Courtois, C. (1979). Characteristics of a volunteer sample of adult women who experienced incest in childhood or adolescence. *Dissertation Abstracts International, 40,* 3194A–3195A.

Darabi, K. F., & Ortiz, V. (1987). Childbearing among young Latino women in the United States. *American Journal of Public Health, 77*(1), 25–28.

DeYoung, M. (1982). *Sexual victimization of children.* Jefferson, NC: McFarland.

Elliott, D. S. & Morse, B. J. (1985). Drug use, delinquency and sexual activity. In C. Jones & E. McAnarney (Eds), *Drug abuse and adolescent sexual activity, pregnancy, and parenthood.* NIDA Research Monograph Series, Washington, DC: U.S. Government Printing Office. (in press)

Finkelhor, D. (1979). *Sexually victimized children*. New York: Free Press.

Finkelhor, D. (1984). *Child sexual abuse: New theory and research*. New York: Free Press.

Finkelhor, D., & Browne, C. (1985). The traumatic impact of child sexual abuse: A conceptualization. *American Journal of Orthopsychiatry, 55*, 530–541.

Fox, G. (1981). The family's role in adolescent sexual behavior. In T. Ooms (Ed.), *Teenage pregnancy in a family context: Implications for policy* (pp. 73–130). Philadelphia: Temple University Press.

Fox, G. L., & Inazu, J. K. (1980). Mother–daughter communication about sex. *Family Relations, 29*, 347–352.

Fromuth, M. E. (1983). The long-term psychological impact of childhood sexual abuse. Unpublished doctoral dissertation, Auburn University.

Furstenberg, F. (1976). *Unplanned parenthood; The social consequences of teenage childbearing*. New York: Free Press.

Garobalo, J., & Hindelang, M. (1977). *An introduction to the National Crime Survey*. Washington, DC: U.S. Department of Justice.

Gebhard, P. H., Pomeroy, W. B., Martin, G. E., & Christenson, C. V. (1958). *Pregnancy, birth and abortion*. New York: Wiley.

Gelles, R. J. (1978). Methods for studying sensitive family topics. *American Journal of Orthopsychiatry, 48*, 408–424.

Herman, J. (1981). *Father–daughter incest*. Cambridge, MA: Harvard University Press.

Huizinga, D., & Elliott, D. S. (1984). *Self-reporting measures of delinquency and crime: Methodological issues and comparative findings*. Boulder, CO: Behavioral Research Institute.

Hunt, M. (1974). *Sexual behavior of the 1970's*. Chicago: Playboy Press.

James, J., & Meyerding, J. (1977). Early sexual experiences and prostitution. *American Journal of Psychiatry, 134*, 1381–1385.

Jehu, D., Gazan, M., & Klassen, C. (1984/85). Common therapeutic targets among women who were sexually abused. *Journal of Social Work and Human Sexuality, 4*, 46–69.

Katz, S., & Mazur, M. A. (1979). Understanding the rape victim: A synthesis of research findings. New York: Wiley.

Kinsey, A., Pomeroy, W., & Martin, C. E. (1948). *Sexual behavior in the human male*. Philadelphia: Saunders.

Kinsey, A., Pomeroy, W., Martin, C., & Gebhard, P. (1953). *Sexual behavior in the human female*. Philadelphia: Saunders.

Loftus, E. F., & Marburger, W. (1983). Since the eruption of Mt. St. Helens, has anybody beaten you up? Improving the accuracy of retrospective reports with landmark events. *Memory and Cognition, 11*, 114–120.

Meiselman, K. C. (1978). Incest: A psychological study of causes and effects with treatment recommendations. San Francisco: Jossey-Bass.

Miller, R. G. (1984). *Simultaneous statistical inference* (2nd ed., p. 67). New York: Springer-Verlag.

National Survey of Family Growth (NSFG) (1984). Sterilization use up, pill use down among married women. *Family Planning Perspectives, 16*, (Jan./Feb), 1.

Peters, S. D. (1984). The relationship between childhood sexual victimization and adult depression among Afro-American and White women. Unpublished doctoral dissertation, University of California, Los Angeles.

Peters, S. D., Wyatt, G. E., & Finkelhor, D. (1986). Prevalence. In D. Finkelhor

(Ed.), *A sourcebook on child sexual abuse*. Beverly Hills, CA: Sage Publications.

Reiss, I. L. (1967). *The social context of premarital sexual permissiveness*. New York: Holt, Reinhart & Winston.

Reiss, I. L. (1971). Premarital sex codes: The old and the new. In D. Grummon and A. Barclay (Eds.), *Sexuality: A search for perspective*. New York: Reinhold.

Robinson, I., King, K., & Balswick, J. (1972). The premarital sexual revolution among college females. *Family Coordinator, 21*, 189–194.

Russell, D. E. H. (1983). The incidence and prevalence of intrafamilial and extrafamilial sexual abuse of female children. *Child Abuse and Neglect, 7*, 133–146.

Russell, D. E. H. (1986). *The secret trauma: Incest in the live of girls and women*. New York: Basic Books.

Schuman, H., & Presser, S. (1981). *Questions and answers in attitude surveys: Experiments on question form, working and context*. New York: Academic Press.

Seidner, A. L., & Calhoun, K. S. (1984, August). *Childhood sexual abuse: Factors related to differential adjustment*. Paper presented at the Second Annual National Family Violence Research Conference.

Silbert, M. H., & Pines, A. M. (1981). Sexual child abuse as an antecedent to prostitution. *Child Abuse and Neglect, 5*, 407–411.

Sorenson, R. B. (1973). *Adolescent sexuality in contemporary America: Personal values and sexual behavior, ages thirteen to nineteen*. New York: World.

Staples, R. E. (1973). *The black woman in America*. New York: Nelson-Hall.

Tsai, M., Feldman-Summers, S., & Edgar, M. (1978). Childhood molestation: Variables related to differential impacts on psychosexual functioning in adult women. *Journal Abnormal Psychology, 88*, 407–417.

Tsai, M., & Wagner, N. (1978). Therapy groups for women sexually molested as children. *Archives of Sexual Behavior, 7*, 417–429.

U.S. Bureau of the Census (1980). *America's black population: 1970 to 1982. A statistical view* (Special Publication Series plp/Pop83). Washington, DC: U.S. Government Printing Office.

Wattleton, F. (1986). Teen sex education campaign launched. *The Los Angeles Times*, Oct. 17, p. 22.

Weis, D. L. (1983). Affective reactions of women to their initial experience of coitus. *Journal of Sex Research, 19*(3), 209–237.

Wyatt, G. E. (1985). The sexual abuse of Afro-American and white women in childhood. *Child Abuse and Neglect, 9*, 507–519.

Wyatt, G. E. (1989a). Re-examining factors predicting Afro-American and white women's age of first coitus. *Archives of Sexual Behavior, 18*, 271–298.

Wyatt, G. E. (1989b). The relationship between child sexual abuse and adolescent sexual functioning in Afro-American and white-American women. *Annals of the New York Academy of Sciences, 528*, 111–122.

Wyatt, G. E., & Peters, S. D. (1986a). Issues in the definition of child sexual abuse in prevalence research. *Child Abuse and Neglect, 10*, 231–240.

Wyatt, G. E., & Peters, S. D. (1986b). Methodological considerations in research on the prevalence of child sexual abuse. *Child Abuse and Neglect, 10*, 241–251.

Wyatt, G. E., Peters, S. D., & Guthrie, D. (1988a). Kinsey revisited, part I: Comparisons of the sexual socialization and sexual behavior of white women over 33 years. *Archives of Sexual Behavior, 17*, 201–240.

Wyatt, G. E., Peters, S. D., & Guthrie, D. (1988b). Kinsey revisited, part II: Comparisons of the sexual socialization and sexual behavior of black women over 33 years. *Archives of Sexual Behavior, 17,* 289–332.

Yankelovich, D. (1974). *The new morality: A profile of American youth in the 1980's.* New York: McGraw-Hill.

Zelnik, M., & Kantner, J. (1972). Sexuality, contraception, and pregnancy among young unwed females in the United States. In F. Westoff and Parke, Jr. (Eds.), *Commission Research Reports* (Vol 1). U.S. Commission on Population Growth and the American Future. Demographic and Social Aspects of Population Growth. Washington, DC: U.S. Government Printing Office.

Zelnik, M., & Kantner, J. F. (1980). Sexual activity, contraceptive use and pregnancy among metropolitan area teenagers: 1971–1979. *Family Planning Perspectives, 12*(5, Sept./Oct.), 230–237.

Zelnik, M., Kantner, J. F., & Ford, K. (1981). *Sex and pregnancy in adolescence.* Beverly Hills, CA: Sage Publications.

12

The Impact of Sociocultural Influences on Adolescent Sexual Development: Further Considerations

John Bancroft

In the second part of the volume we have so far considered social factors from three different viewpoints. Mary Hotvedt provided us with an anthropological, cross-cultural perspective; Jan Trost considered some of the mechanisms by which social influences are mediated; and Gail Wyatt gave us an example of evidence obtained in a careful study of adult women reflecting on their adolescent experiences, in a specific geographic area (Los Angeles), and with a particular emphasis on the comparison of black and white California women. These are three "windows" into the social background to adolescent sexual development. Let me look further through these windows at certain points that deserve added emphasis before moving on to consider and speculate about some specific aspects of adolescent sexuality.

It is difficult to overemphasize the importance of the cross-cultural view that Hotvedt provides us. It is all too easy to reach conclusions and take policy decisions about adolescent behavior after focusing on the relatively narrow range of adolescent experience that we find in our own culture, with consequences that may actually be counterproductive.

There are important differences even between the geographically distinct cultures represented at this meeting—between, for example, Scandinavia, Britain, and the United States. Wyatt has also pointed out differences between ethnic groups living within the same geographic area while at the same time reminding us how easy it is, with methodological inadequacies, to confuse cultural and socioeconomic influences. The

United States in particular is a rich and relatively recent mixture of different cultures, subcultures, and religions. Europe provides another rich mixture, though with a much longer history and hence more time for social integration. There are exceptions of course. The Asian community in Britain is of relatively recent origin and has embedded within British society several cultures that contrast considerably with the indigenous British model.

Hotvedt, in her use of cultural materialism, takes us back to preindustrial societies to consider the basic elements of social systems and how they relate to specific aspects of the human sexual experience, such as the pattern of male–female relationships. She touches briefly and tantalizingly on more recent European and American evidence.

Such evidence is of three types. There is the social anthropology of preindustrial societies, most of which are now social systems of the past, having been reshaped by their contact with Western culture and religion. A second type of evidence is the social history of the last few hundred years of European and American society. In the past, historians have tended to concentrate on the "high and mighty," so that factors influencing the lives of ordinary people have been somewhat neglected. Modern social history is attempting to redress the balance with fascinating and at times seductive accounts such as those of Shorter (1975), Stone (1979), or Gillis (1985), covering in particular the period from the mid-seventeenth to the mid-nineteenth centuries. Finally, there is the comparative evidence of recent years, with some studies showing us change over a relatively short period of time within the same culture, such as those of Zelnik & Kantner (1977) in the United States, and of Schmidt and colleagues in West Germany (Schmidt & Sigusch, 1972; Clement, Schmidt, & Kurse, 1984). There have also been some recent comparisons across cultures, and a particularly valuable example is presented by Jacqueline Forrest in Chapter 14 of this volume. Recently at the International Academy of Sex Research we heard a fascinating attempt to compare and contrast teenage sexuality in East and West Germany (Starke & Clement, 1987).

All three types of evidence confront us with the rich variety of adolescent sexuality. We see the contrasting patterns in different types of preindustrial society, dependent on such factors as the main method of food production, the importance of inherited wealth, and the level of segregation and stratification of males and females. We also find, in the accounts of social historians, evidence of major changes in teenage behavior in Europe, most strikingly around the early stages of the industrial revolution. And, as if the whole social process is accelerating, our recent epidemiological studies show dramatic changes within periods of time as short as 25 years, with the earlier contrasts between male and female sexuality and the "double standard" of sexual morality beginning to lessen. Such short-term changes are powerful indicators of the crucial significance of social factors, although biological factors can contribute dramatically, as with the advent of effective steroidal contraception. The analysis of Forrest (Chapter 14) illustrates the importance of socioeconomic factors in modern societies.

We are left, however, with a need to link together these three sources of evidence—a task of considerable magnitude. How does the evolving European picture of the seventeenth, eighteenth, and nineteenth centuries relate to the patterns of preindustrial societies that Hotvedt described for us? What is the origin of the apparent difference between the northern European and Mediterranean patterns of adolescent sexuality (Bancroft, 1989)? In the north the emphasis in the past has been on fertility and a relatively equal status of male and female in the sexual relationship, and less on the double standard. The Mediterranean pattern, with its view of the female as property of the male, handed on from father to husband, places emphasis on the maintenance of virginity of the unmarried female. It is interesting to speculate to what extent the spread of Christianity through Europe led to a wider dissemination of the Mediterranean model, with northern Europe rebelling in some respects at the Reformation. How much does the religion follow the social system, or vice versa? We do now see a striking contrast between northern European and Mediterranean countries; was this the case in the eighteenth and nineteenth centuries? We see the double standard of sexual morality, which is so crucially important to adolescent sexuality, and which some historians have attributed to the industrial revolution (Schmidt, 1977), receding earlier in northern Europe than in Mediterranean countries where the "machismo" male is still very much in evidence and the women's movement has a larger struggle on its hands.

A Theoretical Model of Sexual Development

Against this background of social influence, let me consider some aspects of adolescent sexual development in closer detail. A model of sexual development that seems helpful involves "strands" and "stages" of development (for more details, see Bancroft, 1989). There are three principal strands, relating to (i) gender identity, (ii) sexual response, and (iii) the capacity for intimate dyadic relationships. These strands develop in parallel during childhood, relatively independent of each other. But, during adolescence they start to integrate to form the beginning of our sexual adult. Early and late adolescence are two stages of the developmental process that concern us at this meeting, but important stages occur later in life also, at such times as the formation of the stable pair preceding marriage, at the onset of parenting, with parenting of adolescents, the effects of aging, and so on.

In this developmental system, sexual preference or orientation is an aspect of sexual identity that typically begins to organize during early adolescence. That is not to say that early childhood experiences are unimportant, but that the child enters adolescence with the ingredients for sexual orientation rather than a sexual orientation per se. The ingredients are principally the three strands already described. The development of each individual strand will subsequently influence the form the orientation takes. This is a view of sexual development akin to Erikson's model of developmental stages, which sees the child entering adolescence with certain relevant skills such as the capacity for intimacy and trust, which are highly relevant to adolescent sexuality but have to be incorporated into the unfolding sexual identity. It contrasts with the Freudian view, which assumes early organization of sexual orientation even if that orientation remains latent, or with the view of John Money who sees the organization of "love maps" or templates of sexual preference laid down within the first 8 years of childhood.

The Importance of Gender Identity for Adolescent Sexuality

The development of gender identity, both during childhood and adolescence, thus assumes considerable importance in our developmental model. Gender identity is for most individuals well organized by the end of childhood; the prepubescent child often feels quite secure in his or her role as boy or girl. Then adolescence throws this stable state into temporary confusion. Many of the previous criteria of successful masculinity or femininity no longer apply. Physical changes occur over which the adolescent has absolutely no control and with no idea when or how they will end. Self-confidence becomes vulnerable and the position in the peer group uncertain. Masculinity and femininity have to be renegotiated in adolescent terms; a significant portion of those terms concerns sexuality, which previously had little relevance to gender. Thus, in early adolescence, sexual behavior serves an important function in the reorganization of gender identity for both boys and girls. Hence, the sociocultural factors that provide the "social scripts" for masculinity and femininity—exemplified in the double standard of sexual morality—are of fundamental importance to our subject. Trost (Chapter 10) contrasts the influence of the family with that of the peer group. In terms of gender identity, these two influences are often concordant, reinforcing each other.

Adolescence as Separation and Transition

A further aspect of adolescence that has a powerful bearing on adolescent sexuality is its function of separating the child from dependence on the parents—the "rite of passage" from childhood to adulthood.

Hotvedt reminds us how in many societies this process is institutionalized in the form of ritual. (It is interesting how often these puberty rituals seem to reinforce gender role differences.) The implication of such a system is that the transition between roles can be achieved within a relatively short time. The young male after his initiation ritual may still have a lot to learn, but he is expected to take on, almost overnight, a new responsibility that goes with the adult role. In modern society we assume that our young people require a much longer period of transition to prepare them for the complexities and demands of modern life, although paradoxically modern adolescents may have to contend with earlier reproductive maturation and the associated effects of sex hormones on their emotions and behavior.

This brings us to another crucial issue: parental responsibility. Although the anthropological evidence may be incomplete on this point, the puberty ritual of a preindustrial society implies that the community takes over, or at least shares responsibility. Hotvedt tells us that in most societies, sexual guidance of the adolescent is clearly not provided by the parents but by others in the community. She describes various models of which the "dormitories" are particularly striking. One model, the Sambian dormitory, is designed for the male as a single-sex system in which younger boys learn from older adolescents and young adults. (On reading this, I could not avoid a comparison with the English boarding school of my own childhood and adolescence, an experience that undoubtedly reduced if not eliminated any likelihood of sex education from my parents, while exposing me to a male peer group culture, which did not prepare me well for my sexual career.) The other model she describes, the Mundo *ghotul,* provides a mixed-sex peer group, which sounds rather more appealing.

Contrast such systems with the modern North American and to a lesser extent, European patterns. Hyman Rodman (Chapter 15) brings the issue of parental responsibility for the adolescent into sharp focus, pointing out the prevailing tendency to delay handing over individual responsibility rather than grant it prematurely. Why is our culture apparently so different in this respect? Is it because the complexities of modern industrial society lead to a degree of anomie in which parents feel little identification with their community and hence are unwilling to hand over the welfare of their adolescent offspring to that community? The tendency for some parents, who can afford it, to send their children to boarding schools that promote (or at least are thought to) values with which they can identify is at least consistent with such an explanation. Or is it that in our society, parents have come to rely for their own self-esteem increasingly on the achievements of their children, so that their own future well-being and status in society as well as that of their children is put at risk during the hazardous phase of adolescent experimentation?

But there is a further important dimension to take into account. Where adolescent sexuality is concerned it is not simply a matter of relaxing parental responsibility. There is also the sexuality of the parent–child relationship to consider. For the prepubertal child this is less of a problem and the parents provide the most natural and appropriate source of guidance on sexual matters. But with the adolescent, sexual tension develops between parent and child. The girl's unfolding sexuality alters her perception of her father, the first man in her life, while at the same time altering the balance of power between the girl and her mother. For the boy, tension also develops though perhaps differing in important ways. The relationship between mother and son has been intimate from infancy, whereas between father and daughter there has always been, by comparison, a distance that enhances the sexuality of that relationship. These changes, together with the physical changes in the adolescent, produce sexual repercussions in the parents. While we rely on the incest taboo to contain these tensions, in the majority of cases successfully, the dramatic increase in awareness of intrafamily child sexual abuse confronts us with the limitations of this control system. Comparison with those social systems in which the sexually emerging child is separated to a considerable extent from the parents is thus of considerable interest.

This issue is of central importance to our vital debate on sex education, and the conflict of opinion between those who advocate sex education outside the home and those who insist that the family is the appropriate educator (in spite of mounting evidence that the large majority of parents are unable to provide effective guidance on sexual matters to their adolescent children: see, for example, Roberts, Kline, & Gagnon, 1978). I personally hold the view that, whereas the parent is the best person to guide the child on sexual matters and sexual morality prior to puberty, after puberty the parent has good reason for *not* being the main guide. Therefore, our teenagers need and deserve access to other responsible adults with whom they can discuss their sexual concerns and uncertainties.

What may well happen, when parents persist in their attempts to hold the reins of their children's development, is that sexuality becomes a "separation issue" (as drugs have become)—a medium by which the teenager asserts his or her independence. In such circumstances influences from the teenage peer group and the family, as Trost points out in Chapter 10, are in conflict. According to this analysis, the caring parent needs a community structure of adults who can be trusted to be responsible, if not necessarily sharing *all* the parents' values, and a confidence that worthwhile moral values have been instilled prior to adolescence and will see them through this risky but vital stage of development.

Sexual Orientation

As mentioned earlier, there are differing views about the timing of development of sexual orientation. In my view, adolescence is of crucial importance in this respect. In the previous Kinsey symposium (Bancroft, 1990), I discussed the possible role of biological factors in the determination of sexual orientation, and put forward the view that if biological factors are important they are probably mediated via their effects on gender identity development, rather than on sexual orientation per se. Adolescence is perhaps the time when social factors are of particular importance to sexual orientation.

The development of sexual orientation can be described as a three-stage process: the prelabeling, self-labeling, and social labeling stages (Bancroft, 1989). In the prelabeling stage the child's behavior is subject principally to the effects of social learning, that is, the reinforcing effects on behavior of its consequences. In the self-labeling stage, typically during early adolescence, cognitive learning holds sway and the individual starts to categorize himself or herself according to the labels (or "scripts") that the social group provides. The adolescent privately compares his or her own responses and feelings with those prescribed in the scripts. It is in relation to this stage that consideration of cross-cultural evidence is of particular importance, as the "social scripts" relevant to sexual orientation do vary from one culture to another. One of the most dramatic examples comes from Herdt (1981), in his ethnography of the Sambian people, referred to in Hotvedt's chapter. In that New Guinea society, which is highly sexually segregated, the young male is provided with a social script of homosexual oral sex as a method of establishing and reinforcing masculinity in preparation for, not a homosexual, but a heterosexual life-style.

As usual there are problems in making connections, in terms of social evolution, between a primitive society of that kind and the complex industrial society of, say, the United States. There is also the confounding effect of the modern gay movement, which has no counterpart in primitive social systems. However, we can at least recognize social scripts in most modern industrial societies that polarize sexual orientation into either heterosexual or homosexual; you are either one thing or the other.

If the sexually unfolding adolescent finds evidence of homosexual interest in himself or herself then, according to such scripts, this places a bar on heterosexuality, or at least undermines confidence in one's capacity for coping with a heterosexual life-style. The polarizing effect of this dichotomous view of sexual orientation (something that Kinsey tried to counter with his scale) on the self-labeling stage of adolescent development is potentially profound.

How the adolescent reacts in the self-labeling stage depends on whether there is confidence and conformity in one's gender identity, whether there is the capacity for coping with intimacy, whether the development of sexual desire has been earlier or later in relation to one's peer group.

This view of sexual development requires us to consider an intriguing sex difference. There is consistent evidence that homosexual behavior is more common among males, and it is possible that there are differences between the two sexes in the determinants of sexual orientation, at least in terms of emphasis. Richard Udry (Chapter 5) presents compelling evidence that the sexual behavior of the boy in early adolescence is predominantly influenced by androgens, whereas with girls at the same stage of pubertal development social factors have a more predictable influence on sexual behavior. Yet, paradoxically, it would seem that the polarizing effect of social scripts on sexual orientation, described above, is more powerful in the male than in the female, as if the greater, or at least more predictable biological drive behind the sexuality of the young male requires more powerful or more systematic social mechanisms to control or direct it. In the studies of heterosexual teenage behavior of West Germans, carried out by Schmidt and colleagues (Clement, Schmidt, & Kurse, 1984), they have found a narrowing of the gap between male and female behavior, with the sexuality of girls becoming more like that of the boys over a period of about 25 years. There is perhaps greater acceptance of bisexuality within the social scripts of girls, or at least of physical affection and intimacy with other females. In recent years, as we learned in the last Kinsey symposium (McWhirter, Sanders, & Reinisch, 1990), bisexuality has been becoming more acceptable and frequent in both men and women. Is it possible that as a result of changing social influences we are seeing a narrowing of the differences between males and females in this respect also, but this time with the male becoming more like the female?

Fertility and Adolescent Sexuality

In conclusion, a comment is in order about the role of fertility in determining adolescent sexuality; this issue is addressed more fully in the chapters by Hofferth and Forrest (Chapters 13, 14). I have already referred to the apparent difference between the north European and Mediterranean patterns of premarital sexuality, with the latter placing greater emphasis on virginity and the former on fertility. The explanation for this apparent social difference remains obscure, but the north European pattern at least hints at a basic need of the sexually unfolding female to demonstrate her fertility. The interaction between such a tendency and the prevailing social influences on adolescent sexual expression could be of crucial importance. In a society or subculture that provides the adolescent female with alternative roles to motherhood as a source of self-esteem, the urge to be fertile may be less important. But when unemployment prevails or the traditional "mothering" stereotype of femininity is strongly reinforced, then this urge may be an important influence on adolescent female sexual behavior and should be taken into account when trying to understand the contraceptive risk-taking of many adolescent girls.

In focusing on social issues, I have allowed this discussion to be speculative. But, while we strive to understand the complex effects of social processes on adolescent sexuality, we should not lose sight of the underlying biological mechanisms. It is in attempting to understand the interaction of the two, biological and social, that we are most likely to throw light on this important aspect of adolescence.

References

Bancroft, J. (1989). *Human sexuality and its problems* (2nd ed.). Edinburgh: Churchill-Livingstone.

Bancroft, J. (1990). Biological Contributions to Sexual Orientation. In D. P. McWhirter, S. A. Sanders, & J. M. Reinisch (Eds.) *Homosexuality/Heterosexuality: Concepts of Sexual Orientation*. New York: Oxford University Press.

Clement, U., Schmidt, G., & Kurse, M. (1984). Changes in sex differences in sexual behavior: A replication of a study of West German students (1966–1981). *Archives of Sexual Behavior, 13*, 99–120.

Gillis, J. R. (1985). *For better, for worse. British marriages, 1600 to the present.* Oxford: Oxford University Press.

Herdt, G. H. (1981). *Guardians of the flutes.* New York: McGraw-Hill.

McWhirter, D. P., Sanders, S. A., & Reinisch, J. M., (1990). *Homosexuality/Heterosexuality: Concepts of Sexual Orientation*. New York: Oxford University Press.

Roberts, E., Kline, D., & Gagnon, J. (1978). *Family life and sexual learning: A study of the role of parents in the sexual learning of children* (3 vols.). A report of the Project in Human Sexual Development. Cambridge, MA.

Schmidt, G. (1977). Introduction to sociohistorical perspectives. In J. Money & H. Musaph (Eds.), *Handbook of Sexology* (pp. 269–282). Amsterdam: Excerpta Medica.

Schmidt, G., & Sigusch, V. (1972). Changes in sexual behaviours among young males and females between 1960 and 1970. *Archives of Sexual Behavior, 2*, 27–45.

Shorter, E. (1975). *The making of the modern family*. New York: Basic Books.

Starke, K., & Clement, U. (1987). *A comparison of students' sexual behavior in the Federal Republic of Germany and the German Democratic Republic*. Paper presented at the International Academy of Sex Research, Tutzing, FRG, June 1987.

Stone, L. (1979). *The family, sex and marriage in England 1500–1800*. London: Pelican.

Zelnick, M., & Kantner, J. F. (1977). Sexual and contraceptive experience of young unmarried women in the United States 1976 & 1972. *Family Planning Perspectives, 9*, 55–71.

13

Trends in Adolescent Sexual Activity, Contraception, and Pregnancy in the United States

Sandra L. Hofferth

Premarital sex among teenagers is a major issue in the United States today. Although this has been primarily due to concern over unwanted pregnancy, it has also taken on an increased importance since the spread of herpes, which is not curable, and the acquired immune deficiency syndrome (AIDS), which is fatal. Highly personal sexual attitudes and practices have come under increased public scrutiny in the past 5 or 6 years. Given the documented negative consequences for teens of bearing children too early, and the increased risk of contracting incurable sexually transmitted diseases (STDs), it is of the utmost urgency to have up-to-date information on the sexual beliefs, values, and behavior of individuals, the trends in these behaviors, and their causes in order to better understand the population at risk. Although major changes in sexual attitudes and practices have taken place over the past several decades, there is very little understanding of what has led to these changes; therefore, we have very little understanding of the individual or social factors that might lead to a reversal of such a trend. Even though there is very little research evidence on which to base them, a number of programs have been established with the goal of delaying the initiation of sexual intercourse until either the later teenage years or marriage. Adequate evaluation of such programs will be very important.

However, given that a large proportion of the teenage population is sexually active, and that there are proven methods to avoid pregnancy and STDs, it is also important to have a better understanding of trends in contraceptive use, the extent to which contraceptive use could be improved, and ways to do so. Thus it is important to identify factors associated with increased use of effective contraception, both to prevent pregnancy and to reduce the exposure to STDs.

The first goal of this chapter is to describe and evaluate what we know about trends in sexual activity among teenagers and about sexual attitudes and practices.[1] The second goal is to describe trends in adolescent reproduction—pregnancy and birth. The third goal is to describe contraceptive practice among teens, particularly whether it has been improving.

Scope of the Problem

There is an increasing gap between the age at which young women become sexually mature and the age at which they first marry. The mean age at menarche declined about 1 year between the beginning of this century and the late 1970s, from about 13.6 years for whites and 13.1 for blacks to about 12.7 years for whites and 12.5 for blacks (MacMahon, 1973).[2] Marital behavior changed even more. Between the 1950s and the late 1970s, the mean age of young white women at first marriage rose from 21.4 to 23.0 (Espenshade, 1983). The mean age of black women at first marriage rose from 21.9 to 26.1 over the same period (Espenshade, 1983). This means that the length of time between average reproductive maturity and average age at first marriage is about 11 years for white women and about 14 years for black women.

The data for teenage women show the same trends. Whereas 60% of female teens in 1960 were still single at age 19, in 1985 this figure had increased to 83% (U.S. Bureau of the Census, 1986). Blacks are even more likely than whites to remain single throughout their teenage years. By ages 18–19, 97% of black and 85% of white female teenagers were still single in 1985. Although it is true that in the recent past teenagers were less likely to be sexually active prior to marriage, white teenagers were also more likely than they are today to be married by the end of their teenage years. A larger proportion of teen sexual activity was marital sexual activity. Is it realistic to expect young people to remain celibate for this increasingly long period of their lives? In fact, the majority do not.

Trends in Sexual Experience

Data from three surveys of youth during the 1970s collected by Kantner and Zelnik (Zelnik & Kantner, 1980, Table 1) show a substantial increase between 1971 and 1979 in the proportion of never-married metropolitan women aged 15–19 who ever had sexual intercourse, from

27.6% in 1971 to 39.2% in 1976, and to 46% in 1979, a relative increase of 67% over the period. Questions about age at first sexual experience[3] were again asked of teens in 1982 in Cycle III of the National Survey of Family Growth (NSFG). According to these data, the proportion of sexually experienced never-married teen women in metropolitan areas apparently declined between 1979 and 1982 from 46.0 to 42.2% for women of all races, although the decline was not statistically significant (unpublished tabulations from the 1982 NSFG). Although the percentage who were sexually experienced declined by only 2 percentage points among whites, from 42.3 to 40.3%, for blacks the percentage who were sexually experienced declined from 64.8 to 52.9%, a decline of almost 12 percentage points, which is statistically significant. Thus the data suggest that for white teenagers sexual experience increased during the 1970s but leveled off at a new higher level between 1979 and 1982. For black teenagers, in contrast, it apparently rose during the early 1970s, leveled off between 1976 and 1979, and declined between 1979 and 1982.

In a recent paper, Hofferth, Kahn, and Baldwin (1986) calculated cohort-specific estimates of cumulative sexual experience using NSFG data. The results show that the proportion of sexually experienced white and black teenage women did increase among those born during the 1950s, who came of age during the late 1960s and early 1970s (Table 13-1). This increase was larger for whites than for blacks, since the levels of premarital sexual experience among blacks were very high even for cohorts born as early as 1938.

Has there been a recent decline in sexual experience? The results of both analyses on the NSFG show that among both whites and blacks, teenage girls continue to become sexually experienced at younger and younger ages, and any leveling off or decline in the probability of initiating sexual activity is limited to 18- and 19-year-olds. The results of a multivariate analysis that estimated the probabilities of first premarital sexual intercourse by age and birth cohort, controlling for the effects of mother's education, Catholic background, age at menarche, and whether the girl lived with both parents at age 14, support these conclusions.

Table 13-1 also divides sexual experience into premarital and marital experience. Except for cohorts born during the 1940s, black marital experience among teenage women has been small. Almost all black teen sexual experience is and has been premarital. For white teens, the table shows that a much larger proportion of teen sexual experience, especially between ages 17 and 19 (by age 20) was marital. Among cohorts born in 1938–40, two of five nonvirgins first experienced sex within marriage, compared with the birth cohort of 1956–58 in which one of eight nonvirgins experienced first sexual intercourse within marriage.

Table 13-1
Percentage of Women Sexually Active by Exact Ages 14, 17, and 20 by Race,
Marital Status at First Intercourse, and Birth Cohort

AGE AND MARITAL STATUS	BIRTH COHORT				
	1938–40	1944–46	1950–52	1956–58	1962–64
White					
Age 14					
Premarital[a]	1.3	0.6	0.5	3.0	3.4
Age 17					
Premarital	10.2	10.7	11.2	25.7	34.8
Marital	2.2	4.6	2.0	0.5	0.6
Both	12.4	15.3	13.2	26.1	35.4
Age 20					
Premarital	33.3	37.0	52.5	64.9	N.A.[b]
Marital	24.5	22.6	13.7	9.5	N.A.
Both	57.8	59.6	66.2	74.4	N.A.
BLACK					
Age 14					
Premarital[a]	8.5	8.0	5.5	7.6	7.9
Age 17					
Premarital	42.7	33.9	34.0	44.5	57.3
Marital	0.8	3.8	0.2	0.5	0.0
Both	43.5	37.7	34.2	45.0	57.3
Age 20					
Premarital	81.7	73.9	83.1	88.8	N.A.
Marital	1.8	6.9	2.8	2.0	N.A.
Both	83.5	80.8	85.9	90.0	N.A.

Source: National Survey of Family Growth, 1982.
[a] All sexual activity by 14 was premarital.
[b] Not applicable.

If both marital and premarital sexual experience are included, the proportion who first had intercourse as a teenager increased 50% between
the cohorts born in 1938–40 and 1956–58, from 57.8% to 74.4%. In contrast, there was a 100% increase in premarital experience. Only about
one third of those born in 1938–40 admitted to premarital experience,
compared with almost two thirds of those born in 1956–58.

Onetime Intercourse as an Indicator of Sexual Activity

One major question is the extent to which having had sexual intercourse once is a good measure of the beginning of a "sexual career."
Apparently it is. In 1976 about 15% of sexually experienced never-married
women had had intercourse only once (Table 13-2). In 1982 only 6.5

Table 13-2
Percentage of Sexually Experienced Never-Married Women Ages 15–19 Who Had Intercourse Only Once, by Age and Race, United States, 1976 and 1982

	1976			1982		
AGE	*All*	*White*	*Black*	*All*	*White*	*Black*
15–19	14.8	14.3	12.7	6.5	7.4	3.7
	(789)	(379)	(410)	(764)	(430)	(316)
15–17	19.9	18.4	18.4	9.3	11.0	5.2
	(423)	(206)	(217)	(294)	(145)	(142)
18–19	8.6	9.3	6.2	4.5	5.1	2.5
	(366)	(173)	(193)	(470)	(285)	(174)

Note: Percentages based on weighted data. Numbers in parentheses represent actual (unweighted) sample size numbers in each age and race group.
Sources: Zelnik and Kantner (1977); National Survey of Family Growth, 1982.

percent of never-married teenagers who ever had intercourse said they had had it only once (Table 13-2). Of course, this figure varies by age and race, with whites twice as likely as blacks to say that they had intercourse only once. And, not surprisingly, twice as many teens aged 15–17 as teens aged 18 to 19 have had intercourse only once. Two fifths of all sexually experienced never-married teenage women had their second intercourse within 1 month of the first, 44.6% of whites and 29.1% of blacks (Table 13-3). Although black teens were slightly less

Table 13-3
Timing of Second Intercourse Relative to First Intercourse Among Never-Married Sexually Experienced Women Aged 15–19, by Race, 1982

TIMING OF SECOND INTERCOURSE	RACE		
	All	*White*	*Black*
Within 1 month (%)	41.1	44.6	29.1
1–3 Months (%)	24.0	21.7	34.1
4–6 Months (%)	12.5	11.1	16.1
7–12 Months (%)	6.5	7.0	5.5
> 12 Months (%)	6.6	5.7	7.0
No Second Time (%)	6.4	7.4	3.7
DK, NA (%)	2.0	2.5	4.4
Total (%)	100.0	100.0	100.0
n (Unweighted)	764	430	316

Source: National Survey of Family Growth, 1982.

likely than white teens to have second intercourse within 1 month of the first, they were more likely than whites to have their second intercourse experience within 1–3 months of the first. Thus they soon caught up. By 3 months after first intercourse, fully two thirds of both whites and blacks had experienced second intercourse.

Frequency of Sexual Intercourse

Having ever had sex does not mean that a young woman is currently sexually active, that is, that she has had sex recently. Data from 1971, 1976, and 1979 (Zelnik, 1983, Table 2-7) show that about two in five did not have intercourse during the past month, and that in this respect there was little change between 1971 and 1979. There was apparently a small increase in the proportion of teen women who had had intercourse six or more times in the past month. This is due to a greater change in the behavior of white teens than that of black teens. While black teens were more likely ever to have had sexual intercourse than white teens, blacks had intercourse less frequently. In 1979 a larger proportion of blacks than whites had ever had intercourse, but a smaller proportion of those who had had intercourse had it six or more times in the past 4 weeks (Zelnik, 1983, Table 2-4).

Table 13-4 shows the frequency of sexual intercourse among unmarried women aged 15 to 24 who had ever had intercourse, from the 1982 NSFG. The question is not identical to that asked in 1971, 1976, and 1979, so the answers cannot be compared. This is because in 1982 the frequency of intercourse was obtained relative to the past 3 months, not the past 4 weeks.

In 1982, of those teenagers who had ever had sex, 18% had not had sex in the past 3 months, 16% had it only once a month, 25% two to three times a month, 21% once a week, 16% more than twice a week, and only 3% daily. Sex was more frequent among the 18- to 19-year-olds than either the 15- to 17-year-olds or the 20- to 24-year-olds.

Comparing blacks and whites, white teenagers are less likely to have had intercourse in the last 3 months, but they are more likely to have had sex once a week or more. This is consistent with the results from the earlier studies mentioned before.

Other Aspects of Sexual Relationships Among Teenagers

Given increased concern about the risk of pregnancy and STDs among teenagers, it is unfortunate that we really know very little about sexual attitudes and practices of teenagers. In particular, the number of partners the young woman or man has had affects the risk of exposure to an STD. The relationship with the partner has been found to be one of the most important factors affecting effective contraceptive use, and is therefore critical for estimating pregnancy risk. The last national survey

Table 13-4

Percentage Frequency of Sexual Intercourse Among Never-Married Females Aged 15 to 24 Who Ever Had Intercourse, by Race and Age, 1982

	AGE			
FREQUENCY OF INTERCOURSE	*15–17*	*18–19*	*15–19*	*20–24*
ALL RACES				
No Intercourse in Past 3 Months (%)	18.3	17.9	18.1	24.3
Once a Month (%)	20.7	13.5	16.4	14.2
Two to Three Times a Month (%)	27.9	23.0	25.0	22.3
Once a Week (%)	21.4	20.6	20.9	18.5
More than Twice a Week (%)	9.8	20.7	16.3	19.3
Daily (%)	1.9	4.3	3.3	1.4
Total Ever Having Intercourse (%)	100.0	100.0	100.0	100.0
n (Unweighted)	295	473	768	626
WHITE				
No Intercourse in Past 3 Months (%)	21.0	20.5	20.7	27.8
Once a Month (%)	14.5	11.1	12.4	14.5
Two or Three Times a Month (%)	29.2	20.8	24.1	20.5
Once a Week (%)	23.2	20.7	21.6	17.0
More than Twice per Week (%)	10.8	22.0	17.6	19.3
Daily (%)	1.3	4.9	3.6	0.9
Total Ever Having Intercourse (%)	100.0	100.0	100.0	100.0
n (Unweighted)	146	175	321	367
BLACK				
No Intercourse in Past 3 Months (%)	11.8	7.5	9.5	15.0
Once a Month (%)	39.5	23.0	30.8	12.6
Two to Three Times a Month (%)	24.9	29.4	27.2	29.8
Once a Week (%)	13.3	21.0	17.4	21.3
More than Twice per Week (%)	7.2	16.9	12.3	18.8
Daily (%)	3.3	2.2	2.7	2.5
Total Ever Having Intercourse (%)	100.0	100.0	100.0	100.0
n (Unweighted)	146	291	437	250

Source: National Survey of Family Growth, 1982.

that obtained information about the number of sexual partners and the relationship with those partners took place in 1979. There may have been substantial changes in the number and relationship with sexual partners since then.

In 1979 among sexually experienced females 15–19 years of age, about half of whites and two fifths of blacks had only had one sexual partner, and 9% of whites and 5% percent of blacks had had six or more premarital sexual partners (Zelnik, 1983, Table 2-6). This represents a drop since 1971 in the number with only one partner, an increase in the proportion with two to three partners, but little change in the proportion with a large number of premarital partners.

Data, again from 1979, show substantial differences in the relationship with first partner by sex (Zelnik & Shah, 1983; Table 2). Among women, about half were engaged or going steady with their first sexual partner; among men, two fifths of white men and only one fifth of black men were engaged or going steady. Two of five white men and three of five black men said that they were just friends with the first partner or that they had recently met. This varies by age, with those who had first intercourse under 15 years of age much more likely than those older at first intercourse to have been friends with or only recently met their first partner (Zelnik & Shah, 1983, Table 3).

Finally, first intercourse usually takes place in the home of one of the teens, with the home of a relative or friend being the next most frequent location. Comparing blacks and whites, the proportion taking place in a home is about the same. Blacks are much more likely than whites to have first intercourse in a motel or hotel, while whites are more likely than blacks to have it in a car or other (unspecified) location (Zelnik, 1983, Table 2-3).

Trends in Pregnancy and Births

The aging of the baby boom cohorts meant that during the mid-1970s there were 60% more teens than the decade before: ten million teen-aged women (Table 13-5). The large number of teens meant a large number of births, almost 600,000 per year. However, even during this period the number of births to teens declined. As a result the birthrates to teens also declined over the period. However, the birthrates to women aged 20–24 and older declined even faster, so the proportion of births to teens actually increased during the 1970s, declining once again in the 1980s.

Although abortion rates rose following legalization in the early 1970s, explaining much of the drop in birthrates, in the 1980s abortion rates have leveled off.

Why then has teen childbearing been considered such a problem? First of all, the decline in birthrates has been primarily among older teens. Birthrates among older teens have declined substantially since their high in the late 1950s; birthrates among younger teens, after first increasing, have not declined as much from their high over the same period (Baldwin, 1986). Second, over this period marriage rates declined dramatically. As women delay marriage, fewer and fewer children are born to married teens. As a result, while overall birthrates have declined, out-of-wedlock rates have been rising for whites. Although they have been falling for blacks, the overall levels are much higher for blacks. The proportion of teen births that occur out of wedlock has increased sharply (39% of whites and 89% of black teen births)

Table 13-5
Reproductive Behavior: United States Women Aged 15–19, 1970–84

REPRODUCTIVE BEHAVIOR	YEAR			
	1970	1975	1980	1984
Total Births	3,731,000	3,144,000	3,612,258	3,669,141
Births at Ages 15–19	644,708	582,238	552,161	469,682
Abortions	59,985	326,780	444,780	410,176
Miscarriages	134,940	149,126	154,910	134,954
Pregnancies	839,633	1,058,144	1,151,851	1,014,812
Total Women Aged 15–19	9,517,000	10,468,000	10,381,000	9,219,000
Never Married (%)	88.8	90.7	91.1	93.4
Total Never Married	8,451,096	9,494,476	9,457,091	8,610,546
Single, Sexually Active (%)	25.0	34.0	40.0	43.0
Total Single, Sexually Active	2,112,774	3,228,122	3,782,836	3,702,535
Total Ever Married	1,065,904	973,524	923,909	608,454
Total Sexually Active	3,178,678	4,201,646	4,706,745	4,310,989
Pregnancy Rate	88	101	111	110
Pregnancy Rate/Sexually Active	264	252	245	235
Birthrate	68	56	53	51
Birthrate/Sexually Active	203	139	117	109
Abortion Rate	6	31	43	44
Abortion Rate/Sexually Active	19	78	94	95
Abortions/Pregnancies	71	309	386	404
Abortions/Abortions + Births	85	359	446	466
Abortions/Births	93	561	806	873

Note: Rate and ratios are per 1000.

(National Center for Health Statistics, 1986). (Out-of-wedlock birthrates have also climbed for women 20–24 years old, suggesting that this is not just a teen phenomenon.) Most of these pregnancies were unintended, and certainly such young women are prepared neither psychologically nor socioeconomically to raise children.

We have discussed the age at first marriage and the age at menarche. What has been happening to the age at first birth? The proportion of women who have a first birth by age 20 among both whites and blacks has been declining since the cohort born in 1940–44. Blacks still have a much more rapid pace of childbearing than whites, with about 41% of those born in 1955–59 having a first birth by age 20, compared to 19% for whites. How do age at first marriage and at first birth compare? For whites, age at first marriage is slightly lower than age at first birth. For blacks, the reverse is true; median age at first birth is lower than age at first marriage by several years (U.S. Bureau of the Census, 1984, 1985, 1986).

What is the trend in pregnancies among teens? Table 13-5 shows the calculations of pregnancy rates for teens from 1970 to 1984. The pregnancy rate for women aged 15–19 rose from 99 per 1000 in 1974 to 108 per thousand in 1984, an increase of 9%. However, we have shown that there were substantial increases in the sexually active population during that time. If only those women are included in the denominator who are sexually active, the pregnancy rate over the period falls from 253 in 1974 to 231 in 1984, a drop of 8.7%.

What is the reason for the decline in pregnancies per 1000 sexually active women? Has contraceptive use improved?

Trends in Contraceptive Use

Recent data suggest that contraceptive use at first intercourse has been improving. The proportion of teenage girls who say that they *never* used contraception declined from 35.5% in 1976 to 26.6% in 1979 and to 14.6% in 1982 (Zelnik & Kantner, 1980, Table 7; NAS, vol II). The proportion who say that they *always* used contraception increased between 1976 and 1979 and then stayed about the same between 1979 and 1982. The proportion who did not use contraception at first intercourse, but used it at some time, increased between 1979 and 1982.

The data on pregnancies show that the risk of pregnancy is very high during the first few months after first intercourse. When is the risk of pregnancy highest? According to data from the 1979 Zelnik–Kantner survey (Koenig & Zelnik, 1982), by 12 months following first intercourse 20% of whites and 30% of blacks have had a first premarital pregnancy. The major factor affecting risk of pregnancy is contraceptive use. Among those who never used contraceptives, 35% would become pregnant within the first year, compared to only 9% of those who always used them. Once contraceptive use is controlled in the data, black/white differences disappear. Differences by age at first intercourse also decline somewhat, but do not disappear.

Thus the pace of adoption of contraception after first intercourse is a very important consideration. Table 13-6 shows the length of time after first intercourse before adopting a method of contraception among those who did not use a method at first intercourse, but who have ever used a method, by age at first intercourse, in 1982. It is clear that the older a young woman is at first intercourse, the faster the pace of adoption of contraception after first intercourse. Only 23% of those under age 15 at first intercourse, compared to 63% of those aged 20–24 at first intercourse, first started using a contraceptive method within the first month. Among those under 15 years of age, 42% delayed more than 12 months until initial contraceptive use, compared with 15% of those aged 18–19 and 14% of those aged 20–24.

Table 13-6
Length of Time After First Intercourse Before Adopting a Method of
Contraception Among Those Who Did Not Use a Method at First Intercourse
but Who Have Ever Used a Method, by Age at First Intercourse, Women
Under 25, 1982

Lag Time To Contraceptive Use (Months)	Age at First Intercourse			
	Under 15	15–17	18–19	20–24
	%	%	%	%
ALL RACES				
0–1	22.6	36.9	53.3	62.6
1–3	14.8	13.4	20.1	8.7
4–6	12.5	5.0	8.6	15.2
7–12	8.0	10.0	2.7	0.0
>12	42.2	34.6	15.3	13.5
Total	100.0	100.0	100.0	100.0
n (Unweighted)	167	293	73	16
WHITE				
0–1	24.4	41.8	55.6	71.0
1–3	20.2	14.2	21.9	5.8
4–6	12.1	6.2	8.6	23.2
7–12	7.6	9.5	1.4	0.0
>12	35.8	28.1	12.4	0.0
Total	100.0	100.0	100.0	100.0
n (Unweighted)	38	111	42	8
BLACK				
0–1	22.9	28.3	43.6	46.6
1–3	10.4	11.6	12.4	14.3
4–6	14.3	2.9	8.6	0.0
7–12	9.2	10.7	8.5	0.0
>12	43.2	46.4	26.9	39.2
Total	100.0	100.0	100.0	100.0
n (Unweighted)	127	179	30	8

Source: National Survey of Family Growth, 1982.

Whites adopted a contraceptive method more rapidly than blacks, except at the very youngest ages, when blacks and whites differed little in pace of adoption of contraception.

Contraceptive use is difficult for everyone. In the NSFG, the percentage who used a method at first intercourse was calculated for women of all ages, by age at first intercourse (Table 13-7). While a higher percentage of those aged 18 or older at the time used contraceptives at first intercourse, still over half of all women reported not using contraception at first intercourse. Among users there was a difference by age in method use, with those older being more likely to use the pill and

Table 13-7
Percentage Who Used a Contraceptive Method at First Intercourse, and
Method Used Among Users, by Age, Women Under 25, 1982

CONTRACEPTIVE METHOD	AGE AT FIRST INTERCOURSE			
	<15	15–17	18–19	20–24
Did Not Use Method (%)	70.0	56.9	52.7	51.4
Used Method (%)	30.0	43.1	47.3	48.6
Total (%)	100.0	100.0	100.0	100.0
n (Unweighted)	885	2933	1740	1135
USERS ONLY				
Pill (%)	14.0	20.6	30.8	39.0
Condom (%)	44.0	43.5	38.3	30.0
Rhythm/NFP (%)	5.1	3.9	7.0	4.7
Withdrawal (%)	30.3	25.3	14.9	13.4
Diaphragm (%)	0.1	0.7	2.2	3.7
Other[a] (%)	6.5	6.0	6.8	9.2
Total (%)	100.0	100.0	100.0	100.0

Source: National Survey of Family Growth, 1982.
[a]Includes sterilization, foam, douch, suppositories, and other methods.

diaphragm, and those younger more likely to use the condom and withdrawal.

Use of a method at first intercourse varied by race and ethnicity, with whites most likely, blacks next, and Hispanics least likely to use contraception at first intercourse (Fig. 13-1). Method used also varies, with blacks more likely to use the pill than whites or Hispanics, Hispanics more likely than whites or blacks to use the condom, and whites more likely than the others to use withdrawal.

Finally, although teenagers at risk of unintended pregnancy are less likely than older women to be currently practicing contraception, still seven of ten are using contraception, compared with eight of ten older women (Bachrach, 1984, Table 3). Among never-married women, younger women are consistently poorer contraceptive users. However, among married women there is almost no difference in contraceptive use by age. The distribution of current method used varies slightly by age, with teenagers more likely than older women to use the pill and condom and less likely to use the diaphragm, intrauterine device (IUD), or sterilization (Table 13-8).

According to recent data (Torres & Singh, 1986), Hispanic teens are just as effective current contraceptive users as non-Hispanic white and black teens: 63% use the pill, 9% other medical methods, 15% the condom, 5% the diaphragm, and 8% other methods (Table 13-9).

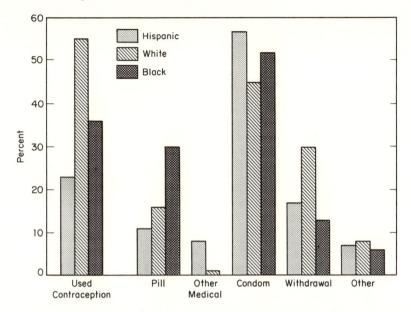

Figure 13–1. Percentage of teens who used contraception at first intercourse, and method used.

Trends in Use at Most Recent Intercourse

Over the past decade there has clearly been an increase in the percentage of never-married teenagers currently using a contraceptive method (Table 13-10). There has also been substantial change among users in the methods used. The use of the pill nearly doubled between 1971 and 1982. There was an increase between 1971 and 1976, followed apparently by a slight decline in pill use between 1976 and 1979, and then a significant increase between 1979 and 1982. During the late 1970s there was a lot of negative "press" about the pill, its side effects, and its possible association with cancer and other problems. This may have been part of the reason for an apparent decline in use between 1976 and 1979. Writings by Zelnik and colleagues based on their 1979 data include remarks about the apparent decline in effective contraceptive use between 1976 and 1979 (Koenig & Zelnik, 1982). If this temporary decline was in fact real, it is also apparent that it was temporary. Along with the increase in pill use occurred a decline in the use of male methods—the condom and withdrawal. It will be interesting to see whether over the next few years the use of the condom will once again increase, as concern about STDs increases, and whether pill use will decline.

Table 13-8
Percentage Currently Using a Contraceptive Method and Distribution of
Never-Married Users Age 15–44 by Method, by Age, 1982

	AGE			
CONTRACEPTIVE METHOD	15–19	15–17	20–24	25–44
Not Using a Method	32.4	40.0	19.0	(19.7)
Using a Method (%)	67.6	60.0	81.0	(80.3)
Total (%)	100.0	100.0	100.0	100.0
n (Weighted) (in 000's)	2872	1081	3291	2519
USERS ONLY				
Sterilization (%)	0.5	—	3.8	10.9
Pill (%)	62.3	63.7	56.1	41.1
IUD (%)	0.9	1.3	4.9	10.3
Diaphragm (%)	6.4	3.6	13.8	19.7
Condom (%)	22.2	25.0	8.3	6.2
Other[a] (%)	7.8	6.4	13.0	11.8
Total (%)	100.0	100.0	100.0	100.0

Source: Bachrach and Mosher (1984), Table 4; Bachrach (1984), Table 3.
[a]Including foam, periodic abstinence, withdrawal, douche, suppositories, and
other methods.

Summary and Conclusions

Teenagers face an increasingly long period of time between sexual maturation and marriage. The trend is toward almost universal initiation
of active sexual careers during this period. There is some question with
regard to whether some retrenchment will occur. There is little evidence so far that decline in sexual activity has occurred. Although there
may be leveling off at the older teen ages, there is apparently continued increase in sexual experience at very young ages. When it is appropriate for young people to initiate sex has been widely debated, as
have the appropriate strategies to delay sexual activity among young
teens. Delaying first intercourse for even 6 months may be very beneficial at young teen ages, less so at older ages. There is little empirical
evidence about the potential length of delay that can be achieved, and
its significance. In any case, by the end of their teen years the majority
of never-married women are sexually experienced and sexually active.
Once teens have become sexually active, it is essential that they have
the knowledge and the means to prevent unintended pregnancies. Teens
apparently have the capability to utilize contraception effectively, and
probably as a result of improved use over the past decade, rates of
pregnancy among those sexually active have declined, and abortion

Table 13-9
Number and Percentage Distribution of Hispanic and Non-Hispanic Women
Ages 15–19 (All Marital Statuses) Currently Exposed to the Risk of
Unintended Pregnancy, by Current Contraceptive Status, 1982

| | | ETHNICITY/RACE | | |
| | | | Non-Hispanic | |
CONTRACEPTIVE STATUS	Total	Hispanic	Black	White and Other
Not Using Contraception (%)	29	32	35	27
Using Contraception (%)	71	68	66	73
Total (%)	100	100	100	100
n (Weighted) (in 000's)	3244	290	630	2324
USERS ONLY				
Pill (%)	64	63	70	63
IUD, Sterilization (%)	2	9	5	0
Condom (%)	21	15	13	23
Diaphragm (%)	6	5	2	7
Other (%)	8	8	10	7
Total (%)	100	100	100	100
n (Weighted) (in 000's)	2302	197	413	1692

Source: Torres and Singh (1986).

rates, after increasing, have declined in the last 5 years. Teens as a group are only slightly less effective contraceptive users than older women. The least effective are the youngest teens. These teens are least likely to use contraception at first intercourse, and are the slowest to adopt contraception afterward. It is this group that has the highest risk of pregnancy in the period right after first sexual experience and probably the poorest prospects if they become pregnant. Strategies to target the youngest teens appear essential.

Notes

1. For a more complete overview of trends in teen sexual activity, pregnancy, and childbearing, and the factors affecting those trends, see Hayes (1987), and Hofferth and Hayes (1987).

2. Data for the 1970s are from unpublished tabulations by Ronette Briefel of the National Center for Health Statistics, U.S. Department of Health and Human Services, from the Second National Health and Nutrition Examination Survey, 1976–1980.

3. "Sexually experienced" means having experienced sexual intercourse at least once.

Table 13-10
Percentage Distribution of Sexually Experienced Never-Married Women
Users Aged 15–19, According to Current Method Used, for the Years 1971,
1976, 1979, and 1982

	YEAR			
METHOD	1982	1979	1976	1971
Not Using a Method (%)	31.4	—	36.6	54.8
Using a Method (%)	67.6	—	63.4	45.2
Total (%)	100.0	—	100.0	100.0
n (Unweighted)	1742	—	786	1225
USERS ONLY				
Pill (%)	62.2	40.6	49.2	33.4
IUD (%)	0.9	2.0	3.4	1.8
Diaphragm (%)	6.4	3.5	—	—
Condom (%)	22.3	23.3	19.9	31.8
Douch (%)	—	2.1	3.6	3.8
Withdrawal (%)	—	18.8	16.7	22.8
Foam (%)	8.0	3.9	—	—
Rhythm (%)	—	5.8	7.1	6.4
Sterilization (%)	—	—	—	—
Other (%)	—	—	—	—
Total (%)	100.0	100.0	100.0	100.0
n	—	665	—	—

Sources: 1982—Bachrach and Mosher (1984), Table 4; 1979—Zelnik and Kantner (1980), Table 11; 1976 and 1971—Zelnik and Kantner (1977), Table 12.
Note: Phraseology used for the different years varied slightly: 1982, "current
method"; 1979, "most recent method used"; 1971 and 1976, "method used at
last intercourse."
[a] Metropolitan United States only.

References

Bachrach, C. A. (1984). Contraceptive practice among American women, 1973–
1982. *Family Planning Perspectives, 16,* 253–259.

Bachrach, C. A., & Mosher, W. D. (1984). Use of contraception in the United
States, 1982. *Advance Data from Vital and Health Statistics, 102,* 1–8.

Espenshade, T. J. (1983). *Black–white differences in marriage, separation, and re-
marriage.* Paper presented at the annual meeting of the Population Association of America, Pittsburgh, PA.

Hayes, C. D. (Ed.) (1987). *Risking the future: Adolescent sexuality, pregnancy, and
childbearing* (Vol. 1). Washington, DC: National Academy Press.

Hofferth, S. L., & Hayes, C. D. (Eds.) (1987). *Risking the future: adolescent sexuality, pregnancy, and childbearing* (Vol. 2). Washington, DC: National
Academy Press.

Hofferth, S. L., Kahn, J., & Baldwin, W. (1986). *Trends in teen sexual activity
over the past three decades.* Paper presented at the annual meeting of the
Southern Regional Demographic Group, Baltimore.

Koenig, M. A., & Zelnik, M. (1982). Repeat pregnancies among metropolitan-area teenagers: 1971–1979. *Family Planning Perspectives, 6,* 341–344.

MacMahon, B. (1973). Age at menarche. In *Vital and Health Statistics* (Series 11, No. 133). Rockville, MD: National Center for Health Statistics.

National Center for Health Statistics (1986). *Advance report of final natality statistics, 1984* (Vol. 35, No. 4, Suppl.), pp. 1–43. Rockville, MD: Author.

Torres, A., & Singh, S. (1986). Contraceptive practice among Hispanic adolescents. *Family Planning Perspectives, 18,* 193–194.

U.S. Bureau of the Census (1984). Child spacing among birth cohorts of American women: 1905–1959. In *Current Population Reports* (Series P-20, No. 385). Washington, DC: U.S. Government Printing Office.

U.S. Bureau of the Census (1985). Marital status and living arrangements: March 1984. In *Current Population Reports* (Series P-20, No. 399). Washington, DC: U.S. Government Printing Office.

U.S. Bureau of the Census (1986). Marital status and living arrangements: March 1985. In *Current Population Reports* (Series P-20, No. 410). Washington, DC: U.S. Government Printing Office.

Zelnik, M. (1983). Sexual activity among adolescents: Perspective of a decade. In E. R. McAnarney (Ed.), *Premature adolescent pregnancy and parenthood* (pp. 21–33). New York: Grune & Stratton.

Zelnik, M., & Kantner, J. (1977). Sexual and contraceptive experience of young unmarried women in the United States, 1976 and 1971. *Family Planning Perspectives, 9,* 55–71.

Zelnik, M., & Kantner, J. (1980). Sexual activity, contraceptive use and pregnancy among metropolitan area teenagers: 1971–1979. *Family Planning Perspectives, 12,* 230–237.

Zelnik, M., & Shah, F. (1983). First intercourse among young Americans. *Family Planning Perspectives, 15,* 64–70.

14

Cultural Influences on Adolescents' Reproductive Behavior

Jacqueline Darroch Forrest

There can be little question that the reproductive behavior of adolescents and adults not only is a function of biology and individual personality but is strongly influenced by sociocultural factors as well. Even among industrialized countries, there is wide variation across societies and over time in the many facets of behavior that culminate in reproduction. Much research and interest has been focused on the levels of adolescent sexual activity, pregnancy, birth, and abortion in the United States. There has been general agreement that the high level of teen pregnancy in the United States is a problem, but this has been accompanied by the notion that this state of affairs is a common characteristic of modern, developed countries.

A recent study by the Alan Guttmacher Institute (Jones et al., 1985) explored adolescent reproductive behavior in developed countries and clearly showed that high adolescent pregnancy rates are not characteristic of all industrialized countries. (For greater detail, see the book by Jones et al. [1986], from which much of this chapter is drawn.) The study combined two separate but related approaches: a quantitative analysis of factors associated with adolescent birthrates in thirty-seven developed countries, and more in-depth quantitative and qualitative case studies of the United States and five other selected countries.

Differences Among Developed Countries

Table 14-1 shows birthrates for women aged 15–19 in thirty-seven countries, which were selected on the following criteria of develop-

Table 14-1
Birth, Abortion, and Pregnancy Rates per 1000 Women Aged 15–19, by
Country, around 1980

	BIRTH RATES		ABORTION RATES		PREGNANCY RATES[a]	
Greater than	Bulgaria	81				
United States	Cuba	80				
	Puerto Rico	78				
	Romania	73				
	Hungary	69				
	Chile	65				
Same as	Czechoslovakia	54	United States	42	United States	96
United States	United States	54			Hungary	96
	East Germany	54				
Less than	Greece	53	Hungary	27	Czechoslovakia	66
United States	Yugoslavia	48	Norway	25	Norway	50
	Poland	46	Denmark	24		
	USSR	41				
	Portugal	41				
	New Zealand	39				
	Austria	35				
	Taiwan	33				
	Scotland	33				
	England and Wales	31				
	Australia	28				
	Canada	28				
	Spain	27	Sweden	21	England and Wales	48
	France	25	Finland	20		
	Israel	25	Canada	18	New Zealand	47
	Norway	25	France	18	Canada	46
	Ireland	23	England and Wales	17	Scotland	44
	Italy	23			France	43
	Belgium	23	Czechoslovakia	12	Denmark	40
	West Germany	20			Finland	39
	Finland	19			Sweden	37
	Denmark	16				
	Sweden	16				
	Singapore	12	Scotland	11	Netherlands	14
	Hong Kong	12	New Zealand	8		
	Switzerland	10	Netherlands	5		
	Netherlands	9				
	Japan	4				

[a]Sum of births plus abortions, with no estimate of miscarriages.
Note: Countries below the upper dotted line have rates half or less that of the
United States. Countries below the lower dotted line have rates one quarter or
less that of the United States.

ment: total fertility rate below 3.5 children per woman, per capita income more than $2000 per year, and at least one million population. Only six countries (Bulgaria, Cuba, Puerto Rico, Romania, Hungary, and Chile) have teen birthrates higher than the United States. Western European countries all have lower rates. There are eleven countries in which adolescent birthrates are between 25 and 50% of the U.S. level and five countries with rates less than 25% of those in the United States (Singapore, Hong Kong, Switzerland, Netherlands, and Japan). Comparison of available information on abortion rates is available for only thirteen countries. These data indicate that the high U.S. birthrates are not the result of less recourse to abortion by American teens. In fact, the U.S. birthrate is high because the pregnancy rate among teens in this country is exceptionally high. The result of this high pregnancy rate is the highest adolescent abortion rate among all countries with available data and the high U.S. birthrate.

Data on abortion (necessary for the calculation of pregnancy rates) were available for so few countries that the focus of analysis of differences between the thirty-seven countries was on birth rates. Variables representing factors that might be responsible for the observed wide differences in birthrates were gathered in the following areas: marriage, childbearing, contraception, abortion, sex, health, education, social integration, general social conditions, employment, and general economic conditions. These independent variables were sought from a wide variety of published sources and a country-level survey, developed and fielded by the Institute, of U.S. embassies, foreign embassies, and family planning organizations in each country. Many desired variables were not included because they were not available for a sufficient number of countries or because quality or comparability was poor. A measure of the level of sexual activity among adolescents in each country was not available and therefore could not be investigated in this part of the study. A total of forty-two independent variables were included in the analysis.

The variables most strongly associated with lower birthrates for those under age 18 were a lower proportion of the labor force in agriculture, less liberal policies on maternity leave and benefits, more equitable distribution of income in the country, and more open attitudes concerning sex. Those associated with lower birthrates for women aged 18–19 were a lower proportion employed in agriculture, less liberal policies on maternity leaves and benefits, more openness about sex, and the lack of a national policy geared to raise the overall level of reproduction. The United States does not fit the general pattern of higher levels of development being associated with lower levels of teen birthrates. It does, however, fit the general pattern seen of higher birthrates in countries with less openness about sex and less equitable distribution of income.

Case Studies of Six Countries

The country case studies attempted to follow leads pointed out in the thirty-seven-country analysis and to investigate important questions that could not be included in the first phase. Countries were picked from the group of thirty-seven on the basis of three further considerations: Their rates of adolescent pregnancy were distinctly lower than the United States; they were generally similar to the United States in cultural heritage and stage of economic development; and important data relevant to the evaluation of adolescent pregnancy were available. From this group, five countries (plus the United States) were selected: Canada, England and Wales, France, the Netherlands, and Sweden. Detailed data were collected on births and abortions, marriage and cohabitation, sexual activity, and contraceptive practice through review of published materials available in the United States and from each selected country. Teams of two investigators conducted interviews in each country with government officials, statisticians, demographers, and other researchers, as well as with family planning, abortion, and adolescent health service providers. These site visits helped identify other sources of data as well as providing opportunities to discuss attitudes and other less tangible factors that might not otherwise have been documented.

Differences in Pregnancy, Abortion, and Birthrates

The five other case study countries have much lower levels of teenage pregnancy than the United States (see Table 14-1). The American rate of 96 pregnancies (births plus abortions) per 1000 women aged 15–19 is about twice as high as those of Canada, England and Wales, and France, three times higher than the rate in Sweden and seven times higher than the Dutch rate. Differences are greatest for the youngest teens, but at each age, U.S. teens have higher pregnancy rates than teens in any of the five case study countries. Although pregnancy rates among black teens are twice those of white U.S. adolescents (165 vs. 83 per 1000 women aged 15–19, respectively), the position of the United States is not due solely to the higher rates among blacks. The international differences are great even when compared to white U.S. teens.

Differences between the United States and the five other case study countries have widened since the early 1970s. As shown in Figure 14-1, in 1973 the pregnancy rate for American adolescents was 23 points higher than the rate in England and Wales. By 1983 the British rate had decreased 15 points but the American rate had increased 13 points, so that the difference had more than doubled to 51 points. Although data for some countries is available only for more recent years, it appears that the United States has been the only one of the case study countries

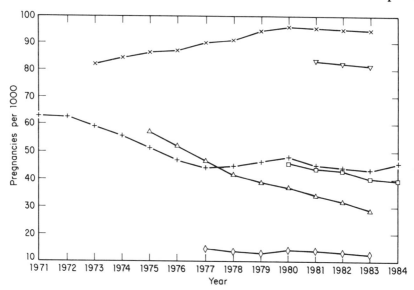

Figure 14–1. Pregnancies per 1000 women aged 15–19 for the years 1971–84, in five developed countries. Key to symbols: Canada □; England and Wales +; Netherlands ◇; Sweden △; United States total X; United States whites only ▽.

in which pregnancy rates among adolescents have risen. They have decreased in Canada, England and Wales, and Sweden. There has been less change in rates for those aged 15–17 than for older adolescents, but at both ages the U.S. rates increased while those of other countries decreased, widening the differences between the United States and other countries.

The abortion rate among U.S. teens rose even more steeply than the pregnancy rate, as shown in Figure 14-2. It rose sharply from 1973 through 1979 and appears to have plateaued since then, with steeper increases among 18- to 19-year-olds. This pattern was not seen in the other case study countries with trend data on abortion. The British rate increased less steeply than the U.S. rate, and Swedish and Canadian teens showed decreasing rates of abortion. In 1975, the Swedish abortion rate for 15- to 19-year-olds was only 2 points below the U.S. rate and it was higher for 15- to 17-year-olds. Since then, the rate in Sweden has dropped steadily, so that in 1983 the Swedish rate was 26 points lower for 15- to 19-year-olds and 19 points lower than the U.S. rate for 15- to 17-year-olds.

Although the U.S. pregnancy rate has risen since the early 1970s,

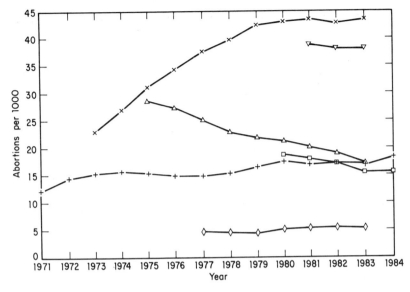

Figure 14–2. Abortions per 1000 women aged 15–19 for the years 1971–84, in five developed countries. Symbols are as in Figure 14–1.

relatively steeper increases in the abortion rate have caused the birth-rate to drop. It declined from 65 per 1000 women aged 15–19 in 1971 to 52 per 1000 in 1978, and since then has varied between 51 and 53 per 1000. Birthrates among adolescents declined even more steeply in the other case study countries, however, so that again the differences between the United States and the others have widened (see Fig. 14-3). In 1971 the U.S. birthrate was only 14 points above that of England and Wales, the case study country with the next highest rate. By 1984 the difference had widened to 23 points.

Comparison of trends over time indicates that not only is the United States different from the other case study countries in its higher rates of pregnancy, abortion, and birth among adolescents, but it has become more different since the early 1970s. While the birthrates in all six countries have dropped, the drop has been less steep in the United States. The available data indicate that in Canada, England and Wales, and Sweden, decreasing pregnancy rates have been an important cause of lower birthrates. Decreases in pregnancy rates in Sweden and Canada were large enough to achieve lower abortion rates as well. In the United States, the increasing pregnancy rate meant that lower birth-rates could be achieved only through a considerable increase in abortion rates.

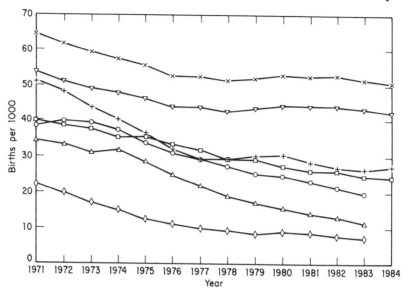

Figure 14–3. Births per 1000 women aged 15–19 for the years 1971–84, in six developed countries. Symbols are as in Figure 14–1, with the addition of France, ○.

Factors Responsible for the Difference

What accounts for these differences between the United States and the other case study countries? The most likely possibilities are higher levels of sexual activity among teens in America, greater desire among adolescents to have children, and lower levels of contraceptive use. (Biological differences in fecundity were not explored because they were judged less likely to exist or to account for such great differences.)

Levels of Sexual Activity

Figure 14-4 shows the percentage of adolescent women who had ever had intercourse for each of the case study countries. These data are estimates from surveys that differ in size and in the population covered (see Jones et al., 1986). The proportions who have had intercourse are higher at all ages in Sweden and lower in Canada than in the other four countries. The median age of sexual debut (the age at which half the girls have had intercourse) is about 17 in Sweden, 18 in England and Wales, France, the Netherlands, and the United States, and 19 in Canada. The differences in levels of sexual activity are neither large enough nor in the right order to account for differences in the preg-

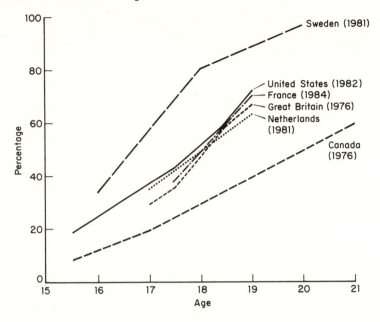

Figure 14–4. Percentage of women who ever had intercourse, by age. The year for which the most recent information was available for each country is given in parentheses. (Reproduced from Jones et al., 1986.)

nancy rates between the United States and the other countries. Higher levels of sexual activity in the United States contribute, however, to U.S. pregnancy rates that are higher than Canada at all ages and higher than France, Great Britain, and the Netherlands at the youngest ages. Interestingly, Sweden, with the highest levels of sexual activity, has pregnancy rates one third those of the United States, and the Netherlands, where rates of sexual activity are similar to the United States, has pregnancy rates only one seventh as high.

Pregnancy Intentions

The higher U.S. pregnancy rate is not due to a high level of intended adolescent pregnancy. The abortion rate among U.S. adolescents is as high or higher than the total pregnancy rates of the other countries studied, as shown in Figure 14-5. More than four fifths of the teen pregnancies in the United States are unintended; the unintended pregnancy rate is approximately 81 per 1000. If only intended pregnancies occurred among American teens, their rate would be about 15 per 1000, between the levels of the Netherlands and Sweden.

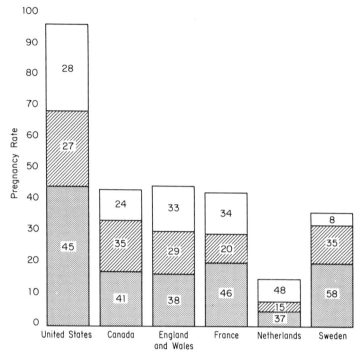

Figure 14–5. Percentage distribution of pregnancies and pregnancy rates, by outcome, for women aged 15–19 for the year 1980/81. The rates can be estimated by measuring the height of the bars against the vertical axis. The numbers inside the bars represent the percentage distributions. Open bars represent marital births; diagonally hatched bars, nonmarital births; shaded bars, abortions. (From Jones et al. 1985.)

Contraceptive Use

Figure 14-6 shows that those adolescent women who are sexually active in the United States appear to be less likely than comparable teens in other case study countries to use any contraceptive method. Comparisons also suggest that those American teens using contraceptives are less likely than those in other countries to use oral contraceptives, which are the most effective reversible method. (Although it also appears possible that American teens using contraceptives are more likely to fail and become pregnant than users of the same method in the other countries, direct analysis and evaluation of comparative contraceptive failure rates was not possible.)

The United States then has outstandingly high rates of adolescent pregnancy, abortion, and birth when compared to these other coun-

Age	United States		Great Britain	France			Canada	Sweden		Netherlands	
	1976	1979	1976	1979	1980	1976	1978	1981	1979 1980	1981
	NM	NM	NM	T	T	T	T	T	T	NM
	Used at last coitus	Used at last coitus	Use currently	Use regularly	Use regularly	Use currently	Used at last coitus	Used in last 4 weeks	Used in last 6 months	Used at last coitus

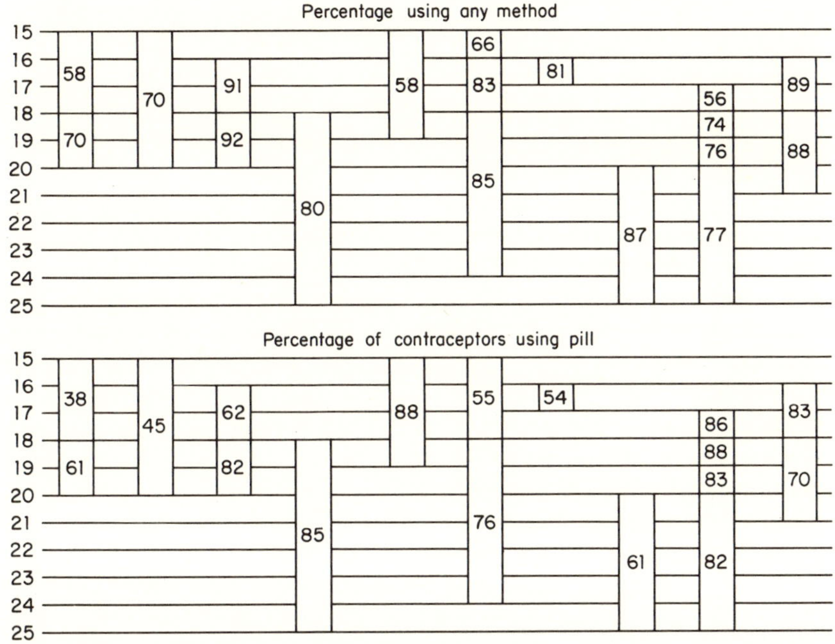

Percentage using any method

Percentage of contraceptors using pill

Figure 14–6. Percentage of sexually active women using any contraceptive method and, among users, percentage using the pill, by age and marital status of woman, and occasion of contraceptive use. The data should be interpreted cautiously because of problems in their comparability and (quality. NM = never married women; T = all women. (From Jones et al., 1986.)

tries not because U.S. teens are more sexually active than others or want to have high birthrates, but because they are managing their sexuality poorly, with less use of contraceptives and less use of more effective methods, especially the pill, than their counterparts in other countries.

Differences in Attitudes, Information, and Contraceptive Accessibility

Why do U.S. teens have poorer control of their sexuality? The answer is certainly a combination of a myriad of differences among the countries (see Jones et al., 1985, 1986). Indeed, even the national rates conceal differences among subgroups that exist in each country. Three areas of investigation are of most direct interest to this discussion and received special focus in the Institute study: attitudes regarding sex and pregnancy for adolescents, ways in which attitudes and information are passed on to adolescents, and the delivery of contraceptive services.

Attitudes About Adolescent Sexuality and Pregnancy

The Institute researchers concluded that, compared to the United States, adults in other case study countries, especially those in Europe, were more open about sexuality in general. Although, as in the United States, they do not all approve of teens having sex, they are more accepting of such behavior than American adults. Professionals and other country representatives interviewed in the site visits generally defined the "problem" in their country (if indeed they felt there was one) to be teen pregnancy, especially births to adolescents. In contrast, many in the United States view sexual activity among adolescents itself as the "problem." This is perhaps most clearly seen in the heated arguments between the federal Secretary of Education and the U.S. Surgeon General over whether the prevention of AIDS among adolescents should focus solely on telling teens not to have sex or should include information on condom use as well.

More than other countries, the United States can be characterized as ambivalent about sexual activity in general and among adolescents in particular. Over time, increasing proportions of Americans feel it is not wrong "for a man and a woman to have sex relations before marriage"—32% of adults surveyed in 1969 compared to 57% in 1985. In a 1979 study, 63% of parents of college-aged youth considered premarital sex acceptable. While sex before marriage is acceptable to many, approval of sex without a commitment to marry, especially among young adolescents is probably less acceptable. Former United States President Ronald Reagan stated that unmarried adolescents should not have sex, and in 1981 a federal governmental program to coordinate and develop services to adolescent mothers was altered to add as a major focus the prevention of sexual activity among unmarried adolescents. While eight in ten American adults support sex education in public schools and most support the provision of contraception by the federal government to sexually active adolescents, vocal minorities see these not simply as inadvisable but as the causes of sexual activity and as evils that should be eradicated, as should nonmarital sexual activity, especially among adolescents.

A 1976 survey of British women aged 16–49 found that 60% approved of sex before marriage, and a 1981 survey found that most women disagreed with the statement that premarital sex usually has more bad than good consequences. Most people in Britain favor sex education in the schools, including contraceptive education, but the proportions are not so high as in the United States.

A 1977 survey found that 40% of Canadians felt that having sexual relations with someone other than the marriage partner was not always wrong, compared to 28% of Americans surveyed in the same year. Public opinion about sex education is about the same in Canada and the United States. English Canada displays the same range of attitudes about sexuality as that in the United States. It appears (though difficult to document) that Canadians as a whole have a more tolerant attitude toward sexuality, however. Canadians interviewed during the site visit said that there is a fair degree of acceptance of out-of-wedlock childbearing, and that more Canadian than U.S. teenagers are cohabiting. Attitudes toward fertility control play a central role in the new, liberated spirit of Quebec, where fertility control is seen as part of a revolt against the church and the burden on women of large families. Quebec has changed rapidly from being more conservative than other provinces to being similar to or slightly more liberal with regard to sexual matters.

In France, issues involving early childbearing, adolescent sexual activity, sex education, and fertility control services for unmarried adolescents have been part of a much broader ideological tug-of-war. On the one side are the feminists, who have successfully championed the causes of contraception and abortion and the rights of adolescents to fertility control and sex education. On the other side are the more traditional proponents of the family, with a fundamentally pronatalist outlook.

Sweden, and the Scandinavian countries in general, seem to have evolved a largely secular view of sexual behavior in which the main concerns are that individuals know what they are doing and are sensitive to the needs and feelings of the other person and to the responsibilities involved. This demystification of sex also includes attention to the right to say no to sex. In fact, in this postliberation period, there is some evidence of a rejection of the ideology of casual sex and a renewed emphasis on the value of commitment.

There has been an enormous change in the Netherlands since the mid-1960s with respect to attitudes and behavior related to reproduction, birth control, and sexuality. Dutch society has become exceptionally open on matters related to sex, and sexual expression has come to be regarded not only as a good thing, but as something to which every member of society is entitled. Contraception, which used to be thought of primarily in terms of family planning, is now also associated with sexual liberation. The Netherlands is a country with a very deep-seated respect for individuals and tolerance of the personal life of others and freedom of choice within broadly prescribed limits. In this context, the investigators were told, on the whole, parents accept the sexual activity of their teenage children, without encouraging it.

Transfer of Attitudes and Information to Adolescents

The case study investigations looked at three ways in which adult society expresses its attitudes or attempts to give adolescents information about sexuality and pregnancy-related behavior: communication with parents, sex education through schools, and the mass media. There were differences across countries in how these channels are used.

COMMUNICATION WITH PARENTS

Research in the United States has shown that most parents do not talk with their teenage children about sex or about birth control. Among those who have talked about sex-related issues, there is a good deal of misunderstanding about what parents think they have communicated and what teenagers think they have heard from their parents. Adolescents most commonly cite friends, reading, media, and schools as the major sources of sexual information.

A 1974/75 study in England and Wales found almost two thirds of 16- to 19-year-olds said it was easy for them to talk to their mothers about things that are important to them, but a much smaller portion had ever talked to a parent about reproduction, sex, and birth control. A little under half of the young people who had talked about intercourse with a parent expressed satisfaction with the discussion.

Only half of the French postsecondary students surveyed in 1982 thought they had been well informed about contraceptive methods. The information source most commonly mentioned was books and magazines (34%) followed by parents (16%), friends (14%), doctors (13%), and teachers (11%). Among women under age 20, friends were the most common source of contraception information but more said parents were their desired source of information. School ranked as the second most common actual and desired source.

There is a considerable amount of communication between parents and their children in Sweden. A long history of sex education in Swedish schools means that parents probably know more and have more accurate information about sex-related topics than American adults. A study in six localities of Sweden found that 58% of adolescents said they had talked about sexuality with their mothers. These same adolescents, however, reported that the best information about sexuality came not from their parents, but from teachers.

A 1981 survey in the Netherlands found that 61% of men and 70% of women aged 16–20 said the topic of sex came up in conversation at home at least from time to time. In contrast, fewer than 20% of those aged 21–64 thought that their parents had been frank and open about sex with them and this proportion decreased sharply with age, suggesting extensive change over time. The main sources of information on the facts of reproduction are parents and schools, each mentioned by more than 40% of teens. Fewer, however, learn about contraception in school (20% of young males and 28% of females) or from their parents (<15%). Young men were particularly unlikely to learn about contraception from either source.

It seems clear that even where there is more communication and probably more accurate information about sexuality and pregnancy prevention passed from parents to adolescents, as in Sweden and the Netherlands, other sources of information may be even more common and teens may have more confidence in them.

Sex Education

The degree to which there is sex education in schools varies among the case study countries and often varies within them as well.

In the United States, local school authorities decide whether to offer sex education and what to teach. About three fourths of adolescents receive some sex education before leaving school; more than half have sex education that includes contraceptive information.

Similarly, in Canada, sex education is a local option, but 87% of Canadian urban school districts offered sex education in 1984, compared to only 75% of school districts in large cities in the United States in 1982.

While sex education is also a local option in England and Wales, there is a national policy favoring the inclusion of topics related to sex and family life in the curriculum. In the mid-1970s sex education was more prevalent in Britain than in the United States, but the proportion getting instruction on contraception did not differ greatly.

Sex education is mandated by French national policy for all adolescents, but in practice local authorities are free to interpret this provision. The proportion of girls taught about contraceptive methods in school may be higher than in the United States.

Sex education has been a compulsory part of the school curriculum for all ages in Sweden since 1956. The underlying philosophy of sex education in Sweden and the content of the curriculum have undergone several transformations. It has evolved from a narrow biological emphasis to include the full context of human relationships. Even the label, "sex education," has been broadened, at first to "education in sex and life together," and then to "education in living together." Whereas in the early days, stress was laid on freedom and the presentation of all points of view, adult value judgments are now clearly stated for young people to accept or to reject. Responsible premarital sex is acceptable, but sex is not to be regarded as an isolated event. Stress is placed on the importance of ethics, fidelity, and equal rights, and on the responsibilities of parenthood.

In contrast, sex education in the Netherlands has been incorporated in the school curriculum only to a very limited extent, with the formal school program usually limited to the biological facts about reproduction. The government has, however, funded the major private family planning association in the Netherlands to provide educational services. Group sessions are given at the association's own centers and education teams make visits to classrooms upon invitation from the schools.

MASS MEDIA

There was an increase in explicit and implicit sexual behavior on television in the United States during the 1970s. The emphasis of the frequent sexual references is on titillation. References to extramarital sex are much more common than to sex between married couples, and programs seldom portray sexual relationships as warm, loving, or stable. Radio and television commercials as well as print advertising often have clear sexual overtones. Portrayals of male–female relationships depict them as highly romanticized or exploitive. There is almost no realistic information about sex and no mention of use of contraceptives (until prompted very recently by the AIDS crisis).

Television and radio news and talk programs do cover topics related to sexuality with increasing frequency, often in the context of adolescent pregnancy. They usually present factual information, sometimes including reference to sources of care. Newspapers and magazines have also dealt with topics related to sexuality over the past few years in news and feature articles, as well as in advice columns.

In most ways, the British media are far more open about sex than the media in the United States. Nudity is seen fairly commonly in programming and in some commercials. Newspapers and magazine feature articles on family planning are quite common and often of high quality. Most newspapers and magazines have "agony" columns, which respond to readers' personal problems, many of them sexual in nature. The columnists regard themselves as agents for information services, and all letters are answered personally with informational material from the various relevant agencies. Phone-in radio programs in which experts give frank advice to people with sexual problems and relationship difficulties are commonplace in Britain. Sex education programs created for schools as well as for general audiences are part of continuing education programs on radio and television. The wording of messages in a mass-media health education campaign to encourage sexually active teens to use contraceptives was deliberately made less explicit, however, because of concerns about promoting promiscuity.

The media in English-speaking Canada reflect the strong influence of the United States, since most of the popular programming comes from the United States. Newspapers carry some of the same advice columnists as in the United States as well. In contrast, the media in French Canada directed much attention to the increased sexual activity of teens in the mid-1970s. There was extensive discussion in the media of the change in sexual behavior and the need for contraceptives. Soap operas discussed and portrayed the use of contraception. Observers interviewed during the study felt that the net effect of the media attention was to encourage acceptance, though not necessarily approval, of the change and to promote a sense of the importance of the use of contraceptives and of responsibility in sexuality.

France made extensive use of television and radio in a 1981 family planning publicity campaign, but there has been very little other information on sex and contraception in these media until recently. Sex is generally romanticized in the media and the presentation of male and female roles is highly stereotyped. Much of what has appeared in the popular press has been sensational rather than objective reporting, but certain women's magazines have carried responsible and informative articles. Although most magazines for youth have not covered contraception, one very popular one carries a column by the leader of the French family planning movement, who answers readers' questions.

It appears that mass media played a minor role in changing sexual attitudes in Sweden. Many of the television programs, imported from the United States, contain considerable violence and portray women as sex objects. The sex education program attempts to counteract these kinds of messages. Growing popularity of video cassette recorders led to a public debate about the showing of violence and pornography and to the passage of an antipornography law in 1981. There have been a few special programs with some positive impact, however, and women's magazines carry numerous articles on contraception. The National Association for Sexual Information carries out major publicity campaigns for specific purposes, such as reducing the prevalence of sexually transmitted diseases.

In contrast, the media were an important factor in the very rapid spread of modern contraception in the Netherlands, beginning in 1972, when a television program prepared to educate doctors on contraception was shown to the general public as well. After this, there was a remarkable increase in the presentation of materials related to the general topic of sex. Even though large parts of Dutch society remained traditional in outlook, the Dutch system of allocating air time to groups representing different points of view made it possible for programs produced by any one group to be seen by everyone. Popular information programs began to appear, and books explaining contraceptive methods were widely distributed. Magazines also took up the topic, although sensational topics, such as scares about the pill, have sometimes been exploited at the expense of more objective reporting. Discussion of sex on radio and television and in the print media has become commonplace. Such discussions range from the biological facts to the emotional side of sexual relationships, and sexual problems. Young people have been exposed to these influences along with their elders, so that, in a sense, the entire society has concurrently.experienced a course in sex education.

Examination of these six countries shows differences in the ways parental communication, school sex education, and mass media are used to convey attitudes and information about sexuality and contraception to adolescents. In general, the United States appears less open about sexuality through these channels and is less likely to use them to convey attitudes and provide information about contraception. Media presentation of sexuality in exploitive relationships and for purposes of titillation is common to all six countries, but in countries other than the United States this media message seems to be offset to a greater extent by formal sex education, by other media, and—especially in French Canada and the Netherlands—by additional programming.

Accessibility of Contraceptive Services

Contraceptive services were found to be least accessible to adolescents in the United States and most accessible in England and Wales, Sweden and the Netherlands, as indicated in Table 14-2. In all but Sweden, adolescents can obtain prescription contraceptives from both physicians and clinics. In the United States the physicians are most likely to be obstetrician–gynecologists, to whom the teen would probably not have gone before, while in the other countries physicians providing contraceptives are usually general or family physicians whom the teenager would probably have visited for other reasons as well. The primary health centers providing contraceptives in Sweden and the health clinics in England and Wales would also be places to which an adolescent would have gone for other care as well. The clinic system that serves about half the teens using prescription contraceptives in the United States is primarily a service system for low-income women and is not likely to be used for other health services by most teens. In all these countries, but especially England and Wales, Sweden, and the Netherlands, special clinics for youth are available in some areas to meet what are perceived to be special needs of adolescents who may be reluctant to obtain services from their regular physician or clinic.

Table 14-2

Characteristics of Current Contraceptive Services in Six Countries

	UNITED STATES	ENGLAND AND WALES	CANADA	FRANCE	SWEDEN	NETHERLANDS
Source of Care	Some physicians, mostly specialists Clinics (primarily for low-income women)	General practitioner Clinic A few clinics for youth	Some physicians Clinics (uneven coverage of country)	Some physicians Clinics	Primary health center Clinic for youth	Family doctor Clinic for youth
Same Source for Regular Health Care	No	Yes	Yes	Yes	Yes	Yes
Cost	Physician care not free Supplies not free Clinic care and supplies low cost or free	Free care and supplies	Free physician care Some clinics free Supplies not free	Free clinic services and supplies for those <18, older reimbursed by insurance	Free care and supplies	Free physician care Small fee at clinics Free prescription supplies until recently
Confidentiality	Physician discretion Most clinics provide confidentiality	Physician discretion for age <16 years Must be confidential for age ≥16 years	Physician discretion Most clinics provide confidentiality	Clinic services, for <18 must be confidential	Doctors forbidden to inform parents	Services must be confidential if teen requests it
Condom Availability	Limited	Widespread	Limited	Limited	Widespread	Widespread

Free medical care for contraception is readily available in all but the United States, because the other countries all have some form of national health system. In some cases, supplies or care by special providers are not available, but teens are charged a low fee. In contrast, private physician care in the United States is expensive and seldom free except to teens on welfare (who in most areas must be poor, unmarried, and already have a child or be a daughter of a poor, unmarried woman). Contraceptive supplies are much more expensive in the United States than the other countries, in part because of the high expense of product liability coverage in the United States. Visits to clinics and supplies from them cost much less than those obtained privately and are sometimes free for adolescents.

Even though other countries tend to be more open about sexuality than is the United States, confidentiality was an important issue in each of the six countries studied. Confidentiality is up to the individual physician or clinic to determine in the United States and Canada and for those under age 16 in England and Wales, but clinics in these countries are more likely than physicians to provide services confidentially. In England and Wales, services to those aged 16 and older must be confidential, and clinic services in France must be confidential as well. In Sweden, providers are specifically forbidden to tell parents if an adolescent requests contraceptives. Clinic services in the Netherlands are confidential, and visits to physicians must also be confidential if the teen requests it.

Sources of nonprescription contraceptives are important, since the condom is generally the second most popular method among teens. Condoms are readily available in England and Wales, Sweden, and the Netherlands through family planning clinics, pharmacies, supermarkets, and other shops and vending machines, but sources are more limited in the United States, Canada, and France.

Discussion

Comparison of pregnancy, abortion, and birthrates among developed countries shows that it is possible to have lower rates than those in the United States. This study has shown that lower rates are possible in a variety of pluralistic societies, which have different patterns of service delivery and different approaches to sex education in schools. While there may be reasons for reducing the level of sexual activity in the United States in and of itself, the case studies illustrate that that is not a necessary condition to attaining lower pregnancy rates. Rather, the other case study countries have lower pregnancy rates because of earlier, more extensive, and better contraceptive use among sexually active adolescents.

Special attention has been paid here to attitudes about adolescent sexuality and contraceptive use and how those attitudes and information are communicated to teens in the six countries. The comparisons suggest that contraceptive use is greater and adolescent pregnancy rates lower where there is less societal and individual ambivalence about sexuality and the appropriateness of contraceptive use. The more matter-of-fact acceptance of adolescent sexual activity and provision of contraceptives in the five other countries contrasts with a high degree of societal ambivalence in the United States about sexuality. American teens are exposed to clear messages on the one side that sex is romantic, exciting, and titillating, and to equally strong messages on the other side that it is bad to have sex outside of marriage. There is little information about contraceptives or the importance of their use for avoiding pregnancy, in part because of concern that such messages will incite more adolescents to have sex.

The experience of the other five case study countries suggests that increased legitimacy and availability of information about sexuality and contraception and accessibility to contraceptive methods can help lower teen pregnancy rates. It appears that being more open about sexuality allows adults to communicate more clearly to teens their expectations for responsible behavior and to provide the information and services necessary for teens to make effective use of contraceptives when they are sexually active.

References

Jones, E. F., Forrest, J. D., Goldman, N., Henshaw, S. K., Lincoln, R., Rosoff, J. I., Westoff, C. F., & Wulf, D. (1985). Teenage pregnancy in developed countries: Determinants and policy implications. *Family Planning Perspectives, 17* (March/April): 2.

Jones, E. F., Forrest, J. D., Goldman, N., Henshaw, S. K., Lincoln, R., Rosoff, J. I., Westoff, C. F., & Wulf, D. (1986). *Teenage pregnancy in industrialized countries.* New Haven, CT: Yale University Press.

15

Legal and Social Dilemmas of Adolescent Sexuality

Hyman Rodman

A poem of Rachel Field describes "the seven ages of elfhood." In the first, "when an elf is as old as a year and a minute, he can wear a cap with a feather in it." In the fourth, when he's 50 or so, "his coat may have buttons all in a row." And in the seventh, "when he's a hundred and a day, he gets a little pipe to play!"

If only selfhood were as clear as elfhood! If only we had more social consensus on the age of competence for particular actions, more consensus on the appropriate age for individuals to wear a cap with a feather in it, or to use a diaphragm with spermicidal jelly in it. Our lives would then be simpler, and we would face fewer psychological, legal, moral, and social dilemmas.

It is precisely because things are not so clear, because we have substantial differences about when it is appropriate to play our pipes, that we encounter quandaries and dilemmas.

My focus will be on the social and legal dilemmas of adolescent sexuality, but I want to refer to two other controversial issues that raise similar questions about when individuals are ready to be independent and to take on certain rights and responsibilities. One issue stems from the abortion controversy: It is the issue of fetal viability.

At what gestational age is a fetus sufficiently developed to be able to survive on its own (if born prematurely)? Of course, not literally on its own, but with use of state-of-the-art technology and with parental care and nurturing. The time of viability has gone from about 28 weeks gestational age (LMP) to about 23 weeks, and although abortions legally may be done in the last trimester, technological advances regarding viability have greatly limited the practical possibility of obtaining an abortion during the final trimester. But attitudes about abortion vary widely and are not all focused on the criterion of viability. Attitudes about when abortion should be legal or illegal range from conception to implantation to quickening to viability to birth, among other criteria.

I will not deal with the abortion controversy here. I only want to point out a rough analogy between age of fetal viability and age of adolescent maturity: Attitudes differ, partisan ideologies clash, and they bring legal, social, and moral dilemmas in their wake.

A second issue stems from a controversy about child-care arrangements: It is the issue of children in self-care arrangements (latchkey children). At what age are children mature enough to spend time at home alone, on a periodic basis, while their parents are at work or are otherwise engaged?

According to some, children are virtually never old enough or mature enough to spend time at home alone. For example, the Special Report of the Governor's Task Force on Day Care for Tennessee (August 1986, p. 26) says the following about school-age children: "Although some older children may be mature enough to handle the circumstances when left alone, most children, *regardless of age*, need supervision by a responsible adult" (emphasis added).

According to others, providing time at home alone for children is an excellent way to teach and encourage responsibility and to prepare children for their soon-to-come independence.

There is a social dilemma here: To what extent are child-care professionals, who are for the most part opposed to self-care arrangements, acting out of a concern for children's welfare? To what extent are they motivated by a vested interest in obtaining additional funds for child-care that would extend the influences of their profession?

Self-care also poses a legal dilemma. Laws about child neglect are rather general, even vague. States typically define neglect in terms of "improper," "insufficient," or "inadequate" supervision. Since most cases of neglect focus on parental supervision, those parents who use self-care are potentially placing themselves in jeopardy. Might someone complain about parents who leave a 10-year-old at home alone for an hour a day, 5 days a week, until they get home from work? Will the state intervene under such circumstances? Generally, child placement workers are not going to intervene. Given the rather large number of children in self-care, there are few such cases of intervention. Yet the possibility does exist.

Again, although it would be unwise to stretch the analogy too far, the controversy about self-care also has an underlying question about maturity: When is a child mature enough or competent enough to do

———— ? What differences of attitude, opinion, and ideology exist, and what is the source of these differences? And finally, what social, legal, and moral issues are raised by these questions?

My reading of the general situation in the United States is that we display a paradoxical culture. There is much concern about how we hurry our children along, about not giving them opportunity to enjoy their childhood, about expecting too much too soon. These views are expressed in books like David Elkind's *The Hurried Child* and receive much sympathetic attention. This viewpoint suggests that we err on the side of granting our children responsibility too soon and of expecting more of them than they are capable of.

In reality, however, I think that we err on the side of stressing children's deficiencies, of not granting them sufficient responsibility, of delay in acknowledging their competence. Overall, I think there is more stress on children's incompetence and irresponsibility than on their developing competencies. More stress is placed on the need for a slow and unhurried childhood than on the transition from childhood to adulthood. More concern is expressed about the premature granting of responsibility than about delays in granting responsibility.

The above themes certainly apply to the areas of self-care arrangements and adolescent sexuality. Regarding self-care, despite very limited and mixed evidence, there has been much said by the media and by some professionals about the dangers of self-care. Some are overgeneralizing from earlier studies of institutionalized children and assuming (without empirical evidence) that time spent alone by children is necessarily harmful. Currently expressed concerns about self-care seem to be repeating earlier expressed concerns about the dangers of maternal employment and day care. There is a dilemma here for feminists and others: whether or not to use suspect data on the dangers of self-care to argue for increased funding for after-school child care.

Regarding adolescent sexuality, despite evidence to the contrary, there is much public and political stress on the need to shield children and adolescents from information about sexuality. Despite strong public opinion support for sex education in the schools, as indicated by numerous surveys, partisan and political fear that sex education will corrupt children and will undercut parental authority has greatly limited the amount of education on human sexuality that is provided to American children. Although the evidence is limited, it suggests that children are capable of profiting from sex education, of behaving more responsibly with sex education. The United States provides less in the way of comprehensive sex education than most European societies, displays less openness on sexual issues, and has higher rates of adolescent pregnancy.

Once again, this suggests that we paint ourselves into a paradoxical corner. We stress children's immaturity and we mistrust their ability to profit from comprehensive courses in sex education. Yet, U.S. adolescents engage extensively in sexual behavior and have higher rates of pregnancy, abortion, and illegitimate childbirth than adolescents in most developed societies. In brief, we don't trust adolescents to do things, but they do them anyhow; and because of our mistrust we don't provide the educational tools that would enable them to develop their competence and maturity and to behave in a more responsible fashion. Equally important, our paradoxical and ambivalent attitudes make it difficult to sharpen and test our tools, to develop more effective education in human sexuality.

Our social and cultural pattern can be characterized as "self-fulfilling mistrust." Many, of course, do not share this cultural pattern, but it is widespread throughout society. This makes the transition from childhood to adulthood more difficult. Our self-fulfilling mistrust, aided currently by the influence of New Right ideology, has several unfortunate consequences:

1. It makes it difficult for parents to use self-care arrangements or to find good sexuality education for their children.
2. It makes it difficult for objective research in these areas to drive out anecdotal evidence and false beliefs.
3. It makes it difficult for many practitioners and policymakers to support, or at least to maintain an open mind about, self-care and sexuality education (the community watchdogs are looking over their shoulders).
4. It makes it easy for some to criticize self-care and sex education, to distort and misinterpret evidence, or merely to ignore the evidence.

In short, these issues become ideological and political. Values loom large on the horizon of self-care arrangements and adolescent sexuality.

Adolescent Sexuality

I now turn specifically to a discussion of the legal and social dilemmas of adolescent sexuality.

Adolescents are undergoing processes of social, psychological, and biological growth and development. These are, generally speaking, gradual processes, as the individual moves from childhood to adulthood. Children are in transition from dependence to independence, as they learn new skills and gradually acquire greater degrees of competence in caring for themselves and making their own decisions. Depending on the cultural setting, adolescents may face greater or lesser pressure to speed up or to slow down the process of becoming adults.

In the legal arena, however, there is a discrete change of status as an individual moves from minor to adult. The law usually pays little attention to distinctions among minors, treating infants, children, and adolescents pretty much alike. All at once, at a somewhat arbitrarily defined age, a minor becomes an adult; a person who has legally required parental protection, guidance, support, and consent now becomes a person who is legally responsible for his or her own decisions and actions. Of course, this overstates the case, since there can be some intermediate legal stages, some points at which a minor acquires certain legal rights before attaining majority status. But in relative terms we are comparing a gradual transition toward social, psychological, and physical competence with a sudden shift to legal competence.

These differently paced occurrences pose a potential dilemma for adolescents and their parents. If parents turn responsibility over to their children "too quickly," they may not be able to cope and may make poor decisions and engage in irresponsible behavior. Moreover, parents may be charged with neglect due to inadequate supervision. If parents maintain strict control over their adolescents, focusing on their childhood vulnerabilities and limiting their activities, judgments, and decision-making, they may impede their children's development.

If adolescents seek greater control than the parent is willing to grant, there may be a great deal of conflict. Parents may call on the state to help enforce their control. Or the adolescent may move out of the house in order to escape parental control. In the latter circumstance, parents may enlist the state to find and perhaps discipline their "runaway child."

The potential conflict between parent and adolescent is perhaps greatest in the area of sexual behavior. If parents and adolescent have different ideas about the adolescent's sexual behavior or fertility control behavior, then the clash may be serious and the legal situation may loom large. For example, does a minor legally require parental consent to obtain certain contraceptives? Does a minor legally require parental consent to obtain an abortion? These are specific legal questions that I will address. But the legal issues occur within the context of minors' physical, social, and psychological development and within a context of social and cultural norms and values.

How do societies deal with the potential conflict between adolescent development and parental control? How do individual parents and children deal with the legal and social dilemmas? I will describe three different solutions that can prevent the occurrence of conflict or minimize the conflict that does occur.

Independence Granting by Parents

The first solution is basic, widespread, and unexceptional. It arises from
the informal interaction of parent and child. Although paradoxical features of our culture make it difficult for parents to know when to hold
on and when to let go, when to accept dependence and when to encourage independence, the actual interactions between parents and
children are marked by a great deal of negotiation. Parents know that
their children are heading toward adulthood and they recognize (at
some level) that they have a responsibility to help children develop
their independence. As a result, most parents informally grant increasing degrees of independence and responsibility to their children. Children are developing their own physical, social, and psychological competence, and are typically eager to explore the world and to undertake
increasing degrees of independence and responsibility. Most of these
explorations involve mundane activities that are beyond the reach of
legal or judicial intervention. In consequence, parents cannot and do
not insist on making all decisions and taking all responsibility until
their children are legally entitled to make these decisions. The changing nature of informal, everyday interaction and negotiation between a
parent and child typically conforms with and encourages the child's
gradual development. As a result, the potential for conflict that stems
from discrepancies between the family domain and the legal domain is
not usually realized. Parents informally grant increasing responsibilities to their children; discrete legal changes do not take parents and
children by surprise.

Of course, while independence granting by parents circumvents potential conflicts, not all conflict can be avoided. Some parents only
grudgingly grant limited responsibility to their children, generating
conflict between parent and child. Some children are impatient with
the rights and responsibilities informally granted to them, and strain
at the bit, anxious to be independent of their parents. What happens
to the minor who is dissatisfied with his family and runs away? What
happens to the minor who becomes pregnant and seeks an abortion
without her parents' knowledge or consent?

Legal Flexibility

This brings us to a second solution that serves to minimize potential
conflict between parent and child: legal flexibility. In principle a child
becomes an adult all at once, at age 18. In fact, however, the law is not
that rigid. For example, minors may acquire certain legal rights and
responsibilities before 18—for example, for criminal behavior, for joining the armed forces, for driving a car, or for taking employment.

Another example, more pertinent to this discussion, is the legal status of emancipation. This provides an avenue for minors to free themselves from the authority and control of parents under certain limited circumstances. Marriage typically emancipates a minor. Living apart from parents and being self-supporting also typically emancipates a minor. In the event that there is conflict between parent and child, emancipation can end the conflict. It frees the parent from the duty to support the child and frees the child from the duty to obey the parent. A California statute defines an emancipated minor as "a minor 15 years or older who is living separate and apart from his parents, whether with or without consent of a parent or guardian, and regardless of the duration of such separate residence, and who is managing his own financial affairs, regardless of the source of his income" (Civil Code No. 64).

Once a minor gains legal emancipation, he or she is treated as an adult and is no longer subject to parental authority. This severs the legal bond but not necessarily the social bond. It eliminates the conflict that may stem from the legal authority parents have over children but not necessarily the social and personal conflict. Without emancipation, many minors face a Catch-22 situation. Because of serious conflict they may want to leave their parents, but their ability to do so depends on their parents' willingness to accept the separation. Parents can call on the state to bring back minor children who have "run away" from home. If children continue to run away they can be charged with incorrigibility and placed in a state institution. With emancipation, however, a "minor" is no longer a runaway, parents cannot use force to bring him or her back, and parent and child are then left to their own devices, as adults, to deal with their differences and conflicts.

In effect, emancipation is an example of the flexibility of the legal system to accommodate parent–child conflict. However, in the area of adolescent abortion, it is not the most important example of flexibility. As we shall see, the concept of a mature minor plays a more important role than the occasional resort to a minor's legal emancipation.

Although state statutes generally are silent about minors' access to contraceptive services, most states have adopted policies that explicitly permit minors to obtain contraceptive medical services on their own consent. Several U.S. Supreme Court decisions on related issues effectively protect minors' access to contraceptive services. The U.S. Supreme Court, in *Carey* v. *Population Services International* (1977), held that states could not prohibit the sale or distribution of nonprescription contraceptives to minors. The Sixth Circuit Court, in *Doe* v. *Irwin* (1980), held that the distribution of contraceptives by public clinics did not violate parents' constitutional rights, and the U.S. Supreme Court refused to consider an appeal. Although many private physicians and some family planning agencies will not provide medical contraceptive services to minors without parental consent, most do provide such services, especially those who are more active in serving young women and thus more familiar with the legal situation. It should be noted, however, that legal access is not the same as actual access, and minors often face a variety of obstacles in gaining access to contraceptive services.

The legal situation regarding minors' access to abortion is somewhat more complicated. When the U.S. Supreme Court's interpretation of the constitution liberalized the abortion situation in 1973, in *Roe* v. *Wade* and *Doe* v. *Bolton,* it did not make a decision on parental consent requirements. It noted that although some states had parental consent requirements, such requirements were not at issue in either the Georgia or Texas cases that it dealt with that day. In the last footnote of the *Roe* decision the Court said, "We need not now decide whether provisions of this kind are constitutional."

Those opposed to abortion saw this as an opportunity, at the state level, to hamper minors' access to abortion. As a result, a number of additional states passed legislation requiring parental consent. We might say that the Court's footnote stimulated some state legislatures to give the boot to minors and to drive them away from access to abortion services on their own consent. Parental consent became one of the most controversial abortion questions after *Roe* v. *Wade.* Lower courts issued many decisions on the question of parental consent for a minor's abortion. The great majority of these decisions ruled that the parental consent requirement was unconstitutional. The issue first came before the U.S. Supreme Court in *Planned Parenthood of Central Missouri* v. *Danforth,* a 1976 decision. One of the restrictions passed in 1974 by the Missouri legislature required parental consent for a minor's abortion unless the abortion was necessary to save the minor's life.

Missouri argued that the law protected minors by ensuring parental counsel regarding an important decision. The state also argued that the law was aimed at preserving parental authority within the family. The federal district court upheld the requirement, but it was reversed by the U.S. Supreme Court. The Court rejected the arguments of the state and expressed doubt "that such veto power will enhance parental authority or control where the minor and the nonconsenting parent are so fundamentally in conflict, and the very existence of the pregnancy already has fractured the family structure." The Court held that "the State does not have the constitutional authority to give a third party an *absolute,* and possibly arbitrary, veto over the decision of the physician and his patient to terminate the patient's pregnancy." In deference to the tradition of parental authority, the Court qualified its decision: "We emphasize that our holding . . . does not suggest that every minor, regardless of age or maturity, may give effective consent for termination of her pregnancy."

In *Bellotti* v. *Baird (Bellotti I)*, decided on the same day as *Danforth*, the Court indicated that its objection to the Missouri statute was the state's blanket requirement for parental consent for all minors, with no exception for mature minors or for minors whose best interest would be served by an abortion without parental consent. When *Bellotti* v. *Baird (Bellotti II)* returned to the U.S. Supreme Court for a second time, in 1979, the Court elaborated its views of children's rights. It emphasized children's vulnerability and the important parental role in children's upbringing—including the constitutional interpretation that recognized parents' claims to authority in their own household. The Court indicated that "legal restrictions on minors, especially those supportive of the parental role, may be important to the child's chances for the full growth and maturity that make eventual participation in a free society meaningful and rewarding." Despite its strong support of the doctrine of parental authority, the Court held the Massachusetts statute unconstitutional. It disapproved of the requirement that a minor seek her parents' consent *before* she was entitled to seek court relief. Because Massachusetts required parental involvement in every instance, and because a judge could deny an abortion even if the minor was mature and competent to make the decision, the statute was ruled unconstitutional.

Some state statutes require parental notification rather than consent. Utah requires a physician to notify, if possible, the parents of a dependent, unmarried minor girl before performing the abortion. The statute was challenged in *H.L.* v. *Matheson*, and it was upheld on narrow grounds by the U.S. Supreme Court in 1981. Since the minor challenging the Utah statute in *Matheson* did not claim to be either mature or emancipated, the Court excluded such minors from its decision. In 1983, in *City of Akron* v. *Akron Center for Reproductive Health*, the Court again rejected a blanket parental veto over a minor's abortion decision. It held that Akron's statute requiring parental consent for all minors under the age of 15 was unconstitutional.

Although the issue of parental involvement in the abortion decision is not fully resolved, the cases decided thus far suggest roughly how far a state statute may go while still passing constitutional muster. It seems that a state may, if it desires, require parental consent or notification for a minor's abortion as long as it provides certain exceptions. One exception is for emancipated minors; another is for mature minors. To pass constitutional muster, the law must provide a confidential and expeditious route for dependent minors to demonstrate to the courts (or some other agency) that they are mature and hence competent to make their own decision. Failing the demonstration of maturity, minors must have the opportunity to demonstrate to the courts that obtaining an abortion without parental involvement is in their best interest. A minor's legal right to bypass her parents by demonstrating maturity or "best interest" to the judicial system is referred to as judicial bypass; state abortion statutes on parental involvement that do not provide for judicial bypass or other comparable alternatives are not being upheld by the courts.

In brief, the demonstration of maturity on the part of a minor is another example of legal flexibility that takes into account individual variation. Such legal maturity can provide an avenue for minors to undertake certain actions on their own consent. As with legal emancipation, this flexibility may serve to buffer conflict between parent and child.

These policies on minors' access to contraceptive and abortion services are an important element of the U.S. situation regarding adolescent sexuality. They provide flexibility to the system and make it possible for minors to have access to certain services (including treatment for sexually transmitted diseases) without parental involvement. Do the U.S. Supreme Court decisions that have produced this breach of parental control suggest that the Court has abandoned its strong concern for parental autonomy and authority? As my colleagues and I have said elsewhere, the answer is no:

> The possibility must be considered that the *Danforth* line of cases are direct responses to what the Court saw as deliberate attempts to thwart the effect of *Roe v. Wade,* and that the Court has merely carved out a special exception to the doctrine of parental autonomy in the reproductive rights area. This interpretation would not be inconsistent with the Court's previous decisions in the family planning/abortion area, where one finds repeated examples of the Court's impatience with legislative policies that are antagonistic to family planning efforts (Rodman, Lewis, & Griffith, 1984, pp. 68–69).

The Passage of Time

Time may not heal all, but many things do get better with the passage of time. Is time also able to exert its healing power over conflict between parent and child?

If a 16-year-old and her parents experience serious conflict over authority and responsibility issues, and if the daughter's legal emancipation or legal maturity cannot resolve the problem, then time may do so. As with any conflict, the situation may change over time so that those facing serious conflict resolve the conflict and may even become staunch friends and allies. Failing that, however, time will bring about a solution because the child will shortly become an adult.The 16-year-old daughter will, within 2 years, turn 18 and be free of the legal control of her parents. The personal conflict may endure, but the legal conflict posed by a clash between demanding parents and a disobedient minor will end when the minor becomes an adult.

The case of Walter Polovchak provides a particularly vivid—albeit atypical—example. In 1980, when his parents decided to leave the United States to return to the Soviet Union, he ran away from his parents to live with relatives in Chicago. He was only 12 years old at the time, and under ordinary circumstances parental custody would have been granted and he would have been turned over to his parents. But political undercurrents and legal actions delayed a decision in the case. The parents' chances of regaining custody diminished with the passage of time, and finally, in 1986 when Walter turned 18, the legal conflict ended. The irresolvable conflict between Walter and his parents about where he should live was resolved as soon as Walter the minor became Walter the adult.

In general, parent–child controversies are not good candidates for judicial resolution. The courts are painfully aware of this and are reluctant to adjudicate such cases. Although a case may focus on a single justiciable issue, a complex problem may lie below the surface, placing severe limits on what the courts can do. As the U.S. Supreme Court said in *Bellotti II*, parent–child disputes, unlike most disputes, have the capacity for self-resolution. Any aspect of the controversy that could be solved through the legal process will be resolved by the child's attaining majority. In many instances the child would reach the age of majority in the time it takes a case to wind its way through the courts.

Viewed from this perspective—that of the incipient capability of many parent–child disputes for self-resolution—the abortion cases can be set apart from the typical parent–child controversy. As the Court notes in *Bellotti II*, the capacity for self-resolution is not operative in an abortion case. The abortion decision cannot wait for several months or several weeks; it must be made quickly.

Summary and Discussion

There are substantial differences from one society to another in the social and cultural norms pertaining to adolescent sexuality, parental control, and the pacing of children's social and psychological development. There are also substantial societal and group differences in the pacing of physical and physiological development, although these are not as great as the sociocultural differences. For the individual child, differences in the pace of development from one domain to another can cause confusion and conflict. Conflict between parent and child may also stem from different perceptions about the pace of development and the growth of independence. When children and parents have different expectations about authority, responsibility, and the development of independence, serious conflict may emerge.

I have focused attention on the social and legal dilemmas in the United States. The United States is marked by a paradoxical culture. We worry a great deal about pushing our children along too quickly and turning too many responsibilities over to them. In reality, however, we err on the side of not granting children enough responsibility and of denigrating their competence. This shows up in exaggerated concerns about the potential danger of self-care arrangements and sex education for children.

On the one hand, U.S. society is marked by social and cultural practices that place great emphasis on adolescent sexuality, for example, through advertising, television series, and movies. On the other hand, there are social and cultural prohibitions of adolescent sexuality, so that directly dealing with the issue creates embarrassment and hostility. For example, in contrast to some developed societies where advertising and education regarding condoms and other contraceptives is widespread, in the United States such advertising and education is limited and fragmented. It is the height of irony that the scare of acquired immune deficiency syndrome (AIDS) has become the major wedge in opening up the U.S. media to condom advertising.

The biological readiness of minors for sexual behavior and the ambivalence or hostility of social norms toward such behavior often translates into psychological conflict for adolescents. Moreover, the potential for conflict between parents and children in the arena of adolescent sexuality is enormous. Several features of the situation, however, minimize the conflict. First, parents and children often negotiate the pace of independence and responsibility that is acquired by children, in sexual as well as other areas, so that the pace is gradual and not marked by a sudden shift from dependence to independence at the age of majority. Second, the legal system is not monolithic, and provides room for minors to take on responsibility in a number of areas before attaining the age of majority. Third, the passage of time resolves many parent–child conflicts; once the minor becomes an adult, the legal battle over authority and control is ended.

The area of fertility regulation, however, does not share the capacity for self-resolution that characterizes other areas of parent–child conflict. Decisions about contraception and abortion have an urgency to them, and cannot wait years, months, even weeks for resolution. As a result, the U.S. Supreme Court, despite its strong support for parental control and autonomy, has carved out the area of adolescent sexuality for special treatment. In this area it has created an exception to the usual deference it gives to parental authority. In this way, too, the potential for parent–child conflict in a highly sensitive area—that of adolescent sexuality and fertility behavior—is minimized by the flexibility the courts have built into the system and by the greater degree of responsibility and control that they have granted to minors.

Acknowledgment

This chapter draws on material from the following sources:

Rodman, H., Lewis, S. H., & Griffith, S. B. (1984). *The sexual rights of adolescents: Competence, vulnerability, and parental control.* New York: Columbia University Press.

Rodman, H., Pratto, D. J., & Nelson, R. S. (1985). Child care arrangements and children's functioning: A comparison of self-care and adult-care children. *Developmental Psychology, 21,* 413–418.

Rodman, H., & Trost, J. (Eds.) (1986). *The adolescent dilemma: International perspectives on the family planning rights of minors.* New York: Praeger.

Rodman, H., Sarvis, B., & Bonar, J. W. (1987). *The abortion question.* New York: Columbia University Press.

The chapter has benefited from a conversation I have had with Harriet Pilpel and from her trenchant comments and suggestions.

COMMENT

Harriet F. Pilpel

Far too little attention is paid to the legal and social dilemmas of adolescent sexuality. Dr. Rodman surveys the field from various angles and does, I think, raise a host of questions that those concerned with adolescents have constantly to take into account and to which there are no final answers.

In some respects I disagree with Dr. Rodman's discussion. I find it very disturbing in the first place that he puts very near the beginning of the paper a comparison between "the age of fetal viability" and "the age of adolescent maturity." There are many of us who do not see any similarity between a nonperson and a person who has already been born. Using this comparison raises a lot of questions that by and large are not central to the issue and for which again there are no answers.

Perhaps Dr. Rodman should address other sensible solutions of the problems inherent in the life of the "latchkey child." That there is such a group of children is, of course, a by-product of the fact that today's economics often makes it necessary for both parents to seek gainful employment outside the home. Actually this points to something that Dr. Rodman failed to discuss—the social and economic environment that has bred a great many of the controversies and problems under discussion.

Dr. Rodman does point out that when it comes to sex education "the United States provides less in the way of comprehensive sex education than most European societies." Yet, as he points out, "U.S. adolescents engage extensively in sexual behavior and have higher rates of pregnancy, abortion and illegitimate childbirth than adolescents in most developed societies." It is necessary for us as a society to find out why this is so and what can be done about it. Little attention is paid to the problem, though it is addressed to some extent in other chapters.

On the other hand, Dr. Rodman comes up with a number of observations that are a genuine contribution to the field. His concept of "self-fulfilling mistrust" is a helpful and original analysis.

He also points out that the "potential conflict that stems from discrepancies between the family domain and the legal domain is not usually realized." That I think is true, and I very much hope that Dr. Rodman will expand on that statement in future writings.

There is a point at which Dr. Rodman refers to "a judicial bypass as a necessary precondition of the validity of an antiabortion statute as applied to adolescents." It should be pointed out that, although the cases that have reached the courts on this have involved "a judicial bypass," the original position of the U.S. Supreme Court, and one to which I believe it still adheres, is that it is up to the state to decide whether it will be a judicial bypass (a court) or an administrative bypass (like a health department), or some other judicial or administrative agency or person. Constitutionally, there must be available to the minor some alternative to involving her parents.

Finally, although I agree that "the passage of time" helps resolve many conflicts, I do not agree that the child's reaching the age of 18 necessarily means that the conflicts—even legal conflicts—will disappear. There will still be questions about authority and there will still be court cases that pose the question of whether a parent or parents remain liable for the expenses of a college education and even of a professional education for their children when the children have passed the age of 18. These questions are most apt to arise when the father and mother have separated, or are in the process of separating and trying to work out a separation agreement or decree; but they are nonetheless real for many people.

I agree that the law has developed some flexibility in the areas that touch on adolescent sex. However, there is still a need for much more sharing of scholars' experience with both parents and their offspring, those under 18 as well as those over 18. My wish would be that this chapter would be but the first of a number on this subject written by Dr. Rodman, which I think would make an invaluable series.

16

Adolescence and Puberty:
An Overview

D. Malcolm Potts

The prime objective of this book is to distill a few generalizations from the many insights gained into human adolescence and to apply them to the social and family issues facing modern America. The papers and discussions cover a wide range of issues, from the exquisite cytochemical study of hypothalamic neurons loaded with GnRH in the monkey hypothalamus (Cameron, Chapter 1), to the most depressing statistics about the current epidemic of unintended pregnancies in the United States (Forrest, Chapter 14). From a larger, biological perspective, this book covers a limited phase of reproduction in a small number of primates that probably had a common ancestor ten or twenty million years ago. Here I suggest some important themes that can be identified from among the many and diverse topics covered in this text.

In the United States today, we are bitterly divided over the policies adults should attempt to set for adolescents. What messages about them should be translated into newspaper headlines instead of into papers for refereed journals?

First, we need to put today's problems into some sort of biological and social context. The youngest age of puberty I know of in mammals occurs in the stoat *(Mustela erminea)*. Mating and delivery are widely separated, and the fertilized egg remains unimplanted for 6 months. In order to breed the following summer, the baby stoat mates in the nest while it is still at its mother's breast, although it postpones all other aspects of puberty until the next year (Gulamhusein & Thawley, 1974). The oldest documented age of mammalian puberty that I know is from the work of Jim Wood and Ken Campbell in Michigan who have studied a human tribe called the Gainj in New Guinea, who did not see a white man until 1953. They report the mean age of the menarche as 20 years and the mean age of the first birth 24 to 25 years (Wood & Campbell, 1986).

For reasons we do not fully understand, the age of puberty has declined by several years in the past century. European data are more extensive than North American data (Parkes, 1976). Johann Sebastian Bach noted that the voices of soprano boy singers in the Leipzig choir broke when they were about 17 years old. While other chapters in this book have been able to explain certain relatively small effects in the age of puberty, we still seem to be a long way from an adequate explanation of why the age of the menarche has declined from around 18 to 20 to about 12 or 13 years.

The social environment affecting adolescents is now more clearly understood. My parents were born in the nineteenth century, and they both left school by the age of 12. Many contributors to this book did not stop accumulating degrees until their later twenties. Our complex society demands education far beyond puberty if individuals are to perform as self-sufficient adults. Sixty percent of American men aged 18–24 and 48% of women in the same age group live at home or in college dormitories and continue to depend on their parents. Teenagers are having intercourse at early ages, and the mean age of marriage is now 10–15 years after the age when sex becomes a possibility. To complicate the matter further, a Finnish study suggests the earlier a girl begins to menstruate, the more rapidly she moves to fully ovulatory cycles (Apter & Vihko, 1983).

Much has gone wrong for the modern adolescent, and the demands of culture and changes in biology have created some unprecedented problems. We are not like the Munda in the dormitories having a happy sex life; U.S. teenagers are getting pregnant at a fearsome rate and are increasingly exposed to sexually transmitted diseases (STDs)—to herpes, which is not curable, and to AIDS, which is lethal.

In summary, then, adolescent America is caught in a colliding world between the apparently irresistible forces of biology and the immovable demands of society. We are animals that have been dropped into a very turbulent civilization, not the other way around. Early puberty is an unmitigated social and health disaster. In Wyatt's Los Angeles study some women had had sexual intercourse with more men than there are adults to talk to in a hunter–gatherer community (Wyatt, Chapter 11).

Second, the academic community must share the empirical data that premarital sexual practices do not seem to be influenced by the availability or nonavailability of the means to control fertility, but access to contraception does reduce the incidence of unwanted pregnancies. Whereas 1 in 10 American teenagers becomes pregnant each year, only about 1 in 100 teenagers in the Netherlands does each year, even though the prevalence of adolescent sexual activity is much the same in both countries (Jones et al., 1985). The difference stems from the better access and more realistic use of contraception in the Netherlands.

Third, many teenage pregnancies are unwanted and will end in abortion. Society as a whole must determine the legal status of abortion, but public health specialists can confirm that, all ethical considerations apart, early legal termination of pregnancy is a remarkably safe and simple procedure, both physically and psychologically (Interdivisional Committee on Adolescent Abortion, 1987).

Statistics suggest that the legal status of abortion has relatively little effect on the total number of terminations that take place in any society, but whatever the number of abortions, most reasonable people prefer contraception to abortion (Tietze, 1973).

The contraceptive needs of young people are partly also determined by the possibility of exposure to STDs as well as pregnancy, both of which can have lifelong consequences. Moreover, where abortion is legal the pregnancy can be terminated, but the infertility that may follow infection cannot necessarily be treated, and the AIDS infection certainly cannot be cured. There is increasing evidence that cervical cancer is related in some or all cases to infection with the human papilloma virus, which is killed by spermicides as well as reduced in its transmission by the condom (Syrjanen et al., 1984).

A recent clinical study of sexually active young women in Bangkok, Thailand found the use of a nonoxynol-9-containing sponge reduced the rate of infection with gonorrhea and chlamydia (Rosenberg et al., 1987; see Fig. 16-1). (The slight rise in candida infection is a recognized effect of nonoxynol-9 on the vaginal flora.) There is excellent laboratory evidence overall that spermicides also kill the herpes and AIDS viruses (Singh, Postic, & Cutler, 1976; Hicks et al., 1985).

Barrier methods also reduce the risks of STDs as well as that of pregnancy, and it seems to me logical to combine the two advantages. I think our fourth message to the outside world should be if you think you are at risk of disease, then use a spermicidally lubricated condom. We have to increase condom use—from more than 13% of 15-year-olds at first intercourse quoted earlier.

I would criticize the Food and Drug Administration, which currently will not permit the relabeling of spermicide packages to say that they are deterrents against STDs; after all, my toothpaste claims fluoride is a deterrent against cavities, and surely it is much more important to tell consumers spermicides are deterrents against STDs.

The United States is also a strange country when it comes to product

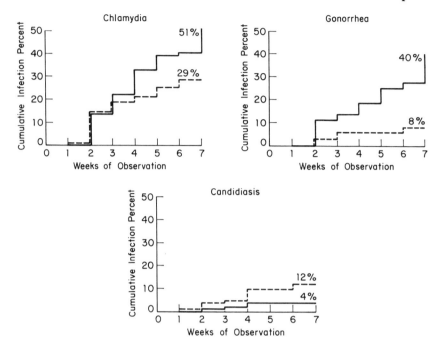

Figure 16–1. Cumulative percentage of women infected by week of observation, parallel cohort, Bangkok, 1986. Numbers refer to percentage of contraceptive sponge users (dashed line) and nonusers (solid line) infected at end of study period.

liability. There has been one legal finding against spermicides for $4.7 million in the case of supposed congenital abnormality. There is no consistent scientific evidence of a relationship, but it is possible we may lose spermicides from the marketplace, which would be an unmitigated disaster.

We need a happier, more forceful attitude toward condoms. San Francisco has set an interesting example and is home to National Condom Week from George Washington's birthday to Saint Valentine's Day. It is celebrated with a rock concert, a condom sculpture, and a competition for the best condom couplet: Recent entries include "Use a condom and you will learn, no deposit no return!" and "Red is for roses, hot nights and safe sex, if you love your sweetie, say it with latex!"

And we need to be saying some positive things about oral contraceptives. One of the greatest public health tragedies of the twentieth century is that the oral contraceptive ever went on medical prescription. If the pill had been invented 5 or 10 years earlier, it would have been an over-the-counter item, like aspirin. The pill has been in human use for

30 years and is among the most intensively studied drugs in the phar-macopoeia. Indeed, there is so much information it is difficult to put it together.

The adverse effects of the pill begin when a woman first takes the pill, and most end when she stops using it. However, the beneficial effects take some time to accumulate and persist for 5, 10, 15 years after use—perhaps even a fertile lifetime. A number of independent studies show that oral contraceptive use reduces ovarian cancer (CDC, 1983a), and the longer you use the pill the more marked the effect, and the effect persists after discontinuing the pill. The same holds true for en-dometrial cancer (CDC, 1983b). The problem is how to portray the risks and benefits of the pill in a single, grand, Einsteinian equation. One practical way is to ask what is the effect on the expectation of life if a woman uses the pill continuously for 5 years in a specified age group (Fig. 16-2). For Western women, it actually increases life expectancy for a tiny but measurable amount in women under 30: it is a tiny chip off the philosopher stone (Fortney, Harper, & Potts, 1986). Basically, the protective effects against cancer more than outweigh the adverse ef-fects on the cardiovascular system. For a woman in the developing world, where the risks of pregnancy are greater, the beneficial effects are correspondingly larger.

Overall, both the risks and benefits of the pill are trivial in relation to other risks and benefits of life. Oral contraceptives increase the life expectancy by 12 days. The worst they can do to the life expectancy of older women is shorten life by 40–80 days. Smoking one pack of ciga-rettes a day decreases the users' life expectancy by an average of 4.6

Figure 16–2. Change in life expectancy attributable to 5 years of oral contracep-tion (OCs) in women aged 20–40 years, United States, 1978.

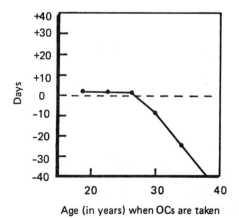

Age (in years) when OCs are taken

years. I stand by my aphorism of many years ago that cigarettes should be on prescription and pills in vending machines!

Oral contraceptive use also reminds us of one important aspect of puberty not mentioned in the other chapters. The earlier a girl begins to menstruate, the greater the risk of ovarian, endometrial, and breast cancers later in life around and beyond the menopause. Beyond the social pain, early puberty is a major disadvantage because it increases the risks of common cancers later in life. The human body does not seem to like frustrated fertility (i.e., repeated ovulatory cycles). There is good evidence, meticulously collected from many parts of the world (MacMahon et al., 1970), of a linear relationship between the age when a woman has her first pregnancy, and the risk of getting breast cancer later in life: the earlier the pregnancy, the less the risk of breast cancer. One in eleven American women gets breast cancer, and one in eighteen will die from this disease. We need a method of either making puberty come later or, as second best, giving a girl anovulatory cycles as an adolescent.

In a way, it is curious that the pill does not have an effect on breast cancer—either positive or negative (Stadel et al., 1985; Lipnick et al., 1986). One of the prime targets to research in the next decade should be how to tease out whether it is possible to formulate a combination of artificial steroids that reduce the risks of breast cancer similar to their preventive effects against endometrial and ovarian cancers.

Contemporary perceptions of the pill are uniformly negative. In 1985, the American College of Gynecologists showed that most Americans think that the pill has substantial risks to health. Family Health International has used the same questions in a number of other countries and found that women, worldwide, have a pessimistic attitude toward the pill (Grubb, 1989). A significant number of people in all countries think the pill causes the very cancers it prevents (Fig. 16-3). They even think it causes stomach cancer. Very few people realize that the pill has any protective effect, in forestalling either cancer or STDs. This latter effect is probably due to the steroids' effect in making the cervical mucus firmer throughout the cycle. Overall, pill users have a relative risk for pelvic inflammatory disease of about 0.5; more research is needed to discover if this reduction in risk is spread across all STDs.

Our next message to the outside world, then, should be that the pill is one of the most misunderstood therapies of the twentieth century; it is an excellent method for young women, especially if they are in a regular sexual partnership. Oral contraceptives are safe, effective, and give long-term protection against two important cancers.

When the world changes rapidly, as it is at the present moment, one option is to deny that change is taking place. And that is what an increasing number of people in our society seem to do. They wish to

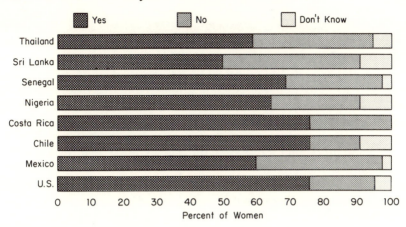

Figure 16–3. Perceptions of the Pill Survey—Health Risk. Are there substantial health risks in taking the pill?

re-create what they perceive as a lost world without pills and legal abortion, where teenagers did not have sex. In fact, if that world ever existed, it was for a few decades in the sixteenth century, but it was a powerful image.

Yet, when groups of people in a society adopt highly polarized points of view, it is usually the case that everybody has some element of the truth. Sexual abstinence is a solution to many problems today's teenagers face, and perhaps we need to pay scientific attention to the issue. The single, most interesting thing I have learned from the Kinsey symposium which was the basis for this volume is that sexual behavior in contemporary adolescents in the United States is largely biologically driven in males, but is influenced more by social factors than by biological maturity in females. In primates the biological sex drive is highly modified by the social context in which the adolescent monkey finds himself or herself. The problem in our society is that young people are not behaving like animals. If they did, then, we would not find, as J. R. Udry did (Chapter 5), that the most powerful predictor of sexual activity in Tallahassee schoolboys is the level of testosterone in their blood. Among women, Wyatt (Chapter 11) found some influence of social factors when girls decide to engage in sexual intercourse, although it only makes 1 or 2 years' difference; even so, the age of first menstruation, at least among the black community, seems too strong a factor predicting the initiation of sexual activity. On the one hand, any prolongation of sexual abstinence by social pressures for a teenager is important: Sex at 17 is a lot better than sex at 15, but on the whole there seems no real possibility that social pressure will prevent any but the most adamant virgin from beginning her sexual career long before the mean age of marriage in the United States, which is now 23 years. The prime predictor of the initiation of sexual intercourse among Los Angeles women was the rehearsal for sex represented by necking and petting. The study also demonstrated that having two parents at home delays the age of initiation of sexual activity for about a year. We do not know how social and biological forces interact. Why is it that two parents in the home delay the age of first intercourse? One simple hypothesis might be that it is merely the degree of parental supervision— old-fashioned chaperonage.

We can learn from other societies that place a range of social controls on biological urges. Perhaps it is useful to remind ourselves that there have been other cultures at other times that appear to have extended the social control over adolescent sexuality much more and for a much longer interval. Wrigley (1969) and other historical demographers in Britain have documented a mean age of marriage in the upper twenties for the peasantry in some English parishes in the sixteenth and seventeenth centuries, and even though many brides went to the altar pregnant, the illegitimacy rate was low. Quaif (1979), in a study of the ecclesiastical and civil cases in seventeenth-century Somerset, a county in Britain, has shown that in high Puritan times, the illegitimacy rate was down to 1 in 200 births (Fig. 16-4). Some of that may have been made easier because of a late menarche, but they also had a late age of marriage. Certainly, the penalties for "bastardy" were explicit and severe. One woman in six was whipped, and a typical punishment for a first offender was severe:

> As soon as she shall be able to travel abroad [after delivery] she shall be brought by the . . . Churchwardens and overseer or some

Figure 16–4. Differences in rates of illegitimacies in sixteenth-century England and in contemporary United States.

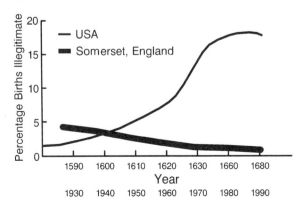

of them unto the next market town to the said parish of Limp-
sham and there they shall cause her to be stripped from the neck
to the girdle and to be openly whipped through the same town
on the market day. And this to be done as that it may be for the
example of others to avoid the like offense. (p. 218)

We heard that half the women in the Los Angeles sample delayed sexual intercourse, at least for a short time, out of fear of parental disapproval or a pregnancy, and there may have been some decline in sexual activity in the black population in the United States between 1980
and 1982. Can such social control be extended without making an un-
acceptably inhumane world? Can we raise the number of adamant or
technical virgins in our society?

Probably not very much. First, there seems to be little doubt we live
in a society that is committed to a high degree of autonomy for young
people, and for that reason we do not take up all the options technology presents. For example, we could, hypothetically, make puberty begin at any time, by giving GnRH antagonists, or extend universal protection against teenage pregnancy by implanting subdermal, synthetic
progestogens that last 5 years—a sort of latter-day, systemically active
chastity belt—in all teenage girls. It would certainly be more humane
than what happened in Puritan England. Second, social pressures,
however expressed, were probably more effective in a homogeneous
society that was dispersed into small villages where everybody knew
everybody else and where even the threat of gossip was a strong deterrent. Today's urban society is vast and anonymous, and young people are highly mobile. When daddy gives his 16-year-old the keys to
the automobile, he is also giving her the privacy necessary for sexual
intercourse. Perhaps if the privacy necessary for intercourse is easy to
come by, that is one very good argument for making contraceptives
easy to come by.

As Hyman Rodman pointed out (Chapter 15), it is difficult to be consistent about puberty. It is hard to create absolute rules about such a
protracted, gradual process. Consequently, we are forced back on
somewhat arbitrary rules that define the slow, individually paced changes
of puberty. For example, public opinion in the United States is divided
over the choice between providing confidentiality for the teenager attending a family planning service and informing the parents. The fact
that we lean more toward the parents in the United States than in
Europe may be one of the reasons for the high pregnancy rate in this
country.

I find a biological perspective on puberty a useful one. I do not think
that society "has laid a different trip on the two sexes." There is nothing in the biology or sociology of puberty we have discussed in this
book that does not make Darwinian sense. Women have a relatively

short fertile life and can only reproduce themselves a very few times, so they are likely to be socially more sensitive and innately more cautious about sex than men. By contrast, on purely biological grounds, it is always in the man's biological interest to copulate if the costs are low enough: there is always the chance that you might leave your genes in the next generation (Symons, 1979).

Biology may also help explain why parents are not good at teaching sex education to their children. Is it that relaying such information, somehow or another, gets mixed up with the incest taboo, which is so deeply ingrained in all of us?

Another thing that makes it difficult to increase the abstinence rate among adolescents is that we have such a heterogeneous society, both in the real world around us and in the world of TV fantasy. Young people can choose from very many social models for themselves.

So, it is possible that contemporary society is put together in a way that, for the foreseeable future, will prevent any widespread abstinence. But, AIDS might just change that. The "wages of sin" are once again death. Many young people have more than six partners. Already 1 in 300 army recruits has antibodies to the AIDS virus, and an increasing number of people in their twenties and thirties will be dying from this awful disease in a few years' time. It may remain incurable forever, and a vaccine might take many years to perfect.

The important fact that follows—and this should be trumpeted from the roof of The Kinsey Institute and everywhere else—is that a case of AIDS that can be prevented now will end up preventing 4, 8, 16, 256 cases by the time we get a vaccine—if we ever get a vaccine.

Perhaps our last message should be to emphasize the need to be realistic. Those genuinely interested in the welfare of the young can applaud sexual abstinence when undertaken by thoughtful, informed people. At the same time, they can and should promote contraceptive availability to those who do not want to abstain from sex. The trouble is that some policymakers see a contradiction here even though none is necessary. Clearly, in this emotional area, judgments are going to differ concerning availability of fertility regulation to adolescents whether you are a 14-year-old, the mother of a 14-year-old, a man running for political office, or the parent of a teenage daughter who has just told you her period is late.

References

Apter, D., & Vihko, R. (1983). Early menarche, a risk factor for breast cancer, indicates early onset of ovulatory cycles. *Journal of Clinical Endocrinology and Metabolism, 57*(1), 82–86.

Centers for Disease Control (CDC) Cancer and Steroid Hormone Study (1983a).

Oral contraceptive use and the risk of ovarian cancer. *Journal of the American Medical Association, 249,* 1596.

Centers for Disease Control (CDC) Cancer and Steroid Hormone Study (1983b). Oral contraceptive use and the risk of endometrial cancer. *Journal of the American Medical Association, 249,* 1600.

Fortney, J., Harper, J., & Potts, M. (1986). Oral contraceptives and life expectancy. *Studies in Family Planning, 17* (3), 117–125.

Grubb, G. Women's perspective of the safety of the pill: A survey in eight developing countries. *Journal of Biosocial Science,* in press.

Gulamhusein, A. P., & Thawley, A. R. (1974). Plasma progesterone levels in the Stoat. *Journal of Reproduction and Fertility, 36,* 405–408.

Hicks, D. R., Martin, L. S., Getchell, J. P., Heath, J., Francis, D. P., McDougal, J. S., Curran, J. W., & Voeller, B. (1985). Inactivation of HTLV-III/LAV-infected cultures of normal human lymphocytes by nonoxynol-9 in vitro. *Lancet, 2,* 1422–1423.

Interdivisional Committee on Adolescent Abortion (1987). Adolescent abortion: Psychological and legal issues. *American Psychologist, 42,* 73–78.

Jones, E. F., Forrest, J. D., Goldman, N., Henshaw, S. K., Lincoln, R., Rosoff, J. I., Westoff, C. F., & Wulf, D. (1985). Teenage pregnancy in developed countries: Determinants and policy implications. *Family Planning Perspectives, 17,* 53–63.

Lipnick, R. J., Buring, J. E., Hennekens, C. H., Rosner, B., Willett, W., Bain, C., Stampfer, M. J., Colditz, G. A., Peto, R., Speizer, F. E. (1986). Oral contraceptives and breast cancer: A prospective study. *Journal of the American Medical Association, 255,* 58–61.

MacMahon, B., Cole, P., Lin, T. M., Lowe, C. R., Mirra, A. P., Ravuihar, B., Salker, E. J., Valaoras, V. G., & Yuasa, S. (1970). Age at first birth and risk of breast cancer. *Bulletin of the World Health Organization, 43,* 209.

Parkes, A. S. (1976). *Patterns of sexuality and reproduction.* London: Oxford University Press.

Quaife, G. R. (1979). *Wanton wenches and wayward wives.* London: Crown Helen.

Rosenberg, M. J., Feldblum, P. J., Rojanapithayakorn, W., & Sawasdivorn, W. (1987). The contraceptive sponge's protection against chlamydia and gonorrhea. *Sexually Transmitted Diseases, 13–14,* 147–152.

Singh, B., Postic, B., & Cutler, J. C. (1976). Virucidal effect of certain chemical contraceptives on type 2 herpesvirus. *American Journal of Obstetrics and Gynecology, 126,* 422–425.

Stadel, B. V., Rubin, G. L., Webster, L. A., Schlesselman, J. J., & Wingo, P. A. (1985). Oral contraceptives and breast cancer in young women. *Lancet, 2,* 970–973.

Symons, D. (1979). *The evolution of human sexuality.* New York: Oxford University Press.

Syrjanen, K., Vayrynen, M., Castren, O., Yliskoski, M., Mantyjarvi, R., Pyrhonen, S., & Saarikoski, S. (1984). Sexual behaviour of women with human papillomavirus (HPV) lesions of the uterine cervix. *British Journal of Venereal Diseases, 60,* 243–248.

Tietze, C. (1973). Two years experience with a liberal abortion law: Its impact on fertility trends in New York City. *Family Planning Perspectives, 5,* 36.

Wood, J., & Campbell, K. (1986). Fertility in traditional societies. In P. Diggory & S. Teper (Eds.), *Natural human fertility: Social and biological mechanisms.* London: McMillan.

Wrigley, E. A. (1969). *Population and history.* London: Weidenfeld and Nicolson.

Author Index

Subject Index

Abortion, 234
attitudes toward, 255
court cases involving minors and
abortion, 261–63
Bellotti v. *Baird* (Bellotti I; 1976), 262
Bellotti v. *Baird* (Bellotti II; 1979), 262
City of Akron v. *Akron Center for
Reproductive Health* (1983), 262
Doe v. *Bolton* (1973), 261
H.L. v. *Matheson* (1981), 262
Planned Parenthood of Central Missouri
v. *Danforth* (1976), 261
Roe v. *Wade* (1973), 261
U.S. Supreme Court and, 261–67
fetal viability, 254–55, 266
minors and, 258, 260–63
minors, emancipated vs. mature, 260,
262–63
parental authority, consent, and
notification, 258, 261–63
judicial and administrative bypass,
263, 267
rates, 224, 230–31
cross-cultural comparisons, 176, 179,
234–39; contraception use, 242–43;
levels of sexual activity, 240–41;
pregnancy intentions, 241–42
U.S., 174–75, 237–43
safety of, 271
Abstinence. *See* Sexual abstinence
Acquired Immunodeficiency Syndrome
(AIDS)
influence on social norms about sex,
180
prevention of, 278
Adjustment problems
age, 104–5
hormones, 101–4, 107–11, 113
Adolescence. *See also specific topics*
definition of, 159
Adrenal androgens, 32, 89, 94–96, 105–7,
111, 113
regulation of, 96–97
Adrenal genital syndrome (AGS), 54
Adrenarche, 32, 89. *See also* Adrenal
androgens; Hormones; Puberty
Affective disorders, 125–27
age trends, 125–26

depressive conditions, 125–26, 132–33,
135–38
cognitive factors, 136
genetic factors, 135–36
hormonal factors, 133
role of experience in, 137–38
frequency during adolescence, 125–27
compared to other forms of negative
mood state, 126
grief reactions, 126
suicide, attempted and completed, 125
age trends, 125
sex differences, 125–26
Age trends
adjustment problems, 104–5
adolescent maturity, 255, 266
aggression, 133
anorexia nervosa, 127
autism, 130
biological maturity and psychiatric
disorders, 132–36
birth, 225, 236
cognitive maturity and psychiatric
disorders, 136
coitus, first, 187–89, 191–200, 202, 219–
20, 240
conduct disturbances, 128–29, 133, 137
developmental disorders, 130
marriage, 169, 182, 218–20
menarche, 218, 270, 274
psychiatric disorders, 125–31, 134–39
puberty, 132, 218, 269–70, 277
sexual activity, teenage, 182
social age and psychiatric disorders, 139
substance abuse, 128
suicide, attempted and completed, 125
Aggression
age trends, determinants of, 133
testosterone, 133
Alan Guttmacher Institute, 234
American College of Gynecologists and
oral contraceptives, 274
Androgens. *See* Adrenal androgens;
Hormones
Anorexia nervosa, 13, 21, 41–43, 96, 127–
28
age trends, 127
ballet dancers, 128, 135